FOUNDATION

OF

JAPANESE BUDDHISM

FOUNDATION
OF
JAPANESE BUDDHISM

VOL. II

THE MASS MOVEMENT
(Kamakura & Muromachi Periods)

BY

ALICIA MATSUNAGA Ph.D.
DAIGAN MATSUNAGA Ph.D.

BUDDHIST BOOKS INTERNATIONAL

LOS ANGELES - TOKYO

Library of Congress Cataloging in Publication Data

Matsunaga, Alicia.
  Foundation of Japanese Buddhism.

  Bibliography: v. 1, p. [271]–275.; v. 2, p. 329
  Includes indexes.
  CONTENTS: v. 1. The Aristocratic age.—v. 2. The
Mass movement (Kamakura & Muromachi periods)
  1. Buddhism—Japan—History. I. Matsunaga, Daigan,
joint author. II. Title.
BQ676.M39   294.3'0952   74-83654
ISBN 0–914910–27–2 (cloth)
              –28–0 (paper)

Printed by Kenkyusha Printing Co.

Tokyo, Japan

TO

TAIE & KEI MATSUNAGA

CONTENTS

CHAPTER FIVE: ROLE OF THE OLDER SECTS DURING
THE KAMAKURA AND MUROMACHI PERIODS

viii / CONTENTS

CHAPTER I

INTRODUCTION
THE HISTORICAL SETTING: A SUMMARY

Buddhism was formally introduced to Japan during the sixth century, and rapidly gained recognition among the aristocratic ruling class as both a vehicle of advanced Chinese civilization and a superlative form of continental magic that introduced a vast new pantheon of deities, and a means of handling the troublesome problem of death. The Soga clan was initially placed in charge of Buddhist affairs, but their downfall at the time of the Taika Reform in 645 did not diminish the fortunes of the new religion, for the leaders of the reform were anxious to promote Chinese civilization and acknowledged the growing importance of Buddhism by placing it under official Ritsuryō government control. The religion quickly became an accepted means of controlling national calamities, curing Imperial illness, putting the dead to rest, and promoting the general prosperity of the nation, as well as the cause of the aristocracy. However, with the major emphasis upon theurgy, the true religious spirit of Buddhism and its path of individual salvation were almost totally neglected. The native Japanese spirit of affirmation had seized merely the hull of the new faith. It was not until the succeeding Heian period when the shell would be cracked, and the bittersweet flavour of impermanence and the transitory nature of life could be accepted as the prelude to a deeper affirmation of the nature of man.

The Six Sects of Nara

The year 710 marked the completion of the first permanent capital of Japan at Nara, epitomizing the apex of Chinese borrowing in the form of a small-scale duplication of Ch'ang-an, the mighty capital of T'ang

China. This move ushered in a new phase of Buddhist activity and during the years 747–51, the famous Six Sects of Nara were imported from China consisting of: the Kusha, Jōjitsu, Ritsu, Sanron, Hossō and Kegon schools. Prior to this, the Japanese had no form of sectarian Buddhism, and even these new schools could scarcely be classified as 'sectarian' insofar as two of them failed to attain independent status, and all six frequently were housed and studied at the same monastery. But the importation of these Six Sects abruptly introduced to the Japanese the major developments of over one thousand years of Buddhism in India and China. Although it was impossible to immediately digest such a vast store of knowledge, and ostensibly Nara Buddhism continued to minister to the theurgic needs of the ruling class—the foundation stone was laid for the future evolution of Japanese Buddhism. Under the mantle of the Six Nara Sects, the seeds of Tendai, Shingon, Zen, Pure Land and even Nichiren were implanted in embryonic form and preserved to develop when their social time was ripe.

The Chinese pattern of a centralized Ritsuryō government based upon equal land distribution and taxation was not suited to Japanese society and Nara Buddhism too successfully became aligned with this concept of government, hence it shared the common fate. As the government succumbed to corruption so did the vast Buddhist institutions that in effect had become part of the bureaucracy.

Aristocratic Mikkyō

In an effort to separate Church and State as well as to institute a vast system of reform, Emperor Kammu moved the seat of government in 794 to the city of Kyoto. At this time two new sects were formally imported from China, the Tendai and Shingon. The former based upon the *Lotus Sutra* was to establish a thriving center of study on Mt. Hiei, becoming the cradle of all later major developments of Japanese Buddhism. In contrast, Mt. Kōya, headquarters of the Shingon sect evolved into a quiet sanctuary of meditation. Both of these new schools of Buddhism advocated *Mikkyō* (Tantrism), which soon won favour among the Heian aristocracy. The numerous esoteric mountain temples became sites of popular pilgrimages and retreats for the worldly court society, who in the midst of their opulence gradually began to think of the fleeting nature of human life in terms of the fragile beauty of the cherry blossom or evanescence of the morning dew—which ultimately proved as lasting as their own way of life.

Rise of the Shōen

Despite the idealism of their founders, the Tendai and Shingon sects also succumbed to the disease of affluence, in the wake of a drastic political change. During the early Heian period a gradual shift in the power-structure had commenced as the aristocratic landowners, great temples and shrines managed to evade taxation and acquire huge landed estates (shōen). The Fujiwara family, who usurped political power by monopolizing the post of regent to the Emperor, became the worst transgressors of the Ritsuryō codes and were largely to blame for the decline of the central government. While the Fujiwaras were firmly in control from the mid-ninth to the late eleventh century, the economic basis of the nation shifted from the Chinese-modeled Ritsuryō system of nationalized land to tax-exempt shōen (estates), and although the organs of central government virtually collapsed, the aristocratic court continued to maintain its affluence by absentee landholdings and other irregular means of support. The Buddhist institutions out of necessity followed suit and shifted their basis of sustenance to the patronage of the aristocrats and development of their own private shōen; such a move however solidified their alienation from the masses and dependency upon the aristocracy.

By the close of the Heian period, the shōen themselves were forced to turn to the bushi (warrior) class to preserve order and protect the interests of absentee aristocratic landowners in the absence of central authority. These bushi arose from the various types of shōen managers, who recruited private armies, and the few local owners who chose to reside upon their estates. They were the individuals who effectively began to control the shōen and resorted to military means in order to protect their interests, assuming the role of militia and police as the control of the central government diminished. Each *shōen* drew up a private military force and, on a larger scale, geographical and family alliances were made. It was not long before *de facto* ownership of the *shōen* passed into the hands of the military and they began to intervene in the political affairs of the capital to promote their interests.

Dominance of the Samurai

The first major conflict in which the *bushi* displayed their power was the succession dispute following the death of retired Emperor Toba in 1156. In this battle, known as the Hōgen War, the great Taira (Heike) and Minamoto (Genji) families allied supporting the retired Emperor Go-Shirakawa, but it was not long before jealousy sundered their relationship and they took to the sword to resolve their differences in the brief struggle known as the Heiji war of 1159–60. The victor of this conflict was Taira no Kiyomori, who became the military master of the capital and soon commanded the remnants of central government. For a brief period of twenty years (1160–1180), the Taira family virtually controlled the court. Kiyomori became Dajōdaijin (Chancellor), married daughters to the Emperor and Fujiwara regents, and in 1180 managed to place his own grandson upon the throne as Emperor Antoku; he even briefly attempted to move the capital to Fukuhara (modern Kōbe).

The aristocrats witnessed this new usurpation of power in a state of mild shock. The disintegration of the central government and irregularity of the *shōen* system had by now eroded the basic reason for their existence, and as their titles became meaningless, bribery and corruption increased. Aristocratic morale had already been undermined by Fujiwara domination, a gradual awareness of dependency upon the samurai and the progressive erosion of their landholdings as the warriors settled disputes. The Hōgen war effectively marked a turning point in Japanese history, since it displayed the visible beginnings of the evolution of feudalism, but the aristocrats were not yet aware of this fact. The samurai in control, and particularly Kiyomori after 1160, managed to preserve an aristocratic veneer while taking an active role in court affairs.

Mappō

Still the mood of the day was extremely unsettled and there were those who questioned the ability of the Taira to maintain control of the nation. Plots, intrigues and corruption abounded, and even the Buddhist temples developed *sōhei* (priest-warriors) to protect their interests and frequently air demands at the capital in raucous demonstrations. It was a period of general uneasiness and the mood of *mappō* (Degeneration of the Dharma) dominated the land. Then in the year 1180, the once-defeated Minamoto family once again raised their white banner and challenged Taira supremacy, this time under the leadership of Yoritomo. For five years the nation was engulfed in violent warfare until the famous sea battle of Dan-no-ura in the spring of 1185 finally annihilated the Taira and established Minamoto Yoritomo as the *de facto* ruler of Japan.

Fall of the Aristocracy

The conclusion of the long Gempei conflict brought a degree of stability to a war-weary land but increased the anxieties of the aristocracy. The lands of the Taira and their allies were now confiscated and distributed among Yoritomo's loyal followers, the child Emperor Antoku had perished at Dan-no-ura, and Yoritomo, wishing to avoid the dangers of aristocratic corruption at the capital, set up his spartan *bakufu* (tent-government) in distant Kamakura. He then attempted to place a personal steward (*jitō*) retainer on every *shōen* in the nation under the higher control of provincial supervisors (*shugo*), selected from among his loyal retainers. Aristocrats who wished to settle any dispute regarding income rights from *shōen*, had now to journey to Kamakura and plead their cases before Yoritomo's samurai court of appeal. It was obvious that their days of survival were numbered and that they were destined to disappear in the manner of their past glory, or as the chronicler wrote in his epitaph for the fallen Taira:

> The sound of the bell of the Jetavana monastery echoes
> the impermanence of all things. The colour of the flowers
> of the Sāla tree reveal the law of the rise and fall of the

powerful. The proud ones do not last long and their
glory is like a spring night's dream. And the mighty
ones too will ultimately perish, like dust before the wind.

Heike Monogatari

These same words predicted the fate of the residue of Heian aristocracy
as they attempted to face the new feudal order which would ultimately
sweep them into oblivion. Court life continued, but its glitter had
tarnished and a gloominess prevailed that could not be dispelled by
witty sayings, clever poetry or seasonal festivals. The natural calamities
of fire, plague, earthquake and famine that had struck the capital area
during the long Gempei war made the advent of *mappō* a reality and the
observant were aware the end was near. The dramatic turning point
came in the year 1221, when the Retired Emperor Go-Toba attempted to
test his strength against Yoritomo's successors, the Hōjō Regents, in the
brief encounter known as the Shōkyū war. With Go-Toba's defeat, the
Kamakura government had an excuse to confiscate the estates of all the
aristocrats who had supported his cause, and the temporal power of
the aristocracy was permanently destroyed.

A New Social Order

What is known in Japanese history as the medieval period, spans four
centuries from the close of the twelfth to the end of the sixteenth, and
encompasses the rise and final establishment of feudalism in what can be
described as three stages. The first stage, representing the evolution of
the feudal state and establishment of the Kamakura government under
Minamoto Yoritomo, was a period of samurai struggle for supremacy
and the development of a strong sense of loyalty between the lord and
his retainers. Yoritomo received the title of Shōgun from the Emperor
in 1192 and attempted to rule the country from Kamakura by a simple
warrior-family type organization. During this period, the samurai
established themselves as a new class in Japanese society and formed
their own code of ethics. The era also coincides with the foundation of
five new Buddhist movements directed towards the masses and needs
of the new social order.

Kamakura Buddhism

One of the most controversial movements was the independence of Pure Land devotion in the form of the Jōdo and Jōdo Shinshū Sects. Previously in Tendai and Shingon thought, Pure Land devotion was regarded as an *upāya* (skillful means) useful to stimulate individuals incapable of performing the more demanding disciplines of meditation and purification. Attainment of such a variety of Pure Land, was viewed as a preliminary stage to the true attainment of Nirvana, for it was believed that Enlightenment was possible only when such individuals became capable of undertaking regular practices. In contrast to such a notion, the rising Pure Land movements emphasized the single-practice of chanting the *nembutsu* (name of Amida) as the path of salvation for even common man, who had been totally neglected by the older sects. In a similar vein, albeit somewhat more exclusive and dogmatic manner, the Nichiren sect also advocated a single-practice and Enlightenment for all by means of chanting the title of the *Lotus Sutra* (*Namu-Myōhōrengekyō*). And finally Rinzai and Sōtō Zen introduced meditation as an independent single-practice. In contrast to the Nara and Heian sects, these new movements turned to the common people for the basis of their support, and for the first time Buddhism in Japan assumed a true Japanese character by embracing the majority of the populace. It was a timely move, since the instability of the government and aristocracy made any other form of patronage unfeasible.

Northern and Southern Courts

After Yoritomo's death in 1199, both of his sons, Yoriie and Sanetomo, died at the hands of assassins, and his wife Masako's family, the Hōjō, assumed the post of regent, maintaining power until 1333, when an attempt was made for a restoration of Imperial power by Emperor Go-Daigo, backed by a group of aristocrats and samurai dissatisfied with the Kamakura government. For three years the Emperor, supported by the warriors Nitta Yoshisada and Ashikaga Takauji, endeavored to assert his control in a brave attempt known as the Kemmu Restoration. This ultimately failed when Yoshisada and Takauji fell out and Go-Daigo supported the losing side. Ashikaga Takauji then seized the capital of Kyoto in 1336 and set up the puppet Emperor Kōgon. Go-Daigo retreated south to nearby Yoshino and established a separate Southern Imperial court that lasted up until 1392 when his successor, through political compromise, was absorbed into the northern court at Kyoto.

Muromachi Culture

The second stage of Japanese feudalism is represented by the Ashikaga or Muromachi period lasting from 1336–1573, which witnessed a line of shōguns who never succeeded in establishing effective control over the nation. The government was set up at Muromachi, a district of the capital. The period experienced rapid social and economic growth with the rise of a merchant class, but at the same time the great war lords, known as Daimyō, began to evolve and gobble up the country and establish miniature kingdoms in their struggle for power. Although the nation experienced a cultural flowering of Zen Buddhist arts and influence from the Chinese Sung dynasty, politically it was a time of extreme instability. The Ōnin war of 1467–77 wiped out the last of the shōen and the Kyoto aristocracy were reduced to complete poverty. One Emperor even had to support himself by selling samples of his calligraphy. But with the final decline of the Heian court aristocracy, new cultural centres began to evolve upon the individual realms of the great Daimyō, who each set themselves up as small autonomous rulers at their private castles. This movement represented the first major diffusion of culture throughout Japan and it abetted the establishment of the new forms of Buddhism that had developed during the Kamakura period.

Mass Movements

At the same time the nation was being divided up among the great warlords, certain other classes were gaining the desire for independence. The medieval merchants and artisans began to form a guild system known as the za, to establish local monopoly rights in production and transportation of their products through the realms of the various

Daimyō, each of whom demanded barrier taxes. The peasants also experienced a growing sense of self-awareness. By the early fifteenth century they began to riot and instigate uprisings (*ikki*) against moneylenders and unfair taxation. They often rallied under the banner of one of the new forms of Buddhism such as the Jōdo Shinshū (*Ikkō Ikki*) or Nichirenshū (*Hokke Ikki*), and by now the new religious institutions themselves began to assert political influence. The general unrest was to usher in the third phase of Japanese feudalism, which ultimately resulted in the unification of the country under the stern control of the Tokugawa government. But before Japan could achieve unification, the nation first had to endure a century of bloody conflict known as the Sengoku (Warring States) period.

After the Ōnin war, one of the interminable succession disputes that began in 1467, Ashikaga authority was effectively broken, although they were to continue nominally in power for over a century longer. But the Ōnin war served as an excuse to plunge the Daimyō from all over the nation into general conflict. Houses rose and fell in rapid sucession as military strength shifted and then the Europeans arrived. In 1543 the Portuguese landed at Tanegashima, off the southern tip of the island of Kyūshū, and introduced firearms, Christianity and western influence to Japan. In view of the century-long chaos now coupled with a foreign threat, the Japanese were pressed to unify if they intended to survive as a nation.

Tokugawa Control

Three great leaders attempted to reunite Japan. The first was Oda Nobunaga (1534–82), who seized authority from the Ashikaga and sought to break the political and military power of the Buddhist sects by arms and the brief encouragement of Christianity. He was finally assassinated by one of his followers. Toyotomi Hideyoshi (1536–98), his successor, was a man of humble origin who briefly managed to unify the nation. Hideyoshi expelled Christianity, which had proven to be a disturbing factor in furthering his political objectives, but his further plans, including the invasion of Korea, ended abruptly with his death, and once again the country was plunged into a struggle for supremacy. The final victor was Tokugawa Ieyasu (1542–1616), who upon defeating the contending warlords at Sekigahara in 1600, proceeded to establish a strong centralized government in Edo (Tokyo). Ieyasu's policies, carried on by his successors, introduced the final stage of Japanese feudal evolution. Europeans and Christian missionaries were expelled, with the exception of the Dutch, who were forced to confine their trade to Dejima Island off Nagasaki harbour. The course of the nation was set upon a policy of isolation and firm control supported by a Neo-Confucian social order that lasted up until the year 1853, when the black ships of Commodore Perry abruptly forced Japan to reopen her doors.

The medieval period represents four violent chaotic centuries of transition in Japanese history, commencing with the decline of the Heian aristocratic *shōen* system, coupled with the rise of the samurai, and concluding with the stern authoritarian Tokugawa feudalistic regime. During these long years of turbulent warfare, political confusion and social change, Japanese Buddhism experienced its golden age, becoming a true religion of the masses. It had completed its centuries of preparation, beginning with the arrival of the Six Nara Sects through the development of Shingon and Tendai philosophy—and out of this long tradition, now thoroughly assimilated, a number of outstanding spiritual leaders emerged, capable of responding to the social and political needs of the day by developing new forms of Buddhism that were no longer the monopoly of a single segment of society. Buddhism at last discovered a means of reaching everyone; from the fading aristocrats to the spartan warriors and their power-hungry leaders, embracing even the newly rising artisans, merchants and downtrodden peasants—this new Buddhism sank deep roots surviving to the present day. And when we observe twentieth century Buddhism in Japan, we have to remember that its foundation traces back to this golden age, during which an alien faith cast aside its foreign garb, assimilated and created new dimensions in Japanese culture.

CHAPTER II

PURE LAND SECTS: THE PATH OF FAITH

A. Antecedents of the Pure Land Buddhist Movement

As early as the Nara period, Pure Land devotion existed in Japan, but it served primarily as a means of putting the dead to rest rather than an agent of personal salvation. This situation changed when Ennin (794–864) popularized the *Jōgyō sammai* (perpetual chanting meditation) on Mt. Hiei, and later Genshin (942–1017) laid a theological basis for the new form of devotion in his *Ōjōyōshū* (Essentials of Salvation) by describing the efficacy of chanting the *nembutsu* and desirability of the Pure Land of Amida. At the same time, Yoshishige Yasutane (d. 997), a distinguished layman, founded a society of classical scholars in 964 that held semi-annual meetings on Mt. Hiei and recited the *nembutsu*.[1] And in affiliation with Genshin's Yokawa followers, Yasutane edited the first record of individuals believed to have been born in the Pure Land entitled the *Nippon Ōjō Gokurakuki*. Such records became quite popular by the end of the Heian period, listing as many as three hundred names.

The Tendai emphasis upon the *nembutsu* in meditation was the direct antecedent of the rise of Jōdo and Jōdo Shinshū, the most popular Pure Land sects in Japan. But there were also a number of important indirect trends, the most significant being the Shingon *nembutsu* faith of Kakuban (1094–1143), of the Daidenpō-in on Mt. Kōya. Although regarded as a means for Shingon followers of inferior ability to attain salvation, this incorporated the *nembutsu* into the Shingon *Three Tantric practices* (physical, vocal and mental). The tradition was carried on by Shōshin during the mid-twelfth century with a gathering of monks and *hijiri* (sages) that eventually established ties with Hōnen's Pure Land movement. And even after the Daidenpō-in was moved to Mt. Negoro, severing relations with Kōyasan and forming the Shingi (Neo) Shingonshū, Hōnen's Jōdo sect managed to maintain cordial relations with both Kōyasan and Shingi-Shingon *nembutsu* followers.

During the Heian period, the most important propagator of Pure Land devotion among the masses was Kūya or Kōya (903–72), who travelled through the countryside spreading the *Yuyaku* (dancing) *nembutsu*. At this time the *nembutsu* was commonly practiced and diffused by such wandering *shami* (those who called themselves laymen believers) as Kūya, as well as the *hijiri*. And until the end of the Heian era, when interest shifted to single-practice, these itinerants mingled the *nembutsu* and belief in Amida with numerous other popular devotions and magical rites. A characteristic of such *nembutsu* faith was the importance attached to the number of chantings, and it was quite common to recite the *nembutsu* as many as 120,000 times a day; the Regent Fujiwara Michinaga was known to practice such a devotion. Among the *shami* and *hijiri*, emphasis upon the quantity of chantings was believed indicative of the degree of religious commitment and numbers were counted by placing beans in a wooden measurement box. Thus a monk could record his daily chantings as 2 or 3 *koku* (currently standardized as 4.96 bushels) of *nembutsu*.

Other means of spreading the faith were by expression in art and music, and the Yūzū Nembutsushū exhibited such characteristics. More than any other, this movement clearly demonstrates the transition from Heian aristocratic Pure Land devotion to the popular Kamakura faith.

B.   Yūzū Nembutsushū, Transmission by Revelation

1.   Ryōnin (1072–1132), the Founder

Born the first day of the New Year in 1072 of a local landlord and the daughter of a Shintō priest in the province of Owari, Ryōnin was gifted from childhood with a beautiful melodious voice. At the age of twelve he entered Mt. Hiei and was ordained under his elder brother Ryōga, taking the religious name of Kōjōbō Ryōnin. At fifteen he received final ordination at the Miidera temple, but since he was interested in furthering his studies in esoteric Buddhism, he went to the Ninnaji when he was eighteen. His abilities and brilliance were so apparent that at the surprisingly young age of twenty-one, he was appointed as a *kōshi* (lecturer) on Mt. Hiei. But by that time Hieizan was far from peaceful, saturated with corruption and constantly menaced by rampaging *sōhei* (priest-soldiers); it was no longer the ideal place for a sincere religious to pursue the quest for Enlightenment. Thus in the year 1045, Ryōnin made a thousand-day pilgrimage to the FudōMyō-ō shrine of the Mudōji temple on Hiezan and decided to abandon the mountain for a small hermitage in Ōhara, a quiet area north of the capital. It was at this time that he changed the second Chinese character in his name to Ryōnin 良忍 (*'nin'* now signifying 'endurance' or 'patience'). During the next twenty years in Ōhara, Ryōnin practiced a variety of Buddhist music known as *bonbai* (a melodic chanting of the sutras),[2] gradually developed a group of followers, and founded the Raigōji and Jōrengeji temples.

On the fifteenth day of the fifth month in 1117 at the age of forty-six, Ryōnin experienced the most significant event in his life. According to his biography, this was when Amida appeared during his *nembutsu* meditation and directly revealed the philosophy of the *yūzū nembutsu* as the pathway to salvation. At the same time, he was presented with a visual *maṇḍala* of Amida surrounded by ten bodhisattvas as the central image to be used for veneration while chanting.

Ryōnin quietly enjoyed his supernal experience until the Indian *deva* Bishamonten (Vaiśravaṇa) appeared while he was engaged in meditation at the Kuramaji temple in Ōhara, and appealed to Ryōnin to teach his revelation to suffering sentient beings, in a manner reminiscent of the legendary appearance of Brahmā requesting the historical Buddha to preach the fruits of his Enlightenment. Thus on the ninth day of the sixth month in 1124, Ryōnin abandoned his solitude and departed for the capital, carrying the booklet recording the names of his followers and their assignments for chanting the *yūzū nembutsu*. When he arrived at Court, Emperor Toba added his name to Ryōnin's list and agreed to accept the assignment of chanting the *yūzū nembutsu* one hundred times daily. Then the Emperor recast his personal Imperial bell into that of a wandering priest to accompany Ryōnin on future missionary journeys. This Imperial patronage attracted many new members to the sect and soon Ryōnin's followers numbered five hundred and thirteen.

The fourth month of the following year, Bishamonten again appeared to Ryōnin while he was engaged in meditation at the Kuramaji, and allegedly presented him with the names of eight million Japanese gods, who had vowed to recite the *yūzū nembutsu* daily. As proof of the visit, Ryōnin received a scroll inscribed with the names of the gods and in view of such encouragement, he decided to extend his missionary activities throughout Japan. In 1127, he visited the Shitennōji in Osaka, practiced the *yūzū nembutsu*, and then moved on to the nearby Shūrakuji temple, originally belonging to the Shingon sect. This temple in later years was renamed the Dainenbutsuji and became the headquarters of the *Yūzū Nembutsu* sect under Ryōnin's successor, Gongen.

Ryōnin's movement had close affinities with both *shinbutsu shūgō* (union of gods and Buddhas) and Shugendō, and in this respect exhibited the eclectic characteristics of late Heian Buddhism. For example, besides gaining the support of eight million native gods to daily recite the *yūzū nembutsu*, Ryōnin also performed a service for lost spirits on the Yamato *Sanzan* (triad of Yamato mountains), at that time the Yoshino deity Katte Myōjin reportedly accepted his *bonbai* (sutra chanting). And Ryōnin was in the habit of always carrying an *oi* (portable altar) on his back, in the manner of the Shugendō followers as they climbed the sacred mountains and communed with the gods and Buddhas.

Ryōnin travelled throughout Japan for nine years, and then becoming aware that his end was near, returned to the Raigō-in at Ōhara to die at the age of sixty-one. Over six hundred years later, during the tenth month of 1773, he was granted the posthumous title of Shōō Daishi by Emperor Go-Momozono.

2. Philosophy of the Yūzū Nembutsu

Yūzū 融通, derived from the *Kegongyō* (*Avataṃsaka sūtra*), denotes the interdependent intercommunicable relationship between existents, and in the form of the *yūzū nembutsu* is considered to be a practical applica-

tion of the Kegon concept of *jiji muge* (the interrelationship of phenomena). The entire philosophy is summarized in the revelation Ryōnin
received from Amida, as follows:

> One man equals all men,
> All men equal one man,
> One practice equals all practices,
> All practices equal one practice;
> This is *ōjō* (attainment) by Other-power.
>
> The ten worlds are within a single thought,
> And if the *yūzū nembutsu* is recited countless times,
> All virtues will be complete.

Due to the interrelated nature of existents, man does not stand alone,
but is inseparably united to the sufferings and fate of all mankind. Thus
the action of a single individual, even though it may seemingly have
invisible immediate consequences, ultimately affects the destiny of the
entire society. In view of this vast interwoven network, the constant
chanting of the *nembutsu* by one individual permeates and purifies the
whole of society, just as the chanting of the group influences the life of
the individual, for the individual contains within himself the totality
of the universe and mirrors all other attributes of existence. If he is
successful in purifying himself, he will in turn expurgate the universe
reflected within him.

The most important aspect in practice was considered to be constant
endeavour and the complete surrender of oneself to the *yūzū nembutsu*.
A *saṃgha* was created by a number of individuals recording their names
in the membership book and agreeing to accept, according to their
ability, a daily assignment to chant 100 or 1,000 or more *yūzū nembutsu*.
The power of the *yūzū* to effect purification was regarded as *Tariki* or
salvation by 'Other power'. The individual surrendered himself to this
power, abandoning attachments and desires of the ego and the inter-
transference of merit accrued by the chanting of the group mutually
affected and purified each member, as well as influencing the greater

society to which he belonged. In this manner, the entire group could attain (*ōjō*) the Pure Land by means of the *yūzū nembutsu*.

Besides the profound Kegon notion of *jiji muge* as the principle of interrelatedness, Ryōnin also used the Tendai concept of ten worlds contained within one thought[3] to express his view of the totality contained within each microcosm. The *yūzū nembutsu* was believed to be the one form of religious practice capable of uniting all individuals, despite their exterior differences in personality, social status, ability and degree of spiritual advancement. By constant recitation, all stages of existence could be purified. The only requirement was complete surrender to faith in the *yūzū*.

Since the *yūzū nembutsu* sect was based upon the direct revelation of Amida to the founder Ryōnin, it recognized no patriarchs or lines of transmission prior to Ryōnin, and its principal scriptures consisted of the verses revealed by Amida and the *Ryōgemon*, (a commentary on Amida's Revelation) composed by Ryōnin. The *Kegongyō* (*Avataṃsaka sūtra*) and *Hokekyō* (*Lotus Sutra*), both from which the idea of *yūzū* was derived, were considered helpful in comprehending the doctrine; of lesser importance was the Pure Land *Triple Sutra* (The Smaller and Larger *Sukhāvatī-vyūha* and the *Meditation sutra*).

3. Restoration of Transmission by a Kami

After Ryōnin's death, his disciple Gongen succeeded him as leader of the sect and transmission of the teachings proceeded smoothly up until the sixth abbot Ryōchin, who died at the age of thirty-five, prior to selecting a successor. Just before his death in 1182, Ryōchin entrusted the membership book containing the names of the followers and their assigned recitations as well as other Yūzū Nembutsu treasures, to the Iwashimizu Hachiman shrine, believing the deity Hachiman would protect the succession of the sect by discovering a talented individual. The wait took nearly one hundred and forty years, creating a serious decline in the sect.

The successor ultimately believed chosen by Hachiman to carry on the Yūzū Nembutsu tradition was Hōmyō, born in 1279, who by the age of twenty-five had already experienced the tragic loss of his parents, wife and children. For a time he had studied at Kōyasan, but his search for a proper teaching led him to Nara and Hieizan as well. Then in 1321 at the age of forty-three, he joined the Ōhara Yūzū Nembutsu group and built a small hut in his native area near Osaka to disseminate the teachings.

Reportedly at midnight on the fifteenth day of the eleventh month (1321), Hachiman appeared to Hōmyō in a dream, announcing that he had been selected to become the seventh successor of Ryōnin. The next morning Hōmyō reported the dream to the priest of the Hachiman shrine and received the membership book and treasures deposited there and was installed as the seventh abbot.

The Yūzū Nembutsu sect claims this transmission through the *kami* Hachiman to be unique in Japanese Buddhist history. It apparently was quite in keeping with the views of the founder, who had established close ties with the indigenous faith. The role of the Shintō shrine in this event is most unusual and implies a relationship between certain shrines and temples that would be unthinkable under modern conditions since the shrines have become institutionalized.

Hōmyō restored the Dainembutsuji temple in Osaka, became its master and established it as the centre of *yūzū nembutsu* practice. He also worked to restore the various branch temples of the sect that had also fallen into ruin during the near century and a half without leadership.

One interesting political aspect of the Yūzū Nembutsushū under Hōmyō was support of Emperor Go-Daigo and his Southern court at Yoshino. While in power, the Emperor had allowed Hōmyō to perform the *yūzū nembutsu* at court and even entered his name with one hundred of his attendants in the membership book accepting daily recitation assignments. Subsequently when Go-Daigo was driven from Kyoto by Ashikaga Takauji, Yūzū Nembutsu members faithfully served him in exile at Yoshino.

The Yūzū Nembutsushū also established a special relationship with Shingon under Hōmyō, who initially had been a monk of Kōyasan. And after Hōmyō's death in 1349 at the age of seventy-one, his successor

Kōzen donated a life-size statue of him to the Annyō-in on Kōyasan. The *yūzū nembutsu* was incorporated into Shingon practice, and even today is frequently used during Shingon funeral ceremonies. A popular belief arose that during life one should practice Shingon teachings and then at death join the Yūzū Nembutsu in order to reach the Pure Land; a different version even reversed the idea. The Yūzū Nembutsu maintained relations with both Shingon and Shingi (Neo) Shingon.

After Hōmyō, who is regarded as the Middle Restorer of the sect, the movement experienced another decline during the late Muromachi and early Tokugawa periods, suffering from division as well as being eclipsed by the more popular Pure Land sects. It ultimately experienced restoration by Daitsū (1649–1716), who became the forty-sixth successor during the Tokugawa period.

Daitsū[4] was born in Osaka in 1649 and during his youth frequently visited the Dainembutsuji with his mother. By this time more than thirty generations had passed since the death of Hōmyō and the morale of the order had collapsed, just as the main buildings had fallen into disrepair. This situation made a profound impression upon the young man. His mother died when he was seventeen and his father seven years later, consequently he decided to enter religion. For a number of years he studied Tendai, Zen and other philosophies under leading scholars of the day, but in 1681 at the age of thirty-three he became a disciple of Ryōkan, the forty-fifth abbot of the Yūzū Nembutsushū.

In an effort to restore the dying order, Daitsū presented a petition to the Tokugawa Shōgun Tsunayoshi, then travelled throughout Japan a number of years engaged in missionary work. And in 1688 when Ryōkan died, Daitsū finally received official permission to restore the sect; the following year he became the forty-sixth abbot.

Daitsū spent the remainder of his life renovating the buildings of the Dainembutsuji, creating rules and regulations for the control of the monks, organizing a study institute and composing two theological works: the *Yūzū Enmonshō* (Treatise on the Complete Teachings of the Yūzū) in 1703, establishing the sect's doctrine of direct transmission from Amida, and the two volume *Yūzū Nembutsu Shingeshō* (Treatise on Yūzū

Nembutsu Faith) in 1705 to clarify the teachings. He also founded the Enmanji temple in 1702 to disseminate the *yūzū nembutsu* in the Kitano district of Kyoto.

The popularity of the sect increased so rapidly under Daitsū's inspiration that soon Emperors and court ladies were listening to the teachings and in Edo even the Shōgun's family joined in its activities. At this time *Dainembutsu-e* (*nembutsu* gatherings) came to be held regularly in January, May and September, festivals that have continued up to present day.

After the success of the order was assured, Daitsū spent the remainder of his life engaged in travelling missionary activities. He is believed to have ordained more than five hundred monks and nuns and built over thirty temples. He died in the second month of 1716 in Edo at the age of sixty-eight, and is considered responsible for the preservation of the sect. Today this order claims some three hundred fifty branch temples under the Dainembutsuji headquarters. Although the Yūzū Nembutsu sect is not representative of the main stream of Pure Land Buddhism, it does symbolize the important transition between Heian Buddhism and the new Kamakura movements.

C.   Theological Basis of the Jōdo and Jōdo Shinshū Sects.

The most significant development of Pure Land belief during the Kamakura period was the rise of the single-practice Jōdo and Jōdo Shinshū sects. Insofar as this has been the most misunderstood form of Buddhism, we will now present an analysis of the historical, textual and doctrinal background of this controversial movement that became the mainstream of modern Japanese Buddhism.

1.   Historical Background and Transmission

Very little is known regarding the inception of belief in either the Buddha Amitābha or his Western Pure Land (Sukhāvatī) in early India, and to date no hypothesis has won general acceptance. The earliest forms of the *Larger Sukhāvatī-vyūha* and *Amitābha* sutras both appeared during

approximately the first century A.D. at the time of the Kuṣāṇa dynasty
in northwestern India, which has led some scholars to theorize that they
were created under the influence of western thought imported from
Persia, Rome and other nations having frequent interchange with India.[5]
But even if we accept such a premise, it is apparent that the theological
concept of the Pure Land is an extenuation within the Buddhist tradi-
tion of such early notions as the Tuṣita heaven of Maitreya and the
Mahāyāna idealizations of Enlightenment in the form of the Buddha-
lands (*Buddha kṣetra*). Descriptions of the Pure Land found in the *Larger
Sukhāvatī-vyūha sūtra* bear striking similarities to the "Mahā-Sudassana
Suttanta," a solar myth of the early Pāli *Dīgha Nikāya*.[6] Contemporary
Japanese scholars find other historical antecedents in the Indian belief in
Uttarakura, a mythical northern continent, as well as the adornments
of the stupas erected in honour of the Buddha, which in themselves formed small sacred Buddha lands with lakes, trees and golden decorations
resembling the descriptions of the Pure Land.[7]

Amitābha

As there also is no clear Indian precedent for the figure of Amitābha,
various attempts have been made, particularly by western scholars, to
establish a foreign origin, such as the Zorastrian heaven of boundless
light corresponding to the name Amitābha (Infinite light), or the Persian
Zervan Akarana, as the possible basis of the Buddha's alternate name
Amitāyus (Infinite life).[8] However, it seems rather uncalled for to search
outside the Indian tradition for varieties of solar myths since that nation
fostered such an abundance of them even prior to the Vedic Age.[9]

Numerous attempts have been made to trace the origin of Amitābha
to the Vedic deities Yama or Viṣṇu,[10] but none has received general
recognition, possibly because the Mahāyāna assimilation of Hindu deities
tended deliberately to blend their traits and characteristics to match
philosophical concepts. The use of the attributes 'infinite life' and 'infinite
light' in relation to the historical Buddha both have a long history dating
back to the days of Early Buddhism. For instance, the *Dīgha Nikāya*
relates how the Buddha mastered *iddhi* (supernatural powers) and attained

the ability to prolong his life for aeons if he so desired, but instead purposely chose to terminate it.[11] The same story is enlarged within the *Larger Sukhāvatī-vyūha sūtra* and can be viewed as representing a justification for the Buddha's finite lifespan as well as reflecting the fervent desire of his followers that he live forever.[12] In a similar vein, frequent references are made to the Buddha in the Pāli canon as symbolizing 'infinite light.'[13] The Mahāsaṃghika school was among the first to unite these two attributes of the Buddha and list them consecutively, thus creating a transition to Mahāyāna development.[14]

Another historical precedent for the concept of Amitābha can be found in the evolution of the theory of the Six Buddhas of the past found in the Pāli canon (Seven, when Śākyamuni is included). These Buddhas, the earliest of whom had near infinite lifespans, were created to idealize the enduring quality of the historical Buddha's Dharma and Enlightenment. Analogous was the historical Śākyamuni's statement that he was merely a 'discoverer' of the path traversed by the Enlightened Ones of former times.[15] Such efforts to idealize the Dharma and Enlightenment in place of the historic individual were the basis of the Mahāyāna devotional evolution of myriads of Buddhas and bodhisattvas.

Fifteen varying *Jātaka* tales attempt to provide a mythical origin for Amitābha, but none grant the Buddha a central role, nor do any correspond to the story of Dharmākara bodhisattva (Amitābha's name prior to Enlightenment), found in the *Larger Sukhāvatī-vyūha*. Despite the obscurity of Amitābha's origin, the Buddha enjoyed considerable popularity in India and Central Asia, and in later Indian Tantrism held an important position as the most ancient of the Five Transcendent Buddhas.[16]

Transmission

Besides the difficulty in determining the source of Amitābha and his Western Pure Land, in the Jōdo school there is also a problem of establishing an official line of transmission or set of patriarchs, since Hōnen made no definitive choices. His followers have set forth various systems,[17] one commencing with Aśvaghoṣa, who in the *Awakening of Faith* allegedly cites faith in the Pure Land of Amitābha as a practice for the weak, however there is a question whether this passage was a later addition. The Jōdo Shinshū sect established seven patriarchs consisting of: Nāgārjuna, Vasubandhu, T'an-luan, Tao-cho, Shan-tao, Genshin and Hōnen. In order to obtain a broad spectrum, here we will briefly attempt to survey the major figures of historical significance in Pure Land transmission.

Nāgārjuna and Vasubandhu

Traditionally Nāgārjuna has been attributed an important role in the development of Pure Land thought in India due to his chapter on 'Easy Practice' in the Daśabhūmika-vibhāṣā śāstra. Some Pure Land apologists believe that this chapter, which describes the easy method of reaching the irreversible state (avinivartanīya) on the path to Buddhahood by means of the upāya of faith, represents the essence of Nāgārjuna's personal belief; for despite the fact that he speaks of this path as inferior and for the weak, his statement is interpreted as a criticism of his own early hedonistic life.[18]

Nāgārjuna does mention Amitābha in this chapter but lists as well all the Buddhas of the ten directions as objects of faith. Considerable devotional significance is read into his treatment of Amitābha as a representative Buddha. Nāgārjuna's twelve homages to Amitābha became important in later Pure Land development and inspired T'an-luan, becoming basis for his verses in honour of the Buddha.

Another important figure in Indian Pure Land development was Vasubandhu, founder of the Yogācāra school and author of the Sukhāvatī-vyūhopadeśa based upon the Sukhāvatī-vyūha. In this work, Vasubandhu unequivocally states his own desire to attain the Pure Land, which he equates with the ideal Nirvana. Vasubandhu was also the initiator of five forms of meditation upon Amitābha consisting of: 1) physical veneration, 2) chanting the name, 3) the single-minded desire to attain the Pure Land, 4) concentration and visualization of the Pure Land, and 5) the return of the virtues acquired in the foregoing practices to benefit others. These meditations became extremely significant in later Chinese Pure Land development.

Although neither Nāgārjuna nor Vasubandhu played a crucial role in the practical application of single-practice Pure Land evolution, their positions in the *theoretical formulation* of the philosophy cannot be underestimated. For although the degree of their Pure Land interest can be debated, the Mādhyamika and Vijñānavāda philosophies that they founded served as the main source of inspiration for both T'an-luan and Shantao, the most important Pure Land theologians in China, through whose efforts Pure Land devotion evolved into the mainstream of Mahāyāna Buddhist philosophy.

Chinese Development

In China the *Pratyutpanna-buddha-sammukhāvasthita-samādhi sūtra* (Chin. *Pan-chou-san-mei-ching*) translated by Chih Lou-chia-ch'an during the latter half of the second century, was the earliest sutra to present meditation upon Amitābha and his Western Pure Land as a method of practice. This sutra was used by Hui-yüan (344–416), the first Chinese allegedly to form a society in honour of Amitābha in the year 402, consisting of one hundred and twenty three monk and lay followers. In later periods this group became known as the White Lotus Society (Pai-lien-she). Hui-yüan was a disciple of Tao-an (314–85), an important figure in the development of the Chinese Buddhist order, who was known to have made a vow in later life with eight of his colleagues to seek rebirth in the Tuṣita heaven of Maitreya in order to obtain answers to all his unsolved theological questions.

After the fall of Hsiang-yang, the capital of the Eastern Chin dynasty in 379, Hui-yüan left his master and fled to Lu-shan in Kiangsi where he established a Buddhist community. Due to his known devotion to Amitābha, Chinese Pure Land followers generally consider Hui-yüan the founder of their sect in China. The Japanese do not share this view, for although they respect his efforts to restore and regulate the Buddhist community during a time of political and moral crisis, they do not regard his Pure Land faith as pure, insofar as it lacked a total commitment to Amitābha and was designed primarily as a practice of meditation and purification, utilizing the visualization of Amitābha as a means of calming the mind. In this respect we can note that all the Southern Chinese Pure Land movements such as that of Hui-yüan, Chih-I (530–97) of Mt. T'ien T'ai, and others based upon *Pan-chou-san-mei-ching* meditation failed to become the mainstream of Chinese and Japanese Pure Land Buddhism.[19] Aristocratic Southern China achieved a flowering of Buddhist culture, but Pure Land philosophy could only develop under the harsh alien rule of Northern China that induced sufficient calamities, instability and fear to lead to the mistrust of human capabilities of attaining Enlightenment.

T'an-luan

The first significant Chinese Pure Land scholar of the north was T'an-luan (476–542), born near Mt. Wu-T'ai during a brief period of prosperity following the Buddhist persecution of 446. As a northerner, T'an-luan was exposed to the Shih-lun sect, which in contrast to the southern San-lun (Three treatise school) added the affirmative *Mahā-prajñāparamitā śāstra* attributed to Nāgārjuna as a fourth treatise. According to legend, it was while T'an-luan was engaged in writing a Shih-lun commentary that he became ill and faced the realization that death would terminate his work. In order to gain time to carry on, he decided to seek the Taoist formula for immortality and travelled throughout China at the age of fifty to find a proper master; finally he met T'ao Hung-ching (452–536) and obtained the secret from him. Joyfully returning north, T'an-luan happened to stop at Lo-yang where he encountered the Buddhist monk Bodhiruci, who convinced him that immortality in the human world was a vain hope and that only the *Meditation Sutra* offered a true means of permanently escaping birth and death. Impressed by Bodhiruci's logic, Tan-luan abandoned the Taoist path and sought to comprehend Pure Land teachings. Although there are certain discrepancies in this legendary conversion, it does appear that a meeting with Bodhiruci affected a turning point for T'an-luan that coincided with the political and natural calamities occurring near 530 A.D.

T'an-luan was responsible for establishing a theological foundation for Pure Land faith based upon his interpretation of the philosophies of Nāgārjuna and Vasubandhu. He wrote the *Wang-sheng-lun-chu*, a commentary upon Vasubandhu's *Sukhāvatī-vyuhopadeśa*, and unlike Hui-yüan, based his views upon the Pure Land *Triple sutra* rather than the *Pan-chou-san-mei-ching*. Using his former Shih-lun studies as a foundation, T'an-luan applied Nāgārjuna's doctrine of *Śūnyatā* (Emptiness) to the concept of the Pure Land, stating that birth in the Pure Land represented the 'birth of non-birth.'[20] In the same manner, T'an-luan was the first to clearly discuss the duality implied in the concept of 'self-power', and to advocate, in contrast to the views of other schools, that although the way of Other-power was 'easy', it was also 'superior', insofar as it transcended all dualism between self and the goal. However, T'an-luan believed that any religious practice could be viewed in terms of Other-power, not merely the recitation of the *nembutsu*. This question was to later stir up considerable controversy and divergent interpretations among the followers of Hōnen. Another important aspect of T'an-luan's teachings was the unique quality he assigned to the name of Amitābha, equating it with Ultimate Reality and thus attributing it with the power to break through the ignorance encasing sentient beings.

Tao-cho

Twenty-one years after the death of T'an-luan, his spiritual disciple, Tao-cho (562–645) was born. By this time the concept of the Degeneration of the Dharma (Jap. *mappō*) had gained popularity in China, and Tao-cho visualized himself as one living during the age of Degeneration, which he believed had commenced in 611 A.D., exactly 1001 years after the death of the Buddha.

Tao-cho theologically clarified the concepts of Amitābha and the Pure Land, which his predecessor had not completed, and developed the distinction between the Holy Path (Jap. *Shōdōmon*) or difficult way of the saints and the way of Pure Land believers (*Jōdomon*), which he believed most in accord with the existing decadent age. The Holy Path represented the traditional means of attaining Enlightenment by self-power through intellectual study, perfection of meditation, and other practices, whereas the way of the Pure Land represented attainment by faith, designed for those capable of recognizing their lack of great intellectual ability and personal sanctity. As Tao-cho described the two paths, 'the Holy Path represented a means of apprehending the great potential of the self through the investigation of the truth, whereas the Pure Land path, by understanding the Original Vow of Amitābha, taught the limitations and frailty of the self, or in other words the art of true self-reflection.'[21]

In his two volume work, the An-lo-chi (Essays on the Pure Land), Tao-cho responded to existing criticisms against Pure Land faith, such as the argument that true Dharma does not exist outside of the individual's subjective mind, and to attempt to transcend the mind in order to attain a Pure Land would be contradictory; or the view that one who is committed to saving sentient beings should desire to be born in the polluted world rather than the Pure Land. To such, Tao-cho replied that considering the Pure Land outside of one's own mind was perfectly in keeping with the doctrine of the two truths (in other words, it represented a conventional truth), and that birth into the Pure Land was actually a preparation in order to save sentient beings.[22]

Although Tao-cho was exceedingly devoted to chanting the name of Amitābha and used small beans as counters, he did not consider recitation as the sole practice to attain the Pure Land and still believed meditation equally important. This problem was clarified by his successor Shan-tao (613–81), who at the age of twenty-nine, after initially studying San-lun philosophy, became a disciple of Tao-cho.

Shan-tao

Shan-tao's principal work consisted of four commentaries on the Meditation sutra in which he attempted to point out the errors of traditional interpretation, in particular, the notion of believing that the main practice of the sutra was visualization meditation, or regarding Queen Vaidehī, the heroine, as a reincarnation of the Buddha.[23] Shan-tao maintained the sutra placed equal importance upon chanting the name of Amitābha and meditation, also that the heroine, Queen Vaidehī, symbolized common suffering man. He was the first Pure Land scholar to approach the sutra with an attitude of total personal commitment devoid of intellectualism, for he believed it offered the only means of salvation for an individual as weak and frail as he regarded himself. According to popular legend, Shan-tao's desire to attain the Pure Land was so great that he ended his life by suicide.

Although Hōnen considered that he had been directly inspired by the writings of Shan-tao to found his sect, there were some further Pure Land activities in China, in particular Shan-tao's disciple Hui-kan, who mastered *nembutsu* (Chin. *nien-fo*) meditation and wrote a treatise to demonstrate how common people could attain the Pure Land, and Shao-K'an known as a 'later Shan-tao', for his ardent faith.[24]

In Japan, Genshin is regarded as the first Pure Land patriarch; and although Hōnen eventually rejected his emphasis upon visualization meditation in the Tendai style, Genshin was the first to combine this form of meditation with the chanting of the *nembutsu* and laid a groundwork for practice as well as a philosophical basis in his *Ōjōyōshū*, where he sought means to justify Pure Land devotion in terms of the scriptures. With such a foundation complete, Hōnen was able to totally commit his life to *nembutsu* practice—and it was also Genshin's statement that 'the *nembutsu* is the principal form of karma (deeds) to be born in the Pure Land'[25] that initially inspired Hōnen.

2. Textual Basis—the *'Triple Sutra'*

The mainstream of Pure Land philosophy in China and Japan is based upon what is popularly known as the *'Triple Sutra'*. Actually this consists of the following three independent works:

a. *Larger Sukhāvatī-vyūha sūtra (Daimuryōjukyō)*

Composed during approximately the first century A.D., this text has a number of Chinese translations of which five are currently extant.[26]

Muryō shōjō byōdō kakukyō

Traditionally believed to have been translated by Chih Lou-chia-ch'an of the later Han dynasty, although modern scholars question this theory, and some place the date as late as the mid-fourth century.[27]

Amidakyō

Generally believed to be translated by Chih-ch'ien of the Wu dynasty, often known as the *Dai-Amidakyō* to differentiate it from Kumārajīva's version of the *Amitābha sūtra* known by the same title. This is currently regarded as the oldest translation of the text.

Muryōjukyō

Traditionally believed to have been translated by Sanghavarman of the earlier Wei dynasty in 252 A.D., most likely this was actually a co-translation made by Buddhabhadra and Pao-yün.[28] It is the official version used by the Pure Land schools.

Muryōju nyorai-e

The fifth section of the *Mahāratnakūṭa sūtra* (Jap. *Dai-Hōshakukyō*) translated by Bodhiruci of the T'ang dynsty.

Daijōmuryōju shōgonkyō

Translated by Dharmabhadra of the Sung dynasty.

This sutra, regarded as the principal text of the so-called *Triple Sutra*, relates the story of Dharmākara bodhisattva, who in his desire to attain Enlightenment and create the most perfect of Buddha-lands for the benefit of sentient beings, makes forty-eight vows[29] to adorn his land and after aeons of practice subsequently attains Enlightenment.

The vows can be basically divided into two parts; half relating to the actual formation and attributes of the Pure Land, and the other half to how sentient beings can attain that realm. Nearly each of the forty-eight vows commences with the condition "If in my land, after I have attained Buddhahood . . . " and ends with the fulfillment clause, " . . . then may I not attain supreme Enlightenment." The subsequent Enlightenment of the bodhisattva as Amitābha Buddha is regarded as theological proof of the fulfillment of the vows. The following presents a brief summary of their essence:

1) The three evil existences (hells, *preta* and animal) will have no place in my land.

2) Men and *deva* of my land will never return to one of the three evil existences.

3) Every man and *deva* in my land will possess golden coloured skin.

4) Men and *deva* in my land will have no distinction in appearance between beauty and ugliness.

5) Every man and *deva* in my land will possess the transcendent power of having perfect knowledge of aeons of the past.

6) Every man and *deva* in my land will possess the transcendent power of being able to visualize an infinite number of Buddha-lands.

7) Every man and *deva* in my land will possess the transcendent power of being able to hear, comprehend and practice the preaching of Buddhas in myriads of Buddha-lands.

8) Every man and *deva* in my land will possess the transcendent mental power of being able to comprehend the thoughts of beings in myriads of other Buddha-lands.

9) Every man and *deva* in my land will possess the transcendent power of being able to rise above the myriads of Buddha lands by a single thought.

10) No man or *deva* in my land will have attachment even to his own physical body.

11) Every man and *deva* in my land will reside in the state 'determined' to enter Nirvana.

12) My light shall be immeasurable.

13) My life shall be infinite.

14) The *śrāvakas* of my land shall be inifinite in number.[30]

15) Every man and *deva* in my land will have an infinite lifespan unless he should chose to limit it.

16) Men and *deva* of my land shall never hear an undesirable name.

17) My name shall be praised by the Buddhas of the ten directions.

18) All the beings of ten directions with sincere profound faith who seek to be born in my land and call upon my name ten times (in Chinese, ten times is interpreted as in a 'complete' or 'perfect' manner), except those who have committed the five cardinal crimes[31] or injured the true Dharma, shall be born in my land.

19) I will appear at the moment of death to all beings of the ten directions committed to Enlightenment and the practice of good deeds, who seek to be born in my land.

20) All beings of the ten directions who hear my name, desire the Pure Land and practice virtue in order to attain the Pure Land will succeed.

21) Men and *deva* in my land will possess the thirty-two marks[32] of a great man.

22) The bodhisattvas of other Buddha lands who come to my land will be in the state of one-birth except those who have made a vow and worked to save sentient beings.[33]

23) Every bodhisattva in my land will be capable of making offerings to all the Buddhas in their myriads of lands within the span of one meal.

24) Whatever the bodhisattvas of my land desire in order to make offerings to the Buddhas will appear.

25) Every bodhisattva of my land will have assimilated the wisdom of the Buddha and be capable of preaching it.

26) Every bodhisattva in my land will have an adamantine-body.

27) Everything in my land will be wondrously beautiful and pure, immeasurable in quantity by man, *deva* or sentient being.

28) Even the lowliest bodhisattva of my land will be able to see the immense *bodhi* tree adorned with infinite lights and colours.

29) Every bodhisattva in my land will be capable of reading, chanting and teaching the sutras without hindrance.

30) There will be no limit to the wisdom or intellectual capacities of the bodhisattvas of my land.

31) My land will be so pure and radiant that it will be capable of reflecting the Buddha lands of the ten directions like a perfect mirror.

32) Every object in my land will be made from wondrous gems and there will be hundreds of varieties of fragrances capable of attracting beings to engage in Buddhist practices.

33) All beings of the ten directions exposed to my light will become flexible and joyful in mind and body exceeding man and *deva*.

34) All beings of the ten directions who hear my name will attain the bodhisattva practice wherein they will reside in the true Dharma without being distracted by appearances, and comprehend the profound *Dhāraṇī*.

35) Any woman in the ten directions who hears my name and desires Enlightenment but hates her female body will at her death never again have to be reborn as a woman.[34]

36) Any bodhisattva in other lands who hears my name will perpetually engage in good works and attain Buddhahood.

37) Men and *deva* who hear my name with joy, venerate me, and practice the bodhisattva way will be respected by the beings of the ten directions.

38) Men and *deva* of my land shall be clothed at their very wish.

39) Men and *deva* of my land will experience joy and comfort equal to that of the monk who has extinguished his ignorant desires.

40) The bodhisattvas of my land will be able freely to perceive the myriads of Buddha lands at their wish reflected in the gem-trees.

41) All bodhisattvas of other Buddha lands who hear my name will have perfect physical organs prior to their Buddhahood.

42) The bodhisattvas of other lands who listen to my name will reside in perfect *samādhi* being able in one thought to perceive myriads of Buddhas without loss of concentration.

43) The bodhisattvas of other lands who hear my name will be born into noble households.

44) The bodhisattvas of other lands who hear my name with joy and practice the bodhisattva way will possess numerous virtues.

45) The bodhisattvas of other lands who hear my name will reside in the *samādhi* wherein they can visualize all the myriads of Buddhas until they attain Buddhahood.

46) The bodhisattvas of my land can upon their desire freely hear the Dharma of their choice.

47) The bodhisattvas of other lands who hear my name will attain the irreversible state.

48) The bodhisattvas of other lands who hear my name will receive the first, second and third degrees of proper perception of the Dharma[35] and thus attain the irreversible state.

Various classifications have been made of the vows and their importance in the development of Pure Land theology. But generally, the most crucial vows are numbers seventeen to twenty, which relate to Amitābha's capacity for salvation. Vow seventeen specifically states that Amitābha will be accepted and praised by the Buddhas of every land. The eighteenth to twentieth vows promise salvation for sentient beings— these became the basis of Pure Land theology.

b. *Amitābha Sūtra (Amidakyō)*

Translated by Kumārajīva ca. 402 A.D. A later translation was made by Hsüan-tsang about 650. Neither of the later translations displayed the skill nor competency of the Kumārajīva text which became the official version of the Pure Land schools.

Theologically, this brief sutra is regarded as the concluding text of the *Triple Sutra*. It presents a description of the Pure Land and its inhabitants, clarifying its spiritual nature, emphasizing attainment of the Pure Land by reciting the *nembutsu* and praising the virtues of Amitābha. In some areas the contents are nearly identical to the former sutra. For example, the section on the attainment of the Pure Land by recitation of the *nembutsu* corresponds to the eighteenth, nineteenth and twentieth vows of the *Larger Sukhāvatī-vyūha*. One interesting revelation is the eternal presence of Amitāyus, which is explained in the sutra as the Buddha preaching at the present moment (whenever the sutra is recited).

c. *The Meditation Sutra (Kanmuryōjukyō)*

Traditionally believed to have been translated by Kālayaśas (383?–442?), however, there is no extant Sanskrit original nor any evidence an original version actually existed in India. It is quite likely that the sutra was composed in China or possibly Central Asia.

The setting is the palace of Rājagṛha where Prince Ajātaśatru, deciding to seize the throne, has his father King Bimbisāra imprisoned and denied food. The Queen Vaidehī manages to keep her husband alive by secretly visiting him and bringing flour and grape juice hidden on her body. But when her son the Prince learns of this deception, he has his mother imprisoned and is only prevented from slaying her by the counsel of his ministers. The Queen, in sorrow from her prison chamber, appeals to Śākyamumi Buddha to reveal to her the land without suffering where she might be born. The Buddha then appears and teaches her the virtuous actions and thirteen preliminary meditations to calm the mind and visualize the *Sukhāvatī* of Amitāyus consisting of:

1) the setting sun	8)	Amitāyus enthroned
2) pure water	9)	the form of Amitāyus
3) earth of the Pure Land	10)	the bodhisattva attendant Avalokiteśvara
4) trees of the Pure Land	11)	the bodhisattva attendant Mahāsthāma
5) lakes of the Pure Land	12)	oneself born in the Pure Land
6) mansions of the Pure Land	13)	the Buddha Amitāyus and his attendants.
7) lotus throne of Amitāyus		

Next Śākyamumi proceeds to reveal three further contemplations in the form of the nine classes of sentient beings with different levels of attainment:

1) Superior—Three classes of descending degrees of merit accumulated by the practice of Mahāyāna virtues.

2) Average—Two classes of higher degrees of merit relating to the practice of Hīnayāna, and a third class comprised of those who have lived virtuous lives but not gained faith in Buddhism until the time of death.

3) Inferior — Three classes ranging from average ignorant man to those who have committed the most serious crimes.

> Here it is revealed that even the lowest individual
> guilty of the worst sins is capable of attaining the
> Pure Land on the eve of death if he recites the name
> of Amitāyus up to ten times.

Queen Vaidehī attains Enlightenment and with her five hundred attendants is promised birth in the Pure Land.

The meditations set forth in this sutra are forms of reflection utilized to purify the mind to such a degree that past transgressions can be washed away. Each so-called sin or crime is regarded as an action hindering the attainment of Enlightenment and damaging for the effect it leaves upon the mind. To give an example of the purpose of the meditations—in the first, the setting sun symbolically represents the Pure Land in the west transcending the phenomenal world, and at the same time drawing within its embracing rays all existents to itself. The serenity induced by this meditation ideally creates an atmosphere of reflection capable of illuminating interior ignorance, just as the light of the sun makes it possible to distinguish phenomena in the exterior world. Such symbolism led to the fall and spring equinoxes becoming periods of self-reflection and meditation upon the 'land beyond' (higan, lit. 'other shore') in the Pure Land Sects.

In the second meditation, consideration of the clear mirror-like still water of the Pure Land, ideally led to reflection of reality-as-it-is mirrored in the pure mind. In this manner, each meditation was designed to create an awareness and longing for the 'Absolute'. Among the three texts, The Meditation Sutra presents the most subjective and instrospective view of human life.

The three works composing the 'Triple Sutra' form the basis of Pure Land theology, however, although the Pratyutpanna-buddha-sammukhāvastita-samādhi sūtra (Jap. Hanju Sammaikyō) failed to become a textual source of the mainstream development of Chinese and Japanese Pure Land thought, it did play a significant role in the evolution of the Japanese movement as the basis of Tendai Jōgyō sammai meditation devised by Chih-I and brought to Japan by Saichō and Ennin. Other works considered important by Pure Land scholars consist of the writings of the various patriarchs.

3. Doctrine of the Pure Land or Realm of Purification

In Early Buddhism the efforts to present the goal of Enlightenment in a tangible form for the benefit of spiritual initiates established one of the first theological precedents for the evolution of the concept of the Pure Land, or what may more aptly be described as the 'Realm of Purification.' The laymen who were unable to grasp the abstract notion of Nirvana, let alone comprehend the reasons for practicing virtue in order to attain such an inappreciable reward were led along a different path than the monks. And although this distinction is commonly described as 'two levels of teaching,' it is not possible to qualitatively differentiate between them in terms of 'superior' and 'inferior' or even 'direct' and 'indirect.' For although to appearances it might seem that the layman was on a circuitous route to salvation, it was quite capable of proving to be more direct than the equally hazardous path of the monk entailing the intellectualization of Nirvana and all the inherent dangers of attempting to conceptualize intuitive truth. Even though the final goal be experiential, the human mind initially requires some form of tangible goal to grasp in the form of either an intellectualized concept or symbol of faith, and this ultimately must be set aside. In this respect it is often easier to approach the 'Absolute' by myth or symbol rather than rational means, since man has less difficulty in eventually discarding clay images and myths than the cherished products of his own cerebrations.

Deva heavens—goal of worldly morality

The Early Buddhist teachings for the laity took into careful consideration the accepted beliefs of India of the day such as the existence of *deva* heavens, which varied in attraction in accord with the popularity of the *deva*, and the undesirable realms of Darkness. The most popular method of instruction was known as the three *kathā* or graduated forms of teaching. These consisted of *dāna kathā* (discussion on the benefits of offering), followed by *sīla kathā* (discourse on proper discipline or morality) and finally *sagga kathā*, the promise that if the instructions on offering and morality were heeded, sufficient merit (*puñña*) would be accumulated to be born in a happy heaven.[36] Belief in the existence of such happy heavens served as an inducement to practice virtue, and at the same time as a practical instruction on the law of cause and effect (*kamma*).

Ideally, the practice of morality served as a conditioning agent, purifying the mind to such a degree that the goal of a happy heaven would eventually be set aside. And it was believed that the practice of *dāna* and *sīla* would lead to the four stages of pure mind: 1. being amenable (*kalla citta*), 2. softened (*muda-citta*), 3. unbiased (*vinīvarana-citta*) and 4. upraised (*udagga-citta*). Faith (*saddhā*) or conversion coincided with this attainment. After this, the layman was considered capable of comprehending the doctrine of the Four Noble Truths and entered the first stage of Arahanthood.

The advancement beyond the goal of a happy heaven also entailed setting aside conventional or worldly morality (*puñña*) that had earlier been desirable:

> Herein he who has transcended both good (*puñña*) and bad and the ties as well, who is sorrowless, stainless and pure, him I call a brahman.
>
> *Dhammapada*, verse 412

For although *puñña* had served as a first step toward the psychological attitude known as Nirvana, it was still merely conventional morality, devoted to worldly or materialistic goals and had to be transcended. Good and evil now would be measured solely in terms of mental purification (*vodāna*) or pollution (*sankilesa*) and the process of purification becomes a major interest to Buddhist theologians.[37] But in the transformation from conventional morality to the path of purification, certain seeming paradoxes or contradictions arise, partially as a result of the confines of human language. To give an example, we will view the Buddhist attitude towards suicide.

At the stage of conventional morality there have always been strong injunctions against suicide, but it often becomes difficult for those first becoming acquainted with Buddhism to reconcile this attitude with the popular stories depicting the self-sacrifice of the bodhisattva. In the *Jātakas* for instance, we find the bodhisattva offering his body as food to animals while assuming human form, or to humans while in animal form, and similarly the *Lotus Sutra* presents the fiery self-immolation of Bhaiśajyarāja bodhisattva, which has served as a model for subsequent incendiary suicides up to present times. How is this contradiction related to the transformation from conventional morality to the pursuit of mental purification?

What is commonly regarded as 'suicide' falls wholly into the sphere of worldly morality and cannot properly be applied to the bodhisattva. For when an unenlightened person commits suicide he is attempting to destroy a false notion of self as an independent entity that has never existed, and in the process happens to destroy what can be termed the 'conventional' self. In contrast, the bodhisattva's act drastically differs in quality for it reflects a purified mental attitude. Comprehending the interrelated nature of all existents, his action is analogous to one part of the body sacrificing itself for the purpose of saving the whole. To the unenlightened outsider this may appear to be 'suicide', since the end result is similar; this is why only an Enlightened One capable of intuiting the mental state of the individual involved, can determine whether such an act can be judged as conventional 'suicide' or a non-worldly action.[38]

Purification became one of the few positive predicates of Nirvana in Early Buddhism. Another was *sukha* (joy or happiness),[39] which was not merely synonymous with purity, but in its usage as an equivalent for Nirvana transcended all conventional notions of happiness. When *sukhāvatī* (place of joy) later became a synonym for the Realm of Purification, it went one step further by combining the former happy heaven goal of the laity (attained by the practice of *dāna* and *sīla*) with Nirvana, the product of complete mental purification. Although it did not promise the sensual pleasures of the *deva* heavens, it offered a suitable reward for the practice of worldly morality and successfully eliminated the need for establishing then abandoning an inferior goal along the way. The same goal served both purposes; for the initiate it appeared as a desirable after-life, the reward for a virtuous life, whereas for those further advanced, with a slight change of spectrum, it transformed into the ultimate mental purification—Nirvana.

Mahāparinirvāṇa

Early Buddhism offered ample philosophical precedents for the evolution of the Realm of Purification. The search for ever increasing perfection led to concepts such as the four stages of the Arahant (entering the stream, once-returner, non-returner, Arahant), the Three Worlds and the *Mahāparinirvāṇa* of the historical Buddha. Of these, the last two are most relevant to the evolution of the Realm of Purification.

The idea of *Mahāparinirvāṇa* evolved during the lifetime of the historical Buddha and served both as an explanation for the fate of the Enlightened upon the death of the physical body, as well as a recognition of the fact that even the most perfect Enlightenment could never be permanent nor completely free of obstacles as long as the individual was encased within the human body, which created its own endless circle of longings and desires. Freedom from the physical body theoretically offered the highest form of purification, although it was never a goal encouraged by the this-life oriented historical Buddha, and even further disparaged in Mahāyāna where it could only be interpreted as falling short of true Enlightenment, which entailed active worldly endeavours to benefit others. But the devotional use of *Mahāparinirvāṇa* as a seeming-state after death among the laity provided both a form of veneration for deceased Arhats and the Buddha, as well as a necessary ground for future individual hope. It thus established an important precedent for the evolution of Pure Land thought.

Buddha-lands

In the same manner, the psycho-cosmic theory of the Three Worlds (Desire, Form and Non-Form) as it was completed by Abhidharma scholars, provided realms and stages of spiritual perfection leading up to but not including Enlightenment. The Realm of Desire encompassed all the lower psychological states of man: suffering (hells), instinctual life (animal), greed (hungry ghosts), reason (man), and pleasure (*deva* heavens). Beyond this range of daily mental states were the planes of meditation, which also appeared in the form of *deva* heavens. Among these, the last five stages of the Realm of Form were known as the abodes of purity (*suddhavasa*).[40] And beyond these, the Realm of Non-form, consisting of four final stages of meditation, which led directly to Nirvana, the final experience beyond the Three Worlds. Such tangible analyses of human psychology and the higher states of meditation set a precedent for the future Mahāyāna explorations of the psychological attributes of Enlightenment that culminated in the creation of Buddha-lands (*Buddha-kṣetra*), reflecting the purified subjective mind of the Enlightened One. The *Vimalakīrti Nirdeśa* describes this development in the following manner:

" . . . if a bodhisattva seeks to attain the pure land, he should purify his mind and in accord with the purity of his mind, the Buddha land will become pure.

At that time, Śāriputra inspired by the Buddha's majestic dignity, had the following thought, "if the Buddha land is purified by the bodhisattva's pure mind, is it because our Bhagavat's mind was not pure when he was originally a bodhi-sattva, that this Buddha land is so impure?"

The Buddha understanding his thought asked, "Are the sun and moon impure because a blind man cannot visualize their purity? Śāriputra replied: "No, Bhagavat, that is the fault of the blind man, not of the sun and moon."

"O, Śāriputra, because of the ignorance of sentient beings they are unable to see the majestic purity of the Tathāgatha's land, but that is not the fault of the Tathāgatha, Śāriputra, this land of mine is pure but you fail to see it."

T. Vol. 14 p. 538

The purity of the bodhisattva's mind and hence his pure land in Mahāyāna Buddhism is based upon wisdom (*prajñā*), yet, because of the inseparable relationship between wisdom and compassion (*karuṇā*), the

Buddha-land could not remain the sole mental domain of the Enlightened One but had to serve as a realm of salvation for sentient beings as well, as the sutra further explains:

> The Buddha spoke to Śāriputra as follows: "See the majestic purity of this Buddha land." And Śāriputra replied, "O Bhagavat, it is something I have never seen nor heard before, but now the majestic purity of this Buddha land appears in its totality." The Buddha then told Śāriputra, "My Buddha land is perpetually this pure, but for the purpose of saving men of inferior ability, I merely show them an impure land filled with numerous evils. It is like the *deva* who may partake of food from the same treasure cup, but according to their merits, the food assumes various colours. Thus Śāriputra, if man's mind is pure, he can see the virtuous adornments of this land.

> T. vol. 14 p. 538

The myriads of Buddha-lands represent man's interminable quest to transcend the sphere of human limitations, the grossness and ugliness of human behaviour, and attain a serene ideal world surpassing the boundaries of time and space. If attainment of these realms is equivalent to Enlightenment, then it must be possible to enter them with the present human body, if only briefly, and this is the self-power interpretation set forth by the other sects of Buddhism. They believe Amitābha's Realm of Purification can be realized by the psychological process of purifying the mind, whereby the entire (subjective) world becomes purified. Many Pure Land theologians object to such a psychological interpretation however, maintaining that it is not conducive to universal salvation.[41] For considering the Realm of Purification as a state of mind reduces it to merely another intellectualized concept and diminishes the power it has as a *desideratum* to draw individuals. Tao-cho recognized this problem in his *An-lo-chi*, wherein he states that the Dharma nature of the Pure Land as 'the birth of non-birth' is not suitable for all individuals—for the purposes of salvation, the Pure Land must be something more than a state of mind, yet cannot belong to the Three Worlds.[42]

The depiction in the *Amitābha Sutra* of the Pure Land as existing beyond 100,000 *koṭis* of Buddha Lands (one *koṭī* = 100 million) in the distance erects a thin disguise for infinity that at the same time symbolizes the vast profundity of suffering and ignorance in the present realm of birth and death. To attempt to intellectualize this infinite 'Absolute' as a mere state of mind is in effect to drag it down into the mire of the relative world and destroy both its nature as an 'Absolute' and its benefits as a soteriological goal. It may actually be a state of mind, but not one that can be grasped by the struggling finite man who has never experienced it. In this respect most Pure Land theologians maintain a philosophical propriety in their utter refusal to speak from the standpoint of the 'Absolute'.

There is also deliberate equivocacy whether the Realm of Purification can be attained during the present life or not. In the *Meditation Sutra*, Queen Vaidehī attains Enlightenment but is promised birth into the Realm of Purification in the future. On the other hand, with proper meditation, she is able to visualize Amitāyus in his realm at any time. Thus just as with Nirvana, the Pure Land can never become a permanent state during the present life. But such an attitude, joined with its replacement of the happy heavens of Early Buddhism for the laity, often leads to overemphasis upon the attainment of the Pure Land after death.

Ōjō

The term *ōjō* 往生 (lit. 'go and be born') theologically refers to the 'attainment' of Enlightenment (the Pure Land), although in modern language it is euphemistically used in reference to death by Pure Land believers, in a manner similar to becoming *hotoke* (Buddha).[43] Properly Pure Land theologians, as those of other sects, can make no definitive pronouncement whether life after death actually *exists* or not. As T'an-luan so aptly explained, birth (*ōjō*) into the Pure Land is the 'birth of non-birth—it is clearly not a birth like the false illusion of birth within the Three Worlds'. On the other hand, the symbol of the Pure Land representing the 'Absolute' possesses so many levels of *upāya* (gradations of truth) that it is capable of representing literal rebirth to the laity as well as non-birth for theologians. In this respect it closely parallels the Early Buddhist view of *Mahāparinirvāṇa*. The Enlightened One can be said to live forever in the Pure Land (for nothing is actually lost or destroyed at the time of physical death), but simultaneously the false notion of the individual as a solid permanent entity can be said to be annihilated by death (for it in fact never existed). Likewise, man can be said to cease his attachments and clinging at death and attain the Pure Land, for 'he' has surrendered the basis object of attachment, his 'self' and achieved a pure *anātman* nature.

Philosophical Foundations

The Mahāyāna philosophical foundations for Pure Land development were laid by Nāgārjuna, Vasubandhu and T'an-luan, who are considered by some Jōdomon theologians as the three intellectual patriarchs most concerned with the nature of the 'Absolute' in contrast to their later followers, who placed prime importance upon the experiential role of man. Despite their intellectual proclivities, each of these philosophers was concerned with the plight of man and his struggle to attain Enlightenment. But the difference between their approach and later Pure Land theologians was a preoccupation with discovering the nature of Enlightenment, whereas their followers tended to be concerned purely with human subjectivity.

Nāgārjuna in his explanation of *Śūnyatā* (Emptiness), found the basic cause of human ignorance to be the false belief in a substantial permanent entity known as the 'self' (subjectivity) and its consequent rational differentiation from 'other' (objectivity) with the ensuing round of false ego-centered attachments arising from such innate dualistic reasoning (i.e. 'this is mine', 'what is mine is superior to yours', and ultimately the subconscious—'my possessions and loved ones affirm my existence as an independent entity'). For Nāgārjuna, Enlightenment or *Śūnyatā* was achieved by the intuitive transcendence of all such discriminative thought and the experience of the interdependent-interrelated nature of existence.

Vasubandhu and the Yogācāra school embellished upon this view by analyzing the false notion of 'self' and determining it to specifically consist of the five sense-consciousnesses (visual, tactile, auditory, olfactory, and mental), mental-functions (*mano-vijñāna*) and the notion of ego or consciousness acting as a centralizing unit. In contrast to this, the 'other' or so-called objectivity was merely another form of distorted subjective consciousness, the *Ālaya Vijñāna* (Store consciousness), assuming the appearance of the outside world.[44] The mistaken attachment between the consciousness appearing as 'self' and the consciousness appearing as 'other' were considered to be the root of human suffering and frustrations. Enlightenment consisted in the mental transformation whereby each of the eight consciousnesses acquired a new purified nature:

Five sense consciousnesses → Action Wisdom
(devoted to the benefit of others rather than a false ego)

Mental Functions → Observation Wisdom
(devoted to gathering data in order to aid the Enlightened One in teaching others)

Notion of Ego → Equality Wisdom
(no differentiation between self and other)

Store Consciousness → Mirror-Wisdom
(reflecting the outside world as-it-is, without the taint of ego impressions)

In his *Sukhāvatīvyūhopadeśa*, Vasubandhu describes the condition of the unenlightened prior to his conversion as the 'Realms of Pollution,' which transforms into the 'Realm of Purification.'[45] He then proceeds to equate these new perfections with the description of the Pure Land found in the *Larger Sukhāvatī-vyūha sūtra:*[46]

	PRAJÑĀ (WISDOM)	*REALM OF PURIFICATION (FUNCTION OF PRAJÑĀ)*

Subjectivity (purification of sentient beings) —

Action Wisdom (purified 5 sense-consciousnesses)

Observation Wisdom (purified mental functions) ⎞ Four bodhisattva perfections

Equality Wisdom (purified centralizing unit) ⎞ Buddha's eight perfections

Objectivity (purification of container world) —

Mirror-Wisdom (purification of Store consciousness) ⎞ Seventeen perfections of the Realm of Purification

These perfections or adornments of the Pure Land can be summarized as follows:

Four Bodhisattva Perfections

Related to the two wisdoms that actively work together for the salvation of sentient beings:

1) While residing in a Buddha-land, to manifest oneself in all directions in various manners and perform Buddha-practices to save sentient beings.

(manifestation and practice)

2) Manifesting at the proper time and utilizing varieties of *upāya* to eliminate the sufferings of sentient beings.

(timing and *upāya*)

3) To illuminate every Buddha-gathering in every Buddha-land and to praise and venerate the virtues of the Buddha.

(attendance at every meeting to praise the Buddha)

4) To visit every land that lacks the Three Treasures and establish them there, making it possible for the people of that realm to practice.

(propagating Buddhism)

Buddha's Eight Perfections

Upon attaining the realization of his oneness with all sentient beings, the Enlightened One manifests himself in order to lead all to share his experience.

1) His flower pedestal—symbol of meditation
2) Physical actions—his glorious appearance transcends all other beings
3) Vocal actions—his voice can be heard in the ten direcrions
4) Mental actions—no discrimination or mind of separation
5) Congregation—ability to lead all gathered together about him to the Ocean of Wisdom
6) Unsurpassed excellence—transcending even the highest mountain
7) Venerated by all as master and leader
8) Power of equality—possesses ability to lead all bodhisattvas to the Nirvana of equality

Seventeen Perfections of the Realm of Purification

Description of how Mirror-wisdom functions by transforming the world into the depiction of the Pure Land found in the *Larger Sukhāvatī-vyūha.*

1) Purity—transcending the Three Worlds
2) Quantity—free from all categorical limitations of time and space
3) Origin—arises from the great non-worldly compassion of the Buddha
4) Appearance—objects appear as if in a mirror-like reflection
5) Variety of objects—each of the various objects of this realm assume a gem-like nature
6) Wondrous colour—the clear light unpolluted by egocentric desires gloriously illuminates all phenomena
7) Sensations—every object is soft to touch, the sensations of harshness and coarseness do not exist
8) Three elements of water, earth and sky—beauty of the landscape; the lakes and ponds are covered with floating gem-like flowers, the earth is adorned with gem-trees, palaces and pagodas, while the air is filled with magnificent jeweled nets and tinkling bells

9) Rain—of fragrant flowers
10) Light—wisdom as bright as the sun illuminates and dispels ignorance
11) Wondrous voice—music in the air and the sound of birds ceaselessly chant the name of Amitābha
12) Master—Amitābha resides in his realm
13) Master's attributes—Amitābha's Enlightenment leads others to be born from the flower of Enlightenment
14) Enjoyment—the residents continually enjoy the Buddha's teachings and *samādhi* as food
15) No-difficulty, no-hindrance—physical and psychological sufferings no longer exist, so the enjoyment is constant
16) Nature of residents—the text mentions that the two vehicles and other perjorative names such as 'women' and 'deformed' are not present. What this actually means is that all the residents enjoy equality and none are forced to endure subservient roles such as Hīnayāna (inferior) disciples, women (those who in the social order of the day were reduced to servile woman-like roles) and the deformed or outcasts[47]
17) Fulfillment of all desires—all wishes are capable of fulfillment

This view tends to emphasize the attainment of the Realm of Purification during the present life, for after the transformation of consciousness has been achieved, the present world symbolically appears as the Pure Land. It became the basis of Tendai and other forms of Pure Land devotion. The Pure Land schools, however, were not satisfied with viewing the Realm of Purification as *merely* a transformation of the subjective mind, as we earlier mentioned, for they sought to use it more broadly as an *upāya* to offer salvation to all classes of individuals, rather than merely religious with ample time for spiritual practice.

Transcendence of the Three Worlds

In reviewing the universal descriptions of the attributes of the Realm of Purification found in the writings of the patriarchs, we find one of the most essential common features is that they all agree the land transcends the Three Worlds, which indicates that they all equated it with Nirvana rather than any form of actual 'existence'. And if we analyze what the statement to 'transcend the Three Worlds' implies, we will gain a clearer notion of their conception of the Realm of Purification[48]

1) Realm of Desire— (*Kāma-dhātu*)

to transcend common sensual impressions. This is the reason why in the sutras, descriptions constantly attempt to portray the lakes, trees, pagodas and even music of the land as being of indescribable beauty. In other words, all represent impressions of the purified senses (after their transformation). Despite the magnificence of this world, it cannot create ordinary desire—or as Tao-cho has stated, 'if we cling to the joy of the Pure Land, how can that land remain pure?'[49] It clearly is the realm of emptiness, non-birth and non-discrimination, but it does create the purified desire to lead one's fellow men into its appreciation.

2) Realm of Form— (*Rūpa-dhātu*)

to transcend all conceptions of material existence, hence to discard notions of time and space that necessarily accompany the existence of matter. In this respect, the Realm of Purification cannot properly be spoken of as the present life or future after-life.

3) Realm of Non-Form— (*Arūpa-dhātu*)

to transcend all forms of conceptualization. In other words, the Realm of Purification cannot properly be spoken of even as an intellectual concept. The moment it is conceptualized, it ceases to be the Realm of Purification for its nature is equivalent to Unconditioned Nirvana.

From this brief summary it is obvious that the Realm of Purification can not be viewed *theologically* as a *land* or *heaven* existing after death, such is merely the shadowy symbolic appearance or *upāya* for the laity and spiritual initiates. Even intellectual thought or conceptualization of the Realm of Purification falls into the same category, reducing it to a mere relative symbol.

Although, the Realm of Purification represents the eternal human longing for the perfection of the 'Absolute' and possesses tremendous soteriological value as a goal, it also appears far beyond the level of attainment for the single finite struggling man, who is incapable of correcting the human injustices surrounding him, and so often feels trapped in an impossibly helpless situation. In this respect, Amida Buddha becomes the essential bridge to realization, for Amida, the master of that Realm, exists within oneself.

4. Amida Nyorai

As we have noted, the Realm of Purification acts as a tangible symbol for the experience of the 'Absolute' Nirvana, while at the same time serves as a transcendent goal for struggling mankind. In a closely related manner, the figure of Amida as the *Nyorai* (*tathāgata*), literally 'one who has come from truth (*tathatā*),'[50] symbolizes the manifestation of Absolute truth functioning within and among men. Both the Realm of Purification and Amida are identical in essence, although their soteriological nature varies. The Realm of Purification acts as a goal, while Amida functions as the effective cause of attainment. And just as the Realm of Purification is capable of changing its appearance from a 'happy heaven' to Nirvana in accord with individual spiritual development, so Amida also is capable of changing appearance from a semi-personified being to Absolute truth.

Scholars may dispute interminably over the historical origin of Amida, but such arguments have little theological significance, for even if it is possible historically to prove the concept of Amida to be of foreign origin, the soteriological role of this *Nyorai* is uniquely Buddhist. The theological source of Amida is based upon certain key Mahāyāna concepts, which we will now proceed to analyze:

Prajñā and Upāya

Prajñā in Buddhism refers to spiritual wisdom and in the early Nikāyas, where it was considered to be one of the three pillars of Buddhist practice, it denoted the wisdom 'to perceive reality as-it-is'[51] and thus was equivalent in essence to the experience of Nirvana. In the Prajñāpāramitā sūtras, where the term 'Mahāyāna' is first used, the perfection of wisdom (prajñāpāramitā) is equated with the Unconditioned Dharma-kāya itself and described as the 'Mother of Buddhas', or the 'wisdom that leads to the other shore.'[52]

In contrast, upāya function as: 1) the means of communicating Enlightenment to sentient beings, and 2) as practical methods employed by sentient beings to attain Enlightenment.[53] As a means of communication, upāya appear in diverse forms, such as the promise of a 'happy heaven' as a reward for virtue for spiritual initiates, and the words of the sutras themselves. Since it is impossible to communicate Absolute truth (paramārtha satya) in the conventional world without gravely distorting its nature and reducing it to various relative truths (saṃvṛti satya), the upāya or means of communication vary in degree of purity in accord with the spiritual level of understanding of the listeners. For spiritual initiates in Early Buddhism, the figures of the Indian deva and promises of attaining a 'happy heaven' served as upāya, while for the advanced, the doctrines of the Four Noble Truths and theory of Interdependent Origination also can be regarded as upāya in the developed connotation of the term. There is of course a natural tendency to regard the former teachings as inferior to the latter, but this is not necessarily true.

Upāya can only be judged by their efficacy in communicating truth or leading toward Enlightenment. If the teachings of the Four Noble Truths or Interdependent Origination are intellectualized, serving merely as sources of spiritual or scholarly pride, then they have failed their purpose and proven to be inferior upāya. In this respect upāya function quite analogous to medicine, and just as it is unthinkable to judge one medicine superior to another without taking into consideration the nature of the illness and condition of the patient, so it is equally impossible to determine the efficacy of a given *upāya* without regard for the spiritual, intellectual, emotional and environmental situation of the individual. And this is the reason why only Enlightened Ones are capable of properly imparting or evaluating the merit of *upāya*—in fact, *upāya* represent the active function of their Enlightenment.

In Mahāyāna Buddhism the attainment of *prajñā* (wisdom) is in essence equivalent to Enlightenment, or the experience of Emptiness (*Śūnyatā*). But at the same time that the attainment of *prajñā* reveals the empty (*śūnya*) nature of all existents, it also involves the realization of interrelatedness (*pratītya-samutpāda*). The Enlightened One experiences reality as-it-is, transforming the false dichotomy between subjective self and others into an intuitive comprehension of the interrelated unity of all existence. Such an awareness arouses the spontaneous need to aid all other sentient beings comprising the whole, of which the Enlightened One now realizes he is merely a part, and bring them into sharing his experience. However, this desire to enlighten can only be accomplished by means of *upāya* or the communication of his experience. And since it is impossible to communicate the experience of the Unconditioned 'Absolute' in human language, *upāya* consist of various means of leading or communicating graduated forms of truth in accord with the individual level of spiritual comprehension.[54]

This inseparable relationship between the attainment of *prajñā* and function of *upāya* has been interpreted by Shinran, founder of the Pure Land Jōdo Shinshū Sect, in the following manner:

> In the *Treatise* (Vasubandhu's *Sukhāvativyūhopadeśa*), it is stated that "*Prajñā, karuṇā and upāya, are all three contained within prajñā and prajñā embraces upāya. So it should be known.*"
> '*Prajñā*' is the name of the wisdom that leads to as-it-isness and '*upāya*' is the name of the knowledge that relates to conventional manifestations (of reality). When one reaches as-it-isness, the functions of mind become tranquil. And comprehension of the conventional in itself is the knowledge that thoroughly reflects the plight of sentient beings. Such knowledge is unknowing. The wisdom that leads to tranquility is also

unknowing, yet it too thoroughly comprehends. Therefore *prajñā* and *upāya* are interdependently dynamic and static. The nature of wisdom is dynamic yet static. And static but dynamic is the force of *upāya*. Thus "*prajñā, karuṇā* and *upāya* are contained within prajñā and prajñā embraces upāya.*" And "*so it should be known*" signifies that *prajñā* and *upāya* are the father and mother of the bodhisattvas. If it were not for these two, the way of the bodhisattva would never be achieved.

Kyōgyōshinshō[55]

In a similar vein the *Vimalakīrti Nirdeśa* states:

Prajñāparamitā is a bodhisattva's mother,
his father is *upāya*,
for the teachers of all sentient beings
come only from these two.[56]

Both *prajñā* and its function *upāya* are inseparably interrelated and just as suffering cannot exist without one who suffers, so wisdom in Buddhism cannot exist without thought of the unenlightened and the means (*upāya*) of communicating to them. Both of these aspects form the essence of Amida as a Nyorai or 'the one who has come from the truth.'

In the Pure Land sects, where emphasis is placed upon the plight of man in the conventional world rather than the 'Absolute', the spontaneous need of the Enlightened One to share his experience in the form of *upāya* is manifested as his 'compassion' (*karuṇā*). For unenlightened man, unaware of the nature of reality, such altruistic actions can only be interpreted as 'compassion'. *Upāya* are viewed as the tangible symbols of this 'compassion', as well as the means by which man can attain Enlightenment. In this respect, the twin names of *Amitābha* (Infinite Light) and *Amitāyus* (Infinite Life) represent both the response to man's longing for the 'Absolute', and the interrelated function of penetrating wisdom (symbolized as Infinite Light) and compassion (Infinite Life or deliverance from birth-and-death). In this manner the essence of Amida is revealed in his name and it is not accidental that Amida's two attendant bodhisattvas Mahāsthāmaprāpta (wisdom) and Avalokiteśvara (compassion) were also chosen to demonstrate these inseparable qualities. In a similar,

albeit horizontal manner, a related theme is found in the Mahāyāna
Trikāya theory.

The Trikāya Theory

The seeds of the *Trikāya* theory appear in Early Buddhism with the
gradual idealization of the historical Buddha and his Enlightenment in
the form of the thirty-two marks of a superior man and ten mental
powers. And during the rise of the Abhidharma schools, the Mahāsaṃghika were the first to declare the historical Buddha totally free from
human desires, possessing an infinite lifespan and infinite powers. The
Sarvāstivādins were not willing to go so far, and declared that the
human body (*rūpa-kāya*) of the historical Buddha possessed human desires, but his Enlightenment and teachings (*Dharma-kāya*) were free from
such limitations. Later in the *Aṣṭādaśasāhasrikā prajñāpāramitā* and Mādhyamika school, this distinction was enlarged upon and the *Dharma-
kāya* was understood to represent Ultimate Reality or As-it-isness
(*tathathā*). Such a distinction was still not completely satisfactory. It was
obvious that the very mention of the Unconditioned 'Absolute' by name
reduced its nature to a relative absolute, but at the same time, man
struggling to transcend his finite self needed to grasp the 'Absolute' in
some tangible form as an object of devotion and longing. This need
ultimately resulted, under Vijñānavāda influence, in the creation of a
Trikāya theory consisting of:

Dharma-kāya—	The Dharma-body or Ulti- mate Reality	(Absolute Truth)
Saṃbhogha-kāya—	Enjoyment body or the idealized Buddha image	(mythical conceptu- alization of Abso- lute Truth)
Nirmāṇa-kāya—	Manifestation body appear- ing in response to the needs of the audience	(relative truths in the conventional world)

Although at a glance this theory appears completely transcendent, we
must keep in mind that the *Dharma-kāya* actually is Enlightenment,
hence is to be found within one's own self—or, as Vasubandhu explain-

ed, is identical to Mirror-wisdom, the transformation of the *Ālaya Vijñāna*. Since Mahāyāna Buddhism recognizes the capability for Enlightenment existing within every sentient being, the so-called Buddha nature is equivalent to the *Dharma-kāya:*

> Buddha nature is Dharma nature,
> Dharma-nature is *Dharma-kāya.*
> *Dharma-kāya* has no colour, or form,
> thus is beyond our comprehension.
> It transcends words and language.
> This oneness, manifests in form,
> showing the appearance of the *Upāya Dharma-kāya,*
> and declares it is Dharmākara Bhikku
> (the name Amitābha prior to Enlightenment).[57]

There is some discrepancy in sectarian efforts to place Amida within the *Trikāya*, since the theory was slightly modified within the various schools. The *Larger Sukhāvatī-vyūha* sutra initially describes Amida as *saṃbhogha-kāya*, and in most descriptions elsewhere, Amida is presented as a prime example of this Buddha-body. But later Chinese translations of the sutra vary, and the Sung version considers Amida both as *Dharma-kāya* and *saṃbhogha-kāya*. The Chinese scholars also had some disagreement over the classification and some, such as Hui-yüan (523–92) and Chi-ts'ang (549–623) contended Amida was merely a *nirmāṇa-kāya*.

The most significant theological view of Amida in China was set forth by T'an-luan, who clearly distinguished two natures existing within Amida, a Dharma body with a Dharma-nature and a Dharma-body with an *upāya*-nature.[58] He contended that these differed in function, although they were identical in essence. The concept of two natures actually arose from the relationship between *prajñā* and *upāya*, insofar as the Dharma-body of the Dharma-nature represented the realization of wisdom, and the *upāya*-body was activated by that wisdom towards sentient beings. The fundamental concept of Amida in the Japanese Pure Land schools is derived from T'an-luan's exposition along with some slight elaboration by Tao-cho and Shan-tao on the *saṃbhogha-kāya* nature of Amida.

The Chinzei branch of the Jōdo sect emphasizes Amida as a *saṃbhoga-kāya* as a result of his *practices*, in keeping with their belief that other practices combined with the *nembutsu* are the means of attaining the Realm of Purification. In contrast, the Seizan branch of the Jōdo school places Amida as a *saṃbhoga-kāya* as a result of his vows. The Jōdo Shin-shū sect shares this view, and in particular emphasizes the crucial Eigh-teenth vow promising he would not attain Enlightenment if any being with sincere faith seeking to be born in his land and calling upon his name should not attain that goal. The Jōdo Shinshū sect also recognizes the importance of the Twelfth and Thirteenth vow, providing the *saṃbhoga-kāya* Amida with his attributes of 'infinite life' and 'infinite light'. In Shinshū theology, the *nirmāṇa-kāya* is viewed as another aspect of the *saṃbhogha-kāya* and believed to be a special manifestation for those who rely upon self-power and practices other than the chanting of the *nembutsu*. But this is considered to be a limited and conditioned form of the Buddha arising out of his Ninteenth and Twentieth vows, which promise attainment of the Pure Land to those who practice good deeds, and this Realm is regarded as a 'manifestation' Pure Land, not the actual one.

According to the Jōdo Shinshū interpretation, Amida appears as a manifestation from the *Dharma-kāya* (as-it-isness) and then further manifests himself in various bodies to lead beings to Enlightenment. Shinran explained this in the following manner:

> Arrival at certain extinction is eternal joy. Eternal joy is ultimate serenity and ultimate serenity is Absolute Nirvana. Absolute Nirvana is the Unconditioned *Dharma-kāya* and the Uncon-ditioned *Dharma-kāya* is Reality. Reality is the Dharma-nature. The Dharma-nature is truth as-it-is and truth as-it-is is Oneness as-it-is. Thus Amida Nyorai coming from as-it-isness manifests various bodies as *saṃbhogha* and *nirmāṇa-kāya*.[59]

In this manner, the figure of Amida embraces the entire *Trikāya* and offers multiple levels of interpretation depending upon the individual degree of spiritual attainment.

It cannot be denied that for the average man on the street, Amida assumes a role closely approximating a deity, with certain crucial differences. There is never any association of judgement or punishment with Amida, nor the separateness of a creator-god, and the belief in the indwelling of Amida within the individual is a constant present factor. In this respect at the most unsophisticated levels, a natural feeling of affinity exists between Amida (and all the other Buddhas) and the Shintō *kami*. This is why it was easy for lay followers of the Jōdo and Jōdo Shinshū sects to accept a modified form of *shinbutsu shūgō* (unity of gods and Buddhas), in which Amida embraced the indigenous deities. And this devotional role relates to another aspect of Mahāyāna Buddhism associated with the origin of Amida—the bodhisattva.

The Bodhisattva and his vows

The notion of the bodhisattva was the result of two closely united movements of thought in Early Buddhism; the idealization of the Buddha and development of popular devotion. As the Indian *deva* were reduced in status and made subservient to Buddhism, it became necessary to establish a new object of devotion in the form of the Buddha himself. This is why the thirty-two marks of a great man, gift of supernatural powers (*iddhi*), the stupa, and other such idealizations increased in importance. Not a great deal of literature is available to demonstrate how this gradual evolution occurred, since present collections predominately represent the interests of the monks, but it is evident that devotion did play a very important role in the budding religion. And those who mistakenly believe that Early Buddhism was merely a rational-ethical philosophy overlook the adequate sources demonstrating the religious nature of the early *sangha* as well as the dependence of the monks upon the laity both for financial support and future recruits. It is apparent that faith played an important role even in the lives of young aspiring monks, who often joined the *sangha* to attain supernatural powers rather than the goal of Enlightenment.[60]

In Early Buddhism, natural movements in the idealization of the Buddha were to proclaim his birth supra-human, such as depicted in the *Mahāpadāna Suttanta*, and his lifespan exceeding that of normal man.

Next by attributing him with former lives, the Buddha was elevated to an immortality capable of appeasing the longings of common man. This must have been a very effective *upāya* for the laity since a whole body of literature developed in the form of the *Jātaka* or Buddha birth-stories, teaching simple cause and effect morality. Unquestionably the main purpose of these tales was didactic, but by using the figure of the Buddha, they also served to propagate devotion to him—and from such stories the devotional figure of the bodhisattva emerged.

Eventually, the idealization of the historical Buddha reached the degree where he became dehumanized and visualized in terms of his Enlightenment rather than personality. This was a natural development as the *sangha* gradually transformed into men who had never known him personally nor even heard directly from those who had. As the personality of the historical man dimmed, his Enlightenment or 'discovery' became of prime importance. In Mahāyāna Buddhism this reaches an apex in the *Saddharma Puṇḍarīka sūtra*, in which the historical Buddha is dismissed merely as a manifestation of Enlightenment or the Eternal Śākyamuni. But the removal of the historical Buddha's personality created a void in the lives of the laity and monks that had to be filled—and as he became intangible, the figures of mythical Buddhas and bodhisattvas emerged to satisfy devotional needs.

The term 'bodhisattva' has two connotations in Mahāyāna Buddhism: first, it applies to every sentient being on the path to Enlightenment (Buddhahood), and secondly, to those who have attained Enlightenment and return to work for the salvation of others. The latter aspect is most commonly represented by the mythical bodhisattvas (often symbolizing the union of *prajñā* and *upāya*), who have become objects of popular devotion.

Inseparable with the bodhisattva, is the concept of his 'vow' (*praṇidhāna*) or 'commitment to save others.' *Praṇidhāna* is a difficult term to translate into a single English equivalent since it has multiple connotations, but it is frequently rendered as 'vow', 'prayer' (generally in the sense of an earnest wish), 'resolve' or 'aspiration.' However, we cannot consider Amida's *praṇidhāna* as described in the *Larger Sukhāvatī-vyūha* simply as a 'prayer' or 'aspiration' since a great deal more is entailed.[61] As Dharmākara bodhisattva, the future Amida Buddha states that he will *not* attain Enlightenment *unless* the conditions of his *praṇidhāna* have been fulfilled. Since he stipulates his Enlightenment is actually dependent upon the fulfillment of the conditions set forth in his vows, we have to assume that by becoming Enlightened as Amida Buddha, the fulfillment of these conditions is a *certainty*. Thus they cannot be regarded as mere 'wishes' or 'aspirations,' and *'commitments'* would be a better term.

For the bodhisattva, *praṇidhāna* represents the spontaneous necessary function of his Enlightenment in his commitment to save others. But to sentient beings in the conventional world, this appears to represent his ultimate compassion (*karuṇā*), expressed tangibly in the form of *upāya*. In this respect, Amida with his forty-eight vows epitomizes the concept of the bodhisattva committed to the Enlightenment of all beings, and the practice of the Six *pāramitā*.[62] Such a figure presents a powerful *upāya* for those emerged in the human world filled with sufferings and imperfections. Amida can fulfill their longing to transcend their present condition by offering them the link to perfection.

But besides acting as a forceful *upāya*, the essence of Amida's role is the inherent potentiality existing within each sentient being for the attainment of Enlightenment, or in other words the innate 'Absolute,' clouded by false egocentric illusions and desires like brass coated with tarnish. This inherent Buddha-nature represents the true essence of Amida, for although he may be tangibly symbolized as existing without, he can only be discovered within. The link between the indwelling Amida and the creature housing him, blinded by its delusive ego, is the *nembutsu*. In the words *Namu Amida Butsu*, the subjective self (symbolized by *Namu*), and its core of being are inseparably united.

We will take up the topics of 'the nature of faith and the *nembutsu*' and 'self-power versus Other-power' under the Jōdo Shinshū sect, since these were systematized and developed under Shinran in the belief he was clarifying his master Hōnen's teachings. We will now turn to the life of the man who inspired the vast Kamakura Pure Land Buddhist evolution.

D. Jōdoshū

The first single-practice Pure Land sect to rise during the Kamakura period.

1. Hōnen, the Founder

Born in Mimasaka (present Okayama) province in 1133, a year after the death of Ryōnin of the Yūzū Nembutsushū, Hōnen's father was a local samurai, Uruma Tokikuni, possessing a small domain and his mother belonged to the Hata *uji*. During this age of political chaos, Hōnen's family symbolized the plight of the provincial gentry attempting to stem the encroachments of the local *shōen* managers, who were anxious to gain territory. Tokikuni's personal adversary was Akashi Sadaaki, manager of the Retired Emperor Horikawa's estates. The struggle between the two reached its climax in 1142, when Sadaaki made a night foray into the Uruma domain and mortally wounded Hōnen's father. The fate of his mother in uncertain, and although a few biographies and an alleged letter mention her later existence, these are so obviously contrived attempts to demonstrate Hōnen's filial virtues, that modern scholars assume she also perished during this night raid.[63] To avoid pursuit, the nine-year old Hōnen fled to a nearby Bodaiji temple, where he spent three years.

There is no question that the traumatic loss of his parents and subsequent exposure to religious life greatly influenced the child Hōnen. In 1145 at the age of thirteen he decided to enter Mt. Hiei and was ordained after two years by Kōen (d. 1169), famous author of the *Fusō Ryakki*. Three years later, evidently due to his dissatisfaction with the worldly atmosphere of the headquarters at Mt. Hiei where the reigning abbot, a son of the Fujiwara regent had recently been unseated by rampaging *sōhei*, Hōnen retired to the Kurodani sector of the mountain. It was here that he first received his religious name Genkūbō Hōnen[64] from his new master Eikū (d. 1174), a former disciple of Ryōnin's. The Kurodani area, together with nearby Ōhara, had long been a centre for the *nembutsu hijiri* and was particularly famous for its practice of the twenty-five Pure Land meditations set forth by Genshin in his *Ōjōyōshū*.[65] This form of Tendai meditation placed emphasis upon the visualization of Amida and the Pure Land, a practice that Hōnen was eventually to abandon; for as he later explained, 'even if spiritual novices are successful in creating a vision of Amida, in beauty it will never rival the carvings of the great masters, nor could a vision of the Pure Land be as lovely as the real flowers of the cherry, plum, peach or pear.'[66]

While at Kurodani, Hōnen visited Nara to study the philosophy of the Six Sects. And most likely it was at this time that he came into contact with the earlier type of Pure Land devotion propagated by the Yōkan (1033–1111), Chinkai (1091–1152), Jippan (d. 1144), and others. In contrast to Tendai *nembutsu* meditation, this devotion stressed *Tariki* (Other-power) and Amida's vows, based upon the writings of Shan-tao.

It was this variety of Pure Land faith that Hōnen ultimately embraced after his long years of spiritual search, during which he reportedly read the entire *tripiṭaka* five times and still failed to attain peace of mind. Finally in 1175, inspired by a passage in Shan-tao's commentary on the *Meditation Sutra*, Hōnen left Kurodani to establish his *senju* (single-practice) *nembutsu*. In effect, this move meant the rejection of his previous thirty years of religious training, and in particular it meant abandoning Genshin's Tendai form of *nembutsu* meditation, with its emphasis upon visualization of the Pure Land mingled with other devotions.

Hōnen settled in Ōtani in eastern Kyoto where he spent the next forty years, except for his period of exile. There are no records of the names of the benefactors who assisted his move, but he was financially able to construct immediately two buildings besides his living quarters.

It was not long after the move to Ōtani that Hōnen began to draw followers from all walks of life and eventually his popularity attracted the notice of the established religious institutions. Reportedly in 1186, a debate was held at Ōhara between Hōnen and leading Buddhist scholars such as Kenshin (1131–92), who later became Tendai abbot, Chikai,[67] Sōshin, Myōhen of Mt. Kōmyō and Jōkei of Kasagi, before an audience of three hundred. According to most biographers this occasion marked official recognition by the established sects of Buddhism,[68] but modern historians question whether the event has not been overglorified, since there was no reason why the established sects should offer Hōnen such an advantageous platform.[69]

At this time Hōnen was successfully attracting a number of aristocratic patrons such as Taira Shigemori, the favourite son of Kiyomori. But the most important follower, who virtually created a turning point in Hōnen's career, was the Fujiwara regent Kujō Kanezane (1148-1207). Kanezane had served at court under the Taira rule and was also trusted by the new Shōgun Minamoto Yoritomo as a capable and circumspect statesman. In fact, during this period under the youthful Emperor Go-Toba (1183-98 reign), Kanezane's position became near supreme at court until a conspiracy caused his removal from power in 1196. Kanezane became one of Hōnen's most enthusiastic patrons.

Even members of the samurai class were drawn to Hōnen, such as the famous Minamoto warrior Kumagai Naozane, who is romantically depicted in the *Heike Monogatari* as deciding to become a priest after being forced to take the life of a brave youth following the Heike defeat at Ichi-no-tani. But growing popularity created two distinct problems for the new movement: first, the difficulty in controlling disciples who sought to use reliance upon faith as a rationalization for hedonistic conduct, and secondly, the jealousy of the established temples who viewed Hōnen's popularity at the time of their decline as a distinct menace.

Hōnen's Personal Faith

When Hōnen completed his principal theological work, the *Senjaku Hongan Nembutsushū* (Treatise on the Selection of the *Nembutsu* of the Original Vow) in 1197 outlining the essence of his sect, reportedly at the request of Kujō Kanezane, he added a postscript that the work was not to be openly revealed since it contained views that could be improperly used; only a limited number of trusted disciples were even allowed to copy it. And Hōnen's fears were not unfounded since in 1227, fifteen years after his death, the *Senjakushū* was censored as damaging to the true

Dharma and publicly burnt. Although the work offered a theological confrontation to the existing sects in its choice or selection (lit. *senjaku*) of the sole-practice of chanting the *nembutsu*, Hōnen's personal position regarding single-practice was somewhat ambivalent. He enjoyed the reputation of being an outstanding ordination master in the Tendai tradition and frequently participated in formal ordination rites using esoteric tantric ritual. In fact, at the request of Kujō Kanezane, Hōnen even ordained laity for the cure of illness. Such activities would appear to contradict the purity of the 'single-practice' he advocated in his *Senjakushū*. Other aspects in Hōnen's personal life also point up this discrepancy, such as his continuing fascination with the Tendai *nembutsu sammai* meditation after leaving Mt. Hiei, which has led modern critics to maintain that Hōnen was actually not very different from his Tendai predecessors.[70] His daily practice of chanting the *nembutsu* 60,000 times, later increased to 70,000, led to the visualization or trance-type meditation advocated in Genshin's *Ōjōyōshū* that Hōnen had challenged. Furthermore, Hōnen's record of his own visualizations of Amida and the Pure Land between 1198–1206 known as the *Sammai Hottokuki*, and notated to be kept secret until after his death, belonged to this variety.[71] In this respect, there appears to be a contradiction between Hōnen's personal life and his theology that becomes further apparent in his interest in *vinaya*.

The Nembutsu to remove sin

Shan-tao, who had the reputation of being a strict *vinaya* master, was particularly drawn to the *Meditation sutra*, which clearly relates the recitation of the *nembutsu* to the removal of sins (hindrances to Enlightenment). In considering himself a latter-day disciple of Shan-tao, Hōnen was also interested in the power of the *nembutsu* recited continuously to purify previous transgressions. As he explained to Kujō Kanezane, if one raises the mind of proper faith and chants the name but stops with that single chanting, then future offences committed will become hindrances to the attainment of the Pure Land, for even the tiniest sin, if not repented, becomes a hindrance. In this respect chanting the name ten times is better than once and a hundred times better than ten, since each chanting serves as a means of purification.[72]

Such sentiment was in perfect keeping with the Tendai *nembutsu* tradition based upon 'self-power' or personal efforts to attain Enlightenment, but again a seeming contradiction to the 'Other-power' Hōnen advocated in the *Senjakushū*. Thus the established sects observing Hōnen's unreproachable life-style and admirable reputation were slow to criticize him personally, but they quickly moved to assail his followers who publicly observed 'Other-power' single-practice. On the other hand, despite Hōnen's view of the *nembutsu* as a means of removing sin, he did not share the same type of interest in *vinaya* that was being revived among his contemporaries of the Nara schools such as Jōkei, as a reaction to *mappō* thought.

Although later his disciples were frequently to be accused of neglecting *vinaya*, Hōnen's own opinion was that 'during the period of *mappō*, there can be no question of either maintaining the *śīla* or breaking the *śīla*,'[73] for his own thought transcended the simple rules and regulations created in a bygone age and lumped together to create the body of precepts known as '*vinaya*.' In Hōnen's view, one could not reach *ōjō* either by eating fish or not eating fish, and he likened contemporary interest in *vinaya* to the householder attached to his *tatami* (straw floor covering) and worrying whether it might wear out or not, or break. His contemporaries assumed the *vinaya* itself was an existent (rather than a spirit) and spent their concern over the refraction of rules.[74] Hōnen sought to emphasize the *spirit* of Mahāyāna *vinaya* and this attitude was inherited by many of his disciples, in particular Shinran.

Conflict with the Established Temples

Due to the revolutionary nature of Hōnen's movement and popularity among the masses at a time when religious fervour in general was declining, the established temples sought to either control the new Jōdo sect or eliminate it altogether by means of government pressure. In the seventh month of 1204, the most serious incident occurred when these foes united uner the Enryakuji of Mt. Hiei to appeal to the authorities. By this time, Hōnen's following had attracted large numbers of individuals from all social ranks and become increasingly difficult even for him to control. The established temples focused their attack against so-called radical disciples, in particular Gyōkū and Junsai (d. 1207). Gyōkū advocated the *ichinen ōjō* (one-calling attainment), which by its simple appeal quickly gained popularity among the poor and uneducated lower classes, while Junsai (also known as Anraku), was a dynamic, handsome young preacher extremely attractive to the women; these two men were the most visible objects of *nembutsu* popular appeal.

When the Enryakuji petition was presented to court, Emperor Go-Toba, who was personally sympathetic to the movement and later during exile on Oki Island became a *nembutsu* follower, attempted to mediate in company with other prominent aristocrats. Hōnen was uncertain of what course of action to pursue, since he was aware that the temples were motivated by jealousy, but also suspected excesses on the part of some of his followers who, under the name of 'Other-power' single-practice, were known to publicly break the *śīla* by eating meat as well as denouncing other Buddhas. Thus Hōnen chose a moderate course attempting to placate Shinshō, the Tendai abbot, and at the same time setting forth a future guide of conduct for his disciples in the form of a Seven-article Pledge. This has been preserved at the Nison-in temple and in essence can be summarized as follows:

1) Not, out of pretext of devotion to Amida, to criticize Shingon, Tendai, or other Buddhas and bodhisattvas.

2) Not to engage in vicious disputes with men of intelligence who maintain other practices.

3) Not to attempt to make individuals of different beliefs and practices abandon their commitments.

4) Not to encourage meat eating, drinking or sexual indulgence in the name of the *nembutsu*, nor to consider those who maintain the *vinaya* as merely practicing secondary works.

5) Not to state one's own beliefs without restraint nor to engage in unnecessary disputes.

6) Not to use the popular style (*shōdō*) preaching to convert the laity.

7) Not to claim one's own improper interpretations to be the teachings of the master.

This pledge offers an insight into the types of abuses Hōnen was aware existed among his followers. A number of those who asserted to be his disciples incensed the monks of the established sects by declaring their own interpretations of the *senju nembutsu* to be Hōnen's. Prominent monks and scholars who personally knew Hōnen could dismiss such allegations, but they rankled the lesser monks who did not and could observe the immense popularity, arrogance, and even hedonism of some of Hōnen's disciples professing to have their master's sanction for their behaviour.

Hōnen signed the Seven-article Pledge on the seventh day of the eleventh month (1204) accompanied by eighty of his disciples; the next two days more of his disciples signed, making a total of one hundred-ninety signatures. But evidently to add weight to the document a number of disciples were not content to sign merely once: Gyōsai signed four times, Ansai three, and as many as seventeen others signed more than twice.[75]

The pledge satisfied the Tendai abbot and for a brief period peace prevailed, then in the ninth month of 1205 the powerful Kōfukuji temple of Nara presented a petition to the now Retired Emperor Go-Toba to halt the *senju nembutsu* movement. This document, known as the *Kōfukuji sōjō*, was believed to have been composed by Jōkei of Kasagi and contained nine points of alleged sacrileges and crimes committed by *nembutsu* followers. Many of these articles touched upon issues of vital political importance to the established temples. The nine points can be briefly summarized as follows:

1) *Error of establishing a new sect without Imperial Edict.*
   This was the first time a sect had risen among the masses or lower segments of society rather than being officially established by the higher authorities.

2) *Error of drawing new Buddhist images, in particular the Sesshu*

Fusha Mandara, in which the nembutsu followers are directly illumi-
nated by Amida's light but followers of other sects are not.

There are no extant representations of this *mandara*, but according to contemporary accounts, it featured Amida in the centre,
issuing rays of light to illumine the ten directions. A number
of laymen, priests, etc. were drawn surrounding Amida and the
rays issuing forth from the central image managed to directly
touch only *nembutsu* followers. Some versions even went so
far as to depict the *nembutsu* followers taking the life of living
creatures and still receiving illumination while pious monks of
other sects chanting the sutra failed to receive it. The *mandara*
irritated the established church for two reasons: first, it appeared to lack proper scriptural basis, although Hōnen claimed
it was inspired by a statement found in the *Meditation Sutra*.
More importantly, the *mandara* proved to be a most effective
and popular means of instructing the laity, who could gain
hope from it for salvation despite their situation in life.

3) *Error of treating Śākyamuni Buddha improperly.*
   Since the emphasis of the sect was solely upon chanting the
   name of Amida, critics interpreted the 'neglect' of Śākyamuni
   as an insult to the founder of Buddhism.

4) *Error of neglecting good deeds other than the nembutsu.*
   The author of this treatise takes the *nembutsu* creed to an extreme
   by stating that its followers despised or even condemned to
   hell the practice of other devotions such as chanting the *Lotus
   Sutra*, building temples, or creating images. He also declares
   that the sect has abandoned the Mahāyāna tradition by refusing
   to chant other sutras.

5) *Error of rejecting the Shintō gods.*
   This was an interesting criticism because it actually was aimed
   at Hōnen's alleged refusal to venerate famous historical shrines.
   At this time, as the Ritsuryō system was collapsing, respect towards these famous shrines, instituted and supported by the
   government with close alliances to the established temples,
   had diminished.

6) *Error of abandoning practices other than the nembutsu that properly
   lead to the Pure Land.*

Here the author cites the traditional combination of practices believed to result in the attainment of the Pure Land.

7) *Error of misunderstanding the significance of the nembutsu.*

Hōnen's followers did not practice the traditional forms of meditation or visualization of the Pure Land in conjunction with the chanting of the *nembutsu.* The criticism here is that chanting alone represents an inferior form of physical practice.

8) *Error of rejecting the vinaya and compromising with the lay life.*

According to this criticism (aimed at *nembutsu* priests), they neglected to follow monastic discipline while claiming that those who worried about such sins as gambling or meat eating failed to place total reliance upon the power of Amida.

9) *Error of bringing confusion to the nation since the nembutsu practice is not based upon the harmony of the Dharma of the Emperor and Buddha.*

This criticism blames the decline of the eight sects of established Buddhism, with the resulting failure of the Ritsuryō government, solely upon the upsurge of the *senju nembutsu* movement. What the author actually meant was that a religion rising from the masses naturally upset the existing authoritarian control, and he used the existing state of political and social confusion as proof of his contention.

The petition also requested that Gyōkū and Anraku especially be singled out for punishment.

This nine-point denunciation was accepted by the court with mixed feelings, and the immediate action the Kōfukuji hopefully anticipated did not occur. Many of the aristocrats in authority to act upon the petition either sympathized with Hōnen's movement or were actually followers. There is little doubt that if untoward circumstances had not arisen the whole affair would have passed away, but the sudden arrest of two of Hōnen's disciples changed the entire situation and no longer allowed aristocratic sympathizers to prevent drastic action. The events leading up to this incident are as follows:

On the ninth day of the twelfth month in 1206, the Retired Emperor Go-Toba happened to be away on pilgrimage to the Kumano shrine, while at the same time two of Hōnen's disciples, Jūren and Anraku, held a *Rokuji raisan* service at the Palace. This ritual consisted of dividing the day into six-hour watches beginning at sunset and ending the following noon, during which special hymns were melodically chanted in honour of Shan-tao, Nāgārjuna and others. The method of chanting initially had been imported to Japan by Ennin, during the ninth century, but Jūren and Anraku popularized it and the nostalgic haunting melody instantly captivated the attention of the court ladies, soon becoming the most popular sought-after music of the day. Both Jūren and Anraku were famous for their appealing voices, while Anraku also had the envious reputation of being the most handsome monk in Japan.

Exactly what happened during the Retired Emperor's absence is unclear and the biographies differ considerably, but even the sympathetic Jien, brother of Kujō Kanezane, states in his *Gukanshō* that the ladies of the *in* (Retired Emperor's palace) secretly invited Anraku and others to their quarters and permitted them to spend the night. We cannot be certain that the priests were guilty of misconduct, since both had been marked as particular targets by the established sects and it is conceiveable that the entire affair was staged as an entrapment. But as Jien added, there was no question that the *Rokuji raisan* fascinated court women, while the priests themselves held the belief that even if one sinned, he need not fear punishment from Amida for salvation was solely dependent upon faith.

When the Retired Emperor returned he was promptly informed of the scandalous happenings by Hōnen's enemies, and since one of the women involved was his personal favourite, the Emperor's immediate anger, in accompaniment with the waiting Kōfukuji petition and importunities from other established temples, made action imperative.

Exile

Thus during the second month of 1207, Jūren, Anraku and two other disciples were sentenced to death, while Hōnen was ordered defrocked and exiled to Tosa province on the island of Shikoku. Seven other disciples received similar sentences of exile: Jōmon, Chōsai, Kōkaku,

Gyōkū, Shinran, Kōsai, and Shōkū, although the latter two were allowed to remain in the capital under the charge of the Mudōji temple master. We can imagine that Hōnen's exile to the relatively accessible Tosa was in consideration of Kujō Kanezane, who since his fall from grace no longer exercised great power but still had influential friends. The event of Hōnen's exile so demoralized Kanezane that he died less than a month later. But Hōnen still was not without many sympathizers at court who were working to gain his pardon. If he had been less respected as a apiritual leader and gifted theologian, his enemies might have been successful in quelling his movement, but Hōnen's friends at court never wavered in their respect for him.

Officially the humiliation of exile and execution of four disciples satisfied the established temples and the court was not bound to further placate them. There had never been any personal animosity against Hōnen at court and an excuse was eagerly awaited to grant him pardon. The occasion of the Retired Emperor Go-Toba's dedication of the Saishō Shitennō-in at the capital on the eighth day of the twelfth month served the purpose, and Hōnen was pardoned although not yet permitted officially to enter the capital. After his ten-month exile in Shikoku, he took up residence at the Katsuodera temple in a suburb of Osaka and remained there until the seventeenth day of the eleventh month (1211), when he was granted permission to enter the capital. Three days later, he returned to Ōtani and the deserted site of his old living quarters. Jien, who was in charge of the nearby Shōren-in, arranged for him to live in a small hillside temple. But the psychological and physical strains of exile had taken their toll and on the twenty-fifth day of the first month of the following year (1212), Hōnen died at the age of eighty. His place of death at Higashiyama Ōtani is presently the site of the Chion-in temple, headquarters of the Jōdo sect.

2. Doctrinal Divisions Among Hōnen's Disciples

At the time of Hōnen's death, a number of crucial theological problems were left unsolved. Primary among these was the critical relattionship between faith, Other-power (*Tariki*) and the recitation of the *nembutsu.* According to the Eighteenth vow of the *Larger Sukhāvatī-vyūha Sutra,* the essence of the cause of attaining the Realm of Purification could be summarized as consisting of three qualities of mind: sincerity, faith, and desire for attainment plus the action of calling upon or thinking of the name of Amida. Hōnen, following the views of Shan-tao, tended to place more emphasis upon the act of reciting the *nembutsu* and included the three qualities of mind within the chanting of the name. He also believed with Shan-tao that constant repetition of the *nembutsu* was capable of purifying the consciousness and increasing the depth of religious awareness:

> While believing that even a man guilty of the ten evil deeds and the five deadly sins may be born into the Pure Land, let us, as far as we are concerned, not commit even the smallest sins. If this is true of the wicked, how much more of the good. We ought to continue the practice of the *Nembutsu* uninterruptedly, in the belief that ten repetitions, or even one will not be in vain. If this is true of merely one repetition, how much more of many![76]

Such constant repetitions of the *nembutsu* would appear to fall into the category of self-power (*jiriki*), but Hōnen denied this was the case:

> Again, to say that frequent repetitions of the sacred name mean the encouragement of the principle of self-effort shows utter ignorance of facts and is a deplorable blunder. Even one repetition or two of the sacred name must be said to be the *Nembutsu* of salvation by one's own power, if one does it with that thought in his heart; while a hundred or a thousand repetitions day and night for a hundred or a thousand days, so long as one does it with an entire trust in the merits of the great Vow, looking up in confidence to Amida with every repetition, constitute the *Nembutsu* of salvation by Amida's power alone. And so the *Nembutsu* of those who possess the so-called mental states, no matter how many times they may call upon the sacred name, moment by moment, day and night, can by no means be called the *Nembutsu* of salvation by one's own power, so long as they

are really looking up to Amida, and trusting in his saving power alone.[77]

Hōnen, however, did not clarify how the relationship between faith and the multiple recitation of the *nembutsu* functioned as Other-power (*Tariki*), nor exactly at what moment the attainment of the Pure Land became assured. There is also a great deal of equivocacy in his writings regarding the benefit of other practices such as monastic *vinaya*, meditation, and so on.

In viewing the *nembutsu* way of life, Hōnen described in his *Senjakushū* the proper attitude of the *nembutsu* follower to consist of four interrelated aspects:[78]

1) *Practice of veneration* (*Kugyōshu*)
   Respecting and honouring in particular Amida's image, but also the images of all the other Buddhas.

2) *Undivided Practice* (*Muyoshu*)
   Upon facing Amida, to dismiss all worldly thoughts and with a concentrated mind to think of Amida alone.

3) *Perpetual Practice* (*Mukenshu*)
   To ceaselessly chant the *nembutsu*, not allowing the mind to be interrupted during the day by disturbing thoughts or false notions. In particular, if a devotee has vowed to chant 10,000 or so *nembutsu* a day, not to complete the chanting in the morning and spend the remainder of the day engaged in idle thoughts, but rather to intersperse chanting with work throughout the day.

4) *Prolonged Practice* (*Chōjishu*)
   To continue practicing from the moment of commitment until the eve of death, realizing that it is never possible to achieve a sufficient number of recitations.

Thus, the *nembutsu* becomes an interwoven element in the progress of daily life. These four aspects of mind offer an important insight into Hōnen's concept of the *nembutsu* and its practice with the influence of *vinaya* apparent.

Although Hōnen considered the Eighteenth vow of the *Larger Sukhāvatī-vyūha Sutra* to be the essential cause for attaining (*ōjō*) the

Realm of Purification, he did not exclude the other two vows relating to attainment. According to the Nineteenth vow, Amida promises to appear at the time of death to those who practice other works and desire the Realm of Purification, while the Twentieth vow promises attainment for those who desire it and practice virtue. The Tendai, Hossō, and other established sects had interpreted all three vows as bearing equal weight and thus incorporated devotion to Amida within the established practices of their sects. In the *Senjaku Hongan Nembutsushū*, by the very nature of its title, "Selection of the *Nembutsu* of the Original Vow," Hōnen set forth the *nembutsu* as the sole-practice for attaining the Pure Land. But in his personal life, as we have previously noted, he did engage in other practices, even Tantric rituals. He also allowed his disciples equal freedom to follow their own predilections. This tolerance plus the fact that Hōnen's principal disciples greatly varied in age, as well as theological training prior to and after their period of study with him, naturally led to divergent interpretations and ultimately even new religious movements.

While Hōnen was alive, disputes arose over issues such as 'the merits of faith versus practice' and 'one recitation of the *nembutsu* versus many.' These problems intensified after his death, and to make matters worse, nearly all of Hōnen's writings other than the *Senjakushū* were destroyed in the 1227 attack on his tomb. In an effort to clarify Hōnen's thought, further theological developments occurred following his death, but the original disciples managed to maintain a great deal of tolerance towards each other. This was not continued by their disciples, who proceeded to accentuate differences along strictly sectarian lines.

The exact number of Hōnen's followers during his lifetime is uncertain. Allegedly one hundred and ninety official members signed the Seven Article Pledge, although as we have pointed out, some were not content with signing merely once. Hōnen also had followers among the established sects. The theories regarding his major disciples vary and alternate between five, nine, fifteen and twenty-four names. In a record of 1257, five names are recorded, in which the name of Shinran was ostensibly omitted. Later Jōdo sectarian developments also excluded

Kōsai and Chōsai as proper followers of Hōnen. Overlooking such sectarianism, however, we can regard six principal disciples of Hōnen as influential in the transmission and development of the Jōdo tradition, these consist of: Shōkōbō Benchō, Zennebō Shōkū, Ryūkan, Kakumyōbō Chōsai, Jōkakubō Kōsai, and Shinran.

Shōkōbo Benchō—Founder of the Chinzei-ha

Born in Chikuzen province of Kyūshū in 1162, Shōkōbō is regarded among the various Jōdo sects as the most powerful orthodox successor of Hōnen. At the age of twenty-two he came to the capital and studied for seven years at Mt. Hiei before returning to his native province. Three years later profoundly disturbed over the death of his younger brother, he journeyed to the capital again to obtain an image for the shrine he was building in his brother's memory, and at that time first met Hōnen and became interested in the *nembutsu*. Two years later in 1199, at the age of thirty-eight, he came to the capital to become a follower of Hōnen.

After five years of study, in 1204 Shōkōbō returned to Kyūshū to propagate the *nembutsu* teachings throughout the northern section of the island, establishing the Kisshōji, Zendōji (later known as the Kōmyōji), and Ōjō-in temples. He also wrote several works clarifying Jōdo doctrine, and in the second month of the year 1238, he died at the Zendōji at the age of seventy-seven.

The essence of Shōkōbō's thought can be found in his *Tetsu Senjakushū* (Absolute Reliance on the *Senjakushū*) and *Jōdoshū yōshū* (Essentials of the Jōdo Sect). In these works, although he emphasizes the *nembutsu*, he also affirms in accordance with the Twentieth vow, the possibility of attaining the Pure Land by a variety of other practices, in this respect he can be viewed as a link with the Tendai tradition. It is not clear why he chose this method rather than sole-practice of the *nembutsu*, but it can be theorized that he was attempting to demonstrate the continuity between Hōnen's movement and the established Pure Land tradition of other sects. Such a conciliatory attitude was undoubtedly important in his propagation of the *nembutsu* movement in Kyūshū, for although he carried on Hōnen's interest in the masses to a degree, Shōkōbō gained his primary support from the local landlords and *bushi*. To appeal to such an audience, his movement needed respectable ties with the established sects. This attitude of coexistence with other practices ultimately allowed his later Chinzei-ha followers to establish themselves in the capital and Kantō area, becoming the most successful branch of the Jōdo sect.

Zennebō Shōkū—Founder of the Seizan-ha

Shōkū was born in the year 1177 in Kaga prefecture and later adopted by the illustrious Minister of the Centre, Koga Michichika. At the age of fourteen to the surprise of his family, he decided to join Hōnen's movement. Gifted with a brilliant logical mind, Shōkū participated in the compilation of Hōnen's *Senjakushū* in 1198, and at the time of the 1207 persecution, was cited as a *nembutsu* conspirator and sentenced to exile, but escaped by being entrusted to the Jien, the influential Tendai abbot. At the time of Hōnen's death in 1212, Shōkū was thirty-six years old and decided to pursue further Tendai studies. He studied Taimitsu under Jien, received the *Kanjō (abhiṣeka)* ordination and took up residence at the Ōjō-in temple. This temple was located within the Seizan Yoshimine-dera, which had long been popular with the *nembutsu hijiri*, practicing both visualization meditation and the chanting of the *nembutsu*.

An aristocrat from birth, Shōkū maintained close association with the aristocracy throughout his life. Among his patrons were the Kujō family, Fujiwara Teika, the Saionji and Tokudaiji families, Emperor Go-Saga and other prominent members of court. Shōkū did attract some following among the masses, but his *nembutsu* primarily appealed to the aristocracy and his theology was strongly Tendai-oriented. He included other practices as a necessary good *within* the *nembutsu* and personally chanted the *nembutsu* 60,000 times a day.

Shōkū's strong influence at court, Tendai affiliations after Hōnen's death, and harmonization of other practices within the *nembutsu* apparently mollified the established sects and enabled his followers to become established at the capital as the official Jōdo sect. At the time of the

1227 persecution, Shōkū again escaped exile, this time on the grounds that he had proven he was not a follower of the single-practice (senju) nembutsu movement by serving as a funeral master at the time of Jien's death and participating in the Tendai rites. As the other nembutsu leaders were exiled, Shōkū's group expanded and replaced them at the capital. Shōkū composed a number of Tendai-oriented theological works, but so many forgeries were later made in his name that it has become impossible to be certain of his actual writings. Shōkū died at the capital in 1247 at the age of seventy-one. One interesting postscript is the fact that Ippen, founder of the Ji sect, rose among Shōkū's later disciples.

Ryūkan—Founder of the Chōrakuji-ryū

Born in the capital in 1148, Ryūkan completed his early education on Mt. Hiei. It is not certain exactly when he joined Hōnen, but it appears to have been quite late in life. In 1204 at the age of fifty-seven he was granted permission to copy the secret Senjakushū, and many historians place this as the date when he joined Hōnen, although it seems he did have some association with the movement earlier.[79] Even on Mt. Hiei he was known to have devotion to the nembutsu, since he resided for a time among Genshin's followers at Yokawa and, according to legend, chanted the Amidakyō 48 times a day and the nembutsu 35,000 times daily prior to meeting Hōnen. After that he ceased chanting the sutra and increased the nembutsu first to 60,000 times and ultimately to 84,000 times a day.

Among Hōnen's disciples, Ryūkan became the advocate of 'many chantings (tanengi) of the nembutsu' versus the principle of 'one-calling' (ichinengi). In Ryūkan's view, attainment was only possible at the moment of death and all chantings of the nembutsu prior to that acted as a prelude for that one moment of ōjō. As a result, the state of mind during the moment of death and attainment could be described in Tendai terms as the state of joy, and common man at that single moment could finally perfect his nembutsu and break the ties of ignorant ego-attachments.

Although Ryūkan was an advocate of multiple chantings, he affirmed the principle of Other-power (*Tariki*) in chanting and attainment. In many respects his notion of attainment at one moment, the time of death, was actually not so divergent from the disciples who advocated one-calling. Ryūkan personally was to state that one should not be caught up in the argument between one-calling and many, since both were inseparable. The many *nembutsu* could be viewed in the Tendai or Kegon manner as the accumulation of the one. Ryūkan's disciples however, appear to have carried his views to greater extremes.

In a short period Ryūkan became an important disciple, and at the time of Hōnen's death in 1212 he officiated at the fifth-seventh day memorial service. Still, he is best known for his *Ken Senjaku* (Revelation of the *Senjaku*), written as a defence of Hōnen in response to Jōshō's *Dan Senjaku* (Denunciation of the *Senjaku*). As the work is no longer extant, we do not know the nature of Ryūkan's arguments, but it did play an important role in the persecution of 1227. Prior to this persecution, Ryūkan resided at the Chōrakuji temple in Maruyama of Kyoto, but as a result of his defence, he was officially exiled to Ōshū in Mutsu. His disciple Jitsujōbō, however, took his place, and Ryūkan went to Sagami where he died the twelfth month of the same year at the age of eighty. After the fifteenth century his movement was absorbed into the Chinzei-ha and the Chōrakuji temple eventually came under the domination of the Ji sect. His disciple Namubō Chikyō later built a Shin Chōrakuji in Kamakura.

Kakumyōbō Chōsai—Founder of Kuhonji-ryū

Born in 1184 in Sanuki province of Shikoku, Chōsai initially came to the capital at the age of nine to study the classics and joined Hōnen's movement ten years later in 1202. At the time Hōnen was seventy, and Chōsai became one of his youngest disciples. Chōsai accompanied Hōnen on his exile, and after his death in 1212 continued studies under prominent scholars of other sects such as Shunjō—the Tendai, Zen and *vinaya* master of the Sennyūji, and Dōgen—founder of Sōtō Zen. As a result of this later training, Chōsai came the closest among Hōnen's disciples to holding the *nembutsu* views of the established sects. Becoming a leading scholar, Chōsai resided at the Kuhonji temple in northern Kyoto where he attracted a considerable number of disciples, prominent among whom were priests of other sects such as Gyōnen, author of the *Hasshū kōyō* (Outline of the Eight Sects).

In contrast to Hōnen's disciples like Shinran, who believed the practice of devotions other than the *nembutsu* in accord with the Twentieth Vow would lead only to an inferior Pure Land presided over by the *nirmāṇa-kāya* of Amida, Chōsai advocated that the Twentieth Vow promised the true Pure Land, presided over by the *saṃbhogha-kāya* Amida. According to his argument, if the *nembutsu* alone represented the Original Vow and sole means of salvation, then Amida would necessarily be an imperfect Buddha, excluding those of other practices from attainment. Chōsai set forth the theory of *shogyō hongangi* (various practices in accord with the Original Vow), making the Original vow of Amida offer equal emphasis to other devotions such as meditation, *vinaya*, and so on, as the means of attainment. This view was in accord with Tendai and Hossō sects but seemingly quite removed from Hōnen's *senju* (single-practice) *nembutsu*. As a result, Chōsai was not considered by later followers of Hōnen to fit into the orthodox Jōdo tradition.[80] Chōsai died in 1266 at the age of seventy-three.

Jōkakubō Kōsai—Founder of Ichinengi

One of Hōnen's most unique disciples, also later excluded from the Jōdo sect, was Kōsai. Born in 1163 of uncertain family and place, according to the legendary biography, Kōsai had been a Tendai priest who joined Hōnen at the age of thirty-six upon the death of his child. (It appears that he had been a married layman prior to entering Mt. Hiei.)

Considerable controversy surrounds the nature of Kōsai's views as well as whether Hōnen personally expelled him from the Jōdo sect as he allegedly did Gyōkū, also a follower of *ichinengi*. Gyōkū's expulsion appears to have been due to the fact that in advocating the *ichinengi* principle, he encouraged the criticism of other Buddhas and abandonment of the *śīla*. Hōnen was unable to accept an *ichinengi* that condoned a deliberate hedonistic life supposedly balanced by the single-chanting of the *nembutsu*. Although critics attempted to place Kōsai's *ichinengi* in the same category, this does not seem to have been the case.

Ichinengi thought appears to have risen among the idealistic *nembutsu* followers who saw little use in endless repetitions of the name with an improper attitude of mind. To a certain degree, the argument of 'many chantings' versus a 'single calling' resembles the age-old Mahāyāna dispute over the merits of 'gradual' versus 'instant' Enlightenment. The *ichinengi* group wished to pinpoint the actual instant of attainment, the qualities of mind present and interreaction between the ignorant self and Amida (Buddha nature) at that moment. Ryūkan, the advocate of many callings, had placed the moment of perfect attainment at death, when the individual naturally cast aside all physical desires and attachments. Kōsai, strongly influenced by Tendai philosophy, most likely kept in mind the Tendai belief in attainment of the Pure Land during this lifetime by the reversal of the 'ignorant' psychological attitude. In Kōsai's view, a single chanting based on the unity of faith and wisdom represented the conversion or turning point, when individual attainment became certain.[81]

Although Shunjō's biography of Hōnen recounts that Kōsai was expelled from the Jōdo sect by Hōnen personally,[82] we have to doubt the truth of his statement. Shunjō belonged to the Chinzei-ha, who numbered among Kōsai's strongest critics, and in his biography, Shunjō completely fails to even mention the name of Shinran as a disciple of Hōnen, for the Chinzei-ha, in their bitterness over the contemporary success of the Jōdo Shinshū sect, went so far as to claim that Shinran had been merely an offspring of Kōsai and never a disciple of Hōnen.

Historically it is doubtful that Hōnen expelled Kōsai, since we find that Kōsai's name appears among the followers of Hōnen sentenced to exile in 1207. At that time Kōsai was sent to Awa in Shikoku and his name also appears among Hōnen's followers exiled in 1227, when he was sent to Kazusa in the Kantō area. Although Kōsai advocated the *ichinengi*, he did not personally condemn the practice of many chantings, nor did he allow his disciples to break the *śīla*.

After Kōsai's death in 1247 at the age of eighty-five, many different variations of his teachings arose, one group was even associated with the hedonistic Tachikawa-ryū, while others divided over further sectarian differences. It cannot be denied that Kōsai's theological approach bears certain similarities with that of Shinran and might have influenced him. Kōsai's views were easily accepted by the masses, although his purist philosophy led to constant confrontation with the established churches. After Kōsai's exile and death, his movement eventually declined due to lack of support among the aristocracy at the capital and the eventual absorption of many of his lay followers into the Jōdo Shinshū sect. Historically, Kōsai remains as one of the most unique and original disciples of Hōnen.

Other Disciples

Shinran also ranks among these major disciples but we will view his life and teachings under the Jōdo Shinshū sect. Other prominent followers were: Tankū (1176–1253) of Saga who had a large following at the Nison-in; Shinkū (1145–1228) of Shirakawa, who Hōnen later named his successor; and Genchi (1182–1238) of Murasakino. The latter two disciples withdrew to semi-isolated hermitages and managed to escape the later persecutions of *nembutsu* followers.

Among Hōnen's disciples we can note two major trends of thought: first, conciliation with the established sects by advocating practices other than the *nembutsu*, and secondly, a movement towards further purification of the *senju* (single-practice) *nembutsu* in the form of *ichinengi* (single-calling), excluding all other forms of practice. The former appears in keeping with Hōnen's personal life, and the latter a development of the theology he set forth in the *Senjakushū*. With the passing of time these differences increased and sectarian lines arose that ultimately fragmented the Jōdo sect.

3. Later Developments—Foundation of the Chinzei and Seizan branches

The year of Hōnen's death the secret *Senjakushū*, previously read by only a chosen few, was published for the first time and although this led to an increase of followers, it also stirred up a bitter persecution of the Jōdo sect. Prior to this, the members of the established sects were only able to judge Hōnen on the basis of his personal life, which seemed in accord with their principles. The publication of the *Senjakushū* made it obvious to their eyes that his theology offered a direct challenge to their institutions and that the arguments of Hōnen's disciples, which they had considered to be so obnoxious, actually were based upon their master's views. Prominent priests such as Myōe Kōben (1172–1232), who had respected Hōnen during his lifetime, upon actually reading the *Senjakushū* for the first time were stirred to write theological denunciations. Ultimately the Tendai *sōhei* were to confiscate the original wood-blocks of the *Senjakushū* and burn it in the courtyard of the Enryakuji in the name of 'returning gratitude to the Buddhas of the Three Worlds' by destroying a work harmful to the Dharma. A major reason for such an outbreak was the rapidly expanding popularity of the Jōdo sect among both aristocracy and masses.

Although there had been a number of *nembutsu* bans imposed by the court in earlier years, in 1227 a violent persecution was led against the Jōdo sect at the instigation of the Enryakuji *sōhei*.[88] By importunity and coercion, they received Imperial permission to destroy Hōnen's tomb, the original wood-block printing plates of the *Senjakushū* and the exile of Hōnen's leading disciples.

The bases of this persecution were complex. The priest Jōshō challenged Hōnen's disciple Ryūkan to debate by sending him the *Dan Senjaku* (Denunciation of the *Senjakushū*). In Ryūkan's skillful refutation, the *Ken Senjaku* (Revelation of the *Senjakushū*), he made certain 'inflammatory' statements such as calling Jōshō s work 'a pebble thrown in the dark,' which so incensed Jōshō that he appealed to the Tendai abbot Engi (1186–1238) to petition the court to ban the *nembutsu* movement. The reason for the court's acquiescence on this particular occasion was closely related to the socio-political problems of the day. The capital for sometime had been politically unstable, completely lacking law and order. Many temples had been looted, and arson and pillaging were common. The seat of the *de facto* government was in the hands of the Hōjō regents at Kamakura, who did little to control the civil disturbances. Since the masses constituted the largest number of Hōnen's followers, it was simple matter for the established temples to declare the *nembutsu* movement sympathetic to the disturbances, if not inciting them. A crucial factor was that the *sōhei* of Mt. Hiei formed one of the largest military bodies in the vicinity of the capital and were quite capable of enforcing their objectives upon a reluctant court.

The Enryakuji charged three individuals as ringleaders of the *nembutsu* movement: Ryūkan, Kū Amida Butsu (d. 1228), and Kōsai. Briefly Shōkū was also named, until he asserted proof that he was not a follower of the *senju* (single-practice) *nembutsu*. On the seventh day of the seventh month an edict was issued for the exile of Ryūkan to Mutsu in the Tōhoku area, Kū Amida Butsu to Satsuma in Kagoshima prefecture of Kyūshū and Kōsai to Oki Island, but by the end of the month not one of the three could be found. Since their disappearance appeared to undermine the authorities, and the Enryakuji importunities continued, by the thirtieth day of the following month, forty some *nembutsu* followers were sentenced to exile, mainly the disciples of these fugitives. As a result of this persecution all major centres of *nembutsu* activity in the capital and its periphery were destroyed, with the exception of Shōkū's Seizan-ha.

At the same time efforts were being made to have leading *nembutsu* disciples exiled, an attempt was carried out against Hōnen's tomb at Higashiyama Ōtani, which had become an important centre of *nembutsu* devotion. Special officers were sent by the Enryakuji on the twenty-second day of the sixth month in 1227 to destroy the tomb and throw Hōnen's body into the Kamo river. But before they could carry out their order, a retainer of the Hōjō regents charged to observe court activities in the office of *Rokuhara Tandai*, sent Naitō Morimasa, who later became a Pure Land priest, to halt the Enryakuji *sōhei* violence at the tomb. Although Morimasa attempted to prevail upon the *sōhei* to stop their attack until they could receive proper *bakufu* approval from Kamakura, he was unsuccessful, and finally had to send for arms to turn them back.

During the temporary period of quiet following this initial attack, loyal disciples such as Hōrembō Shinkū, Kaku Amida Butsu and others appealed to the influential Ryōkai (1184–1242), eighth son of Kujō Kanezane, who was to become Tendai abbot in 1229,[84] for permission to secretly move Hōnen's body before the *sōhei* could resume their attack. At that time they moved the remains to the Nison-in at Saga, which geographically seemed far enough removed from Mt. Hiei, as well as in the proximity of several important *nembutsu* centres. The body had only been there a few days when another attack by the Tendai *sōhei* appeared imminent. So once again on the twenty-eighth day of the same month, they transferred it to the Raigōbō of the Kōryūji. There the body rested until the anniversary of Hōnen's death on the first month of the following year when the decision was made to cremate it.

There is no explanation why Hōnen's body, in keeping with Pure Land practice, was not immediately cremated at the time of his death. We can merely surmise that Shinkū, to whom he bequeathed all his belongings and made successor at the time of his death, might have lacked adequate authority since many of Hōnen's disciples were still scattered from exile. In any event, when cremation finally took place in 1228, the ashes were supposedly entrusted to Kō Amida Butsu, a disciple of Shōkū's, who privately kept them in his residence, later becoming the site of the Kōmyōji temple—this action created certain problems.

The Higashiyama Ōtani site of Hōnen's death and original tomb had been severely vandalized, and all writings and memorabilia were destroyed. Under normal circumstances this area would have become the centre of the Jōdo sect with the caretaker of Hōnen's remains becoming his officially recognized successor. But now the ashes, and with them the official successorship, rested in the hands of Kō Amida Butsu, a disciple of the very Shōkū who had escaped the 1227 persecution and seemingly capitalized upon the situation by declaring he was not a follower of the *senju nembutsu*. This rankled many of the loyal disciples. Hōnen's appointed successor Shinkū died and thus could not protest the situation, but his close friend Tankū, also an original disciple who controlled the

Nison-in Temple at Saga where the remains had briefly rested, eventually decided to take matters into his own hands and forcefully seize them. Learning of Tankū's plan, Kō Amida Butsu locked his residence, hid the remains and absented himself to Kyūshū. Nevertheless, Tankū's followers allegedly found the ashes and moved them to the Nison-in, which for a century and a half after the death of Hōnen remained the centre of his personal veneration. While at the same time, the followers of Seikambō Genchi of Murasakino quietly began to restore the original tomb at Higashiyama Ōtani.

Of the many schools and branches of the Jōdo sect that developed after Hōnen's death, two are of major historical significance: the Seizan-ha founded by Zennebō Shōkū and the Chinzei-ha of Shōkōbō Benchō. As we previously mentioned, Shōkū and his followers avoided arrest during the 1227 persecution on the grounds that Shōkū proved he was not a follower of the *senju* (single-practice) *nembutsu* movement by serving as a funeral master at the death of Jien (four times Tendai abbot). When all other influential *nembutsu* groups were exiled from the capital and its vicinity, Shōkū's followers remained and officially established themselves as the Jōdo sect. In later years Kō Amida Butsu's control of Hōnen's remains abetted the exclusive monopoly of this group until the close of the thirteenth century.

Eventually Shōkū's Seizan-ha divided into subsects under four of his leading disciples:

Jōon (1201–71)	—	Nishitani-ha
Enkū (1212–84)	—	Fukakusa-ryū
Shōnyū (?–1244)	—	Higashiyama-gi
Shōe (1194–1264)	—	Saga-gi

The Higashiyama and Saga schools disappeared while the Nishitani and Fukakusa temporarily united as the Seizan-ha during the Muromachi period only to later divide into smaller sub-sects.

In contrast to the powerful stronghold of the Seizan-ha at the capital, the Chinzei-ha established its roots in northern Kyūshū where its founder Shōkō had propagated its teachings, and in the Kamakura area where Shōkō's disciple Ryōchū (1198–1287) became second abbot and extended the hegemony of the school. Ryōchū's group became a particular target of Nichiren's attacks against the followers of Hōnen, and Ryōchū personally was instrumental in the Kamakura government indictment of Nichiren.

During the latter half of the thirteenth century, three of Ryōchū's principal disciples (Ryōkū, Nenkū and Ryōe) decided to move to the capital and establish the Chinzei-ha in that prestigious centre that was still more influential than all the provincial areas combined. But due to the absence of their founder Shōkō from Kyoto even prior to the 1207 persecution, as well as opposition from the already established Seizan-ha, it was nearly impossible for them to obtain recognition as legitimate transmitters of Hōnen's teachings. This problem was solved when they decided to absorb the small group of isolated Murasakino followers of Genchi, who while being recognized as orthodox transmitters of Hōnen's tradition at the capital, also in their seclusion had managed to avoid sectarian quarrels and government persecution. Genchi's disciples furthermore had unostentatiously taken control of the Higashiyama Ōtani site where Hōnen had spent most of his life and died. When the Chinzei-ha assimilated this group, they built the Chion-in temple upon the site of Hōnen's first tomb and in a very short period successfully gained recognition swiftly becoming the most influential school of the Jōdo sect.

Gradually the veneration of Hōnen came to centre around the Chion-in temple, although where Hōnen's ashes finally came to rest is still uncertain. They were either kept secretly at the Nison-in or were later transferred, although there is no record. In fact, the present Kōmyōji temple claims Tankū's disciples did not successfully remove the ashes and that they still remain in a stone pagoda at that temple. It is quite possible that the story of Tankū's seizure is somewhat fanciful and that at the time of cremation, portions were distributed among the various disciples, with Tankū's efforts being directed against Kō Amida Butsu's share. In any event, the secrecy to protect them ultimately resulted in their loss.

During the Muromachi period the powerful Chinzei-ha was dominated by two powerful personalities Shōgei (1340–1420), considered the seventh successor, and his disciple Shōsō (1365–1440). For the first time under the leadership of Shōgei, the Jōdo sect was able to break its forced legal affiliation with Tendai and allowed to ordain its own priests. Shōsō, founder of the Zōjōji temple, is considered to be the eighth successor of the school due to his leadership and propagation of the teachings. Together these two men established powerful samurai patrons in the eastern portion of the Kantō area, with temples so prosperous that they were able to establish branches.

The Chinzei-ha headquarters in Kyoto was also active during the Muromachi period, and the Chion-in made a popular appeal at court. By this time, although the aristocracy no longer exercised much political power, their sanction still carried prestige and respectability and was avidly sought by the new religious sects. In contrast to the Jōdo Shinshū movement, which was to make the masses its basis of support, the Chinzei-ha continued the aristocratic-landlord appeal established by its founder. It became popular among the newly rising samurai, who founded *ujidera* (family temples), much in the style of the old days when Buddhism was first introduced to Japan, or Bodaiji (patron temples). During the Warring States (Sengoku) period, the main work of such temples was to pray for battle victories for their lords or prosperity for the warrior family. As a result, the rise and fall of the Daimyō families became a crucial matter affecting the existence of the temples. Due to this aristocratic tendency, the Chinzei-ha and other branches of the Jōdo sect failed to achieve the spectacular growth of their contemporary, the Jōdo Shinshū.

Despite the early theological divisions within the Jōdo sect, the Chinzei and Seizan schools successfully have transmitted the teachings of Hōnen to modern day. We can only theorize that all of Hōnen's various disciples, including Kōsai, Shinran and Chōsai, believed they were actually transmitting the views of their versatile and charismatic master. During his lifetime, Hōnen was capable of gaining respect from the volatile and jealous Enryakuji as well as the common masses, who for the first time found themselves attracted to the hitherto intellectual and aristocratic religion of Buddhism. He was also able to draw some of the finest minds and greatest names of the day as his followers. If more of Hōnen's writings had survived, we might be able to estimate the nature of his genius, as well as reconciling the reasons for the seeming disparity between his personal life and theology. As it is, we can merely present hypotheses—but it is only fair to assume that each of Hōnen's disciples received a major portion of their inspiration from their master, and that he was basically responsible for the future developments of the Jōdo tradition in the form of new sects and movements.

E. Jōdo Shinshū

The Pure Land philosophy capable of capturing the allegiance of the masses and becoming the dominant form of Japanese Buddhism.

1. Shinran, the Founder

Shinran was born the son of Hino Arinori, a minor bureaucrat of Fujiwara descent, in the vicinity of Kyoto in 1173 and ordained by Jien at the age of nine. It is uncertain why he entered the priesthood at such an early age, and some biographers cite family problems, since Shinran's grandfather is known to have had such a notorious reputation that it was difficult for later members of the family to hope for successful civil service careers. At the same time, Shinran's ordination occurs a year after the Genji revolt that initiated the bloody five-year Gempei war, and also coincides with the beginning of the great famine described in the Hōjōki. In all, it was an unsettled time of political and social upheaval during which religious life offered one of the safest havens and most suitable careers for a child who could not aspire to a government position.

After his ordination, Shinran went to Mt. Hiei to study, and there he eventually joined the Eshin-ryū founded by Genshin, and became a dōsō at the Jōgyōdō. At that time, a dōsō was a monk practicing the perpetual nembutsu in accord with one of the four varieties of Tendai meditation known as *jōgyō sammai*. Shinran remained in that position until he reached the age of twenty-nine in the year 1201, and then he left Mt. Hiei to join Hōnen.

Shinran's reasons for leaving the Tendai sect are unclear. Although Mt. Hiei had been relatively free from extreme violence during his stay there, the conditions were far from conducive to an ideal spiritual life. The abbots were involved in the worldly affairs of the court and catered to the aristocracy, while the *sōhei* (priest-soldiers) of the mountain represented the most powerful military force at the capital and were frequently involved in disputes. And although the mountain was still an intellectual centre, institutional corruption had alienated many scholars, who chose to either leave or live in secluded areas.

Prince Shōtoku's Revelation

Before severing ties with the Tendai sect, Shinran made a one-hundred day retreat at the Rokkakudō (Chōhōji temple) in order to receive inspiration for his future course. The temple was then believed to have been founded by Prince Shōtoku and the main image, a Guze Kannon, was regarded as the *honji* (true nature) of the Prince. According to legend, and the newly discovered letters of Shinran's wife Eshin-ni written after his death, it was on the ninety-fifth day of this retreat that he received a revelation in the form of a dream, in which Kannon appeared as Prince Shōtoku and spoke to Shinran. Today, we do not know the nature of this revelation, but two theories exist:

The first is that Prince Shōtoku spoke the verse believed to have been inscribed in his mausoleum in Shinaga, in which he states that 'he is actually Guze Kannon, his wife Seishi bosatsu, and his mother Amida, representing as-it-isness or truth manifested in three bodies. Since his karma in Japan has been exhausted, he is returning to the western Pure Land, but for the benefit of sentient beings in declining ages, the physical body he received from his parents will be left in Shinaga—and those who visit there even once can be certain of attaining the Pure Land.' Some consider this to have been Shinran's inspiration for joining Hōnen's *nem-*

butsu movement.[85] It is certain that Shinran was aware of the legend, as he later copied the verse in his writings.[86]

Most scholars today however, believe that the revelation of the Rokkakudō was the dream in which Kannon, speaking through Prince Shōtoku, promised Shinran that if, as a consequence of past karma he should marry, Kannon would then appear as a beautiful maiden, enter into conjugal relationship with him, serve him through life and at the time of death lead him to the Pure Land.

Those who accept the first theory believe that the second dream occurred later in Shinran's life, motivating him to preach to the masses. However, the first dream is so vague in nature that it is difficult to consider it as sufficient motivation to join Hōnen. On the other hand, if we accept the second more popular hypothesis of Kannon offering to become Shinran's wife, then a problem of interpretation arises. Some modern scholars have viewed the erotic implications as representing Shinran's struggle with priestly celibacy.[87] If this was the case, it would not seem to be an adequate reason for leaving Mt. Hiei, as it was a common practice for priests to keep secret wives, although Shinran might have been too idealistic to engage in such hypocrisy. Celibacy does appear to have been an issue, but it is extremely simplistic to consider this to be his sole motivation for leaving Mt. Hiei, for in Buddhism sexual indulgence is regarded as merely one of the one-hundred and eight hindrances to Enlightenment.

According to popular legend, as a result of this dream, Shinran shortly thereafter married Tamahi, a daughter of Kujō Kanezane, and had one son, Inshin.[88] However, there is no historical proof in the Kujō family for the existence of such a daughter, and we have to presume that this marriage was fictionalized by later followers, who placed momentous historical significance upon Shinran's marriage and wished to imagine that he forsook the *śīla* for a member of the nobility rather than merely the daughter of a provincial landowner.

If we interpret the revelation of Kannon in the light of Shinran's subsequent life, we can view this incident as his motivation to preach the *nembutsu* to the masses and carry the Mahāyāna *śīla* one step further in Japan. For when Saichō decided to establish the independence of Mt. Hiei, he renounced the Hīnayāna *śīla* of Nara, seeking to extend the teachings of Buddhism to all levels of individuals and to embrace them within his Mahāyāna *śīla*. Prior to this, the established Six Sects of Nara had even prohibited the semi-slave class (*nuhi*) from receiving ordination, and Saichō sought to put an end to such discrimination. But by Shinran's time the Tendai sect itself had become aristocratic and no longer practiced the spirit of its founder's equalitarian ideals. To a certain degree, Hōnen's movement was a fulfillment of Saichō's dream, but Shinran was to carry the ideal further by even abolishing the separation of the elite clergy from the laity in his concept of *hisō hizoku* (neither monk[89] nor layman). In this respect, Shinran's dream of taking Kannon, the symbol of compassion, as a wife was a revelation of his personal role among the masses, as well as a promise of hope for every householder who aspired to reach the Pure Land—and directly after joining Hōnen's movement, Shinran began to make his interest in the plight of the common man apparent.

Marriage

Shinran's marriage ultimately became one of the most prominent aspects of his life noted by later writers, for it resulted in the creation of blood succession, a unique feature of the Jōdo Shinshū sect. But at the time Shinran took a wife, his action was not such an unheard of phenomena. From approximately the ninth century on, monks had been taking secret wives, and it was a known practice among those living on Mt. Hiei. There were even a few cases where monks openly married, and Shinran cannot be historically regarded as the first Japanese Buddhist priest to take a wife. But it was an important aspect of his life, and he was the first founder of a sect to establish such a principle.

There is still no certainty of when Shinran married or exactly how many wives he had. This is not surprising when we consider that up until fairly recent times serious questions were even raised regarding Shinran's historicity. The discovery in 1921 of the letters of Shinran's wife Eshin-ni, written to her daughter Kakushin-ni in Kyoto after Shinran's death, did dispel the notion that Kakushin-ni, who cared for him in his later years, might have been a wife.[90] But there are still those who maintain that Shinran had two wives, one in Kyoto prior to his exile, and Eshin-ni who is believed to have been a native of Echigo province. The only tangible evidence for the possible existence of two wives is found in a letter written by Shinran to his son Zenran (24th day fifth month 1256) at the time he disowned him. In that letter, Shinran quotes a portion of a previous letter from Zenran stating that Shinran had been 'fooled by (Zenran's) step-mother' (mama-haha).[91] Those who interpret this passage literally believe that Zenran must have been the son of a first wife of Shinran. However, mama-haha is a pejorative for stepmother, and it is most likely that Zenran was using it to insult his mother. In fact, Shinran admonished Zenran for 'calling his mother such a name while she was still living.'[92] If we accept the Honganji geneology listing the names of Eshin-ni's children, Zenran appears as the second of six offspring.[93]

Even if we hypothesize that Shinran had only one wife, there still exists the dispute over whether Shinran married Eshin-ni in Kyoto or after his exile to Echigo. Some scholars place his marriage to Eshin-ni as taking place a few years after he joined Hōnen,[94] but there is no definitive historical proof. In fact, since Eshin-ni is believed to have been a native of Echigo and daughter of a provincial landlord, the only way Shinran could have married her in Kyoto would have been if she were temporarily living in the capital, perhaps for education. Without further proof, we have to regard Shinran's marriage as taking place after his exile.

Joining Hōnen

Shinran is known to have joined Hōnen's movement in the year 1201, and first assumed the new religious name of Shakkū, which he later changed to Zenshin. In 1207 at the time of the nembutsu persecution, when he was exiled to Echigo province, he received the lay name of Fujii Zenshin. It is not certain why Shinran was selected to be among the disciples of Hōnen exiled in 1207, but it can be theorized that it was due to the fact that he was one of the trusted few allowed to copy the *Senjakushū*. After parting in 1207, Shinran and Hōnen were never to meet again, but throughout the remainder of his life, Shinran believed that he was merely transmitting the teachings of his master.

Exile to Echigo

The experience of being defrocked and exiled at thirty-five must have been traumatic for one dedicated to the religious life since the age of nine. The fact that his master and fellow disciples suffered equal if not worse fates offered little comfort. Although Shinran was not alone in his disgrace he nonetheless must have felt humiliated and suffered a loss of confidence. It was at this time that he began to call himself *gutoku* (lit. ignorant bald head), or *gu*, 'lacking in learning' and *toku*, a pejorative for a monk who does not maintain the *śīla*. The choice of this name was inspired by Saichō, who upon entering Mt. Hiei had vowed to extend the Mahāyāna *śīla* to all beings while calling himself 'an ignorant among the ignorant.'[95]

Through his exile Shinran was formally released from the government *sōniryō* regulations for the clergy, which insisted that monks reside at temples, maintain the *śīla*, engage in study, pray for the peace and prosperity of the nation, and ostensibly refrain from activities among the masses. No longer a servant of the government, he was now in fact a criminal outcast in an extremely authoritarian society. But since he had not assumed the layman quest for material comforts or worldly power, he could truly consider himself to be 'neither monk nor layman.'

Shinran is believed like Hōnen, to have continued to preach the *nembutsu* during his exile in Echigo, but a later list of his followers dated 1343 lists only one member in Echigo. We can merely wonder if his confidence flagged during his four-year exile. The area was not unsympathetic to the *nembutsu* movement, since a number of followers had migrated north prior to 1207 and successfully propagated the teaching. The question is why did Shinran fail to establish a following in Echigo? During his exile Shinran's material concerns were evidently provided through his marriage to Eshin-ni, who was nine years his junior.

Although the family does not appear to have been very wealthy, Eshin-ni's father is commonly believed to have been a minor bureaucrat.

Move to Kantō

On the seventeenth day of the seventh month in 1211, Shinran was pardoned by the Court the same day as Hōnen, but chose not to return to the capital at that time. One reason might have been due to the fact that Hōnen died two months after the pardon. Also, the year coincided with the birth of a son, Shinrenbō, the only child whose birthdate is mentioned in Eshin-ni's letters. Yet three years later in 1214, at the age of forty-two, Shinran accompanied by his wife and children did move to Inada in Hitachi province (present day Ibaragi). The reasons for such a change are unclear, but a contemporary theory cites possibly a large migration of farmers at the time, and hypothesizes that Shinran decided to preach the *nembutsu* to the masses.[96] His activities and residence for the next twenty years in the Kantō area are also uncertain, although it is known that he acquired a sizeable following.

Shortly after moving to the Kantō area, Shinran again had a major religious experience. Although he had early embraced the *senju* (single-practice) *nembutsu*, his past Tendai heritage of other devotions still must have influenced him, for he made a vow to chant the *Triple Sutra* one thousand times for the benefit of sentient beings. After the fourth or fifth day of chanting, however, he realized anew that one single recitation of the *nembutsu* was sufficient and that he was presumptuous to think that he could save other sentient beings when faith itself was a gift from Amida; he thus stopped his chanting. But sixteen or seventeen years later when he lay ill of fever, the remembrance came to mind, and he reminded himself of the folly in believing he personally was capable of helping others.[97]

Although Shinran moved to various places in the Kantō area, it is generally believed that by 1224 he completed the first draft of the *Kyōgyōshinshō* (Teaching, Practice, Faith, Attainment), his major theological work that he continued to revise up until the time of his death. The year coincided with further attempts on the part of the Enryakuji to cease *nembutsu* practice, which perhaps increased Shinran's deter-mination to commit his beliefs to writing. But it is doubtful whether many of his Kantō followers were ever capable of reading his work. Shinran on occasion remarked on the lack of education of the country-side people, and there is no doubt that he regularly had to deal with near illiterate followers.

Nembutsu dōjō

Shinran's method of propagating the teaching was to establish a meeting place at a modified private home known as a *nembutsu dōjō*. Around this centre a congregation (*monto*) would form that in turn assumed a geographical name such as the Takada *monto* or Yokosone *monto*. This system was not unique, since the existence of *dōjō* was mentioned in the *Sōniryō* code of the early Nara period. At that time they represented unauthorized temples or private religious gatherings that were forbidden by the government. The priest Gyōgi (668–749) frequently worked among the masses in this manner and became a target of the Ritsuryō government.

The *nembutsu dōjō* and its congregation (*monto*) was unique insofar as it presented a sharp contrast to the official government-sponsored tem-ple institution, and as such offered a constant challenge to the establish-ment. From the inception of Japanese Buddhism, the government and aristocracy had financed and controlled the temples. The congregational system, which was also used by Hōnen and Ippen, represented a demo-cratic gathering where the members themselves formed their own rules and precepts, and often held regular monthly meetings. Genshin on Mt. Hiei had originally set aside the fifteenth day of each month for *nembutsu* meetings. During the lifetime of Shinran, meetings came to be held on the twenty-fifth day of each month, marking the anniversary of Hōnen's death. Later, after Shinran's own death, the monthly meeting date was changed to the twenty-eighth day (or its eve) in honour of his memory.

Many problems arose with the *nembutsu dōjō* during Shinran's lifetime. Since he personally was unable to supervise each one and later even had to counsel their leaders by letter from Kyoto, a great number of abuses occurred. The *dōjō* leaders tended to become authoritarian and frequently used the *dōjō* and all donations collected as private property. Some even went so far as to teach the countryside people that whether they became large or small Buddhas depended upon whether they offered large or small donations.[98] Often the leaders of the *dōjō* held views radically different from Shinran, which eventually created social problems. To make matters worse, around 1234-5 Shinran decided to return to Kyoto, and his control over the *dōjō* in the Kantō area further weakened. Thus in 1235 (eleventh day seventh month), the Hōjō Regents, who had been relatively silent during the 1227 and other court persecutions of *nembutsu* followers, finally issued an edict against such abuses as eating meat, bringing women and having drinking parties at the *dōjō*. The Hōjō made it clear that they did not intend to punish serious *nembutsu* followers, but did want to put a stop to such abuses. Thirteen days later they further requested the court in Kyoto to deal with morally degenerate *nembutsu* followers wandering through the provinces.

When Shinran returned to Kyoto, his wife and children probably accompanied him, but at some later date Eshin-ni and several children are known to have returned to Echigo. It may have been that she returned to manage property she inherited. It does not appear that she was able to send Shinran and her daughter Kakushin-ni financial aid, although she did send them servants on occasion. During later years in her letters to Kakushin-ni she frequently speaks of her own difficult circumstances and requests small items to be sent from the capital. It still remains puzzling why she did not remain with Shinran.

From Kyoto, Shinran attempted to guide his followers in the Kantō area by letter. There is no certainity how many *dōjō* leaders he had or how many followers they in turn had gathered, but existing records contain considerably less than one hundred names; the seeds of the order at this point were still uncertain.

Zenran

One of the most painful events for Shinran must have been the necessity to disown his son Zenran. Between approximately 1248–56, Zenran went to the Kantō region, probably at the request of Shinran, to attempt to regulate the conduct of the Kantō followers. However, once Zenran arrived, he began to create his own following, assuring those members that what they had previously learned from Shinran was not the real teaching, since Shinran had secretly communicated this to Zenran late one night. Such a claim created immediate confusion among the followers and some expressed an unwillingness to believe Zenran. These he charged before the government authorities with moral corruption and sacrileges against the native gods.

Shinran, upon initially hearing the garbled versions of what was happening in Kantō, was unable to determine the true situation, and his efforts to make peace were unsuccessful. When he ultimately realized his son Zenran was responsible, in 1256 at the age of eighty, Shinran disowned Zenran, denouncing both him and his teachings.

During the winter of 1262, Shinran became ill and, as he faced death, began to be concerned about the welfare of his daughter Kakushin-ni, now widowed and with children. Since Kakushin-ni had been born in the Kantō area, he wrote somewhat hesitantly to the Kantō members on the eleventh day of the eleventh month, requesting them to support her as in the past they had supported him.[99] This was evidently not an easy thing to do, but he obviously felt the responsibility to provide for the future of the daughter, who had faithfully cared for him during his last years. Finally, on the twenty-eighth day of the eleventh month (1262) he died at the age of ninety and was cremated the following day at the Enninji temple at Higashiyama.

Comparing the lives of Shinran and Hōnen, it is obvious Hōnen was the famous scholar, Shinran the nonentity. Why then did Shinran's movement develop and surpass that of Hōnen? Some might say it was an historical accident, the result of later influential propagators such as Rennyo, who arose at the perfect time in history to diffuse the movement. But if this was the case, why the lasting success of Jōdo Shinshū? The institution met severe crises and yet survives, just as Shinran's works today still manage to attract the interest of modern thinkers. Other's might attribute Shinran's entire teaching to Hōnen, as Shinran in his humility was wont to do—but Shinran's approach and lifestyle was far more consistent than Hōnen's appears to be. Thus although we certainly have to question the degree of the master's influence, we cannot fail to attribute a certain uniqueness to Shinran that it appears his master lacked. Perhaps the answer lies in Shinran's conception of faith.

2. Faith and the Nembutsu

If, upon the attainment of Buddhahood, all beings in the ten quarters who aspire in sincerity and faith to be born in my land, recite my name up to ten times and fail to be born there, then may I not attain the Supreme Enlightenment. . .

Eighteenth Vow

In Jōdo Shinshū theology, faith assumes the principal role as the means of attaining the Realm of Purification. But this 'faith' (shinjin) has a un-precedented character in the evolution of Buddhist thought. In Early Buddhism, when faith (Skt. śraddhā) is mentioned, it generally referred to the acceptance or belief in the Three Treasures (Buddha, Dharma and Sangha) as well as the law of cause and effect. As such, it represented a volitional decision or choice on the part of the individual. Such a 'faith' in Jōdo Shinshū, exists merely as a practical effect or phenomenological reality, not as a theological principle. In other words, if we objectively examine the nature or quality of faith among the mass members of the sect, we will find that it differs little from the Early Buddhist belief in the Three Treasures—its nature is primarily volitional, even though there may be certain cognitive elements present. The individual chooses to believe in what may or may not have received support from his reason. Furthermore, when we objectively observe that the Pure Land sects set forth a 'way of faith' in contrast to the intellectual approaches of other sects, we are still speaking of a soteriological method whereby individual devotees volitionally accept a non-rational or trans-rational goal that entails varying degrees of suspension of reason. This may be termed 'conventional faith' and it conforms to our normal understanding of the term, but as it falls completely within the scope of self-power (jiriki), it differs from the Jōdo Shinshū theological concept of faith and ultimately must be abandoned prior to Enlightenment.

If we examine conventional faith based upon human volition and all the ensuing religious and ethical actions arising from such a faith in the light of Mādhyamika philosophy, we find that it is based upon a false dualistic comprehension of reality, or the ignorant assumptions that form the basis of the unenlightened man's daily existence. Separating the subjective self from its container world and falsely believing the self to be an independent entity capable of possessing and controlling other independent entities, was how Nāgārjuna viewed the situation of unenlightened man when he set forth his famous Eight denials and concept of *Śūnyatā* (Emptiness). *Śūnyatā* became equivalent to Enlightenment because it indicated freedom from the false conventional discrimination of reality or *prapañca*, 'the expression of reality based upon categorical reasoning.' All human language and thought fell into this realm and had to be discarded in order to attain the intuitive realization of the true interrelated nature of existence, free from the attachments and distortions of the subjective ego. In the same manner, in Jōdo Shinshū, all forms of volitional faith and action have to be abandoned, for as long as views such as 'I believe,' 'I meditate' or 'I fast' exist, there is no escape from the clutches of the self-centered ego. Volitional faith and actions, which constantly become objects of self-conscious reflection and self-glorification, merely serve to feed the ego and ultimately become hindrances to Enlightenment equally as great as attachments to possessions, fame or honour. Shinran set forth the ideal of a pure faith, totally free from the distortions of the egocentric self and the subjective colourings of self-power (*jiriki*) action.

Experiential Realization of Man's Inability to Attain Salvation

Theoretically, in the light of Mādhyamika philosophy, the pitfalls of volitional faith and volitional religious actions are obvious, but if the realization is merely confined to a theoretical level, then the insidious danger of intellectually rationalizing laziness appears. This is one reason why the heady atmosphere of the *theology* of Jōdo Shinshū is not an appropriate starting point for spiritual initiates. Even in this sect they are weaned upon the pabulum of volitional faith and conventional moral actions until they reach the level of spiritual maturity capable of comprehension. Jōdo Shinshū *theology* is basically oriented towards those individuals who have already entered the stage of self-awareness and are capable of recognizing the constant deceitful guises of the ego—toward those who have nobly struggled but still failed to scale the mountain of religious perfection.

Shinran attained his realization of the nature of man after twenty years of religious endeavours upon Mt. Hiei, which finally led him to understand that despite such a long struggle, he was in effect no further advanced than the layman groping in the slime of worldly attachments for a grubby bit of wealth or spark of recognition. Renunciation of such goals itself becomes a snare of pride for the religious, and the ego, with its consuming desires, feeds and grows upon such spiritual feats as sleepless nites, countless hours of meditation, meagre food and other hardships. Ultimately the end result, despite the nobility of purpose, is identical—food for the ego—be it spiritual or worldly. And it was in this light that Shinran uttered his famous statement, "If even a good man can be born in the Realm of Purification, much more so an evil man."[100] For he had attained the realization that religious self-complacency and social recognition as a spiritual person were perhaps the greatest handicaps of all in the search for Enlightenment.

The basis of the Jōdo Shinshū attitude towards life is a profound self-reflection—the most extreme form of coldly calculating objectivity that man is capable of realizing by his own efforts. This is just far enough to allow him to realize the total futility and absurdity of all his actions. To go further is to bask and glory in one's own misery. But a detached self-reflection upon past endeavours and experience is sufficient to arrive at an awareness of the egotistic pleasures hidden within so-called spiritual practices.

The Tendai sect, by advocating the existence of the Buddha nature in all existents had firmly rejected the theological existence of the *icchantika*, or group of individuals who were forever incapable of attaining Enlightenment. Theoretically their view was unapproachable, but practically they overlooked the fact that the vast majority of mankind never attains Enlightenment. To these people Shinran offered hope through the unique understanding of the nature of faith as a total gift of Amida, rather than the product of one's own generally misdirected ego-dominated efforts. The historical Buddha admonished his followers to rely upon themselves and make personal efforts to attain Enlightenment. But this was merely the first, although extremely essential, step towards spiritual progress. The second step entails the realization of the insidious lurking of the ego behind *every* attempt for spiritual perfection—and thus demands the complete abandonment of the egocentric self, a feat that can only be accomplished through the spontaneous workings of the 'Absolute' itself.

Three Minds Equivalent to One

According to the Eighteenth vow of the *Larger Sukāvatī-vyūha Sutra*, three qualities of mind are necessary for the attainment of the Realm of Purification consisting of:

1) sincerity (*shishin*)
2) faith (*shingyō*)
3) aspiration for attainment [of the Realm of Purification] (*yokushō*)

The important point regarding these three qualities in Jōdo Shinshū thought is the fact that they belong to Amida alone and are in effect a reflection of the single mind (*isshin*) of Amida.[101] As the qualities are interrelated, the possession of one presumes the existence of the other two and determines the future attainment of Enlightenment as well:

Thus we truly understand that 'sincerity', 'faith' and 'aspiration for attainment' are different words but in essence they are one. The reason is because the three minds never have any taint of doubt. Thus they form one mind, which is called the indestructible (*vajra*) mind.[102]

Each of these qualities it devotionally regarded as a product of the merits accumulated by Amida over his long aeons of practice as a bodhisattva. He transfers them to sentient beings, making in effect the mind of the unenlightened sentient being his own mind. This is equivalent to the Vijñānavāda notion of transforming the tainted *Ālaya Vijñāna* (Store Consciousness) into Mirror-wisdom; the difference is that the conversion is not accomplished by the finite individual himself, but rather by the workings of the 'Absolute' (Amida) within him. In this respect the philosophy represents an evolution from the Mādhyamika-Yogācāra concept of man and the nature of Enlightenment.

The possession of these three qualities of mind is given by Amida in conjunction with the Name (*nembutsu*), which is the means of fulfilling the conditions for attaining the Realm of Purification. It is essential in Jōdo Shinshū thought to note the inseparable relationship between the three qualities of mind (one mind of Amida) and calling the *nembutsu*. As we previously noted, Hōnen and Shan-tao tended to emphasize recitation of the *nembutsu*, believing that by its purifying nature the three qualities of mind were established. In contrast, Shinran considered the three qualities to be a necessary condition to properly recite the *nembutsu*:

> The indestructible true mind is called true faith and true faith is certainly provided with the Name. However, the Name is not necessarily provided with the faith supported by the power of the Vow. Therefore [Vasubandhu] the author of the *Jōdoron*, at the beginning states: 'I, with one mind.' And further adds: 'It is the practice truly in accord with the significance of the Name and Reality-as-it-is.'[103]

In Shinran's view, recitation alone without the proper three qualities of mind would in effect be a work of self-power. Thus to call the Name properly can only be a gift of Amida combined with the three qualities of mind.

The next question that arises is how Amida grants the three qualities of mind, transforming the mind of the unenlightened one into his own pure mind? This is accomplished at the moment the unenlightened one interiorly hears the calling of the *nembutsu*.

As all sentient beings hear his Name, joyful faith is awakened
in them leading to one thought, for [Amida's] sincere mind
is 'transferred' to them. When they seek to be born in that
land, they will instantaneously attain (*ōjō*) it and reside in the
irreversible state.[104]

In other words, the 'Absolute' within calls out, and as the self irresistably
responds to this call by hearing the *nembutsu*, the layers of ignorant
egocentric delusion are cracked and penetrated. Figuratively, the active
cause of salvation is the Name (representing compassion) and the passive
cause is Amida's light (symbolizing wisdom). But who is saved? For
pragmatically it is obvious that every individual in the world is not
interiorally hearing the call of Amida. The answer must be that those
who have begun to feel their alienation from the 'Absolute' are the
first to be saved. Salvation is manifested to those who are most in need,
just as "those about to drown are in greater need to be saved than those
standing upon the shore."[105] The first response within the individual to
this call is a profound awareness of his own limitations and shortcomings,
coupled with the reliance upon the compassion of Amida. Shan-tao
described this relationship in his analysis of the two qualities of the 'profound mind' within the sentient being:[106]

Subjective mind (sentient being) *ki*	1)	to recognize oneself as an ignorant sentient being enmeshed and perpetually submerged in the evils of birth-and-death from beginningless time with no hope of overcoming them.
Dharma mind (Absolute) *hō*	2)	to acquire firm faith in the vows of Amida and setting aside all doubts to be assured of salvation.

These two qualities of mind are joined within the *nembutsu* with *Namu*
representing the subjective self-awareness of the individual joined to the
'Absolute' in the form of Amida Buddha.

NAMU——————————*AMIDA BUTSU*

(sentient being)   (Absolute)

The more the individual becomes aware of the hopeless nature of his condition, the greater his reliance upon the 'Absolute' until the moment arrives when perfect faith is established and the *nembutsu* is chanted completing the conditions for attainment of the Realm of Purification. Both self-awareness and the acceptance of belief are considered to be the result of Other-power.

Other Power (Tariki) and Natural Actions (Jinen)

Although the newborn baby is incapable of dualistic rational thought or separating itself from the unity of its environment, its condition is very different from the experience of Enlightenment. For prerequisite to Enlightenment is the rise and eventual shipwreck of categorical reasoning. This is essential because the unity of Enlightenment is based upon the multiplicity of existence—the realm of the 'Absolute' is dependent for its existence upon the phenomenal conventional world. And once the individual has experienced Enlightenment, he must return to work in the discriminative world of daily life.

Just as the shipwreck of reason is essential for the attainment of Enlightenment, so the shipwreck of self-efforts are the essential prerequisite for complete dependence upon Other-power. Without initial efforts and the final realization of their futility, Other-power merely descends to the role of a deity at the relative level—and in most cases becomes another mask of the ego. Undoubtedly Amida is quite often viewed in this manner by the unenlightened, but that is a distortion of Amida's true significance—and also the reason why at the conventional level, the Jōdo Shinshū sect advocates the practice of ethical actions and conventional morality. Self-power is still a potent *upāya* at the conventional level, and as the chain of karma relentlessly drags on, the unenlightened individual is forced to use self-effort in the choice of good actions that will bring beneficial results. There can be no splurge into immoral volitional actions with the idea in mind that Amida will eventually bring salvation, since the individual must still feel the painful results of improper actions. As Shinran wrote:

> When one is miserable all the time,
> misery increases all the more.

Like a man who loves to sleep,
the more sleep he has, the more he feels sleepy.
It is the same with lust for indulgence and *sake*.[107]

On the other hand, the moment he realizes the source of his misery and
alienation, he has begun to respond to the call of Amida and is on the
path to salvation despite the weight of his past deeds.

The fruits of self-effort can lead to a cessation of suffering and the
goal of Enlightenment as long as there is no attachment to them. Continually the individual must observe the weakness of his will and be
aware that the very mind that rejects his finite miserable state is the
same mind that clings to it and prevents him from attaining realization
of the 'Absolute.' The consciousness of 'self' in his efforts must be replaced with the awareness of Amida working as the Other-power
within him, until ultimately this sense completely absorbs him and he is
able to act spontaneously (*jinen*) totally with the mind of Amida. This
does not mean, however, a total surrender to some form of Cosmic consciousness, for in the first place as we have seen, Amida is not an onto-
logical being, and secondly, the individual never totally loses his own
identity, merely his attachment to it. The interrelated relationship between the 'Absolute' and sentient being is essential for the continued
existence of both.

The question arises, how does the Other-power function? From the
standpoint of the sentient being, it would seem that Other-power represents the 'compassion' of Amida. As we have earlier noted, on the
behalf of Amida, this is not properly 'compassion,' but in the eyes of the
sentient being it appears to be such. In fact devotionally it resembles
the Christian concept of grace, yet there are certain theological differences. The results of Other-power are not bestowed by a separate superior entity, nor can they be freely rejected, for they require no obvious
cooperation from the sentient being. Above all, at the *theological* level,
it is not a free gift of the 'Absolute', but the fulfillment of a spontaneous
need similar to the daily necessity for the sun to shed its illumination
over the world, oblivious to the concerns of those touched by its rays.
For the action of leading all sentient beings to Enlightenment is a spon-

taneous function of Enlightenment (the 'Absolute') itself. The 'Absolute' must manifest and call its own, just as man must respond to the atavistic (primeval) glimpse of perfection within himself, and without even realizing it, attempt to establish some form of that perfection in the world about him.

The soteriological manifestation of the 'Absolute' Other-power within the sentient-being is known as merit-transference (Skt. *pariṇāma*), which forms the basis of *Tariki* and has two functions:

1) Outgoing merit-transference (Jap. *ōsō-ekō*)
2) Returning merit-transference (*gensō-ekō*)

Outgoing merit transference consists of the 'Absolute' functioning within the sentient being to draw it towards Enlightenment. Figuratively we can describe this as the voice of Amida calling the individual away from the distractions of the world. In contrast, returning merit-transference consists of the awakened sentient being in turn helping others to attain Enlightenment. These two functions in Mahāyāna Buddhism demonstrate the ceaseless active relationship between wisdom (*prajñā*) and its necessity to communicate itself (*upāya*).

The individual who has received the benefits of the Other-power and the three qualities of mind equivalent to the mind of Amida, henceforth acts in a wholly natural or spontaneous (*jinen*) manner, completely free from egotistical self-awareness and in complete accord with the Dharma. All his actions are aimed at leading others to share his realization, or to assist them in listening to the voice of Amida. Finally, at the moment of death, he is assured of permanently residing in the Realm of Purification.

It might be questioned, if the Realm of Purification is not to be confused with an after-world at the theological level in Jōdo Shinshū thought, why is it spoken of as a permanent attainment only at the time of death?[108] In this respect, the Shinshū view of the Realm of Purification closely resembles the Early Buddhist concept of *Mahāparinirvāṇa*. But we must remember when the Tendai or even other Pure Land sects speak of attainment of the Realm of Purification during this lifetime, they are not actually imagining a permanent state of experience. Just as with Nirvana, it is impossible to consider the experience permanent as long as man has a finite human body and paradoxically, once he has discarded his finite body we cannot in Buddhism properly say he either 'exists' or does 'not exist.' It is possible, however, if he was Enlightened at the time of death, to state that he has permanently attained *Mahā-parinirvāṇa* or the Realm of Purification, since we are not speaking in terms of existence.

In his idealistic search for purity, Shinran discarded even the slightest implication that Nirvana or the Realm of Purification could be solidified and reduced to a finite state. He idealistically rejected the notion that 'I can become Buddha' not only on the grounds that it implied dichotomy between two entities joined by self-power, but because it also implied that the finite can permanently ascend to an 'Absolute' state. The ceaseless functioning of the 'Absolute' does not permit a static moment, the Enlightened One must constantly work for the benefit of others and to accomplish this, he has to live and work in the conventional phenomenal world. There is no permanent area of retreat from daily life, and with the return to active work, the world of discriminative reasoning must again be entered. Thus the movement from the experience of Enlightenment to the resumption of daily life forms a cycle— which can be described as the rise and decay of Enlightenment within the sentient being.

Although Shinran did not permit the notion of permanent attainment of the Absolute Pure Land with this finite body, or by extenuation the attainment of true 'Buddhahood,' which can only be an appellate of the 'Absolute,' he did believe that future attainment of the Realm of Purification was 'determined'[109] the moment the individual recited the *nembutsu* with the three qualities of mind (or mind of Amida):

> The Name in the Original Vow is the practice of certain [attainment]. The [Eighteenth] Vow of sincere faith is its cause. To achieve awakening and to attain Ultimate Nirvana are due to the fulfillment of the [Eleventh] Vow assuring deliverance.[110]

This view was in contrast to the Pure Land tradition that maintained final attainment could not be assured until the moment of death. The instant Amida's mind is established within the sentient being, no further purification is necessary. The egocentric self has been shattered and henceforth actions no longer can be viewed from the good/evil standpoint of relative morality. The 'Absolute' now functions spontaneously within the individual free from all ego hindrances:

> When faith is firmly established, attainment is achieved through Amida's means, our own contrivance is not involved. The more we realize our limitations, then the more we look up to the power of the Vow, and as a consequence of Naturalness (*jinen*) a mind of harmony and tolerance will arise.[111]

Shinran defined this spontaneity or 'naturalness' of action (*jinen*) as 'beyond man's efforts or discrimination,' hence it transcends the mind of dualistic thought and acts from the intuitive comprehension of the interrelated nature of all existence:

> When we speak of Naturalness (*jinen*), *ji* signifies 'by itself.' It is not a conscious effort of man. *Nen* denotes 'to cause to come about.' 'To cause to come about' is not a conscious effort of man. Since it is what the Nyorai has vowed, it is 'in accord with the Dharma' (*hōni*). The Nyorai's vow is in accord with the Dharma therefore, it causes [things] to come about in accord with the Dharma. Since the vow is in accord with the Dharma, all man's conscious assertions cease as a result of the virtue of the Dharma. Then for the first time, man ceases self-conscious endeavour. Thus it should be known that 'non-reason is reason.' The original meaning of *jinen* was 'to cause to be.' Amida Buddha's vow from its beginning was his attempt to embrace those who recite *Namu Amida Butsu* relying upon the Buddha without conscious effort. So I have heard that when man abandons his own conscious effort and ceases to speculate regarding good or evil, that is Naturalness (*jinen*). The essence of the Nyorai's vow was his pledge to make [the man of the *nembutsu*] a Supreme Buddha. The Supreme Buddha does not possess any physical form, and since it does not possess any

form we call it Naturalness (*jinen*). When it manifests a form we cannot call it Supreme Nirvana. In order to reveal the formless it is called Amida, so I understand. Amida Buddha is the mode by which we know the way of Naturalness (*jinen*). Once this principle is understood Naturalness should not be discussed. If we constantly discuss Naturalness [the principle] of 'non-reason is reason' begins to assume reason. This is incomprehensible Buddha-wisdom.[112]

Once having established faith, the individual no longer has any need to perform conscious ethical actions or recite the *nembutsu* for the sake of Enlightenment, for in effect, although he is unable to reside permanently in the Realm of Purification, he is able to experience it for brief periods. Devotionally this would be described as Amida revealing the Pure Land, just as it was revealed to Queen Vaidehī in the *Meditation Sutra*. At this point further recitation can only serve as a reaffirmation of one's intuitive comprehension, or in devotional terms, an act of thanksgiving for the compassion of the 'Absolute.'

3. Shinran's Attitude Toward the Native Gods and Popular Beliefs

At the close of the Heian period, the gradual movement toward purity of practice began to accelerate. This move favouring simplicity, was a logical development to clear up the religious clutter that had materialized and actually served as a hindrance to concentration of mind. Numerous Tantric rites and rituals, devotions to various Buddhas, bodhisattvas and deities had been combined with popular beliefs, shamanism, geomancy and astrology. creating a serious deterioration of Buddhist spirit. Many of the abuses that the historical Buddha preached against in the *Brahmajāla Sutta* of the *Dīgha Nikāya* had once again crept in and eroded personal responsibility and self-reliance. Members of the aristocracy would not venture out of their houses on days judged inauspicious by the zodiac or calendar, and the priests who worked among them often assumed the roles of diviners, or worked with the diviners to offset ill-omened predictions through the use of special Tantric rituals.

The *nembutsu* movement was one means of restoring the Buddhist spirit to its pristine simplicity, similar trends were devotion to the *Lotus Sutra* and Zen meditation. The groundwork for the return to purer practices was laid by the *hijiri*, the idealistic sages who ironically had first been responsible for combining and popularizing various *shinbutsu shūgō* devotions. They were also the first to recognize the fact that a multiplicity of devotions was quite capable of creating a distracted state of mind rather than the concentration so essential for spiritual advancement. Gradually they reverted to a minimum of practices, heralding the notion of the single-practice.

The same situation appeared at the leading monasteries such as the Tendai headquarters on Mt. Hiei, where Genshin's movement had gathered at Yokawa. Hōnen carried this one step further by eliminating visualization of Amida and the Pure Land meditation and stressing simply the chanting of the *nembutsu* and faith in Other-power. But as noted, in his personal life Hōnen still exhibited an ambivalent attitude toward other practices.

Shinran was one of the first to perfectly observe single-practice in both his teachings and lifestyle. As a result, the Jōdo Shinshū sect is frequently referred to as an 'exclusive' or 'intolerant' sect and these views are attributed to Shinran. The crucial question is whether purity of practice is necessarily equated with exclusive intolerance, and if Shinran taught such.

Those who believe Shinran rejected the native gods and even the Buddhist *deva* cite the section in the chapter "Keshindo" of the *Kyōgyō-shinshō*, where Shinran counsels his followers 'to take homage in the Three Treasures and do not believe in the *deva* gods.'[113] On the other hand, in the verses of the *Genzeriyaku Wasan*, Shinran states:

> When one chants *Namu Amida Butsu*,
> Brahma and Indra pay homage
> and all the good *deva* gods
> protect him day and night.

> When one chants *Namu Amida Butsu*,
> the Four *Deva* Kings together

protect him day and night,
keeping evil spirits away.

When one chants *Namu Amida Butsu,*
the gods of earth pay homage.
And just as the shadow pursues the object,
they protect him day and night.

When one chants *Namu Amida Butsu,*
the Dragon king and multiple dragon gods
pay homage to the devotee
and protect him day and night.

When one chants *Namu Amida Butsu,*
King Yama pays homage
and together with the Judges of the Five Existences,
protects him day and night.

When one chants *Namu Amida Butsu,*
the King of the Paranirmita vaśavartin heaven
appears before Śākyamuni
and makes his pledge to protect.

All the gods of heaven and earth
should be called good spirit gods.
Together these good gods all,
protect the man of the *nembutsu.*

The faith of incomprehensible vow-power
is the great mind of Enlightenment.
The evil spirit gods which fill heaven and earth
all fear that faith.[114]

How can we reconcile such diverse attitudes? In the first place in the
Kyōgyōshinshō, Shinran is presenting the essence of *Tariki* faith. In keeping with perfect *Tariki* (Other-power) faith, it is impossible to consider
devotion to the native gods or even other Buddha's or bodhisattvas, for
such would fall into the realm of self-effort and serve as a hindrance
for perfect faith (or the mind of Amida) to function. On the other hand,
this in no way implies that devotion to other Buddhas, bodhisattvas, and

even gods may not be included *within* *Tariki* faith. The devotee receives
the mind of Amida (Enlightenment) and within that Mind, everything
favourable or in harmony with Enlightenment is reflected. The difference is that the *nembutsu* follower goes *through* Amida to show respect
or veneration for other Buddhas, bodhisattvas and deities. And it is due
to this respect that Shinran was able to write in one of his letters that
'those who profoundly believe in the Buddhist Dharma are protected
by the gods of heaven and earth, just as the shadow pursues its object,
and that it is unthinkable that anyone with faith in the *nembutsu* abandon
the gods of heaven and earth.[115] He particularly stresses in this letter
that it has been through the guidance of the Buddhas, bodhisattvas and
gods that *Tariki* faith has been established, therefore the follower is
bound to be grateful and express thanksgiving. What he meant by the
need for such gratitude, is that all the Buddhas, bodhisattvas and gods
are manifestations of Enlightenment, hence interrelated. And although
the *nembutsu* devotee finds his soteriological goal in Amida, he nevertheless must respect all the other manifestations, who undoubtedly
assisted him to ultimately find Amida.

As a product of self-effort, faith in other Buddhas, bodhisattvas or
gods cannot as such continue after *Tariki* faith has been established, but
this does not mean that respect and veneration for them is not contained
within Tariki faith. To assert contrary would not be proper Buddhism.
But there is also a problem, at the level of self-effort prior to the establishment of true *Tariki* faith, of *improper* reliance upon the gods. The
historical Buddha was the first to point out that reliance on gods, astrological signs and such presented an improper escape from one's own
personal responsibilities and ethical practices. In the passage in the
Kyōgyōshinshō following his counsel against 'believing in the *deva* gods'
Shinran proceeds to condemn certain astrological practices, which is
very reminiscent of the Buddha's stance in the *Brahmajāla Sutta*.[116]
Shinran obviously considered such beliefs as hindrances to individual
moral and ethical conduct. In fact they represented a furtherance of the
interests of the ego, since man appeals to the gods to order the world
to his own liking. And in due time the gods he appeals to become the

products of his own illusions, whereby he transforms favourable experiences into the actions of beneficent deities and unhappy experiences into the machinations of evil spirits.[117] Ultimately he loses all control over his own destiny and is swayed merely by chance events, taking no hand in ordering his own life in a manner to avoid the results of improper karma (actions).

Some individuals might question whether Shinran was referring to the native Japanese gods when he included 'gods' within the *nembutsu*, and if so, why so many charges were leveled against the Pure Land followers for neglecting the indigenous gods. In the first place, as a man of the early Kamakura period, it would be extremely difficult to imagine that Shinran would distinguish between the India *deva* imported under the mantle of Buddhism and the native Japanese gods. For centuries the two groups had been so mixed that the average Japanese was incapable of distinguishing between them. Furthermore, the *honji-suijaku* (True nature-manifestation) theory had, by the dawn of the Kamakura period, successfully assimilated the indigenous gods within the folds of Buddhism. There is no conceivable reason why at this point Shinran should be distinguishing between the native gods and Indian *deva* without so stating. In fact Yama and the Judges of the Five existences, to which he refers in the *Genzeriyaku Wasan*, were by the Kamakura period, products of the assimilation of Buddhist and Taoist deities in China. It is not logical that Shinran would accept Chinese assimilations while rejecting native Japanese gods, particularly when the nature of the indigenous gods was such in Japan that respect for them equalled respect for the very mountains, trees and soil of the land. Finally, in his letter stating that it is inconceivable that the gods of heaven and earth be abandoned by those with faith in the *nembutsu*, Shinran was specifically answering a question referring to the so-called neglect of the native gods by *nembutsu* followers.

The next question is why were charges so frequently raised with the government that *nembutsu* followers neglected the native gods? The answer to this lies in the political situation of the day. When the Minamoto family seized control of Japan and established their *de facto* government at Kamakura, they placed personal stewards (*jitō*) on each existing *shōen* (manorial estate) and the stewards in turn were placed under the control of local protectors (*shugo*), also picked from loyal retainers of the Minamoto. This system created endless conflicts over property income rights and distribution. As the *nembutsu* movement spread through the countryside, it became a further issue inserted into the quarrels. If a local steward (*jitō*) happened to be a *nembutsu* follower in a dispute, the *shōen* manager would charge him before the government with neglecting the native gods, a charge tantamount to treason since the native gods controlled the fortune of the nation. Or if a *shōen* manager happened to be a *nembutsu* follower, he might be charged by the steward. Charges of immorality among *nembutsu* followers undoubtedly also served the same purpose and were frequent at this time. During later periods, with the rise of the *Ikkō ikki* rebellions, the peasants deliberately rejected the protector gods of the samurai and warlords they sought to overcome, but we will examine that struggle in detail in a separate section.

In summary, if we view Shinran's attitude toward the native gods, we note that he first placed them in their proper perspective at the conventional level, admonishing against the type of reliance that leads man to forfeit control over his own destiny. And secondly, at what might be described as the level of Enlightenment or the attainment of *Tariki* faith, his attitude was not exclusive, insofar as it did not entail intolerance or rejection. Rather, the gods and all other Buddhas and bodhisattvas were embraced *within* the *nembutsu*, and this attitude was developed by his successors.

4. Institutional Foundation of Jōdo Shinshū

At the time of Shinran's death in 1262, his ashes were placed in an ordinary tomb at Ōtani in Kyoto. Ten years later this was transferred by his followers further west near Yoshimizu, to the residence of Shinran's daughter Kakushin-ni and her second husband, Onomiya Zennen. There a small hexagonal mausoleum enshrining an image of Shinran was built by his disciples on the property belonging to Zennen.

The year before his death in 1275, Zennen deeded the land, which is believed to have been located within the grounds of the present Chion-in temple, to Kakushin-ni, and in 1277 she officially donated it to Shinran's followers with the stipulation that although the memorial hall and land would belong to all of Shinran's followers, permanent maintenance and protection would be provided by Kakushin-ni and her descendants. This provision was made primarily because few of Shinran's followers resided in the Kyoto area, but it ultimately became the origin of Jōdo Shinshū blood succession.

After the death of Kakushin-ni, her eldest son, Kakue (1238-1307), succeeded to the post of caretaker. But even at this stage the succession was not without problems, and later it became involved in disputes and intrigues equalling the Imperial throne. Kakue was the issue of Kakushin-ni's first marriage to Hino Hirotsuna. Since the land for the mausoleum had been donated by her second husband, Onomiya Zennen, the son of that marriage, Yuizen, challenged Kakue's position and later the succession of Kakue's son, Kakunyo. The dispute was ultimately resolved in the favour of Kakunyo by the abbot of the Tendai Shōren-in together with the Retired Emperor.[118] But as a result of this conflict the minor position of custodian of the tomb assumed public prominence and increased in prestige.

Kakunyo

When Kakunyo assumed the position of custodian in 1310 at the age of forty-one, he was faced with other challenges to his legitimate succession. In the first place, although he was the great-grandson of Shinran, his blood line was established through Shinran's daughter. Traditionally in a Japanese family, unless a son-in-law is adopted into the family and assumes the family name, upon marriage, a woman and her offspring are considered to belong to her husband's family. Thus Kakunyo by birth could not properly be considered an heir of Shinran. This situation was resolved in a unique manner.

Kakunyo's father, Kakue had been a spiritual disciple from the age of thirty of Nyoshin, the son of Shinran's disowned son, Zenran. Kakunyo met Nyoshin in 1287 and also became his disciple. Although Shinran had formally disowned Zenran, it seems the family relationship was not totally severed, and the grandson Nyoshin led the Ōami congregation of Ōshū. Evidently there was not any problem concerning the orthodoxy of Nyoshin's teachings, and as a result of the efforts of Kakunyo, Nyoshin became the first proper hereditary successor of Shinran.[119] In effect this meant that although Kakushin-ni and Kakunyo's father, Kakue, had held the position of custodians of the tomb, they were not considered as Shinran's proper blood successors. Kakunyo became the first of Kakushin-ni's line to combine the position of blood succession with custodian of the tomb. And this was arranged due to the fact that since Nyoshin did not have a son, Kakunyo as his spiritual disciple, and at the same time the actual great-grandson of Shinran, became Nyoshin's successor.

Kakunyo wrote two treatises, to establish his position, the *Kudenshō* (Treatise of Oral Transmission) and *Kaijashō* (Essay correcting False Faith), setting forth the theory of legitimate succession of three generations, not only in blood but in Dharma. In these he emphasized Shinran's indebtedness to Hōnen his master, and the blood and Dharma succession of Nyoshin and himself.

In view of Kakunyo's justification for his legitimate succession and the subsequent letters he wrote to Shinran's followers in order to obtain their sanction, it might seem that he was overly ambitious to establish his position. But Kakunyo was a man with a vision and a driving goal, allowing no divergence. In fact disagreements with his own two sons, who were both capable men, made it impossible for them to succeed him. Kakunyo's dream was to consolidate all of Shinran's followers into one order under control of the mausoleum. He envisioned creating the mausoleum into a mother temple, and making the congregations (*monto*) in the provinces its branches. Although this was the method used by the established Buddhist institutions, the idea of a Shinshū temple was still a novelty. Shinran had never personally erected a conventional Buddhist temple during his lifetime.[120] And the *nembutsu dōjō* that he founded did not generally begin to assume the title of temple until the late sixteenth or seventeenth century. But Kakunyo had definite reasons in mind. He had watched the other groups of Hōnen's followers establish themselves into the Seizan and Chinzei-ha, and he was also aware of the growing strength in the capital of the congregation of Shinran's followers known as the Bukkōji. Certain powerful congregations in the Kantō area were also expanding such as the Takada, Yokosone and Kashima, and he realized that without centralization these would inevitably develop into independent sects.

Kakunyo's plan to consolidate Shinran's movement first entailed establishing the tomb into a proper temple. To a certain degree, by doing this, and attempting to establish an order, he was destroying Shinran's unique conception of his movement. The congregations (*monto*) that Shinran had established were democratic groups, whereas a sect inevitably would impose authoritarian control. Furthermore, the *nembutsu dōjō* lacked all the rich paraphernalia of established conventional temples. Shinran had been the first to put into actual practice Hōnen's concept, based upon the *Meditation Sutra*, of abolishing wooden images or pictures of Amida. Although Shinran had not objected to such images in existing temples, in the *dōjō* he founded he used the Chinese characters of the name of Amida as the principal image and he personally created three types of character scrolls:

> 10 character—*Ki-myō-jin-ji-ppō-mu-ge-kō-Nyo-rai*
> Homage to the Nyorai illuminating the ten direc-
> tions without hindrance.
> 8 character—*Na-mu-fu-ka-shi-gi-kō-Butsu*
> Homage to the Buddha of Incomprehensible
> light.
> 6 character—*Na-mu-A-mi-da-Butsu*
> Homage to Amida Buddha

Besides such, the early *dōjō* often had portrait scrolls of the seven patri-archs and Prince Shōtoku. Shortly after Shinran's death a popular illumi-nated scroll appeared that became the focal point for the arrangement of the first Shinshū sanctuaries and temples. This contained eight or ten written characters pictured with rays of light issuing forth. On the right and left of the characters, as well as top and bottom, portraits of the Buddhas, Pure Land patriarchs and historical Buddha were drawn. But eventually, as Shinshū *dōjō* transformed into conventional temples, the scrolls once again gave way to images of Amida set in ornate sanctuaries.

It is rather unfair to blame Kakunyo for losing Shinran's original spirit in his dream of establishing a Shinshū sect with conventional temples, for Kakunyo was responding to what he believed to be the pressing needs of his time. Shinran could not have forseen the movements of his fellow disciples under Hōnen developing into the powerful Seizan and Chinzei branches of the Jōdo school, nor could he have imagined the proliferation of his own movement. During his lifetime he is known to have stated:

> I, Shinran, do not have a single disciple. The reason is, if on my own I should lead others to recite the *nembutsu*, I might claim them to be my disciples. But it is unthinkable to consider them my disciples when they recite the *nembutsu* completely through the work of Amida.[121]

A modern edited version of the *Kōmyōchō* listing Shinran's known followers during his lifetime contains forty-eight names.[122] Granted there were probably considerable more than those listed, but at the time of Shinran's death we can scarcely call the Jōdo Shinshū a separate movement for it closely approximated the followings of Hōnen's other disciples. With the gradual growth and popularity of Shinran's following, Kakunyo realized that something had to be done. Although he might be accused of making Shinran's movement sectarian, this was an inevitable development. And the history of Buddhism presents a definable pattern in the rise, prosperity, and ultimate corruption of Buddhist institutions, with the idealistic days of struggle and hardship of the founder replaced by the wealth, prosperity and social prestige that inevitably leads to corruption.

To initiate his plan, in the summer of 1312, Kakunyo publicly declared Shinran's mausoleum to be the Senjuji (Single-practice) temple by hanging a plaque in front of the temple. This action immediately stirred up protest from the monks of Mt. Hiei, who demanded the plaque be removed on the grounds that since the single-practice *nembutsu* had been legally prohibited, this was an unacceptable name for a temple. After this failure, Kakunyo then began to refer to the mausoleum by the title of Honganji (temple of the Original vow). The first appearance of this name in a public document occurred in 1321, and by eleven years later the temple had received official recognition. However, the government legally considered it as an affiliate of the Tendai Shōren-in, and this fact must have created certain social and legal restrictions.

Kakunyo's movement to consolidate Shinran's followers under the Honganji met considerable resistance from certain prosperous congregations that were beginning to develop temples in their own right. He managed to win initial approval of the Takada monto, the most powerful congregation located in Shimotsuke province and founded by Shinran's direct disciples, Shinbutsu (1209–1258) and Kenchi (1250–1334). In order to strengthen his position, Kakunyo began to cultivate friends among the aristocracy, and even took the old Ritsuryō title of *Chūnagon Hōin*.

After his death in 1351 at the age of eighty-two, Kakunyo was succeeded by his nineteen year old grandson Zennyo, who became head of the Honganji the following year. Kakunyo's eldest son Zonkaku (1289–1373), who was his logical successor, had been disowned by his father on several occasions. Despite failing to become fourth successor,[123] Zonkaku became exceedingly important in the Shinshū movement by establishing its theology. The younger son, Jūkaku (1295–1360), father of Zennyo and editor of Shinran's letters (*Mattōshō*), had also been unable to get along with his strong-willed father and was passed over in favour of his young son, Zennyo.

During the time of Zennyo and his descendents Shakunyo (1350–1393), Kōnyo (d. 1440), and Zonnyo (1396–1457), the Honganji faced serious financial problems and developed very slowly. In fact the new congregation of the Bukkōji, founded by Ryōgen a student of Zonkaku, eclipsed the Honganji during this period. The main reason for the lack of growth was due to the fact that Kakunyo's vision of a unified order alienated many of the provincial congregations. Kakunyo's successors were faced with the task of struggling to keep the congregations in line, which required their presence in the provinces, creating a neglect of the Honganji headquarters at Kyoto. Despite their strenuous efforts, powerful congregations like the Takada monto gradually drew away to compete with the Honganji, and before long the powerful congregations were faced with subdivisions within themselves. Ultimately the hard work of the fourth to seventh successors in the provinces was reaped by Rennyo, the eighth successor, who is considered to be the 'Restorer of the Middle Period' of the Jōdo Shinshū sect.

Rennyo

Born in 1415, Rennyo was the son of the seventh successor, Zonnyo, and experienced an unhappy family life as well as the economic difficulties of the Honganji. When he became eighth successor in 1458 upon the death of his father, he was forty-four years old and had the maturity and qualifications necessary to successfully lead the order. Rennyo had not been head of the Honganji long when the monks of Mt. Hiei stormed down and destroyed the temple. The probable reason for this attack was due to the fact that Honganji teachings had spread to Ōmi, next to Mt. Hiei. But the destruction of the headquarters was not a serious event, since by now the congregations under the Honganji had established firm roots in the provinces. In fact Nyokō, leader of the Mikawa monto, interpreted the *sōhei* attack simply as an intimidation to receive payment, and suggested that the Honganji was powerful enough to purchase peace. This was in effect what happened, for the Honganji decided to pay dues temporarily as a branch of Mt. Hiei and came under their jurisdiction.

With the destruction of the Higashiyama Honganji, Rennyo went to Ōtsu province and requested protection from the Miidera, the age-old enemies within the Tendai sect of the monks of Mt. Hiei. Then in 1471 he went to Yoshizaki in Echizen province, which he made the centre of his activities. It was during this time that the Honganji order developed a massive following and individuals came in large numbers from the northern provinces to listen to Rennyo. This sudden popularity of the Shinshū sect was not the result of Rennyo's abilities alone. A foundation had been carefully laid in the countryside by his four predecessors. And above all, the Shinshū faith filled a need of the peasant masses during what again was to mark a drastic change in Japanese society. After the Ōnin war of 1467–77, the authority of the Ashikaga shōguns virtually collapsed and the nation embarked upon a century of bloody conflict between the warlords (Daimyō) competing for power. But this time the socially conscious peasants were not to stand idly by to suffer warlord oppression and destruction of their lands. The Jōdo Shinshū faith offered them the rallying spirit to group together and under the banner of *Tariki* power and the *nembutsu* they formed religious organizations (*kō*) and confidently faced those who threatened them. Since the Shinshū priests taught the peasants that Amida alone was necessary for salvation, they were no longer intimidated by the local gods the Daimyō and great samurai families claimed as protectors. And as the peasants banded together, they posed an awesome threat to the landlords and samurai, who patronized the older established temples and shrines.

Rennyo's presence at Yoshizaki during this tense situation served as the catalyst for violence. In an attempt to break Shinshū strength, the local lords began a series of attacks, which in turn led to peasant uprisings.

Ikkō Ikki

In the tenth month of 1474 Togashi Masachika, who had been forced into exile in Echizen province when his brother Kōchiyo seized the lands originally divided between them, returned to Kaga and captured the domains of Kōchiyo, forcing the latter to flee to Kyoto. In his efforts to regain his lands, Masachika had become a friend of the Honganji, promising to protect Shinshū followers in exchange for their aid. The peasants agreed to help him, although they were aware they could expect little assistance from Masachika in the way of alleviating taxation and Daimyō oppression. But after his victory, Masachika became wary of his erstwhile allies and precipitated an attack on the Honganji at Yoshizaki, the centre of Shinshū activities. On the twenty-first day of the eighth month in 1475 Rennyo escaped, ultimately to seek sanctuary south in the Kinki area as the tide of oppression went against the Shinshū followers. In 1481 a group fled to the adjoining province of Etchū, bringing sullen embers of revolt with them. And although the Shinshū followers fared poorly in the beginning, they were ultimately successful in a battle against Togashi that began in 1487 and lasted until the summer of the following year as the peasants were joined by other ambitious warlords. After this dispute, Kaga became known as the 'province without a master' and for nearly one hundred years Shinshū priests, peasants, and local samurai jointly controlled, making it in effect a feudal domain of the Honganji.

The success in Kaga had a strong influence on neighboring provinces and soon Echizen, Etchū, and Noto were engaged in similar conflicts. The *Ikkō* (Single-minded) *ikki* or rebellions by Jōdo Shinshū followers, geographically broke out in the most prosperous provinces of Japan throughout the one hundred years known as the Warring States (Sengoku) period. During the time of Rennyo and his son Jitsunyo, the *Ikkō ikki* predominately represented the struggle and competition between peasants and local Daimyō for land. Eventually, near the end of the era, the Honganji itself was to become one of the most powerful feudal institutions with a network of trained peasant armies.

Since Rennyo was unable to continue his presence in the northern provinces, he nourished the faith and encouraged followers by letter-messages (*Ofumi*) sent to the various congregations. At this time he also published Shinran's popular *Shōshinge* (Verses of True Faith) and *Wasan* (Hymns). Another effective means of teaching and solving simple doctrinal issues was the *dangibon*, a form of storybook designed to explain Shinshū to the masses. Most prevalent among these were the type of books that dealt with the problems of *shinbutsu-shūgō* (union of gods and Buddhas) for this was a major interest. These works were so concerned with efforts to compromise with folk beliefs that later theologians were to declare many of them heretical.

At this time Rennyo was in a very difficult position. The rapidly growing Shinshū movement naturally created resentment among the established sects and fear among the authorities, whose power was extremely unstable. If the Honganji was believed to incite peasant rebellions, then the Daimyō would quickly move to suppress it in their realms. On the other hand, the peasants were difficult to control, often had just grievances, and frequently arose only after direct attacks against Honganji temples. As head of the Honganji, Rennyo had to tread a narrow path, establishing precepts and counseling against violence or rebellion in general, to satisfy the Daimyō, and at the same time encouraging the peasants in what he considered to be just rebellions. The situation was often reflected by the Honganji attitude towards the native gods, who symbolized the local authorities. Rennyo established a number of precepts warning against sacrilegious acts toward the gods, but at the same time encouraged the *Ikkō ikki* in their rejection of the particular gods representing the Daimyō and landlords they sought to overthrow. This became one means by which the Shinshū sect received massive conversions from the Jishū.

Ippen, founder of the Jishū had been born in a landowning samurai family and since his sect originated from a divine revelation of the Kumano god, it had a close relationship with local Shintō shrines, where members frequently practiced the *nembutsu*. Since the shrines in turn were supported by the local landlords, when the peasants showed signs of restlessness, the Jishū taught them that economic resistance against the landlords would be a sign of disrespect to the native gods and incur their punishment. Thus the fear of the indigenous gods was used as a weapon to maintain passivity. As the peasants gradually became aware that Shinshū followers believed in the *Tariki* of Amida without subservience to the local gods by obeying landlords, they converted in large numbers. The same situation occured with the older established temples whose Buddhas or bodhisattvas were thought to favour the local landlord patrons. Rennyo had to handle such matters with extreme skill, and he did so by following the precedent established by Shinran—emphasizing that respect to the native gods as well as other Buddhas and bodhisattvas was *included* in respect to Amida and that it was unnecessary to show them any special veneration. The *dangibon* storybooks further demonstrated in simple tales exactly how the gods respected Amida, hence the peasants could feel confident in the powerful aid and protection of Amida even if they did act contrary to the wishes of the shrine priests or established temples. And in adopting *honji-suijaku* (true nature-manifestation) thought, these works divided the relationship between Amida, the Buddhas, and bodhisattvas into a three-fold system:

Amida—*honji* (true-nature)
Buddhas and bodhisattvas—divided-body *honji*
native gods—*suijaku* (manifestations)

Rennyo also had problems in controlling the masses who were led by greed in their rebellions, or who sought to disturb exceedingly dangerous Daimyō. In this case, if they failed to heed his counsel he resorted to expulsion from the order, in effect cancelling their *ōjō* (attainment of the Pure Land). The notion of institutional interference with individual faith seems antithetic to the teachings of Shinran, yet we must realize that this 'faith' existed at a very primitive level. Even Shinran is known to have on occasion resorted to expulsion as in the case of his son Zenran, although he did not approve of such a method of control. It set a dangerous precedent, for there was never any assurance that a worldly abbot might not abuse the power. But as a result of the use of expulsion, the feudalistic position of the Honganji became established and the abbot came to have a role analogous to the Catholic Pope, serving as an intermediator or 'voice of Amida.'

Rennyo was successful during his lifetime in balancing relations of the Honganji with the peasants, Ashikaga shōguns, bureaucrats and Daimyō. And in 1478 he began construction of a new Honganji headquarters at Yamashina in the Yamashiro area. As a result of his popularity he managed to bring a number of alienated factions such as the Bukkōji, Sanmonto and Kibe in various provinces temporarily into the

Honganji fold. Then in 1489 at the age of seventy-five, Rennyo retired and spent the last ten years of his life engaged in missionary activities in the various provinces, also constructing a Honganji temple in Osaka. By Rennyo's death in 1499, Honganji influence had geographically spread as far north as the Tōhoku and even into the Ezo (Hokkaidō) area, and south to Kyūshū. This is very near the expanse it covers today, and marked a dramatic growth in a short period.

Rennyo was succeeded by his son Jitsunyo who carried on Honganji activities at Yamashina. This headquarters was ranked as a temple of the Imperial vow (*chokuganji*) but still regarded as a branch of the Tendai Shōren-in. Jitsunyo attempted to continue Rennyo's policy of cordial relations with the Daimyō, authorities and rebellious peasants, but gradually as the political situation changed, the Honganji was forced to choose sides. *Ikkō ikki* uprisings had spread throughout the entire nation in accompaniment with the quarrels between local Daimyō. Civil authority had virtually collapsed and the control of the land fell to whoever was powerful enough to forcefully seize and hold it.

Move to the Ishiyama Honganji

In 1532 the Yamashina Honganji was attacked and destroyed by an attack of Nichiren followers. The tenth successor, Shōnyo, was seventeen years old at the time and managed to escape with the statue of Shinran, which he transferred to the Osaka Honganji built earlier by Rennyo. This became the new Shinshū headquarters and ushered in the Ishiyama Honganji era, when the Honganji feudal role reached its peak.

As the localized *ikki* rebellions spread like wildfire engulfing the nation, a gradual change was taking place in Honganji membership. Even during the time of Rennyo, some samurai had joined the movement. But now under Shōnyo, many Daimyō began to express a desire to join. Realizing the strength of the *nembutsu* peasant power, they recognized that this was one means of protecting their status and stabilizing authority in the provinces. Since the *nembutsu* faith was the peasant's rallying point, it could also be used as a force to control them. Some Daimyō also saw the *Ikkō ikki* peasants as a powerful military force capable of aiding them to acquire new lands and become warlord leaders. Of course, such motives were not the only reasons Daimyō and samurai sought to join the Honganji. Undoubtedly many were truly impressed by the power of the faith to motivate and stir the masses and sought to join out of sincere interest. The membership of such individuals increased both the prestige of the Honganji and the feudal role of its leader.

In 1559 Kennyo became the eleventh successor and was finally granted the official title of abbot (*monzeki*) of the sect by Emperor Ōgimachi. With this recognition of independence the Honganji at last was capable of establishing political relations with the warlords. Institutionally it was now equal to any of the major temples in Nara or Kyoto, and it also was powerful enough politically to match the strength of any aristocratic or military family in the nation. But this strength ultimately led to catastrophe as the powerful Daimyō Oda Nobunaga swept through Japan in his drive to control and unify the nation.

Downfall of the Ishiyama Honganji

It was not long before Nobunaga realized that his most formidable enemy was the Honganji with its vast network of *Ikkō* followers and political allies throughout the provinces. In 1570 he first entered into a skirmish with Honganji followers in Kyoto and was forced to retreat. The following year, in an effort to secure Kyoto, he destroyed the powerful Tendai Enryakuji temple and laid waste to Mt. Hiei. But the Honganji, in alliance with his enemies, still offered a formidable obstacle.

In the first place, the headquarters at Ishiyama was located in a nearly impregnable position overlooking Osaka Bay and surrounded by waterways. Nobunaga made numerous attempts against the headquarters and in 1576, in one such attack, was slightly wounded. Finally, he decided to isolate the temple and cut off all reinforcements and sources of supply in surrounding areas. This he accomplished by the spring of 1580 and, after over ten years of battle, finally forced the Honganji into surrender. Emperor Ōgimachi served as peacemaker, and the abbot Kennyo was forced to withdraw from Osaka to the Kii (present Wakayama) province. This marked the decline of the Honganji's worldly and political power. It also brought a close to the *Ikkō ikki* rebellions, although numerous scattered peasant uprisings continued for some time. At the time of settlement, Kennyo's eldest son and logical successor, Kyōnyo, had not wished to surrender to Nobunaga. As a result of this dispute Kennyo temporarily disowned his son and expelled him from the Honganji, but Kyōnyo's sentiments were shared by many of the members who had fought long and hard for victory.

Nobunaga was assassinated in 1582 and succeeded in power by Toyotomi Hideyoshi. In 1591 Kennyo was granted land by Hideyoshi at Horikawa in Kyoto, the site of the present Nishi (Western) Honganji headquarters, and finally, one hundred and twenty years after Rennyo's retreat, the Honganji order again became established at the capital.

In the eleventh month of 1592 Kennyo died and was succeeded by his eldest son Kyōnyo, but soon after a legal dispute arose. Kennyo's widow, Nyoshun, appealed to Hideyoshi's court using a will written by her husband stating that Junnyo, his third son, should be his proper successor rather than Kyōnyo, whom he had earlier disowned. As a result of this dispute Kyōnyo was forced to retire in favour of his younger brother, who was named twelfth successor, but this was not the end of the matter.

5. Major Division of the Honganji Order

When Kyōnyo had refused surrender at Osaka he received the support of many temple congregations throughout the nation. Thus when he was later divested of his title by Hideyoshi's ruling, he received a great deal of sympathy. In 1596 he returned to Osaka and restored the Ōtani Honganji there, acting very much in the role of abbot. His younger brother Junnyo, who was later to become a scholar primarily interested in ritual, was only seventeen at the time of his succession, and scarcely able to control the activities of his elder brother, who had been trained to be the future abbot. In fact, prior to his return to Osaka, Kyōnyo had briefly controlled matters behind the scenes at the Honganji in Kyoto.

In 1598 when Hideyoshi died, the nation once again underwent a power struggle for leadership. At that time shortly prior to the decisive victory at Sekigahara, Kyōnyo took the risk of visiting Tokugawa Ieyasu on his march to the capital, while he was staying at Ōtsu. Later after Ieyasu's victory over the contending warlords, he remembered Kyōnyo's support and granted him title to land located on Karasuma Street in Kyoto that today is the headquarters of the Ōtani-ha, more popularly known as the Higashi (Eastern) Honganji. In 1603 Shinran's image was enshrined at the temple built on that site, and this marked the beginning of a new branch of the Shinshū faith.

The split, which was based upon institutional rather than doctrinal grounds, did irreparable damage to the powerful Jōdo Shinshū movement. Popularly it is generally believed that the division actually was an act representing Ieyasu's religious policy of controlling the church, but as we have seen, the basis of the division existed before Ieyasu's intervention. The split tested loyalties of congregations and followers throughout the nation, and by 1619 the two were recognized by the government as separate independent entities.

6. The Schools of Shinshū

The ten divisions of the Jōdo Shinshū sect that exist today came into existence during the medieval period. And unlike the branches of the Jōdo sect, were primarily made for institutional rather than theological differences. These branches can be divided into two categories: sects based upon blood succession and those founded by disciples:

Blood   1) Honganji-ha (Nishi Honganji)
succession 2) Ōtani-ha (Higashi Honganji)

Disciples 3) Takada-ha—founded by Shinran's direct disciples Shin-
                butsu and Kenchi in the Kantō area with headquarters
                at the Senjuji. Temporarily it was affiliated with the
                Honganji during the period of Kakunyo. In 1465 the
                tenth successor moved the Senjuji to Ise, where it is
                located today. In 1872 it received the official name of
                Shinshū Senjuji-ha, this was changed nine years later to
                Takada-ha.

4-5) Bukkōji-ha and Kōshōji-ha of Kyoto

Although the Bukkōji claims Shinran as its original founder, it is historically considered to have been established by Ryōgen (1294–1335), a disciple of Ryōen of the Takada congregation over half a century after the death of Shinran. Initially the temple was known as the Kōshōji and located in Yamashina but when it moved to Kyoto it received the new name of Bukkōji. Ryōgen's teachings had tremendous appeal to the masses, and for a time the temple surpassed the Honganji. Kakunyo wrote the *Kaijashō* (Essay correcting False Faith) against Ryōgen's method of popularizing his teachings by promising *ōjō* to all who signed his membership booklet and using a pictorial geneology to prove his succession. Ryōgen was murdered in 1355, and in 1352 the monks of Mt. Hiei nearly destroyed the temple. Finally Kyōgō (1451–1492) and a group of followers split the congregation by joining Rennyo's Honganji movement. The dissident group built a new Kōshōji temple in Yamashina and became known by that name. As a result of the division, the Bukkōji declined. When Hideyoshi decided to build his great Buddha in Kyoto, he moved the Bukkōji to its present location in the Shimogyōku area. The Kōshōji continued to maintain its affiliation with the Honganji and at the time of the division of that school, relocated beside the Nishi Honganji, where it was granted a special status among the Nishi branches. In 1876 it became independent.

6-8) Jōshōji, Yamamoto and Sanmonto-ha of Fukui, Echizen

These three schools were also established by disciples of the Takada-congregation, although they claim to have been founded by Shinran. All three practiced the chanting of *wasan* (hymns) in loud voices and the dancing *nembutsu*. They were all significant congregations up until the time of Rennyo when they suffered a decline. During the Tokugawa period, due to their small sizes, they were treated as legal branches of the Tendai Shōren-in temple. In 1878 they all received independent status. The Yamamoto-ha maintains its headquarters at the Shōjōji and the Sanmonto-ha at the Senshōji.

9) Izumoji-ha of Fukui, Echizen

Founded by Kakunyo's disciple Jōsen (1274–1357) at the site of Izumoji in Kyoto, this group initially had close ties with the Honganji. The original Gōshōji temple was destroyed during the Ōnin war and the group moved to Echizen. During the Tokugawa period it was also treated as a branch of the Shōren-in, not receiving independent status until the Meiji era. The Gōshōji in Fukui is its present headquarters.

10) Kibe-ha of Ōmi

Originally belonged to the Yokosone congregation founded by Shinran's direct disciple Shōshin (1187–1275). Members of this group moved to Shiga province on the western side of Lake Biwa. Jikū, who maintained close ties with the Honganji, was responsible for its popularity but later the group was splintered by Shōe who took a sizeable following to join Rennyo's Honganji, and after this the group entered into decline, finally being restored during the Tokugawa period. In 1872 it became an independent sect and maintains its present headquarters at the Kinshokuji at Ōmi.

Among these schools, the Nishi and Higashi Honganji remain dominant today, and in combination form the largest Buddhist congregation in Japan.

Besides the Jōdo and Jōdo Shinshū sects, Pure Land Buddhism motivated another popular mass movement of quite a different nature.

F. Jishū

Unlike the single-practice *nembutsu* inspired in Japan by Hōnen, the Ji sect approaches much closer to the esoteric Shingon *nembutsu*, while at the same time sharing an affinity with the native gods, reminiscent of the early Yūzū Nembutsu of the Heian period. The characteristics of the Jishū were defined by the life and revelations of its founder, Ippen.

1. Ippen, the Founder

Born the second month of 1239, as the second child of the powerful Kōno samurai family in Iyo province on Shikoku, Ippen was known as Chishin during his childhood. His family earlier had suffered political persecution for allying with Imperial forces during the Shōkyū war and Ippen's father had become a Buddhist priest with the name of Nyobutsu. At the age of ten, Ippen's mother died, and four years later his father sent him to Dazaifu in Kyūshū to study under Shōtatsu of the Jōdo Seizan-ha.

In 1263 upon the death of his father, Ippen briefly returned home to handle the affairs of his family, but when an inheritance dispute arose, he gave up worldly affairs and embarked upon a religious pilgrimage. For three years he lived in the vicinity of his home on a mountainside practicing the *nembutsu*. Then in 1274 he visited the Kii province planning to visit Mt. Kumano, which in those days was believed to be the earthly counterpart of Amida's Pure Land.

According to legend, on his way to the Kumano shrine, Ippen encountered an unknown monk and sought to present him with a *nembutsu* tablet, while advising him to chant the name of Amida with faith. But the monk rejected his offer on the grounds that since he lacked faith in Amida, such chanting would be hypocrisy. The event troubled Ippen's confidence, and at Kumano he sought a solution for the problem of those who lacked faith. It was then that the *gongen* (manifestation god) revealed that Amida's Enlightenment determines the individual's *ōjō* (attainment), therefore faith or purity is immaterial and all Ippen need do was to practice *fusan* (handing out the *nembutsu* tablets).[124] Ippen later expressed his understanding of this revelation in a verse, the *Rokujūmannin*, named for each of the first characters forming its lines:[125]

> Six character name is Ippen's (lit. one universal) Dharma
> *Rokuji myōgō Ippen hō*

Ten worlds relying upon truth form Ippen's body
Jikkai eshō Ippen tai
Liberation from ten thousand practices is Ippen's attainment
Mangyō rinen Ippen shō
This is the superior and wondrous flower among men
Nin chū jōjō myōkōke

Linking together the universal (*ippen*) Dharma-body and attainment, the individual becomes a wondrous flower (*myōkōke*) rising above the muddy defilement of the world. It was as a symbol of this subjective realization that he assumed the new religious name of Ippen, and also made *yugyō* (travelling about the countryside) and *fusan* (handing out *nembutsu* tablets) the major practices of his religious movement.

Ippen travelled throughout the provinces of Japan the next sixteen years and was attended by many happenings believed to be miraculous, such as the appearance of purple clouds in the sky and showers of flower petals. He also initiated the *odori* (dancing) *nembutsu*. In 1289 while visiting Shikoku, he became ill and, realizing his death was approaching, crossed the Inland sea to visit the historic place associated with a *shami* (layman practitioner) he respected, named Kyōshin (d. 866), in Hyōgo province. There on the tenth day of the eighth month he took a few of the scriptures he had carried with him to the Kannon-dō temple and burnt the rest, saying that all the scriptures in the world merely equalled *Namu Amida Butsu*. On the twenty-third day of the same month he died at the age of fifty-one at the Kannon-dō temple, which later became the Shinkōji. His mausoleum still stands on the grounds of that temple. In the year 1806 he was granted the posthumous title of Enshō Daishi.

2. Philosophy of Jishū

The theological foundation of the Ji sect is basically derived from two sources: first, Ippen's period of study with Shōtatsu of the Jōdo Seizan-ha, and secondly, his strong interest in Shingon Tantrism. During Ippen's early pilgrimages he visited Mt. Kōya and travelled in the footsteps of Kūkai. At the time of his revelation from the Kumano *gongen*, Mt. Kumano was not only considered to be the earthly counterpart of

Amida's Pure Land, but the Kumano god, under Tantric influence, was believed to be the *suijaku* (manifestation) of Amida. The Shingon influence upon Ippen can clearly be seen in his belief that once an individual takes sincere homage in Amida and recites the *nembutsu*, then the "I is no longer the I, mind becomes the mind of Amida, actions the actions of Amida, words the words of Amida, and life the life of Amida."[126] Thus in a Shingon manner, he believed that with his present physical body he could become Amida Buddha (*sokushin jōbutsu*).

In accord with his revelation from the Kumano god, Ippen achieved the conviction that whether the individual possessed faith or not, he could be certain of *ōjō* (attaining) the Pure Land by chanting the *nembutsu*, as a result of Amida's *Tariki* (Other-power). And he considered the *nembutsu* to therefore transcend all forms of physical, mental and vocal karma. Or, as he stated, the '*nembutsu* itself chants the *nembutsu*.[127] In other words, the individual totally surrenders to the force of the power of Amida as represented by the *nembutsu*. And to make this surrender easier, Ippen counseled the complete renunciation of all objects of human attachment such as family and property. His disciples followed the simple lifestyle of wandering hermits and were known as *sute hijiri* (sages who abandon all). Ippen was very strict regarding the observance of poverty, celibacy and detachment, and those who broke his precepts were subject to expulsion. In fact, even in the case of a deceased member already listed in the register of followers as having been certain of *ōjō* (attainment), if later transgressions came to light the listing would promptly be changed to 'non-*ōjō*.'

As the latest founder of a Kamakura Buddhist movement, Ippen faced the task of establishing relations with the existing sects. According to the *Honchō Kōsōden*, Ippen studied Zen under Kakushin (1207–1298). Although there is no existing historical evidence to support such a claim, Shinji Kakushin was known as a Zen master affiliated with the Shingon *nembutsu* tradition, and considering Ippen's own Shingon orientation, such a relationship would not seem unusual.[128] Ippen also managed to carefully handle relations with the Nichiren sect and when questioned by his followers regarding the superiority of the *nembutsu* over the *Lotus sutra*, he answered in the following manner;

> The *Lotus* and Name are one,
> the *Lotus* is material Dharma,
> the Name is psychological Dharma.
> Since matter and mind are inseparable,
> the *Lotus* is the Name.[129]

Although theologically, the Ji sect is believed to be based upon the revelation of the Kumano god, Ippen also considered the Pure Land 'Triple sutra' and its commentaries important. Above all he placed emphasis upon the *Smaller Sukhāvatī-vyūha*, which stressed the significance of the name of Amida, for in the Ji sect, the Name was considered to represent the Absolute essence of Amida.

3. Foundation of the Ji Sect

During the lifetime of Ippen his movement merely constituted one variety of *nembutsu hijiri*. Having no intention of founding a sect, Ippen called his group the Jishū 時衆 (lit. *Ji* Congregation rather than sect). The name *ji* (time) signified that its followers did not neglect a single moment of chanting the *nembutsu* whether they be walking, sitting, eating or sleeping, and each chanting was believed to be equivalent to the *nembutsu* at the moment of death. Ippen also divided the day into six watches, assigning eight disciples to chant constantly during each period, establishing perpetual chanting.

The practice of constant *yugyō* (travelling) demanded considerable sacrifices from the followers of Ippen. Arranged in groups of approximately twenty, they would tour the countryside handing out *nembutsu* tablets, while enduring painful hardships and renouncing all attachments to property or family. Each monk or nun was limited to twelve personal items to carry with him, and besides these, each also carried on his shoulders twelve small boxes. At night these were arranged in blocks to form a barricade separating the monks from the nuns. Each member spent the day handing out the small *nembutsu* tablets. It has been theorized that during his sixteen years of *yugyō*, Ippen personally handed out over two million tablets.

In later periods, householders unable to participate in the *yugyō* activities became associated with the Ji sect as *zoku jishū* (layman), who practiced the six-watch *nembutsu* or *kechienshū* (affiliates), who provided food, finances and lodging for the wandering priests and nuns. After Ippen's death, various names were assigned to the movement such as "Shinshū," "Nembutsu Sammai Shinshū," "Jinchoku-shū" (God Revelation sect), "Amidakyō-shū," "Yugyōshū," and so on. It was not until the mid-Muromachi period that the title Jishū was finally established.

Since Ippen had no notion of founding a sect, he failed to name a successor at the time of his death and his disciples were left in considerable confusion. Seven of them followed their master in death by drowning themselves, and others dispersed. But Ippen's closest disciple Shinkyō, who had taken the religious name of Ta Amida Butsu, gathered a group and went to Mt. Tanjō where they planned to chant the *nembutsu* and fast to death. The local landlord heard of their presence and visited them to hear their teachings. At that time Shinkyō was persuaded to succeed Ippen and carry on the practices of *yugyō* (travelling) and *fusan* (handing out *nembutsu* tablets).

Shinkyō had originally been a Jōdo Chinzei-ha priest when he met Ippen in Bungo province in 1277. As his closest disciple, Shinkyō was familiar with the routes Ippen had established during his travels, and led his remaining group over these paths commencing in the northern Hokuriku area and then east to Kantō. In 1302 Shinkyō conducted the thirteenth memorial for Ippen in Hyōgo province, and the following year, suffering from the after-effects of a stroke, he retired to the Taima-dōjō in Sagami province, entrusting his missionary activities to his disciple Chitoku (Ryō Amida Butsu), and also bestowing upon him his own religious name of Ta Amida Butsu. It became a future custom of the sect to pass this name on to the active successors.

Shinkyō's retirement created a new life-style within the Ji movement. The founder Ippen had practiced *yugyō* up until the time of his death, but he had died at the age of fifty-one. It was impossible for elderly members of the sect to continue the life of deprivation and hardship required by constantly moving missionary activities. Thus Shinkyō was the first to initiate a retirement known as *dokujū* (living alone) in a fixed residence. The Taima-dōjō became the Muryōkōji temple and developed around the reputation of Shinkyō into a centre of Ji activities. Shinkyō spent sixteen years in 'retirement' up until his death in 1316 at the age of eighty-three.

At the time of Shinkyō's death, his successor Chitoku turned over his missionary duties to his disciple Eei, known as U Amida Butsu (1265–1327), and also retired to the Muryōkōji temple where he spent the remainder of his life up until his death in 1319. But upon his death the Jishū split into two branches. Since Eei, more popularly known as Donkai, had already succeeded to Chitoku's *yugyō* activities, upon Chitoku's death, he naturally expected to follow his example and retire to the Muryōkōji, but was prevented from doing so by other disciples already in residence at that temple. They claimed that Chitoku had once expelled Donkai from the order, hence he could not become a proper successor. However, Donkai was in possession of the membership register of the sect, which he had received from his master Chitoku, that certified the names of those who had achieved *ōjō*. Without this register the Muryōkōji temple could not continue the sect's missionary activities. Since they were unwilling to accept Donkai as their leader, they were forced to abandon the practice of *yugyō* and recording names in the membership register. To offset this disadvantage they had the privilege of housing the tombs of both Shinkyō and Chitoku, and as a result managed over the years to attract local samurai patrons; they thus became the Taima-ha branch of the Ji sect.

Denied the right to establish himself at the traditional Muryōkōji temple, Donkai and his followers established a new headquarters nearby in Sagami at the Fujisawa-dōjō. This later became known as the Shōjōkōji temple, although popularly it was called the Yugyōji (temple of wandering practice), since Donkai established the custom that the temple serve as the final resting place after missionary activities. Donkai's followers developed into the powerful Yugyō-ha of the Ji sect. When

Donkai died in 1327 at the age of sixty-three, he was succeeded by his disciple Ankoku who made the Fujisawa-dōjō his headquarters and established the custom that retired priests live there, while active travelling priests used the Konkōji in Kyoto as their base. During the mid-fourteenth through the early sixteenth century the Jishū attained its apex of popularity, becoming the foremost Pure Land sect. Ceaseless groups practiced *yugyō*, temples were founded and editions of the scriptures of the sect were published. By the early fifteenth century the travelling monks received protection from the Ashikaga government and also from powerful Daimyō in the provinces. In return their now affluent temples performed rituals for the peace and prosperity of the nation; finally they had achieved acceptance as an established institution. They also played an important cultural role during the Muromachi period that has been referred to as the 'Jishū Ami Culture'[130] due to the fact that individuals affiliated with the sect frequently assumed *Ami* (an abbreviation for Amida) into their names. This suffix often appears in the names of leading *renga* poets of the day, famous *Nō* dramatists (i.e. Kan-Ami, Ze-Ami), and also among prominent physicians who served the Daimyō in battle.

In 1387 Sonkan (d. 1400), a son of the Imperial court at Yoshino, became the twelfth successor of the Yugyō-ha and is generally regarded as the 'Middle Restorer' of Jishū. Under his influence the movement established close ties with the Yoshino court in exile. And as the Ji sect grew in prosperity, it also began to institutionally divide until it eventually became 'twelve schools.' Among these the Yugyō and Ikkō branches were most distinguished. The latter was founded by Ikkō Shunjō, a contemporary of Ippen. The relationship between Ikkō and Ippen was so uncertain, however, that a continual dispute lasted up to the Meiji period between the two branches over the question of whether or not Ikkō was a proper disciple of Ippen, and hence legitimate transmitter of his teachings. The so-called twelve schools of Jishū, based upon institutional rather than doctrinal differences, are as follows:

1) Taima-ha
2) Yugyō-ha

3) Ikkō-ha founded by Ikkō Shunjō
4) Okutani-ha by Sen-A
5) Rokujō-ha by Shōkai
6) Shijō-ha by Jō-a
7) Kaii-ha by Kai-A
8) Ryōzen-ha by Koku-A
9) Koku-A-ha (same founder as above)
10) Ichiya-ha by Sa-A
11) Tendō-ha (the temple where Ikkō Shunjō died)
12) Goedō-ha by Ō-A

As the idealistic activities of travelling and handing out *nembutsu* tablets devised by Ippen gradually were replaced by formalized temples, corruption began to set in. The Ji sect became too closely identified with the establishment at a time of social disintegration and disorder. The register carried by the travelling monks degenerated into a donation booklet that no longer listed the name of anyone as arriving at 'non-*ōjō*.' In fact the priests promised that upon receiving a proper donation and inscribing the name of a person already deceased in their register, the dead could even be brought out of hell to enter the Pure Land. Another sign of decline was the moral corruption of the travelling monks and nuns. Even during the days of Ippen the constant association of men and women over such extended periods of time presented constant danger. Now many of the travelling groups wantonly abandoned the strict discipline their founder had imposed upon them. And a main area for criticism against the sect became the dancing *nembutsu*, which degenerated into a form of entertainment.

Although during its days of popularity, the Ji sect was for a time the most important Pure Land movement, it declined swiftly. Travelling priests were unable to properly conduct missionary activities during the time of civil war between the Daimyō, and many Jishū temples were destroyed by warlord and peasant revolts. In particular they began to lose support among the peasant masses, who sought to rebel against all forms of the oppressive establishment and its allies. And as the Ji sect commenced to decline, the Jōdo Shinshū Honganji movement under the leadership of Rennyo quickly moved in to fill the void, in company with the Zen sect that appealed to many of the former samurai followers of Ippen. During the Tokugawa period the national system of temple registration (*terauke*) also endangered the spirit of *yugyō* missionary practice and the major activity of the sect became the development of theology and editing sacred scriptures. It was during this time that the Tokugawa government recognized the leadership of the Yugyō-ha over the Jishū and legally unified the sect under the abbot of the Shōjōkōji temple.

CHAPTER III

THE NICHIREN-SHŪ, FOLLOWERS
OF THE LOTUS

A second single-practice new religious movement to develop during the Kamakura period that was also faith oriented was the Nichiren sect, where belief was placed in reciting the name of the *Lotus Sutra*.

1. Nichiren, the Founder

Nichiren is unique among the founders of Japanese Buddhism in that the major incidents of his life have all been carefully recorded and preserved. During his later years, he copiously wrote and interpreted the events and miracles that led him to the ultimate realization that he was the embodiment of Jōgyō (Viśiṣṭacāritra) bodhisattva, whose mission was to protect the *Lotus Sutra* and nation of Japan.

Nichiren was born the sixteenth day of the second month in the year 1222 in Kominato of Awa Province. Later followers were to attempt to portray Nichiren's family as aristocratic but in his own words, he was the 'son of an untouchable along the beach.'[1] This statement has caused certain confusion, but today it is generally believed to imply that his father professionally dealt with fishing—a livelihood that was not favourably regarded by idealistic Buddhists since it entailed the taking of life. Nichiren, however, was very proud of the lowliness of his birth.

At the time of Nichiren, the village where he was born was an estate of the Ise Shrine. And the sacred atmosphere undoubtedly served to stimulate his awareness of Japanese tradition and strong feeling of nationalism. As he later wrote while in exile:

> The area of Tōjō in the province of Awa is a remote place
> but it appears to be the centre of Japan. The reason is because

Amaterasu Ō Mikami dropped her manifestation (*suijaku*) there. Originally in the past she dropped her manifestation at Ise but the rulers of the nation offered her little respect while profoundly venerating Hachiman and the Kamo gods, therefore she was angered. Minamoto Yoritomo by petition ordered Kodayū of Auga to receive her and the Outer shrine of Ise was reverently and secretly brought to this place satisfying Amaterasu, and thus he became Shōgun holding all of Japan in his hands. This man set the area of Tōjō as the residence of Amaterasu Ō Mikami and therefore the great god does not reside in Ise but rather in the Tōjō area of Awa province . . . Nichiren, in the Tōjō area, province of Awa in Japan of Jambudvīpa, for the first time has begun to propagate the true Dharma.[2]

We do not know anything about Nichiren's early education but by the time he reached the age of twelve, he arrived at two crucial questions in life and the search to answer them determined his future course:[3]

The first dealt with the misfortunes of the Imperial family, which Nichiren believed should have been divinely protected by the gods and temples of the land. He had been born the year following the Shōkyū war, an Imperial revolt against the Hōjō regents that resulted in the exile of Emperor Go-Toba (1180–1239). And he questioned why the Divine ruler of the nation was permitted to suffer disgrace and be ousted by usurpers. He also sought to know why the child Emperor Antoku had earlier been 'allowed to drown and become food for fish' at the close of the Gempei war that had placed Minamoto Yoritomo in charge of Japan. Nichiren believed that such Imperial ignominies must have had a reason for happening, and he sought to discover it.

Secondly, Nichiren questioned the nature of Buddhism. Observing the numerous sects and immense volumes of sutras, he came to the conclusion that 'just as a nation cannot peacefully function with two rulers, if Buddhism is to be effective there can only be one true sect and one true sutra,' these he also sought to discover. Thus making a vow to Kokūzō (Ākāśagarbha) bodhisattva, that he would become the 'foremost man of wisdom in Japan,' he entered neighboring Mt. Kiyosumi in 1233 to study Buddhism.

In those days, Mt. Kiyosumi belonged to the Tendai sect and had ties with the Yokawa *nembutsu* followers on Mt. Hiei. Dōzen, Nichiren's master was a *nembutsu* monk and in later years Nichiren was to write that while young, he had studied Zendō (Shan-tao), Genshin and Genkū (Hōnen).[4] The Kiyosumi-dera later became affiliated with the Shingon sect, and in 1392 its temple master belonged to the Shingon Sambōin-ryū. At that time forged historical records were made to prove the temple had always belonged to Shingon but during Nichiren's lifetime it officially was a branch of the Sanmon Tendai.

Upon arriving on the mountain, Nichiren was first given the child-name of Yakuō-maru and after four years of study when he was formally ordained, he received the religious name of Zeshōbō Renchō. In 1239, feeling confined by the lack of material for study at such a poor countryside temple, Nichiren decided to visit Kamakura, the *de facto* seat of government. Most historians surmise that it was then he completed further studies in Zen and Pure Land Buddhism, but we have to question exactly what forms of Zen and Pure Land were in Kamakura at the time.

According to legend, Nichiren studied Pure Land under Dai Amida Butsu but as this master died in screaming agony, Nichiren became convinced that Pure Land followers were fated to hell and abandoned the teachings. The story appears to be a later fabrication although it is known that Hōnen had a follower known as Dai-A, who signed the Seven Article Pledge. We can imagine that Nichiren must have had some unpleasant experience that turned him so bitterly against Pure Land Buddhism, and in particular against Hōnen, who had died eleven years prior to his birth. Historically this was the period when Ryōchū of the Chinzei-ha, a powerful future enemy of Nichiren, was becoming established in Kamakura, and although Shinran was also active in the Kantō area at the time, it is most likely Nichiren never heard of him.

If Nichiren studied Zen in Kamakura at this early date, it must have

been an impure form of Zen in the *Enmitsuzenkai* tradition such as propagated by Eisai at the Jufukuji, in accord with the wishes of the Kamakura leaders. For Nichiren's stay in Kamakura considerably antedated
the arrival of Rankei Dōryū in 1246, who led the procession of Chinese
priests transmitting pure Zen in Japan.

Study on Mt. Hiei

In 1242 when Nichiren returned to the Kiyosumi-dera, he wrote a
small work entitled the *Kaitai Sokushin Jōbutsugi* (Essay on attaining
Buddhahood with this body through the essence of the *śīla*) that summed
up his religious studies. The interesting point about this is that he placed
Shingon esoteric doctrines superior to the *Lotus* exoteric teachings.
This was an opinion he was later to radically change, however, we can
only assume that he was profoundly influenced in Kamakura by esoteric
teachings and the concept of attaining Buddhahood with this body
(*sokushin jōbutsu*) was to become a cardinal feature of his later philosophy.
As a further preview of his future course, he also attacked the Pure
Land sect in this short work and declared the *Lotus Sutra* closest to the
truth. Nichiren's anti-Pure Land attitude was enforced the same year
when at the age of twenty-one, he decided to go to Mt. Hiei for further
study and became a disciple of Shunban, the monk in charge of academic
affairs on the mountain, who was known to be a strong opponent of
the *nembutsu*, Zen and Shingon.

In view of Nichiren's later theological position, we can imagine that
he must have been influenced by the Eshin-ryū on Mt. Hiei founded
by Genshin. This group, which tended to oppose Tendai esoterism as
expressed in Taimitsu (a stand Nichiren also adopted), set forth the
doctrine of *hongaku hōmon* (Teaching of the Dharma of Original Enlightenment), which emphasized all sentient beings as intrinsic Buddhas
—a concept Nichiren used as a foundation for his philosophy.[5]

In his search for the 'true' Buddhism, Nichiren established certain
rules. He refused to accept any sect based upon a treatise rather than a
sutra and thus automatically ruled out the Kusha, Jōjitsu, Hossō and
Sanron schools. Furthermore, while in Kamakura he had already decided

that Zen and Pure Land sects could not represent 'true' Buddhism and soon dismissed Kegon as inferior to Tendai. His final choice fell between Tendai and Shingon, but before he finally left Mt. Hiei, he was to decide that the Tendai sect alone represented 'true' Buddhism.

Nichiren's stay upon Mt. Hiei proved to be one of the most influential events in his life and we can place the movement he was later to found within the framework of the Tendai order. It was while there that Nichiren became firmly convinced the *Lotus Sutra* was the perfect culmination of Buddhist truth and the sole hope of salvation for men during the days of *Mappō* (Degeneration of the Dharma). He also came to envision himself as having the responsibility of restoring the Tendai sect to what he believed to be the original ideals of Saichō, its founder.

Initially, Nichiren traced his own unique reception of Tendai transmission in a direct line from Śākyamuni Buddha through Chih-I to Saichō, and finally to himself.[6] Later in life he was to omit the Tendai mediators and declare that he had received a direct transmission of the teachings from Śākyamuni Buddha, but even then, Nichiren never abandoned the conviction that he had a mission to restore the Tendai order. Undoubtedly one reason for his violent attacks against *nembutsu* followers was his belief that the popularity of Hōnen's movement had resulted in a serious decline for the Tendai sect.

During Nichiren's stay on Mt. Hiei, he left the mountain for several years to study other sects of Buddhism. In his letters he mentions having visited the Onjōji, where Enchin's Jimon-ha of the Tendai sect had its headquarters, also Mt. Kōya and the Shitennōji in Osaka where the teachings of the older sects of Buddhism were studied. Strangely enough he makes no mention of ever going to Nara, but perhaps he felt the doctrines of the Nara sects were adequately represented at the Shitennōji.

Beginning of his mission—Shakubuku

When Nichiren decided finally it was time to leave Mt. Hiei, he had the answers to his previous questions. The Tendai sect represented 'true' Buddhism and during the age of *Mappō*, the *Lotus Sutra* alone could offer salvation. The reason the Imperial family had been forced to suffer humiliations was due to the fact that the nation of Japan failed to take homage in the *Lotus* and had allowed heretical teachings to dominate the land, causing the protector gods to abandon it. This was to become the message he transmitted throughout the rest of his life.

On the twenty-eighth day of the fourth month in 1253, Nichiren at the age of thirty-three returned to Mt. Kiyosumi, believing the time had come to preach his doctrine to the world. Accordingly, as in the case of the historical Buddha, Nichiren first wished to preach to his former fellow disciples, and also to his old master. And although the *Honmon-shūyōshō* (Essentials of the Honmon sect) attributed to Nichiren is now generally considered to have been a forgery, the first preaching of Nichiren's had some similarities to the account found there:

> *Nembutsu* followers will fall into the Avīci hell,
> Zen followers are devils,
> Shingon will destroy the nation,
> The Ritsu are enemies of the state,
> Tendai is an outdated calendar.[7]

The first four lines were to be frequently repeated on later occasions and formed the basis of Nichiren's method of *shakubuku* (conversion).[8] Throughout life Nichiren was known for intemperate emotional language, which he used as a deliberate weapon to shock and antagonize his opponents, at the same time attracting the more timid and fearful to his dynamic and confident cause. It is dubious whether on this first preaching that he criticized Shingon, for he did not begin overt attacks on that sect until after the threat of the Mongol invasions, when Shingon rituals gained great popularity throughout the nation. And the attack on Tendai seems to be a fabrication by later followers, since Nichiren personally did not speak ill of that sect. Most likely the initial attack at Mt. Kiyosumi was against the *nembutsu* and Zen, and since his old master and the majority of the monks practiced the *nembutsu*, his charges must have been as astonishing as the mission he claimed to propagate the *Lotus*.

In the audience during this first preaching was the powerful local warlord, Tōjō Kagenobu, a *nembutsu* follower who was so incensed by Nichiren's remarks that he planned an ambush as he descended the mountain. Dōzen, Nichiren's old master, learned of the planned attack and in order to protect Nichiren, publicly disowned him, while secretly sending two monks to accompany him down the mountain. Tōjō's initial plan failed, but as a lifelong enemy of Nichiren he was to try again and be more successful the next time.

Subsequently, Nichiren was invited to the dedication of a local Amida hall. Those who requested his presence merely assumed he was a bright young scholar returning from study on Mt. Hiei and had no idea he entertained such radical views. Accepting the invitation, Nichiren enraged the audience by declaring that since Amida was the master of the western world and not this one, here Śākyamuni and not Amida should receive veneration. The reactions Nichiren deliberately provoked served as stimuli to carry on his *shakubuku* methods, since he astutely interpreted anger as a form of success, proving that he had indeed touched the people. In fact later in life he was to announce that he was 'the greatest man in Japan since he was the most hated person.'[9] For next to acceptance and recognition, hatred and criticism reflect human importance in society,—the most ignoble fate is to be ignored.

First converts

On his way to Kamakura, Nichiren stopped at the home of his parents and although they initially entreated him to cease his offensive style of preaching, ultimately they became the first converts to his movement. His mother received the new religious name of Myōnichi and his father, Myōren. According to legend, this is when Nichiren took the last characters from each of their new religious names to create his own name.

Arriving in Kamakura, Nichiren took up residence at a small hut in Matsubagayatsu on the southeastern outskirts of the city and commenced practicing *shakubuku* by denouncing the Zen and Pure Land sects. It has commonly been believed that Nichiren delivered his sermons on street corners, but contemporary historians question this view since street preaching was a later invention and not practiced at that time.[10]

Most likely he spoke at the homes of laymen or in public meeting places. At first he was met with derision, but in time began to attract disciples. In 1253 Jōben, a former Mt. Hiei monk a year Nichiren's senior, became his first disciple and received the religious name of Nisshō. The following year this monk's nephew, approximately ten years of age, joined Nichiren and received the name of Nichirō.

Risshō Ankokuron

During the years 1254–60, a series of major calamities in the form of earthquakes, drought, famine and epidemic struck Japan and Nichiren decided the time had arrived to warn the nation that these calamities were principally the result of the growing popularity of Hōnen's *nembutsu* movement. He wrote two essays to this effect, and then in the summer of 1260 summarized all his convictions in an official petition to the government entitled the *Risshō Ankokuron* (Treatise on the Establishment of Righteousness for the Peace of the Nation). This he submitted to the former regent, Hōjō Tokiyori, who still ruled from behind the scenes. The essence of this work, written in classical style as a dialogue between a traveller and master of the house, was that the calamities befalling the nation were due to the return of the *deva* and good gods protecting Japan to heaven as a result of the popularity of the teachings of Zendō and Genkū. In order to save the land, all support of the *nembutsu* heresy should be stopped and the country should take homage in the *Lotus Sutra*. If this advice was not heeded, foreign invasion and civil disturbances would be unavoidable.[11]

Exile to Izu

One interesting point about this treatise is the fact that Nichiren, being aware the Hōjō regents personally belonged to the Zen sect, significantly omitted any denuciation of Zen, placing total blame upon *nembutsu* followers. Despite this, his first warning to the nation was ostensibly ignored by the government. Perhaps it was out of kindness, since public notice would have inevitably resulted in charges against Nichiren. But the contents of his petition gradually became known and finally incited an attack upon his hut by *nembutsu* followers. Barely escaping, Nichiren temporarily retired to Shimofusa province, yet when he returned to Kamakura the following year he resumed practicing *shakubuku* as violently as before. It was then that *nembutsu* followers made an official appeal to the Kamakura government to have Nichiren charged with slanderous speech, which under article twelve of the *Jōei Shikimoku* feudal code was punishable by death or imprisonment. As a result, Nichiren was exiled to Izu Peninsula, but he was to have the satisfaction of knowing that Hōjō Shigetoki of the Gokurakuji temple, who had instigated the petition against him, fell ill twenty days after his departure and died before the close of the year; Nichiren interpreted this as divine punishment.

In 1263, the same year that Hōjō Tokiyori died, Nichiren was pardoned and returned to Kamakura. And the following year when a great comet appeared in the sky, Nichiren interpreted the event as a portent of future disaster. He considered again warning the government, but the illness of his mother persuaded him to return home.

According to legend, Nichiren's mother was already dead upon his arrival, but due to his fervent prayers, she was restored to life for four more years. While in the vicinity, Nichiren decided to visit his old master Dōzen, now living at the Rengeji temple in Hanabusa, in order to rebuke him for continuing to practice the *nembutsu*. The old master, despite his affection for Nichiren, was not about to change his ways and years later after his death, Nichiren was further to address him a spiritual admonition.

While visiting his master, an invitation arrived from the warlord Kudō Yoshitaka, and Nichiren set out for his residence accompanied by six or seven disciples on the wintry eve of the eleventh day of the eleventh month (1264), but on the way met an ambush set by his old enemy Tōjō Kagenobu, the local warlord. This time one of Nichiren's disciples was killed, two seriously injured and Nichiren himself received a wound on his forehead as well as a broken left hand. Hearing of the attack, Kudō Yoshitaka and two retainers immediately came to aid but met death in the skirmish. Nichiren barely escaped and a month later upon describing this assault to a follower, announced that he felt more convinced than ever in the divine inspiration for his mission; his confidence was to increase with future events.

In 1268 an envoy arrived in Japan demanding tribute from Kubhilai Khan, the great leader of the Mongols who had recently become Emperor of China. Unlike earlier Chinese messages, this was couched in polite language and clearly implied that the Khan was seeking peaceful tributary relations. The Korean representatives that accompanied the messenger informed the Kamakura *bakufu* that the Khan merely sought tribute as a formality to increase his prestige and suggested the *bakufu* comply with the request.

At the time of the messenger's arrival, Hōjō Masamura was about to turn over the regency to the eighteen year old Tokimune, and as one of his last moderate acts, after debating over the message for nearly a month, decided to turn the matter over to the Court in Kyoto. Shortly thereafter Tokimune became regent and with his more militant advisers firmly rejected the Mongol demand. It was evident that the Hōjō regents were annoyed although not seriously disturbed by the Mongol message, but by notifying the Court, it was not long before rumours spread throughout Japan that the Mongols were about to invade. To placate the people, the *bakufu* sent requests to the established shrines and temples for rituals to safeguard the nation and also cautiously took steps to prepare in the event of an invasion.

Hearing the news, Nichiren went to the Government Bureau of Retainers (*Samurai dokoro*) to submit another petition to the Regent, this time pointing out that the *Risshō Ankokuron* written nine years previously, had predicted foreign invasion if Japan failed to reject heretical teachings and take homage in the *Lotus*. And that now if the government allowed the Buddhist priests, whom he charged as being heretics, to perform rituals for the nation, it would anger the gods to destroy the land. Only he, Nichiren, could prevent the devastation that would inevitably occur and obliterate all within its wake (with the exception of the sacrosanct Mt. Hiei).

On the eleventh day of the tenth month (1268), Nichiren also sent eleven letters addressed to the Regent, major figures of government, and the senior monks of the various temples. The essence of these, with the exception of his letter to Hōjō Tokimune, was to demand support of the temples be stopped, that faith be placed in him rather than in heretical teachings, and finally, that if any doubted the truth of his words, they should prepare to meet him in public debate. Doing this, he prepared to meet persecution or possibly another exile and forewarned his disciples, but the government ignored his advice, and at the leading temples his messengers were either met with derision or refusal to accept his letter.

Since Japan's initial rejection of Kubhilai Khan's demands stirred up no immediate retaliation, public excitement over the matter gradually subsided and was replaced by contemporary affairs. But a subsequent message the following year created further panic, and the nation psychologically prepared for a possible invasion. At this point Nichiren's timely predictions gained more appeal but once again when the invasion failed to materialize, the people lost interest.

Then in the spring of 1271 a drought hit Japan. By summer the situation was so severe that the government requested Ryōkan of the Gokurakuji, the most influential priest of the capital, to perform a rain ritual. When Nichiren heard of this, he made a public challenge to Ryōkan's followers promising that if their master could bring rain within seven days, he, Nichiren, would abandon his faith and become a disciple. But if Ryōkan should fail, then his hypocritical pretence of observing the *śīla* would be exposed.[12]

Supposedly some one hundred-twenty monks participated in the ritual but at the end of seven days there was no sign of rain. Nichiren then sent three messengers to Ryōkan informing him that if he could not perform a simple task like making rain, how could he expect to accomplish something as complicated as becoming a Buddha? After further prayers, allegedly the drought worsened; such failures increased Nichiren's popularity and it is believed that year his followers in Kamakura reached two-hundred sixty.

Because of his constant accusations and demands, Nichiren's opponents, led by Gyōbin, a disciple of the Jōdo priest Ryōchū of the Kō-myōji, brought charges against him to the government claiming amongst other things that of the teachings of Buddhism, only Nichiren exclusively rejected all others, and that his followers were known to throw sacred images of Amida and Kannon in the fire or river; finally, that he kept a group of armed followers as well as a cache of secret weapons at his residence.

The government was not overly concerned about the religious charges against Nichiren since such had been heard before, but they seriously considered the complaint that he kept armed soldiers and weapons. Nichiren had been known publicly to state that all the improper heretical temples should be burned and the leading priests supported by the Hōjō beheaded, thus if the charges were true that he kept a private army, there was a strong possibility that he actually intended to make good his threats. As a result, Nichiren was called to the Court of Appeals (Hyōjōsho) during the ninth month and questioned whether he had indeed made such inflammatory statements, and if it was true that he kept armed followers and weapons. In reply, Nichiren unhesitantly stated that he did believe all heretical temples and priests should be destroyed and that it was true he kept armed followers at his residence for his own protection.

Such an admission placed the authorities in a quandry. If Nichiren actually intended to fulfill his threats and attack the established temples and shrines, he would in effect be attempting to overthrow the government. In fact his frequent criticisms of the Zen sect, to which the Hōjō family belonged, were considered indirect attacks against the Regents themselves. Particularly since Hōjō Tokiyori had been ordained a Zen priest seven years before his death by Rankei Dōryū, Nichiren's contention that Zen followers were inspired by devils and destined to hell was considered a criticism of the current Regent Tokimune, the son of Tokiyori. Furthermore, Nichiren's pro-Imperial views presented a challenge to the legitimacy of Hōjō rule. It was quite simple to establish a case of treason and conspiracy against him.

That day Nichiren was allowed to return home while the situation was debated. On the twelfth day of the same month, a detachment of warriors led by Hei no Saemon was sent to arrest Nichiren. After several hours in court, he was sentenced to exile on Sado Island, but secretly it was arranged that he was to be executed on the way.

Reprieve from Execution

Late at night with an armed guard escort, Nichiren departed on horseback for the place of his secret execution. Midway he halted to call upon the god Hachiman for aid and shortly after midnight the group reached the public execution grounds of Tatsunokuchi where Nichiren was forced to dismount. He was about to be beheaded when a special reprieve from Tokimune arrived entrusting him instead to Honma Shigetsura, the governor of Sado Island.[13] It is not certain why Tokimune decided to commute Nichiren's secret sentence, but some historians believe certain supporters of Nichiren in government were able to use the pregnancy of Tokimune's wife in their campaign to save him.[14] Legendary accounts were to describe Nichiren's escape from execution as miraculous with a blinding light striking the executioner just as he raised his sword. Still, the near execution became a traumatic experience for Nichiren and changed the orientation of his spiritual life. After escaping this fate he felt spiritually reborn—found his convictions to be stronger than ever as well as his sense of divine mission, and the majority of his theological works were written after this event.

Exile on Sado

Nichiren stopped at the mansion of Honma Shigetsura in Sagami briefly before being sent to exile and arrived on Sado Island during the tenth month of 1271, there he was confined to a small abandoned temple-hall that had served as a place of disposal for the dead. He had extreme difficulty in surviving the cold snowy winter in the drafty hut, but gradually won a few converts who helped supply him with food and warm clothing. It was during this time that Nichiren wrote the *Kaimokushō* (Eye-opener Treatise) in which he made his famous vows:

I will be the pillar of Japan
I will be the eyes of Japan
I will be the ship of Japan[15]

and became aware that he was the embodiment of Jōgyō (Viśiṣṭacāritra) bodhisattva, the protector of the *Lotus Sutra*. In essence, the work declared the *Lotus Sutra* to be the only true sutra during the era of *mappō* and that although Śākyamuni was the leader of all sentient beings during his lifetime, now in the age of *mappō*, Nichiren alone was to be regarded as the rightful leader.

Gradually Nichiren's treatment improved, and the following spring he was permitted to take up residence with a farm family at Ichinosawa and his followers on Sado Island increased. At the same time, his movement on the mainland lost much of its vigour without Nichiren's presence.

During the year 1272, a second prophecy of Nichiren's appeared to be fulfilled as a leading member of the Kamakura *bakufu*, Hōjō Tokimune's half-brother Hōjō Tokisuke, who served in the post of *Rokuhara Tandai* (court watcher) in Kyoto, was charged with conspiracy and attempt to revolt. This scandal convinced Nichiren's followers that his prediction of political disturbance if the nation failed to take homage in the *Lotus*, had been fulfilled.

The Daimandara

While on Sado in 1273 (eighth day, seventh month) for the first time, Nichiren created the principal image of his movement in the form of a *Daimandara* (Great Maṇḍala). This portrayed the characters of *Namu Myōhōrengekyō* springing up from the earth like a great stupa and uniting with the heavens to symbolize the affirmation of eternal life. Surrounding these characters, were the figures of the Buddhas Śākyamuni and Prabhūtaratna in company with the four bodhisattvas who rose from the earth to protect the *Lotus*, led by Viśiṣṭacāritra (Jōgyō). In the next level various Śrāvaka such as Śāriputra and Maudgalyāyana are placed among Mahāyāna bodhisattvas such as Mañjuśrī and Samantabhadra. Finally, in the lower level the Sun Goddess Amaterasu, Hachiman and various other deities are depicted along with the names of Tendai Daishi (Chih-I) and

Dengyō Daishi (Saichō). Thus we can see the final crystallization of Nichiren's thought. Earlier he had considered himself to be the spiritual successor of Chih-I and Saichō, but now, as the embodiment of Jōgyō bodhisattva, he stands directly in the company of Śākyamuni. Later certain minor modifications and variations were made in the *mandara*, but its essence remained unchanged.

Return to Kamakura

Nichiren's activities on Sado were carefully watched by the local countryside priests and in 1273, realizing that they were unable to compete with his learning, went in a delegation to Kamakura to appeal to the government that either Nichiren be banished from Sado or else be imprisoned to ensure the safety of their congregations. They also brought the charge that he acted like a madman, for day and night he would climb to the highest mountain on the island and rant and scream at the sun and moon. Little did they realize that this was the way Nichiren communed with the gods and scolded them for derelection of their duties.

Finally in 1274 Nichiren was pardoned by Hōjō Tokimune and on the twenty-sixth day of the third month once again arrived in Kamakura. The reasons for Nichiren's pardon are historically uncertain. It was granted just eight months prior to the first actual Mongol invasion attempt, and the mood of the *de facto* capital of Kamakura was gloomy. Nichiren had some supporters in government and during such uncertain times it was believed that the nation needed all the help it could get. The feelings against Nichiren had changed as the psychological mood of the city had changed. Even prior to his pardon a member of the ruling family, Hōjō Tokimori, had sent a sword to Nichiren requesting him to perform a ritual, and in reply Nichiren had sent a stern but respectful letter urging the old warrior to be strong in his faith.

Upon his return to Kamakura, Nichiren was immediately besieged with requests to perform rituals for the benefit of the nation and even received an invitation from Hei no Saemon, head of the Bureau of Retainers, the same man who earlier had been so insensitive to his petitions and officiated at his arrest. Saemon politely inquired if Nichiren could predict the date of the actual Mongol invasion. Nichiren replied that the sutra did not contain actual dates, but from his interpretation of various celestial signs, he was certain the invasion would arrive within the year. He added that he alone was capable of protecting the nation, and that the government should immediately abandon all Tantric rituals.

Although the government authorities listened respectfully to Nichiren at this time, they still were not convinced his remedies offered the only solution for the dangers confronting Japan. And during the fourth month, in the face of a new season of drought, they called upon Kagahōin Jōchō of the Amida-dō temple to perform a rain ritual. Since rain fell the day after his rite, Nichiren's critics were overjoyed, while his disciples became confused. Nichiren confidently explained to them that in the past many men had been proven capable of making rain, but it also happened that such rain was accompanied by severe damaging winds. Nichiren's prediction was fulfilled as sudden winds afflicted heavy damage in the area.

Retreat to Mt. Minobu

During the fifth month of the year 1274 Nichiren finally decided to retire from the world. He had made three formal appeals to the government commencing with his *Risshō Ankokuron*, then his defense prior to exile, and lastly his appearance upon his return to Kamakura. These had all been ignored and it was time to abandon hope and retire.[16] He was firmly convinced that the Mongol invasion would shortly destroy Japan, and thus sought sanctuary on remote Mt. Minobu, where he believed he could strengthen the faith of his followers and be prepared to return to Kamakura after the heretical sects had all been destroyed.

Mt. Minobu was nearly four thousand feet high surrounded by steep peaks and densely forested with cedar trees. To Nichiren it symbolized Vulture Peak where Śākyamuni had preached the *Lotus Sutra*. From October to April the mountain was covered with deep snow and nearly inaccessible. Nichiren built a crude hermitage where he lived with his small band of disciples. The group underwent extreme hardship lacking sufficient food and clothing and during the winter a number died. Nichiren himself contracted a form of dysentery, but with the coming of spring more disciples joined his group bringing donations of food, clothing and precious salt. Eventually it would seem that Mt. Minobu developed into the centre of the Nichiren danka (lay member) organization providing memorial services and rites for the laity as well as religious education for the monks.[17]

First Mongol Invasion

While Nichiren was encountering his first fall on Mt. Minobu, the first Mongol invasion attempt occurred. On the twentieth day of the tenth month in 1274, a fleet of 900 Korean-style vessels entered Hakata Bay and commenced to land from three directions. Besides a crew of 15,000, which Japanese historians might have exaggerated, their vessels contained an estimated mixed force of 25,600 Korean, Chinese and Mongol troops, a number of whom were soldier-farmers carrying agricultural implements and prepared to colonize Japan. The first skirmish was in the Mongol's favour, but as they returned to their ships for the night a typhoon struck, dashing their vessels against the ragged cliffs of the bay, and according to Japanese accounts, some 13,500 men were lost. The remainder of the fleet limped back to safety in Korea.

Although the first invasion had not borne the results Nichiren anticipated, he interpreted it as a warning, indicating that his prophecy would soon be fulfilled. And indeed the first invasion merely strengthened Kubhilai Khan's attitude towards Japan. Early the following year he sent another envoy to Kamakura, but unbeknown to him this messenger was put to death. The Japanese attitude had also hardened. By 1280 the Khan was preparing a massive six year invasion plan in which he was determined to make Japan a territory. But contrary to Nichiren's predictions, Kubhilai Khan warned his general against a large scale massacre of the populace since he believed a conquest of land alone was futile.

After the failure of the first Mongol invasion, Nichiren turned from political prophecy to writing one of his most important theological works. Undoubtedly his retreat to Mt. Minobu had been intended as a period to establish his theology and train future disciples. The first work he wrote there was entitled *Hokke-shuyōshō* (Treatise Selecting the Essentials of the Lotus Sect), in which he set forth his doctrine of the three secret Dharmas existing during the time of *mappō*.

Nichiren decided to make Mt. Minobu, which he considered to be symbolic of Vulture Peak, the centre of the universal propagation of his teachings. And gradually the hermitage became filled with disciples ranging by the year 1278 from a minimum of forty up to sixty residents. As a result, his solitude was interrupted, but his dream of establishing a centre for his order was being fulfilled; ultimately this hermitage developed into the famous Kuonji temple.

Second Mongol Invasion

From his retreat, Nichiren patiently awaited the second Mongol invasion that he believed would devastate the nation. This finally occurred in the year 1281 when Kubhilai Khan sent a five times larger invasion force than during the first attempt, the number being estimated at approximately 140,000. But the plan was ill-fated from its inception. A force sailing from South China had been scheduled to meet a fleet from Korea but failed to arrive on time. The Korean armada attacked first but their pace was slackened by the wall the Japanese had completed about the strategic points of Hakata Bay. Finally the Chinese arrived, but before the invading forced achieved any decisive victory a typhoon struck on the first day of the seventh month and 70–80% of the invading fleet was destroyed.

At the *de facto* capital Kamakura, the Shingon priests and others who had participated in the rites to safeguard the nation hastened to claim credit for the victory while Nichiren remained forlornly silent. His disciples were thrown into doubt and confusion at the failure of his predictions. But he had been ensnared in the age-old trap of mingling worldly prophecy with spiritual insight. From the time the first Mongol invasion failed to meet his anticipations, he began to observe silence or revert to ambiguity when forced to make a statement. Now as the second invasion met the same fate he found it exceedingly difficult to face his neophyte disciples who trustingly looked to him for worldly as well as spiritual answers. To a follower in Kyoto he wrote:

> An autumn wind destroyed the enemy's ships, but now the people boast of great success as if the commander of the enemy had been captured. And the priests pretend it was due to the efficacy of their rituals. Ask them if they took the head of the Mongol king? Whatever they say, they can make no reply to this.[18]

And then Nichiren lapsed into silence. Inexorably drawn into the role of worldly prophet, he was now to endure the harsh social consequences of failure and his enemies ridicule. But this time Nichiren was too ill and tired to fight back.

Final Illness

During the year 1278 a dysentery epidemic had swept the area and aggravated Nichiren's chronic problem. By 1282 the year following the Mongol invasion attempt, Nichiren became seriously ill and during the fall of that year in an effort to benefit his condition, he embarked on a trip to a hot spring in Hitachi province, also hoping to visit his old home. However, he became worse at Ikegami (Musashi province) where he had to rest at the house of a follower. As his condition deteriorated, his disciples gathered from the various provinces, and to his trusted attendant Nikkō (1245–1332), he dictated the names of the six disciples chosen to succeed him:

Nisshō	Nikkō 日向 (1253–1314)
Nichirō	Nitchō
Nikkō 日興 (1245–1332)	Nichiji

stating that after his death each was to rotate a monthly custodianship of his tomb. A few days later he divided his remaining belongings, and on the thirteenth day of the tenth month at the age of sixty-one, he passed away. Two days later he was cremated and according to his will, after the seventh day memorial, his ashes were transferred to Mt. Minobu. On the one-hundredth day memorial of his death, a mausoleum was built in his memory which exists today. Seventy-six years after his death he was granted the title of 'Daibosatsu' (Great bodhisattva) by Emperor Go-Kōgon and finally in 1922 he was given the posthumous name of Risshō Daishi (Master of the Establishment of Righteousness).

B. Faith in the *Daimoku*

The unique aspect of Nichiren's philosophy was his contention that salvation was attainable solely by chanting the sacred title (*Daimoku*) of the *Lotus Sutra*. As the last of the great Kamakura leaders, we can undoubtedly see an historical affinity in the choice of chanting with the *nembutsu* movement, however, Nichiren's application was based upon the Tendai tradition and in that respect can be viewed as an evolution of Tendai thought. To understand its basis, we have to take into consideration two fundamental Tendai concepts: the theory of Original Enlightenment, and the tradition of interpreting the *Lotus Sutra*.

1. *Hongaku shisō* (Theory of Original Enlightenment)

The Tendai view of 'Original Enlightenment,' which ultimately became quite controversial within the sect itself, was extremely influential among all the new movements of Kamakura Buddhism and served as a foundation of Nichiren's philosophy.[19] The concept was derived from the *Awakening of Faith*, which maintains the intrinsic nature of Enlightenment, contending that if man was not originally Enlightened, he would have no hope of ever attaining Enlightenment. The condition of the unenlightened is simply regarded as accidental and all that is necessary is for the individual to realize or actualize his 'Original Enlightenment.'[20] Hui-szu (515-77), the nominal founder of the Tendai sect equated 'Original Enlightenment' with the 'Buddha-nature,' 'as-it-isness,' and the '*Dharma-kāya*.'[21]

In Japanese Tendai, the concept of 'Original Enlightenment' was introduced by Saichō, and under the esoteric influence of Ennin, Enchin and Annen was linked to the *honjishin* (true nature body) of Dainichi Nyorai. Later, after the abbot Ryōgen and a renewal of Tendai (rather than esoteric) theology, the concept was related to the *Hosshin* (Dharma-body) of Amida as well as the second half of the *Lotus Sutra*, known as *honmon* (Section of the Origin). It was this latter philosophy that Nichiren used as a basis for his own interpretation and emphasis upon the second half of the sutra. In Tendai, the concept was advocated by the Eshin-ryū, in contrast to the theory of gradual or 'beginning' (*shigaku*) Enlightenment set forth by the Danna-ryū, and later identified with the *shakumon* (Section of Manifestation) of the *Lotus Sutra*.[22]

The difference in emphasis between 'gradual' versus 'instant' Enlightenment, and the 'relative' versus 'Absolute' approaches to Enlightenment had a long tradition in Buddhism. As a purist reformer and a product of the Kamakura age, Nichiren sought to obliterate all forms of expediency and approach the 'Absolute' directly. We find a similarity of attitude in the Zen schools and even to some degree in the Pure Land,[23] but Nichiren's emphasis upon the 'Absolute' Buddha particularly resembles the Shingon idealization of Dainichi Nyorai. In both Shingon and Nichiren thought the impulse towards the 'Absolute' is so consuming that everything in its pathway is reduced in significance. But we must keep in mind that in these sects, the 'Absolute' still serves as the very ground of one's own being, hence this is not a drive to an Other but rather a search within. Nichiren's idealism was such that he believed perfect Enlightenment possible for all beings and that as a result, the relative world could be transformed into a veritable Utopia. He interpreted the Shingon view of Enlightenment with this body (*sokushin jōbutsu*) on a grand scale and was willing to accept nothing short of perfection or the 'Absolute' itself.

In contrast, those who placed emphasis upon the manifestation (*shakumon*) section of the *Lotus Sutra* and the relative world, were concerned with the actual difficulties involved in attaining Enlightenment and the *upāya* methods of doing so. Nichiren was impatient with this attitude of the Tendai sect because it generally evolved into theorizing rather than practice and became a synonym for compromise with folk belief and superstition. This is one reason why certain later Nichiren followers were to narrow the definition of *upāya* into 'falsehood' and even question whether the *upāya* chapter of the *Lotus Sutra* should be read. Anything other than focus upon the 'Absolute' and the single-practice of faith in the *Lotus* was to be cast aside as impure. And the Nichiren drive toward purity was epitomized by placing the essence of the 'Absolute' within the five Chinese characters forming the title of the *Lotus Sutra*.

2. The Role of the *Lotus Sutra* (*Myōhōrengekyō*)

In Tendai tradition, the *Lotus Sutra* had a long history of title exegesis. Allegedly Vasubandhu was the first to examine the significance of the title in his *Saddharmapuṇḍarīkopadeśa*. The custom was continued in China where one of the most significant interpretations can be found in Chih-I's *Hsüan-I*. Title analysis became very popular in Chinese Buddhism since the Chinese characters naturally lent themselves to multiple interpretations and efforts were made to depict the entire doctrinal content of the sutra within the title itself. This tradition was continued in Japan by Saichō, Ennin and Enchin and formed the foundation of Nichiren's conviction that all the merits and teachings of the *Lotus* were expressed within the five Chinese characters forming its title, with merely the vocalization of the title being equivalent to chanting the sutra.

Another aspect of *Lotus* exegetical studies was the critical division of the sutra into *honmon* (Section of Origin) and *shakumon* (Section of Manifestation). The Kumārajīva Chinese translation of the text most commonly used, had twenty-eight chapters and these were divided by Chih-I, with the first half of the sutra desginated as *shakumon* (Chin. *chi-men*), since it referred to the historical or 'manifestation' Buddha. The second half that spoke of an Eternal Śākyamuni existing from all ages, and the basis of the historical manifestation, was appropriately labeled *honmon* (Chin. *pen-men*). Each of these sections was based upon a key chapter believed to express its essence. In the case of the *shakumon* section, the second chapter in which the historical Buddha reveals his numerous methods (*upāya*) of teaching and leading sentient beings to Enlightenment was considered to be the essence. The Tendai sect came to place their emphasis upon this chapter and section of the sutra since it dealt with the means of attaining Enlightenment.

In contrast, the essence of the second half of the sutra was believed to be expressed by the sixteenth chapter wherein an Eternal Śākyamuni reveals his existence from the beginning of time with the historical Buddha being one of his numerous manifestations. This Eternal Śākyamuni represents the idealization of the Buddhist Dharma itself or Absolute Truth and with his focus upon the 'Absolute,' Nichiren considered this section of the sutra most significant.

Analyzing the title of the sutra in conjunction with the critical *honjaku* divisions, Chih-I made the following analogy:

The Lotus
    1. For the sake of the fruit there is the flower
    2. Open the flower and reveal the fruit
    3. The flower drops and the fruit is established
A. *The first half of the sutra (shakumon)*
    1) For the sake of the true there is the provisional
    2) Open the provisional and reveal the true
    3) Abandon the provisional and establish the true
B. *The second half of the sutra (honmon)*
    1) From the origin the manifestation is dropped
    2) Open the manifestation and reveal the origin
    3) Abandon the manifestation and establish the origin[24]

In keeping with this analogy and the philosophy of 'Original Enlightenment,' Nichiren discarded the manifestation in the form of the historical Buddha and all other teachings, and placed his entire faith in the 'Absolute' or Eternal Śākyamuni. In later years the dispute over 'emphasis upon the Origin section' (*honshō shakuretsu*) versus treating both sections of the sutra equally (*honjaku itchi*) was to divide Nichiren's followers.

3.   Nichiren's Five-Fold Interpretation of the *Lotus*

While in exile on Izu Peninsula, Nichiren set forth his own analysis of the *Lotus Sutra* that actually defined what he considered to be his mission in life based upon his religious realization. Later this became a support for his sect. In Nichiren's view, proper application of the *Lotus Sutra* consisted of five related aspects:[25]

1. *Teaching (kyō)*
The doctrine of the sutra itself.

2. *Object (ki) of Teaching*
Since any true teaching must be directed towards an object, Nichiren was convinced that the particular object of the *Lotus Sutra* must be those who damage or destroy the Dharma (heretics). These were the individuals to whom the teachings of the sutra must be administered.

3. *Time (ji)*
Even if the true teaching and its object be established, unless the time is right for reception, it cannot be set forth successfully. Nichiren believed that the historical Śākyamuni preached the *Lotus* at the exact appropriate moment in time and that the legendary eight years it took to preach the sutra could actually be identified with the present moment of the *mappō* era. Thus in contrast to the Pure Land feeling of despair during the age of *mappō*, Nichiren took joy in the realization that this was the crucial moment for salvation.

4. *Master (shi)*
The subjective realization that the present moment was the chosen time to preach the *Lotus Sutra*, as well as an awareness of the existence of the teaching and its object, led Nichiren to the natural conclusion that he was the master who had the responsibility to preach to the heretics. He considered this belief confirmed by the persecutions he experienced, which he interpreted as fulfilling the prophecies of the sutra.

5. *Country (kuni)*
Japan was the one nation in the world where all the foregoing components were present. It was a nation filled with heresy during the age of *mappō*, possessing the *Lotus Sutra* and being the ground upon which Nichiren achieved his subjective realization of his mission as master; therefore, it represented the chosen land for his ministry.

In this application we can observe the basis of Nichiren's sense of destiny as well as the nature of his nationalism. Japan was viewed as the sacred soil for his activities, yet if the nation chose to ignore his warnings, he was capable of turning away from it and leading his band of followers into an isolated retreat. Although he was born in an area steeped in the tradition of the Sun Goddess, he was not concerned with championing the cause of the Emperor against the usurping Kamakura government. In fact, he was perfectly capable of even admonishing the Sun Goddess herself if he found her remiss in her obligation to protect the followers of the *Lotus*. Thus Nichiren's nationalism was confined to the dream of establishing a Buddhist state, or as he expressed it himself on a grander scale, of making Japan the nucleus of a world community of *Lotus* followers, just as India (Jambudvīpa) had once been regarded as the centre of the world.

4. *Ichinen Sanzen* and the Three Secret Dharma

Closely related to Nichiren's five-fold application of the *Lotus Sutra*, was the Tendai concept of *ichinen sanzen* (one thought equals three thousand worlds). For he believed that his personal awareness that the *Lotus* was to be propagated at the present time was in fact the subjective awareness of the Eternal Śākyamuni of the Origin section of the sutra. In other words, Nichiren conceived that the entire universe of the Eternal Śākyamuni (Absolute Truth) was revealed within his individual awareness.

In Nichiren's teachings, *ichinen sanzen* became the metaphysical doctrine that was tangibly expressed in the religious practice of chanting the five characters forming *Myōhōrengekyō*. In effect, those sacred five letters contained the three thousand worlds symbolizing the 'Absolute,' and as a method of practice, this fact was revealed in the Three Secret Dharma:[26]

1. *Honmon Honzon (Principal Image of the Origin Section)*
The Eternal Śākyamuni or 'Absolute' as revealed in the 'Duration of the life of the Tathāgata' chapter of the *Lotus Sutra*. As in the case of other Buddhist sects, this image is to be found within the subjective individual mind through self-reflection—or the stripping

away of the layers of ignorance to reveal the 'Original Enlightenment' within.

2. *Honmon Daimoku (Sacred Title of the Origin Section)*
The chanting of the sacred name of the *Lotus Sutra*, which effectively acts as the medium between ignorant man and the object of his veneration, or the 'Absolute' dwelling within him.

3. *Honmon Kaidan (Ordination Platform of the Origin Section)*
The true value of an ordination platform, whereupon one is granted the *śīla*, depends upon the quality of that *śīla* itself. Nichiren believed that all the good deeds of myriads of Buddhas and bodhisattvas were condensed within the title of the *Lotus Sutra*, hence wherever one chants that title becomes the *śīla* platform.

In later years these three Dharma were given added interpretations by Nichiren followers until eventually twelve theories evolved. These can be summarized as follows:[27]

1. One of the most popular intepretations considers the three Dharma representative of the traditional Three Buddhist learnings:

> *Honzon*....*samādhi* (meditation)
> *Daimoku*....*prajñā* (wisdom)
> *Kaidan*....*śīla* (discipline)

This view is partially derived from Nichiren's writings.

2. Indirectly implied in Nichiren's works is the possibility of equating the Three Dharma with the Three Treasures and extending the equation in the following manner:

> *Honzon*....Buddha....Śākyamuni
> *Daimoku*....Dharma....*Lotus Sutra*
> *Kaidan*....Sangha....Nichiren

3. Another view utilizes the Three Treasures also but in this instance, the Sangha is interpreted as the 'subjective individual' or devotee rather than Nichiren.

4. Utilizing three qualities of the Tendai interpretation of '*Myō*,' the first character in the title of the *Lotus Sutra*:

> *Honzon*....Original cause (*honin*)
> *Daimoku*....Original effect (*honga*)
> *Kaidan*....Original Land (*honkokudo*)

5. Another popular interpretation makes the *Trikāya* the basis of the Three Dharma:

    Honzon....*Dharma-kāya*
    Daimoku....*Saṃbhogha-kāya*
    Kaidan....*Nirmāṇa-kāya*

6. In analyzing the nature of various sutras, Chih-I and other Tendai scholars established five criteria:

    a) Interpretation of title
    b) Clarification of the fundamental spirit of the sutra
    c) Essential points forming the basic framework of the sutra
    d) Soteriological efficacy of the sutra
    e) Criticism of the sutra's doctrine

Among these the following were equated with the Three Dharma:

    Honzon....Clarification of the spirit of the sutra
    Daimoku....Essential points of the sutra
    Kaidan....Soteriological efficacy

This interpretation was probably derived from Nichiren's frequently expressed view that within the very title of the *Lotus Sutra* all of these points could be found.

7. Body, wisdom and manifestation

    Honzon....Body
    Daimoku....Wisdom of the Original Buddha
    Kaidan....Manifestation

8. Original Buddha, Dharma and Residence

    Honzon....Original Buddha
    Daimoku....Dharma
    Kaidan....Residence of Buddha and Dharma

9. Essence, Manifestation and Practice

    Honzon....Essence (*tai*)
    Kaidan....Manifestation (*sō*)
    Daimoku....Practice (*gyō*)

This theory was devised by Nikkan (1665–1726)

10. Practice, Subject and Object

    Daimoku....Practice
    Honzon....Subject
    Kaidan....Object

attributed to Nikki (1800–59)

11. Man, Dharma and Location (as objective principles)
     Honzon....Subjective man who reaches attainment
     Daimoku....Dharma, the object of attainment
     Kaidan....Place where man and Dharma exist
     attributed to Nichirin (1793–1823)

12. Realm, Wisdom and Unification (Subjective interpretation)
     Honzon....Realm or object of perception
     Daimoku....Wisdom (man's subjectivity)
     Kaidan....Unification of object and subjectivity

Nichiren avoided limiting the Three Secret Dharma with a single precise but confining definition, thus his followers were able to offer systematic interpretations within the Buddhist tradition. Each of these twelve interpretations present basic philosophies expressing the essence of Buddhism.

3. *Shōdai jōbutsu* (Chanting the *Daimoku* and Becoming a Buddha)

In keeping with his view of *ichinen sanzen*, Nichiren saw the fate of the individual inseparably linked to the destiny of society. Thus his effort to realize an ideal world, as expressed in the *Risshō Ankokuron* was based upon the notion that the evil and sufferings of the society could be reduced to the evil and sufferings of the individual and vice versa. If individuals could be saved, the inevitable result would be a perfect harmonious society, or to express this in a formula:

> *Eternal Enlightenment (Absolute Truth)*
> $\downarrow \quad \uparrow$
> *Manifests* as the five character *Daimoku*
> *Myō-hō-ren-ge-kyō*
> $\downarrow \quad \uparrow$
> In *actual practice* adds the further two Chinese characters *Na-mu* (I take homage) symbolizing the subjective individual.

Thus the 'Absolute' assumes reality or is realized within the individual and man can be said to become part of the Enlightenment of the Original Buddha, who has existed from eternal aeons in the past. And on a wider scale, as each individual becomes Enlightened, the society itself assumes the entirety of the body of the Original Buddha. In this respect, Nichiren's philosophy bore certain similarities to the Tendai influenced Yūzū Nembutsu and Ji movements, both of which emphasized the interreaction between individual religious practice and society, in definite contrast to the subjective and highly introspective emphasis of Jōdo Shinshū.

Through his belief in attaining Buddhahood with this body (*sokushin jōbutsu*), Nichiren envisioned making this world the ideal Buddhaland. With such a distinct emphasis on this world and the acceptance of present reality, he encouraged the performance of rituals for worldly benefits. In effect, these served as a form of *upāya* (although that term is presently avoided) to attract and confirm frail individuals in their faith, as well as to improve society in general. And like all other sects of Kamakura Buddhism, Nichiren extended hope of salvation to those who were outside the domain of the established church. We can particularly note the role of women in his movement, for of the one hundred sixty-two historically identifiable direct followers of Nichiren, forty-seven were women. Nichiren even offered the hope of salvation to those professionally engaged in the taking of life, such as fishermen, all that was necessary was faith in the *Lotus*.

C.   Nichiren's Attitude Towards the Native Gods and Other Beliefs

By the resolute practice of denouncing other sects of Buddhism through *shakubuku*, Nichiren exhibited his complete unwillingness to tolerate any form of truth other than his own. Repeatedly in his writings he states that Dengyō Daishi (Saichō) and he alone are the only two followers of the *Lotus* in Japan,[28] and in his later works he tends to minimize the role of Saichō. As Nichiren refused to grant other forms of Buddhism even a right to exist, we are forced to consider his movement 'exclusive' as well as 'purist.'

The major thrust of Nichiren's theological writings tend to be his denunciation of other sects, in particular the Pure Land and the followers of Hōnen. It would be interesting to count the vast number of times the name of Hōnen is condemned. In the *Risshō Ankokuron*, he begins by recounting the burning of the woodblock plates of Hōnen's *Senjakushū* and the exile of his disciples,[29] and in the *Senjishō*, written on Mt. Minobu, Nichiren concludes by stating that after his death in order to revenge his exile, Hōnen became an evil spirit and entered the bodies of the leaders who had charged him with sedition as well as various temple priests, and created revolt.[30] Nichiren did not seem to waste much energy condemning other Japanese Pure Land followers by name with the exception of Genshin,[31] whom he specifically charges on several occasions. But Nichiren did focus an attack against Tendai esoterism claiming that just as the founders of Shingon, Zen and Jōdo were 'three worms' (*sanchū*), so in Tendai the 'three worms found in the lion body of Dengyō Daishi Lotus belief were: Jikaku (Ennin), Annen and Eshin (Genshin).'[32] Elsewhere he includes Chishō (Enchin) and the abbot Jien in his condemnation.[33]

Nichiren's attacks against the Zen sect were aimed primarily at the controversial Dainichibō Nōnin and his disciple Butchibō.[34] It is obvious that Nichiren closely observed the growth of Zen in Kamakura and the arrival of Rankei Dōryū in 1246, as well as the invitation to Enni Bennen in 1257 to correct the Zen discipline at the Jufukuji. After this period his attacks against Zen intensified, for he interpreted the popularity of Zen as being detrimental to the Tendai sect and a factor contributing to the decline of *Lotus* teachings. Thus he even risked the hostility of the Hōjō Regents by attacking their faith. In particular, Nichiren criticized Zen for their belief in 'transmission outside the scriptures' and doctrine of 'no-words (*furyū-monji*), which he pointed out was after all expressed in words.[35]

Some historians question why Nichiren failed to specifically mention the name of Shinran, who was known to have been active in the Kantō area, or Dōgen, whom legend asserts he met.[36] They theorize that perhaps Nichiren deliberately ignored Dōgen's following because he considered it too intellectual for the masses, and perhaps believed that Shinran's affirmation of the present life bore similarities to his own views, in contrast to Hōnen's 'other-worldliness,' a product of late Heian thought.[37] This is an interesting point, however, historically neither

Shinran nor Dōgen enjoyed the prominence during their lifetimes that they received during later generations, and most likely Nichiren did not consider them of consequence. The specific targets of Nichiren's attacks were the priests who enjoyed the most popularity, and Hōnen by far led the list, albeit posthumously. In fact, Nichiren's preoccupation with Hōnen was so great and knowledge of the *Senjakushū* so thorough, that some modern critics consider this to have exerted a tremendous influence upon his thought.[38] Most likely Nichiren included all of Hōnen's followers in his criticism of their master. A similar situation existed in the case of Dainichibō Nōnin, a controversial Zen exponent, although Nichiren's charges against Nōnin constitute merely a small fraction of those levelled against Hōnen. The only actual contemporary that Nichiren spent efforts to discredit was the Ritsu priest Ryōkan (also known as Ninshō) of the Gokurakuji, who had the somewhat questionable reputation of being an ambitious miracle-worker.

Other Buddhas and the Native Kami

In the year 1271, when the priest Gyōbin officially charged Nichiren with sacrilegious actions against Amida and Kannon, Nichiren denied the accusations. Although he did not personally believe in the efficacy of Amida and Kannon, there is no indication that he displayed disrespect toward them. But this did become a problem among his followers and the intensive practice of *shakubuku* tended to be accompanied by often times violent behaviour against other Buddhas as well as the Shintō gods.

Nichiren was confronted with the same problem all Kamakura leaders faced in respect to the role of the native gods. Like the founders of other movements, he instinctively identified the *kami* with the land of Japan itself and was keenly aware of the importance of the gods and folk beliefs to the masses, whom he sought to influence. In order to explain the role of the gods within his teachings, Nichiren used the *honji-suijaku* (true-nature-manifestation) theory. He considered every Shintō god commencing with the Sun Goddess to be a *suijaku* (manifestation) of the Eternal Śākyamuni of the *Lotus Sutra* and he also believed that the gods had an obligation to protect the followers of the *Lotus*, as well as to punish their enemies. Faced with what he considered to be so many heresies dominating the land, Nichiren could merely conclude that the gods had abandoned the nation and returned to their heavenly abodes.

On the fourteenth day of the eleventh month (1281), shortly after the news of the failure of the second Mongol invasion reached Kamakura, the shrine of Hachiman at Tsurugaoka caught fire and burned to the ground. As Hachiman was regarded as the god of war, the event was considered portentous. The following month Nichiren wrote a petition to Hachiman (*Kangyō Hachimanshō*), in which he claimed that Hachiman had agreed to protect the followers of the *Lotus Sutra* but failed to punish those who had persecuted Nichiren and his adherents, thus the destruction of his shrine was Hachiman's punishment for derilection of duty.[39] When efforts were made to rebuild the shrine, Nichiren objected, claiming that Hachiman had abandoned Japan and returned to heaven, therefore why should the government waste efforts to rebuild a hollow and empty shrine?

The fourth month of 1281 when some of Nichiren's followers were called upon to assist in the reconstruction project, they asked his approval and he allowed their participation. But when wind blew down the first frame, Nichiren interpreted the event as the will of Śākyamuni, demonstrating that Hachiman had indeed abandoned the land.

Nichiren's attitude toward the native gods tended to be quite ambivalent. On Sado Island, observers who watched him cry out on a mountain top to the sun and moon, believed he had gone mad, but this was Nichiren's method of communing with the gods, imploring them to fulfill their obligation, and strike down the enemies of the *Lotus* and end the heresies prevailing throughout the land. He also scolded them for neglect of their duties. Thus he wavered between hostility when he considered them derelict, to the certain belief that they hovered above him and protected him against evil.

Upon Nichiren's death, his followers had increasing difficulty in maintaining cordial relations with the Shintō shrines. Many claimed that the gods had abandoned Japan therefore, there was no point in honouring empty shrines, while others contended the gods had returned to protect *Lotus* followers and this dispute created a serious division. Another complication was the single-practice of the *Lotus*, that naturally led to a certain exclusiveness. Just as in the case of Jōdo Shinshū, later zealots confused purity of practice with intolerance and deliberately sought to obliterate all veneration of the Shintō gods. Such views as the foregoing, combined with *shakubuku* practice and the later doctrine of *fuju-fuse* (no giving, no receiving) made intolerance a characteristic of many of the Nichiren schools.

D. Development of the Nichiren Order

During Nichiren's lifetime he attracted individuals from all walks of life despite the handicaps of two painful exiles and his last years of isolated retreat on Mt. Minobu. The majority of his direct disciples had been drawn from the clergy of the established churches, primarily Tendai, but from the start he also received the children of his faithful lay followers.

The major financial support for Nichiren's movement came from the local warlords or the stewards (*jitō*) of the Kamakura and later Muromachi governments. As a result of such patronage, Nichiren temples gradually assumed the form of *ujidera* (clan temples). A warlord patron would establish a temple in his domain and through his family connections and alliances, assist in propagating the sect to new areas. Also the sons of these patrons frequently became priests and would officiate at the local clan temples, such a method of propagation created firm established roots. But the development of the Nichiren sect became exceedingly complex due to doctrinal disputes.

The Six Direct Disciples

At the time of Nichiren's death, six direct disciples besides the six he had appointed as custodians of his tomb, decided to take turns in handling the affairs of his mausoleum on Mt. Minobu. Since many had active congregations in distant provinces, this plan soon became unworkable and Nikkō 日興 (1245–1332), whose activities centred in the area took charge with his followers. He was joined by Nichiren's other chosen disciple Nikkō 日向 (1253–1314), who came from Kazusa province to become Master of Theology on the mountain in charge of training disciples. But this arrangement came to an abrupt end in the twelfth month of 1288, when the senior Nikkō departed from Mt. Minobu and created the first division in the Nichiren order.

Departure of Nikkō 日興 (1245–1332) from Mt. Minobu

The relationship between the two Nikkō's had not been smooth from the start. The manager of the mausoleum was a strict dogmatic purist, who considered the Master of Theology to be far too worldly. Furthermore, the latter had managed to ingratiate himself with Mt. Minobu's patron, the stewart Hakiri Sanenaga, and the dispute that divided the order centred around what the senior Nikkō considered to be Sanenaga's sacrileges.

It seems that Sanenaga paid a visit to the Mishima Myōjin shrine and also made a donation of horses and lumber to a Shintō shrine on Mt. Fuji. Such actions stirred up the old issue of whether it was proper to worship the Shintō gods and if not, the propriety of a Nichiren follower making offerings to those considered to damage the Dharma (heretics). Sanenaga contended that his donation to the local shrine had actually been a social gift to a friend without religious implications. And he won the support of Nikkō, the Master of Theology, in relation to his visit to the Mishima shrine, since that Nikkō maintained the gods would come on behalf of a *Lotus* follower.

The senior Nikkō refused to accept such arguments and insisted that not venerating the Shintō gods was based upon Nichiren's theory in the *Risshō Ankokuron* that the good gods had abandoned the land and returned to heaven, thus it was improper to worship an empty shrine. He also pointed out that Nichiren had banned all forms of offerings to those considered to damage the Dharma, and interpreted shrine offerings as destructive to the purity of *Lotus* faith.

Sanenaga, who took pride in the fact that he had been a direct lay follower of Nichiren was not about to accept a rebuke for his actions, particularly since he had the support of Nikkō, the Master of Theology. As a result he decided to install that Nikkō as permanent caretaker of Mt. Minobu and the Kuonji temple. Since the issues of the status of Shintō gods and offerings to heretics were to be a constant theme in later Nichiren internecine quarrels, it was prophetic that they created the first division in the order.

The senior Nikkō left Mt. Minobu to found the Daisekiji and Omosu Honmonji on the foothills of Mt. Fuji, his movement became known as the Fujimonryū or Nikkōmonryū. His activities often created confrontations with the other direct disciples of Nichiren such as Nisshō and Nichirō; furthermore, he never forgot his disagreement with Mt. Minobu. His group however, met with great success and during the latter part of Nikkō's life, spread from the northern area of Tōhoku down to the southern island of Shikoku. In 1332 he entrusted the Omosu Honmonji, where he later died, to his disciple Nichidai[40] and the Daisekiji to Nichimoku (1260–1333), but it was not long after his death that his disciples divided into further schools.

Initially Nikkō's group had adopted the theological view of *honshō shakuretsu* (Origin superior, Manifestation inferior) in contrast to those who maintained both sections of the *Lotus Sutra* were equal, but this disagreement was carried even further by his disciples. By the Muromachi period the Fujimonryū had divided into five independent temple groups in the Mt. Fuji area:

1) Honmonji of Omosu
2) Seizan Honmonji
3) Daisekiji of Mt. Fuji
4) Myōrenji of Shimojō
5) Kuonji at Koizumi

The main body of this movement developed into the modern Honmonshū.

Nikkō 日向 (1253-1314) *of Mt. Minobu*

The other Nikkō remained in charge of Mt. Minobu until his later years when he entrusted it to his disciple Nisshin (1259-1334), and returned to the Myōkōji of Kazusa province. His following became known as the Mobaramonryū (location of the Myōkōji) or alternately the Nikkōmonryū or Minobumonryū. The site of the present day complex on Mt. Minobu was built by Nitchō (1422-1500), the eleventh successor of Nichiren, who was considered the second coming of the founder and vastly developed the site of the mausoleum. The Minobumonryū developed into the modern Nichirenshū school.

Nisshō (1236-1323)

The Tendai monk who became Nichiren's first disciple, Nisshō made the Hokkedō temple in Kamakura, later known as the Hokkeji, the centre of his activities. His group became the Nisshōmonryū or Hamamonryū, and among the various Nichiren schools was the closest to the Tendai sect. In fact during the Muromachi period, the Nichiren monk Nisshin (1407-88) even charged this group as being an offspring of Tendai, for the monks were in the habit of studying on Mt. Hiei as well as receiving ordination upon the Tendai *kaidan*. In this respect Nisshō's following represented Nichiren's early ideal of reforming Tendai.

Nichirō (1242-1320)

During Nichiren's lifetime, Nichirō was active along with Nisshō in the Kamakura area and made the Myōhonji the centre of his activities. But after Nichiren's death, with the help of lay followers, he also established the Hondoji in Hiraga and Honmonji in Ikegami and alternated his work between the three temples.

Nichirō had nine brilliant disciples among whom was Nichizō (1269-1342), the first to bring the *Lotus* teachings to the capital of Kyoto in 1294. Nichizō laboured there for twenty-eight years being banished three times, but finally in 1321 was successful in building the Myōkenji temple and three years later when that temple was granted the Imperial title of *Chokuganji* (Temple of Imperial Vow) won official recognition for the Nichiren sect, since acceptance in the capital still determined the legitimacy of a Buddhist sect. The modern Honmon Hokkeshū traces its tradition to Nichizō's line.

In Kamakura, Nichirō was succeeded by Nichirin, who established residence at the Myōhonji and Honmonji and played and important social role during this period.

Nichirō's followers were initially known as the Nichirōmonryū or Hikigayatsumonryū (site of the Myōhonji). The debate over the superiority of the Origin section of the *Lotus Sutra* versus the equality of the two also broke out among Nichirō's followers and created further divisions. Nichi-in (1264–1328) and his disciple Nichijō (1228–1369), were among the most ardent supporters of *Honshō shakuretsu* (Origin superior, Manifestation inferior) and gathered a large following.

Nichiji (1250–1295)

At the time of Nichiren's death, Nichiji had established the Eishōji in the province of Suruga and was active in that area. Although he was one of the six chosen disciples of Nichiren, his direct master had been the Nikkō who left Mt. Minobu and founded the Daisekiji. Gradually relations with this master became strained, and in 1294 Nichiji entrusted his affairs to his disciple Nikkyō, and in 1295 left to propagate the teachings abroad. He is known to have proceeded north through the Tōhoku area to Hokkaidō and into northern China and Manchuria where his fate is unknown.

Nitchō (1252–1317)

At the time of Nichiren's death, the centre of activities of this disciple was the Guhōji temple in Shimofusa province. However, he was later pressured out of this area by Nichijō, the former samurai warrior Toki Jōnin, and retired to Suruga province. As a result, the activities in Shimofusa fell under the control of Nichijō and his follower Nikkō, who had also been a late direct disciple of Nichiren. Nikkō was place in charge of the Hokkeji temple in Wakamiya and he also converted his own birthplace into the Honmyōji (later known as the Nakayama Hokekyōji). This movement eventually became the Nakayama Hokekyōjimonryū.

Besides these six chosen disciples of Nichiren, there were a number of others who established their own congregations and temples. One of the major problems in the order was the fact that Nichiren's early successors merely imitated his dogmatic theological expression without comprehending the depths of his spiritual realization,[41] thus the dogmatic quality was present without the religious experience. It took nearly two centuries before serious commentaries began to appear upon Nichiren's theology, by then numerous schisms had already occurred in the order, in many cases representing a superficial understanding of Nichiren's views or scholarly quibbles. Although to outsiders the Hokkeshū or Nichirenshū appeared to be a vast unified sect, internally it continued to divide and faced continual doctrinal confrontations. As a result, during the medieval period the Nichirenshū was never successful in uniting into any single powerful congregation comparable to the Jōdo Shinshū Honganji.

Veneration of the Thirty Protector Gods

The debate over whether or not to show veneration to the indigenous Shintō gods raged through the sect and caused numerous divisions between those who maintained the purist attitude that the sole practice of the *Daimoku* was sufficient, versus those who wished to compromise and cited Nichiren's own familiarity with the gods and belief that they protected followers of the *Lotus* as a precedent. There was also considerable pressure from the lay followers, who felt a certain loyalty to local shrines as well as community suasion to participate in shrine festivities.

A form of compromise that developed after Nichiren's death was the cult of thirty protector Shintō gods, who were believed to take daily turns in protecting the Dharma. The devotion had existed in the Sanmon Tendai sect and by the late Kamakura period, the Nakayamamonryū and Nichizōmonryū are believed to have been the first to accept it. Gradually other schools also joined and halls were built at Nichiren temples in honour of the Thirty gods (Sanjūbanjindō). The devotion was never accepted by some of the purists and the listing of the gods did not become uniform.

1. Honshō shakuretsu (Origin Superior, Manifestation Inferior)

This was one of the most crucial theological issues to divide the entire sect and by the late Kamakura period those who advocated the superiority of the Origin section of the Lotus Sutra had formed three major groups:

1. Myōmanji-ha
founded by Nichijū (1314-92), a successor in the line of Nichiren's direct disciple Nichijō. In 1383 Nichijū built the Myōmanji in Kyoto. This group in modern times has become the Kempon Hokkeshū.

2. Happon-ha
founded by Nichiryū (1385-1464), a disciple in the tradition of Nichirō. Nichiryū built the Honnōji in Kyoto and Honkōji in Amagasaki. The group was called the school of 'eight chapters' (Happon-ha) since they considered the essence of the Lotus Sutra to consist of chapters fifteen to twenty-two. In modern times this school has become the Honmon Hokkeshū.

3. Honjōji-ha
established by Nichijin (1339-1419), a disciple of Nichijō in the tradition of Nichirō. In 1406 Nichijin founded the Honzenji in Kyoto. In modern times this school became the Hokkeshū.

Besides theological differences over the interpretation of the Lotus Sutra, divisions also occurred over the method of teaching and relations with other Buddhist sects.

2. Fuju-Fuse and Shakubuku

Generally there were two major trends in regard to relations with other sects and teaching methods. Those who considered both sections of the Lotus Sutra equal (honjaku itchi) were inclined to be moderate in their dealings with other Buddhist sects and avoided the violent shakubuku method of propagation. As examples of such a conciliatory attitude, the Myōhonji of Kamakura and Hongakuji of Kyoto both made peace with government authorities by performing rituals for the benefit of the nation, while Nisshō's tradition became completely absorbed in the study of Tendai theology.

But the purists, exemplified by priests such as Nichijū (1314–92) of the Myōmanji, Nisshin (1407–88) of the Honpōji and Nichijin (1339–1419) of the Honjōji, rigidly adhered to the single practice of the daimoku and the use of shakubuku against all who differed with their views. They also adopted the principle of fuju-fuse (no giving, no receiving) toward those who did not believe in the Lotus.

Fuju-fuse first appears in a written document of the Myōkakuji-monryū school in Kyoto in the year 1413, in which articles were formulated disallowing any veneration of Shintō shrines, offerings or receiving items. The complete refusal to contribute in any form or receive anything from those considered heretics came to be the characteristic of the purists who espoused this doctrine.

One attitude important in the propagation of Nichiren teachings shared among the purists was the belief that the entire family of a Nichiren follower should convert to the faith. For example, the Myōkakuji and Honnōji demanded the conversion of a wife within three years after her husband had entered the sect. Strong pressure was even placed upon servants and retainers to join to the extent of making membership a condition of employment. This attitude led to a rapid spread of the teachings among all the members of a family, extending to entire clans and finally even to whole villages and communities. For example, all the inhabitants of Tanegashima and three adjoining islands became members of the Nichiryūmonryū and Nisshin is popularly attributed with the conversion of the entire Hizen province in Kyūshū.

Along with such mass conversions by means of the often violent shakubuku, the principle of fuju-fuse spread causing a distinct threat to the established churches. After 1469, the Sanmon monks of Mt. Hiei began consistent onslaughts against Lotus followers, publicly charging that their exclusive organizations in the provinces were constantly engaged in sacrilegious acts against the gods and Buddhas to the extent that they ultimately threatened to destroy the established church, thus those who practiced *shakubuku* became objects of assault. During the late sixteenth century, the *fuju-fuse* spirit gradually developed into a movement. This was partially due to the fact that after Oda Nobunaga's destruction of Mt. Hiei in 1571, many of the Tendai monks joined Nichiren schools and their presence led to a renewed study of Tendai theology. To counteract what the purists considered to be a degeneration of the Nichiren spirit, strict reformers led by Nichiō (1565–1630), a monk of the Myōkakuji in Kyoto, initiated a *fuju-fuse* school.[42] During the ninth month of 1593, Nichiō was invited by Toyotomi Hideyoshi to the dedication of a great Buddha hall at the Myōhōin. The plan included one hundred monks from each of the ten recognized sects of Buddhism. But Nichiō refused to participate and as a result was ostrasized by fellow Nichiren monks who did attend, forcing him to leave the Myōkakuji. After temporarily becoming a recluse, Nichiō was ordered by Tokugawa Ieyasu in 1599 to debate his views at the Osaka castle. But even this Nichiō considered contrary to the principle of *fuju-fuse* and he refused, resulting in his exile in 1600 to Tsushima island. Twelve years later he was pardoned and returned to the capital, managing to attract many followers to his cause. Another example was Nichiju (d. 1631) of the Honmonji in Kantō, who in 1626 refused a funeral donation for the shōgun Tokugawa Hidetada's wife. He further charged the monks of Mt. Minobu of betraying the founder's spirit by accepting such a donation. At that time Nissen (1586–1648), abbot of Mt. Minobu, brought charges to the *bakufu* government against the *fuju-fuse* advocates. Ultimately they were exiled and Nichiō, who supported Nichiju, was again sent to Tsushima island but died on the way.

As a result of this agitation and the refusal of *fuju-fuse* followers to obey the government's orders, the movement was officially banned, but it still continued to surface and finally in 1876 was officially permitted to become the Fuju-fuse-ha. A second group founded by Nikkō (1628–98) was allowed to take the name of Fuju-fuse Kōmon-ha in 1882.

3. *Hokke Ikki* and Nichiren Activities in Kyoto

As the popularity of the Nichiren sect grew in the capital, the hostility of the monks of Mt. Hiei heightened until in 1387 the Myōkenji temple was destroyed by the *sōhei* (priest-soldiers). Persistent attacks continued, but the popularity of the *Lotus* sect was not diminished. Primarily the followers of Nichiren lived in the southern part of the capital, the residence of merchants, artisans and commoners, in contrast to the northern section which housed the aristocrats. At the time of the Ōnin war (1467–77) and subsequent Bummei wars, the aristocratic northern part of the city was destroyed and the southern merchant residents became fearful of the possibility of further attacks. They were particularly concerned with the neighboring peasant revolts and apprehensive that they might encroach upon the rich storehouses of the city, thus the merchants decided to form a self-defense militia to protect themselves; gradually these forces developed into armies.

After the Ōnin war the spread of Nichiren teachings in the capital was phenomenal and the movement coincided with the organization of the merchant protection groups. The Nichiren banner soon began to serve as a rallying points and the period of 1532–36 is known as the era of *Hokke ikki* (*Lotus* rebellions).

As the Nichiren sect prospered in the city it attracted aristocratic support and soon the headquarters of twenty-one different schools were established, each with massive landholdings. Many of these temples literally became armed fortresses during wartime that served as headquarters for local Daimyō. The temples also, justified by Nichiren's own precedent, created standing armies incorporating the merchant militia groups. Occasionally these armies clashed with each other to solve theological debates, for the advocates of *shakubuku* maintained that the most perfect way to accomplish their aims was by force of arms.

The first significant *Hokke ikki* occurred in 1532 when Nichiren followers in Kyoto, disturbed by neighboring peasant *Ikkō ikki* armed themselves. Then during the sixth month, a popular Nichiren samurai was killed in an *Ikkō ikki* revolt in nearby Sakai. Rumours spread throughout Kyoto that the Honganji abbot Shōnyo, who had just completed a skirmish at the Kōfukuji in Nara, was about to assault the city. In fear of such an attack, Nichiren followers of the various temples joined with the local Daimyō Hosokawa Harumoto and struck a first blow against the *Ikkō ikki* followers in Sakai, and then destroyed the old site of the original Higashiyama Honganji in Kyoto. The initial encounters led to Nichiren success and a force of 30–40,000 troops was gathered for a precipitate strike against the Yamashina Honganji. That resplendent headquarters was totally destroyed but the Honganji abbot Shōnyo fled to the powerful Honganji base in Osaka, and the destruction of the Yamashina Honganji proved of little strategic importance against the *Ikkō ikki*, although it was a powerful victory for Nichiren morale. Finally in the sixth month of 1533 the Daimyō Hosokawa Harumoto and Honganji abbot Shōnyo signed a peace agreement and the *Hokke ikki* died down, however, the Nichiren still faced the enmity of the monks of Mt. Hiei.

As Nichiren followers began to dominate the capital of Kyoto, the Sanmon monks of Mt. Hiei and other established churches as well as local warlords began to feel a distinct threat. Although the Mt. Hiei *sōhei* had participated in the Yamashina Honganji attack as allies of the Nichiren, after a peace accord was signed, they began to fear possible physical attack from the armed Nichiren congregations. Legal action had already been taken to prevent the Nichiren congregations from using the title of Hokkeshū, which the Tendai monks claimed properly belonged to their sect. Tensions increased up until the year 1536, when according to tradition, the heckling of a Nichiren follower embarrassed a Tendai priest and a confrontation occurred. Whether this was the real reason or merely an excuse to attack the Nichiren headquarters is questionable. The Mt. Hiei *sōhei* were joined by the Daimyō Rokkaku Sadayori, another erstwhile Nichiren ally who had begun to resent *Lotus* power.

During the spring an embargo was placed on the city and by summer a massive army from Mt. Hiei attacked the twenty-one Nichiren headquarters temples, during what is commonly known as the Tenmon persecution. The southern half of Kyoto was burnt to ashes, and even the northern section suffered widespread damage. The majority of Nichiren followers escaped to the outskirts and neighboring cities but the Sanmon *sōhei* relentlessly hunted them down.

After the devastation, the Nichiren temples gradually sought to return to the city but met with government objections until finally in 1542 the Court approved. By 1545 fifteen headquarters had been restored but the full number never returned. Mt. Hiei appealed to the Muromachi government to force the Nichiren temples into becoming Sanmon branches, but after 1547 their activities against Nichiren ceased.

If we examine the major characteristics of the *Hokke ikki* between 1532–36, we can note that the revolts generally resulted as a concerted effort of Nichiren followers and merchant self-protection forces. These were frequently joined by mercenaries and unengaged samurai (*rōnin*). The initial attacks were always in alliance with powerful Daimyō requesting assistance such as Hosokawa, Rokkaku and Kizawa clans, who took advantage of the urban dwellers fear of massive peasant uprisings. Unlike the *Ikkō ikki* peasant rebellions that were spreading throughout the provinces, the *Hokke ikki* were confined to the area of the capital Kyoto, and their purpose was to protect the Nichiren faith as well as the property of the city. But the Tenmon persecution was a blow from which the Kyoto Nichiren temples never fully recovered.

4. Schools of Nichiren Followers

After the long years of doctrinal and institutional division, the Nichiren sect was officially established into the following major schools during the Meiji era:

> 1874—Nichirenshū (former Minobumonryū) advocating the equal treatment (*honjaku itchi*) of both sections of the *Lotus Sutra* with headquarters at the Kuonji—
> plus five schools maintaining *honshō shakuretsu:* (Myōmanji, Happon, Honjōji, Honryūji and Fuji-ha)

> 1876—The Fuju-fuse-ha was restored and became independent, along with the Fuju-Fuse Kōmon-ha in 1882.

1891—The five advocates of *honshō shakuretsu* officially changed their titles:

Myōmanji-ha....Kempon Hokkeshū (Myōmanji, Kyoto)
Happon-ha....Honmon Hokkeshū (Honnōji, Kyoto)
Honjōji-ha....Hokkeshū (Honjōji, Niigata)
Honryūji-ha....Honmyō Hokkeshū (Honryūji, Kyoto)
Fuji-ha....Honmonshū (Honmonji, Shizuoka)

1900—The Daisekiji of Shizuoka split from the Honmonshū and took the name of Nichirenshū Fuji-ha. In 1913 this was renamed the Nichiren Shōshū, the school popularly associated with the lay organization known as the Sōka Gakkai (Value Creation Society). Most Nichiren geneologies conspicuously omit this new school from Nichiren tradition,[43] although it has a sizeable following and plays an important role among the so-called 'New Religions' of Japan.

CHAPTER IV

ZEN, THE WAY OF MEDITATION

Chronologically, Zen cannot be considered the last of the new Kamakura Buddhist movements, but it stands in time as a bridge to the new-Confucian social philosophy of the sequestered Tokugawa government. And it was under the sponsorship of Zen learning that Neo-Confucianism first gained *entrée* to Japan, ultimately to become the guiding principle of the merging new feudalistic society, whilst Buddhism entered into more than a century and a half of inanimate political suspension—taking the opportunity to establish its roots. The arrival of Zen in Japan also generated a new cultural surge from China after so many centuries of neglect, conveying in its wake a renewed interest for everything Chinese, and a delayed appreciation for the magnificence of the Sung dynasty.

Of the various types of Zen imported to Japan, two major traditions became dominant: Rinzai (Lin-chi) and Sōtō (Ts'ao-tung).

A. Rinzai Zen

1. Eisai, the First Transmitter

Eisai was born the twentieth day of the fourth month in 1146 into the Kaya family of Jōmawari in Bitchū (modern Okayama) province. It is popularly believed that his father was affiliated with the Kibitsu Shintō shrine and had once studied at the Tendai Miidera (Onjōji). At the age of eleven, Eisai entered the nearby Annyōji temple and studied under the priest Jōshin (d. 1157), who belonged to the Mikkyō tradition of the Miidera and reportedly had been a classmate of Eisai's father. Two years later Eisai entered Mt. Hiei and was ordained in 1154.

When Jōshin of the Annyōji died, in accordance with his master's last request, in 1158 Eisai went to study Taimitsu under Senmyō in Bitchū province and the following year received the Tantric Kokūzō Gumonjihō. It is possible that he commuted to Mt. Hiei during this period and in 1159 he permanently returned to the mountain to study Tendai under Yūben, and practice *shikan* (Tendai meditation).

In 1162 when an epidemic broke out in his native province, Eisai returned and at that time studied Taimitsu under Shūzembō Kikō of Taisenji, who belonged to the Taimitsu Anōryū. Finally, Eisai returned to Mt. Hiei and received the Tendai *kanjō* (*abhiṣeka*) ordination from the master Keni. Thus we can note that the major portion of Eisai's education was devoted to Tantric Taimitsu. He has been credited with founding the Yōjōryū (later known also as the Kenninjiryū), an offspring of the Taimitsu Anōryū on Mt. Hiei, and Tantrism was ultimately the platform upon which he attempted to introduce Zen to Japan.

Eisai's first knowledge of Zen resulted from a fortuitous meeting with the Chinese interpreter Li Te-chao (Jap. Ri Tokushō), while he was waiting in Hakata in 1167, the year prior to his first journey to China, and at that time he first learned of the popularity of Zen in China. Eisai was unfamiliar with the Chinese situation as over a hundred years had passed since a significant Japanese monk had visited China and the *Kentōshi* (Embassy to China) system had been abandoned for more than two hundred-fifty years. The Japanese attitude was simply that China no longer had anything of consequence to offer, and Eisai's dream of visiting China was often met with derision. But Eisai was convinced that during the age of *mappō*, the true Dharma could be rediscovered in China and thus it would be possible to correct the serious abuses and corruption of Japanese Buddhism.

As the age of twenty-eight, Eisai sailed to China and spent less than six months during his first visit, leaving Hakata during the fourth month and returning the ninth. But while in China he happened to meet the Japanese monk Shunjōbō Chōgen (1121-1206), who had arrived the previous year and together they visited the Wan-nien-szu on Mt. T'ien T'ai and other sacred sites. Although this meeting was to prove providential for Eisai's future in Japan, Eisai did not transmit Zen on his first voyage. In the fall when he returned to Japan he brought some sixty volumes of T'ien T'ai scriptures that he presented to the abbot Myōun of the Enryakuji. And since Eisai had observed the popularity of Zen at the Hung-hui-szu temple in China, he decided to study the Tendai tradition of Zen on Mt. Hiei, which had been transmitted by Saichō, Enchin and Annen. For the next twenty years he continued this study in accompaniment with further esoteric teachings.

Evidently Eisai decided shortly after his return to Japan that he would again visit China, in fact he even hoped for a trip to India to bring back the true Dharma, but he was destined for a long wait. During this time he taught in the area of his home province and neighboring Bizen, then spent the last ten years or so in Kyūshū. The reasons for his presence there are uncertain, but the period coincided with the defeat of the Taira family in the Gempei war and rise of Minamoto Yoritomo to power. At that time Eisai's home province was a battleground, and it is also conjectured that his patron was Taira Yorimori, whose domain was located in Kyūshū.[1]

During the Kyūshū period, Eisai did considerable writing although he indicated that he had difficulty in gaining access to the *Tripiṭaka*, which in those days could only be found at large temples in the big cities, where travel was difficult during the time of civil war. The last period of waiting was spent at the Seiganji at Imazu in Chikuzen province, where he read the works of the Chinese pilgrims such as Hsüan-tsang in preparation for his anticipated trip to India. Finally on the nineteenth day of the fourth month in 1187, he sailed from Hakata, but when he arrived in China and requested passage to India was refused by the Chinese court. Thus he sailed along the coast and once again went to T'ien T'ai, where at the Wan-nien-szu he studied Lin-chi (Jap. Rinzai) Zen of the Huang-lung school under Huai-ch'ang, who shared an interest in esoteric Buddhism. From this master Eisai received the Bodhisattva *śīla*[2] and proceeded to study *vinaya*. Eisai had officially received the Bodhisattva *śīla* at the age of fourteen on Mt. Hiei, but at that time the *vinaya* rules and regulations had little significance for they were no longer respected by the monks. In China, Eisai came to realize the importance of observing the precepts, which served as a foundation stone in the life of the Zen monk. When he later returned to Japan, Eisai set a pattern of strict *vinaya* observance, and his precedent in conjunction with the transmission of Zen *vinaya*, led to the restoration of Japanese monasticism during the thirteenth century.[3]

Following his Chinese master Huai-ch'ang, Eisai went north to the Ching-te-szu on Mt. T'ien-t'ung, another centre of Zen. There finally in 1193 he received the *inka* (seal of approval), permitting him formally to teach Zen. As a result of this transmission, Eisai later was to claim to be the sixtieth successor in the tradition commencing with the Seven Buddhas of the past.

While in China, Eisai spent considerable time working to restore temples on Mt. T'ien T'ai and Mt. T'ien-T'ung. It is not clear how he raised the money for these projects, but most likely he personally donated funds, and when he returned to Japan he sent lumber and other materials. This assistance along with Eisai's personal character, won him considerable Zen respect in China and resulted in growing interest among the Chinese monks to visit Japan.

Finally in 1191, after four years in China, Eisai returned to Japan and built the Hōonji temple in Chikuzen province, reportedly the first Zen temple in Japan. The choice of location within the domain of Taira Yorimori beside the Kashii Shrine, to which Eisai had sent a *bodhi* tree while in China, strengthens the hypothesis that Yorimori was Eisai's patron. For the next three years Eisai laboured to propagate Zen at this temple, teaching the first Zen *śīla* and founding other temples in the area.

Eisai's most famous accomplishment was the introduction of tea to Japan. It is not certain whether he brought seeds of the plant on his first or second visit to China, but they were first planted in northern Kyūshū. In 1211 he wrote a two volume work entitled the *Kissa Yōjōki* (Drinking Tea for Health), in which he stressed the stimulative qualities of the drink for keeping a monk physically and mentally awake to practice meditation as well as its beneficial nature, presenting an esoteric interpretation of the human organs.

But even while in Kyūshū, Eisai's activities came to the attention of Mt. Hiei, since he aroused the jealousy of Rōben of Chikuzen province and a complaint was lodged at court to prohibit his activities in conjunction with the teachings of another Zen master, Dainichibō Nōnin.

Contemporary Zen Movements

Eisai was not the first Japanese monk to renew interest in Zen during the Kamakura period. Shortly after his first visit to China, Kaku-A (1143–?), a Tendai priest of Mt. Hiei heard of the popularity of Zen from a Chinese merchant, and in 1171 went to China to study under Hui-yüan of the Ling-yin-szu temple. In 1175 he received the *inka* from his master and returned to Japan, he is generally believed to be the first to receive proper Zen transmission. But Kaku-A was not able to stir up interest in Zen in Japan. Supposedly he was invited to Court by Emperor Takakura, who inquired into the essence of Zen, and Kaku-A's sole response was to play a single note upon his flute. The Emperor and his attendants were annoyed rather than Enlightened.

While Eisai was in China, Dainichibō Nōnin was propagating Zen at the Sambōji of Settsu province and called his movement the Darumashū, after Bodhidharma, the same name that Eisai subsequently used for his new teachings. Since Nōnin's background was unknown and he could prove no orthodox transmission, he immediately came under attack by the established churches. To defend himself and establish his orthodoxy, he sent two of his disciples to China in 1189 to study under the respected Lin-chi master Te-kuang of the Ta-hui school with a letter explaining his own religious state of mind, and managed to receive an *inka* by correspondence. With this confidence he increased his dissemination of Zen and promptly was reproved by Mt. Hiei. In this instance their concern was not wholly unjustified, Nōnin's true spiritual master and qualifications were unknown, and further he failed to emphasize any form of *śīla*, which was a common fault of the Japanese Zen masters who had not been to China; their Zen tended to be a superficial imitation of *zazen* (meditation) lacking the essential strict discipline. When the Darumashū was prohibited by the Court as being 'incomprehensible' and circulating nonsense, Eisai was called to the capital in 1195 by Imperial order to face a formal inquiry. At that time he attempted to persuade the monks of Mt. Hiei by pointing out that Saichō had established Zen within the Tendai tradition and if they denounced it, they were in fact rejecting the teachings of their own founder. He further began the *Shukke Taikō* (Essentials for Monks), which outlined *vinaya* rules for monastic clothing, ritual and lifestyle, this was completed in 1200. The *Genkō Shakusho* even records a debate he had at this time with Nōnin.

The summons to Court in 1195 represented a turning point in Eisai's life during which he strengthened his determination to propagate the new sect, but it was obvious he could not begin in Kyoto. The Tendai attack represented the normal reaction of an established institution to change. They sensed the challenge of the new single-practice orientation within Eisai's thought, and his argument that Saichō had introduced Zen was not acceptable, since Saichō had only viewed it in the tradition of *Enmitsuzenkai* (Tendai, esoteric, Zen meditation and *vinaya*), not as an isolated practice. There was no clear way for Eisai to meet the criticisms of Mt. Hiei, and he was aware that a formal confrontation would be suicidal. Thus rather than irritate the Tendai and Nara sects by his proximity, he decided to return to Kyūshū and there under the sponsorship of Minamoto Yoritomo built the Shōfukuji temple.

Eisai also began his principal work, the *Kōzen Gokokuron* (Treatise on the Propagation of Zen for the Protection of the Nation). In the introduction he cited the four major points of criticism made by Mt. Hiei against his movement: 1) that Zen clung to Emptiness—or that its followers believed they were Enlightened without study, 2) Zen was not the Dharma of *mappō*, 3) Zen was unnecessary for Japan, and finally, 4) that Eisai lacked the qualifications, ability and proper social position to propagate Zen. These charges Eisai easily refuted, although the last must have been most painful, and undoubtedly influenced his later belief that respect for the Dharma was inseparably related to respect for the monk disseminating it. Apparently Eisai submitted his treatise to the

Court, where he had some sympathizers, and then went to Kamakura in 1199.

Some biographers theorize that Eisai's journey to Kamakura was a result of losing his patron, the Regent Kujō Kanezane in Kyoto, who fell from power in 1196,[4] and had proven to be a firm supporter of Eisai, just as he had been Hōnen's staunchest patron. The year Eisai chose to go to Kamakura also coincided with Minamoto Yoriie's brief succession to his father Yoritomo, and this had led other biographers to hypothesize that Yoriie, who hated the *nembutsu* black robes, might have requested Eisai to perform an esoteric ritual.[5] Eisai's name first appears in Kamakura in relation to a Fudō Myō-ō rite held the twenty-sixth day of the ninth month.

Somehow during that period of intense political intrigue, Eisai managed to gain the respect of both Yoriie and the conspiring Hōjō family. In the year 1200 Eisai was chosen to conduct the first memorial service for Minamoto Yoritomo and the same year his widow, Hōjō Masako, made a vow to build the Jufukuji temple and place Eisai in charge. Early records indicate that this temple initially engaged in performing esoteric rituals, although later it became one of the five great Zen temples of Kamakura. It would appear that Eisai was careful to recognize the interests of his benefactors and did not try to force Zen upon an audience that was unready for it. But in 1202, Eisai finally did receive the opportunity officially to introduce Zen to Kyoto, when the Shōgun Minamoto Yoriie granted him the land to found the Kenninji temple. Under Court order, the new temple was obliged to teach Shingon esoterism and Tendai *shikan* (meditation) as well as Zen, and establish special halls for these practices. Furthermore, it was made a *betsuin* (branch temple) of Mt. Hiei, thus Eisai was forced to introduce Zen in the *Enmitsuzenkai* tradition rather than the pure single-practice he had studied in China.

The building of the Kenninji ran into problems from the start, as Minamoto Yoriie was replaced as Shōgun by his brother, Sanetomo, the year of its construction. Fortunately for Eisai, the new Shogun as well as his mother Masako, supported the project, but the Court and people of Kyoto were not so quick to accept him. Thus any unusual phenomenon occuring within the city was attributed to Eisai's strange new religion. As late as 1205 he was blamed for wind damage, allegedly due to the fact that his followers wore robes of an alien land. According to legend, he replied to such charges that he was not a wind god and thus incapable of creating a wind storm, but if the people actually believed he was responsible, then they should have respect for his powers. Allegedly this argument even impressed the Emperor.

Tōdaiji Restoration Project

Eisai apparently commuted those days the difficult distance between Kyoto and Kamakura and worked at both the Kenninji and Jufukuji, establishing at the same time, relations with the aristocracy at court and samurai *de facto* government. Then finally in 1206, his talents were publicly recognized when he was selected to complete the restoration of the Tōdaiji temple.

The history of this project dated back to 1180, when Taira Kiyomori attacked the Tōdaiji, Kōfukuji and other powerful temples in Nara in retaliation for their participation in the anti-Heike revolt of Minamoto Yorimasa. The Kōfukuji, clan temple of the Fujiwara family, was privately restored at their expense but the restoration of the Tōdaiji became a great national project headed by Chōgen, the Japanese monk Eisai had befriended during his first visit to China. Eisai apparently kept close watch on the project, for in 1195, the year he founded the Shōfukuji in Kyūshū, he sent a *bodhi* tree to the Tōdaiji that he had brought from Mt. T'ien T'ai in China.

Since the Nara temples, and in particular the Tōdaiji, still represented the centre of national faith, the restoration project received support from throughout the nation and assumed tremendous social significance. Minamoto Yoritomo took political advantage of it by personally attending the eye-opening ceremony for the Great Buddha after it was recast, indirectly calling attention to the fact that his former enemies had been responsible for the devastation. The restoration project was nearly complete after twenty-five years of endeavour when Chōgen died in 1206, at the age of eighty-six, and that fall Eisai was appointed to succeed him. The reasons for his selection are uncertain, but his friendship with Chōgen must have been a factor, as well as the prestige of his study in China and the patronage of the Shōgun and Hōjō family in building the Jufukuji and Kenninji temples.

Before Eisai could complete the Tōdaiji project, lightning struck the nine-storied pagoda of the Hosshōji destroying it, and Eisai was given the additional task of restoring the pagoda. Reportedly when the Emperor came to attend the dedication ceremony of the Hosshōji pagoda in 1213, Eisai requested the title of *Daishi* (Great Master) as a reward for executing the two projects. Since this honour in the past had always been bestowed posthumously to the greatest Buddhist leaders, Eisai's request caused enormous criticism and was immediately opposed by the Tendai abbot Jien and others. Even Emperor Go-Toba allegedly regretted his patronage of Eisai in view of such an outrageous request. But Eisai was granted the priestly rank of *Gonsōjō* by the Emperor as well as honorary purple robes.

It is unclear why Eisai made such an unusual demand, but it can be imagined that he believed this was the way to overcome the lack of social recognition that had earlier proven to be a handicap in propagating Zen, feeling that his own honour would in turn result in respect for his teachings. There are no indications that Eisai ever sought wealth or power for personal enjoyment, but merely to promote the Dharma. He counseled his followers that one should never delight in receiving public donations but consider them as offerings to the Three Treasures rather than to oneself.[6] And he wrote that monks should set forth a good and dignified appearance, for failure to do so would lead to rejection of their teachings and insult to the Dharma.[7] The purity and simplicity of Eisai's lifestyle at the Kenninji was frequently eulogized by Dōgen, who became a disciple shortly before Eisai's death, and in the *Shōbōgenzō Zuimonki*, Dōgen relates how Eisai even gave the nimbus of a Yakushi Buddha to a needy layman as well as an offering for the monks dinner at a time when they were forced to go hungry.[8] On the other hand, Eisai was careful to drive an impressive new carriage whenever he went to Court to be certain that he created a proper image as a representative of the Dharma, at the same time maintaining the life of simplest poverty at his temple.

Eisai died the fifth day of the seventh month in 1215 at the Kenninji in Kyoto at the age of seventy-five.[9] He later received the posthumous title of Senkō Kokushi (Master of a Thousand Lights), allegedly for the miraculous lights that had once issued forth from his body as he had performed an esoteric rain ritual in China.

Although Eisai is considered to be the founder of Japanese Zen and legitimate transmitter of the Rinzai school, his teachings are generally regarded as impure Zen due to his own esoteric interest as well as the necessity during his age of presenting Zen in the *Enmitsuzenkai* tradition of Mt. Hiei.[10] Eisai planted the seed and it was nurtured by the monks who came from China stimulated by Eisai's reputation there, and finally developed by later disciples at a time when Japan was psychologically ready to accept it into pure Zen, in keeping with the single-practice orientation of the Kamakura period.

2. Historical Background and Transmission

To attempt to view the development of Zen historically is a near hopeless task, for in the Buddhist tradition Zen followers tend to deny the validity of chronological history, but more than any other sect they treat historical facts with a certain vengeance. Just as tantric initiates must have amused themselves with the layman's shock over their deliberately distorted language, so the earthy Zen masters undoubtedly derived pleasure from projecting their thoughts and ideas onto semi-mythical founders such as Bodhidharma and Hui-neng in the form of pungent anecdotes. Although Zen is not an esoteric form of Buddhism, it does share certain common features with tantrism in the method of transmitting its teachings—both emphasize that all forms of Enlightenment are identical to the original Enlightenment of Śākyamuni, and Zen figuratively describes the transmission from master to disciple as merely water transferred from one container to another. To argue the historicity of Zen patriarchs is to miss the point of Zen, or for that matter of Buddhism. However, we can be fairly certain that all the Chinese patriarchs commencing with Bodhidharma were historical personages, although very different individuals from how they are depicted in modern Zen. In some respect the scholarly problem of Zen transmission and the determination of historical facts in the lives of the Zen patriarchs can be compared to the endless controversies over 'forged' versus 'authentic' sutras. If we consider historical chronology, we must dismiss all Mahāyāna sutras as 'forged', since they purport to have been preached by the historical Buddha. Similarly, even the so-called 'Original' Pāli scriptures can be considered largely as forgeries, insofar, as the monks inserted their own views and teachings of their schools in pretense of being actual preachings of the Buddha. Later scholars in collecting the scriptures, were to declare those to be forgeries that contradicted the spirit of Buddhism, failed to concur with established views, or lacked sufficent historical tradition to gain acceptance. Comparable to the problem of the sutras, the writings attributed to Bodhidharma, Hui-neng and other Zen patriarchs proliferated in later generations. The validity of such works cannot properly be judged by the determination of authorship, for these patriarchs have lost their historical nature and become semi-mythical beings; their sayings and works can only be assessed by whether or not they match the accepted spirit of Bodhidharma and Hui-neng and possess soteriological value.

The Rise of Zen

The origins of Zen (Skt. *Dhyāna* or meditation) date back to the long Indian tradition of Yoga, which subsequently became a basic practice of Early Buddhism. The belief that self-control and meditation lead to the peace of Enlightenment can be found in the *Sutta-nipāta*, one of the oldest Buddhist texts. Abhidharma scholars classifed meditation into a complex arrangement of four *dhyāna* and eight *samādhi*, a system that philosophically is quite divergent from modern Zen.[11] This tradition arrived early in China with the translator An Shih-kao, who came to Lo-yang during the mid-second century and proceeded to translate a number of sutras on meditation. The Chinese immediately found Indian meditation similar to Taoist practices and in particular were drawn to the ascetic hermit life it offered as an escape from worldliness and the unbending Confucian social system. A second attraction was the belief that Indian meditation led to the acquisition of supernatural powers, known as *iddhi* in Early Buddhism, granting the ability to perform miracles.

During the fourth century under the influence of Tao-an (314–85), the early Hīnayāna meditation sutras translated by An Shih-kao were linked with the Mahāyāna philosophy of the *Prajñāparamitā*, and the groundwork was laid for a more advanced study of Abhidharma and Prajñā literature, and the arrival of Kumārajīva (350–413), the famous Mahāyāna translator, whose disciples such as Seng-chao (384–414) and Tao-sheng (ca. 360–434) were to elevate Chinese meditation to lofty heights. Another important contemporary was Buddhabhadra (359–429), who translated and practiced a mixture of Hīnayāna and Mahāyāna meditation.

Basically five varieties of Indian meditation were brought to China consisting of:

1) Breath control as a means of concentration.
2) Visualization of impurities, such as the decomposition of a corpse.
3) Visualization of compassion, extended towards all beings.
4) Visualization of the functioning of the law of cause and effect.
5) *Nembutsu* (Chin. *nien-fo*) visualization, utilizing Amida's image and chanting the *nembutsu* to attain purity of mind.

Bodhidharma

The so-called founder of Chinese Zen (Ch'an) is Bodhidharma, who arrived in China during the first half of the sixth century and whose life has been so legendized that certain modern critics even question his existence. But this seems to be a form of scholarly myopia, as there is adequate source material to verify an historical existence, although not as the person he appears to be in later legends.[12] The question is, how did this shadowy figure come to be regarded as symbolizing the essence of Zen?

Bodhidharma's role in Chinese Zen grew in retrospect as the new Zen movement began to assume a distinct shape and became aware of its differences from other forms of meditation, in particular T'ien T'ai, but this did not occur until the late sixth and seventh centuries. Neither Bodhidharma, his successor Hui-ku'o (484–590 or 487–595), nor the third patriarch Seng-ts'an (d. 606) can, except from hindsight, be credited with actually founding a sect. What they evidently did initiate was a slightly different system of meditation that under the fourth patriarch Tao-hsin (580–651), and his successor Hung-jen (601–74), developed into a monastic social institution. Tao-hsin was the first to establish a form of community life and meditation halls, in effect the basic structure of modern Zen. This was further developed by Hung-jen, the fifth patriarch, and it was at this time that the newly rising sect began to contrast its differences with T'ien T'ai, the school that had dominated the Sui period and now gradually was commencing to decline.

T'ien T'ai meditation had been formulated by Chih-I (538–97) in his *Chih-kuan* into a monumental system based upon the Buddhist concept of Emptiness (*Śūnyatā*). This type of meditation was so dominant that efforts were later made to make Chih-I indebted to the Zen tradition by claiming his master, Hui-szu, a disciple of Bodhidharma. Such a contrived effort might have been useful in granting Zen a seeming upperhand in their rivalry with T'ien T'ai, but it was obvious that Zen meditation and T'ien T'ai were quite different, and this is the discovery that was made by Tao-hsin and Hung-jen when they had the opportunity to study the *Chih-kuan* and *Hsüan-i* written by Chih-I. The meditation he devised was divided into four major categories:[13]

Basic types
1. Perpetual Sitting
2. Perpetual practice (walking and venerating a Buddha image)

Secondary Alternates
3. Half-walking, half-sitting
4. Non-walking, non-sitting

These appealed to different spiritual levels and successfully managed to unite the practice of meditation with the normal activites of daily life. The two basic types he outlined ultimately developed into two distinct trends of meditation in China: the first, (perpetual sitting) became the form of meditation propagated by Zen, and the second (perpetual practice), by the Pure Land movement. Yet theologically we cannot state that Zen meditation is an evolution of Tendai *Chih-kuan*, although it did prove to be a considerable stimulus in Zen development.

When Tao-hsin and Hung-jen became fully apprised of the similarities and differences between their form of meditation and T'ien T'ai *Chih-kuan*, they sought to gain the edge of superiority over T'ien T'ai by antedating the origins of their own order. Thus we find the first instance when Bodhidharma was elevated to the role of symbolic founder of the movement that began to assume tangible form more than a century after his death. But this initial Zen order, despite its burgeoning size of over five-hundred followers, still lacked a philosophical basis adequate to satisfy the intellectuals of the great centres of Chang-an and Lo-yang; this was finally accomplished when Zen meditation was linked to the metaphysics of Hua-yen, the *Awakening of Faith*, and *Laṅkāvatāra Sūtra*.

Tao-hsin was the first to incorporate the concept of 'Original Enlightenment' from the *Awakening of Faith* into his meditation sessions and moved visibly away from earlier meditation sutras to the concept of the 'Fundamental Mind.' This trend was carried on under Hung-jen and finally made a characteristic of Northern Zen by his disciple Shen-hsiu (d. 706).

Divisions Within the Sect

The first significant schism in the Chinese Zen community was the movement founded by Fa-yung (594–657), a disciple of the fourth patriarch Tao-hsin. Prior to studying Buddhism, Fa-yung had been a Confucian scholar and after he completed his instructions, retired to Mt. Niu-t'ou, where he founded the Yu-hsi temple. His teaching had the reputation of being so universal that it reached even the beasts and animals, becoming known after its place of location as Niu-t'ou (Jap. Gozu) Zen. The succession extended to six patriarchs, the last being

Hui-chung (683–769), and by the Sung dynasty began to decline.

Northern and Southern Traditions

The fifth patriarch Hung-jen had a number of capable disciples among whom, two were responsible for the future course of Zen and had claims to the title of sixth patriarch; Shen-hsiu (d. 706) and Hui-neng (638–713).

Shen-hsiu was a distinguished scholar, allegedly exceedingly tall, who had studied the classics during his youth. He was first ordained in 625 at the T'ien-kung-szu temple in Lo-yang but it was not until he reached the age of fifty that he met Hung-jen and became his disciple, spending six years of trying study. After his master's death, Shen-hsiu became affiliated with the Yü-chüan-szu in Ching province. Upon the request of Empress Wu, he preached in the palace and subsequently received the Tu-men temple. He died at the T'ien-kung-szu in Lo-yang at an age of over one hundred years. He was later granted the posthumous title of Ta-t'ung Ch'an-shi, which is often believed to be the first such award in China.

Shen-shiu's school developed into what is known as Northern Zen in contrast to the Southern movement attributed to Hui-neng, although it is extremely doubtful whether the two leaders actually entertained the differences of opinion ascribed to them by their followers. The Northern school, following the concept of 'Original Enlightenment' of the *Awakening of Faith*, advocated liberation from discriminative thought. This view in the capital of Chang-an quickly came under the influence of the popular Hua-yen metaphysics and a highly sophisticated philosophy developed. After Shen-hsiu's death it was carried on by his disciples P'u-chi (651–739) and I-fu (658–736), both of whom enjoyed tremendous influence among the aristocracy. But upon their deaths, a lack of creative leadership commenced a decline of this form of Zen, hastened by the invasion of Southern Zen under the command of Shen-hui (668–760), a disciple of Hui-neng.

Not many historical facts are known regarding Hui-neng, who is considered next to Bodhidharma, as the second founder of Zen. From available sources he would appear to be the exact opposite of Shen-hsiu—a short, unattractive, illiterate countryside priest. But it is very likely that even this description was devised by later followers in order to make Hui-neng appear to be an earthy individual in contrast to the suavity and polish of Shen-hsiu. It is not even possible to ascertain what Hui-neng's philosophy was, although fragments appear in the *Platform Sutra*, which is believed to have been composed after Hui-neng's death by his disciple Fa-hai recording his master's sayings—or possibly by Shen-hui's followers in their effort to discredit Shen-hsiu's Northern school. It is in this work that the famous legend appears describing how Hui-neng, in place of Shen-hsiu, legitimately received the transmission to become sixth patriarch. Although we cannot accept the veracity of this so-called transmission, the verses allegedly composed by Shen-hsiu and Hui-neng do reveal the philosophical differences between the two schools.

According to the legend, the fifth patriarch Hung-jen promised to pass his transmission on to the disciple who could best compose a verse expressing the essence of how to attain Enlightenment. Shen-hsiu secretly submitted the following verse by inscribing it upon the monastery wall late one night:

> The body is the *bodhi* tree,
> and the mind a clear mirror standing;
> polish it constantly, and
> allow no mote of dust to collect.

Hui-neng, who allegedly was a humble rice thresher at the time unable to read or write, heard of the verse and asked a monk to read it to him. He then composed his own reply and found someone to write it on the wall:

> *Bodhi* (Enlightenment) is not a tree,
> nor does the mirror stand.
> Since originally there was no thing,
> whereupon can the dust cling?

The legend relates that the fifth patriarch secretly called Hui-neng to his chambers and granted him the robe of transmission, at the same time sending him forth from the monastery to avoid the jealousy of the other monks.

The philosophies expressed within these two verses illuminate the major differences between Northern and Southern Zen. Shen-hsiu and his Northern followers considered the mind to be 'Originally Enlightened' and that the path to salvation lie in the internal reflection upon purity and pollution, sweeping the imperfections away like dusting a mirror, and allowing the true nature of 'Original Enlightenment' to awaken. Popularly this method is known as 'Gradual Enlightenment,' since it encompasses two actions: first, wiping away false discriminative thought, and secondly, the awakening of 'Original Enlightenment.' Hui-neng's disciple, Shen-hui and his Southern group strongly criticized this view, arguing that the mind is not a static entity and cannot reside at any given point, hence it is futile to attempt to reflect upon the mind with the mind; furthermore, such a self-conscious effort inevitably involves false dualism. Shen-hui advocated direct penetration of the 'Originally Enlightened' mind, without any preliminary attempt at self-reflection, consequently his method is known as 'Sudden Enlightenment.' Shen-hui maintained his views to be totally derived from his master Hui-neng, although this is impossible to substantiate.

Modern scholars no longer believe that Shen-hui's Southern Zen was an actual confrontation with Shen-hsiu's Northern school since both groups ultimately used meditation as the means of attaining Enlightenment. Instead, they believe that Shen-hui's Southern followers were actually striving to clarify and perfect the Hua-yen philosophy that the Northern School had absorbed.[14] Also, Shen-hui was ambitious to prove the orthodoxy of his own form of Zen by establishing Hui-neng as the proper sixth patriarch in place of Shen-hsiu, and this is perhaps what he is best known for, although his success was largely due to the lack of capable disciples in the Northern school.

Shen-hui's group, which became the Ho-che sect, eventually reverted into another form of northern Zen in contrast to the followers of Hui-neng, who remained in the south and under Tao-I, better known as

Nan-yo Huai-jang (677–744) and his disciple Ma-tsu (707–86), became the genuine heirs of Hui-neng.

The philosophy of Shen-hui's Ho-che school reached the heights of metaphysical perfection, incorporating Hua-yen thought and the Mahā-yāna sutras into what had formerly been a simple system of meditation under Bodhidharma, but unfortunately, the philosophy became divorced from daily life and actual practice, hence it declined. Tsung-mi (780–841), who also happened to be the fifth patriarch of the Hua-yen school, was the last significant proponent of this school. The refinement of his philosophy is apparent in his analogy of the *maṇi* gem, wherein he criticizes the original Northern Zen of Shen-hsiu, the flourishing Southern tradition of Ma-tsu and finally the Niu-t'ou school of Fa-yung. The following briefly summarizes his arguments:

The *maṇi* (Buddhist symbol of Ultimate Reality) is a perfect transparent gem possessing an infinite potentiality to reflect every existing colour and hue. Among the various shades it reflects is a solid black, and although the gem itself completely differs from this blackness, a foolish man would be unwilling to believe that the stone was transparent since his senses would reveal merely blackness. Such manifestations of the *maṇi* can be approached from three different viewpoints:

Shen-hsiu's Northern Zen	1)	Finally accepting the fact that the black stone is actually a *maṇi* gem, the foolish man still believes that the gem must be encased within the blackness, and hence attempts to polish it in order to discover its inherent *maṇi* quality. (caught in the discrimination between ultimate and relative)
Ma-tsu's Southern Zen	2)	Another individual, unable to perceive the transparent gem manifesting blackness, would instead accept whatever the present shade be as its essence. Hence even if it were to turn to blue or white, he would continue to regard the colour as the essence of the stone. Such a person would also mistake other gems of these colours for *maṇi* gems, and if he ever

happened to find a true transparent *maṇi* gem, would
fail to recognize it.

(caught in the phenomenal world)

Fa-yung's   3)   Lastly, a third person would consider the spontaneous
Niu-t'ou   colours the gem manifests, and arrive at the conclu-
School   sion that both the gem and its colours are empty
                  and dismiss them, terming the essence of the gem
                  void.

(caught in affirming the existence of Emptiness)

Tsung-mi interpreted this analogy explaining that the Northern Zen of
Shen-hsiu sought to eliminate ignorance (blackness) to attain Enlightenment, while in contrast Ma-tsu's followers considered ignorance equivalent to Enlightenment, or the function identical with the essence.
Finally, by ignoring colour and the gem itself, Fa-yung's followers
reverted into utter nihilism. The ideal approach, which Tsung-mi considered to be the belief of Shen-hui, the founder of his school, was to
regard the essence (体) of the gem as embracing its function (用). The
perfection of the gem lies in its quality to reflect every colour, hence
Original Knowledge (Ultimate Reality) makes no differentiations and
perfectly reflects every existent. The proper way should be to quietly
observe the no-thingness (Jap. *Mu*) of the essential quality manifesting
itself.

The sophistication of this argument is apparent and in typical sectarian
style it manages to simplify the views of its opponents, but the question
arises whether this method is effective soteriologically and accomplishes
anything more than providing a sense of intellectual superiority? This
was the pitfall for the Ho-che school, and it came to an end under
Tsung-mi, hastened undoubtedly by the revolt of An Lu-shan that led
to the decline of its aristocratic patrons. But the metaphysics of this school
were quitely absorbed into Southern Zen, although not becoming a
dominant feature.

In contrast to the philosophical approach of Hui-neng's followers
who went north, Ma-tsu and his disciples introduced a radically new
earthy flavour that was to become the hallmark of modern Zen. Origi-

nating in the fertile agricultural province of Hung-hou, this form of of Zen ultimately spread throughout China, just as the masses began to assert themselves with the slow disintegration of the mighty T'ang empire. The mystical hermits were replaced by realistic Zen masters who spoke in common place terms dealing with tangible topics, and who were more than apt to box the ears of an obtuse disciple. They sought to capture the essence of Zen in ordinary living, and as a result elevated the master Hui-neng to become the symbol of the earthy illiterate, capable of perceiving a truth far more profound than intellectuals might ever capture in their wildest fantasies. This new form of Zen introduced a tremendous affirmation of life that was to prove exceedingly attractive to both the Chinese and Japanese. To a certain degree it did set forth the view Tsung-mi criticized,—that all the functions of the human mind were manifestations of the Buddha nature. This attention to daily reality with its ensuing rejection of formalistic practices reached an apex under Lin-chi I-hsüan (d. 867), who sought the essence of Zen within the humblest of human actions, affirming the raw activities of man as representing the spontaneous workings of the Buddha nature. The normal state of mind became the way to attain Enlightenment and daily activities such as eating, drinking, sleeping and defecating were suddenly elevated as equivalent to meditation.

Such a realistic approach met with severe criticism not merely from Tsung-mi, but also from the Neo-Confucian scholar Chu-hsi (1130–1200). Both argued that the functioning of blind human nature could scarcely be considered divine. Certainly there was a dangerous potentiality in this new Zen orientation that could easily degenerate into sheer hedonism, as demonstrated by the critic's argument that if the function of the hand could be regarded as expressing the Buddha nature, then if that hand elected to raise a sword and commit murder, such an action must also be regarded as a function of the Buddha-nature. But such moral laxness was obviously not what Ma-tsu and Lin-chi had in mind. They first demanded the practice of harsh discipline before they sanctioned the effort to transcend all efforts—thus, this philosophy closely resembles the 'Other Power' concept of spontaneous action developed in the Pure

Land schools.[15] Lin-chi's admonitions such as 'destroy the Buddha' or that 'those who practice the Six *Pāramitā* will fall into hell' were not intended for spiritual novices, but rather for the monks who had already mastered the techniques and were on the verge of slipping into complacency or religious pride. The Zen approach is perhaps more abrupt and brutal than the Pure Land, but ultimately accomplishes the same goal—the affirmation of human life and the practical application of religion to daily experience.

The Five Houses of Zen

Among the many worthy disciples of Hui-neng such as Ch'ing-yuan Hsing-szu (d. 740), Nan-yo Huai-jang (677–744), Shen-hui (670–762), Hui-chung (d. 775) and Fa-hai, only two lines of transmission survived: that of Nan-yo Huai-jan with his illustrious disciple Ma-tsu, and the line of Ching-yuan Hsing-szu. The so-called Five Houses of Chinese Zen all belong to these two traditions and developed in the following manner:

1) *Wei wang (Jap. Igyō) School*
Ma-tsu's disciple Po-chang Huai-hai (720–814) laid down the precepts for Zen monasticism and his tradition later divided into two schools: the Wei-wang and Lin-chi. The first to emerge was the Wei-wang founded by Ling-yu (771–853) in 806 and subsequently developed by Hui-chi (814–90). The sect survived some one hundred-fifty years before it gradually declined and merged with the Lin-chi school.

2) *Yün-men (Unmon) School*
Founded by Yün-men Wen-yen (d. 949), who resided on Mt. Yun-men and began to form a sect around 930, assimilating the thought of his two masters Tao-tsung and I-ts'un (822–908). During the Sung dynasty this sect equalled the Lin-chi in prosperity, but by the Yüan had completely disappeared.

3) *Ts'ao-tung (Sōtō) School*
Traces its transmission from Ch'ing-yuan Hsing-szu, the disciple of Hui-neng to the fifth generation Liang-chiai (807–69), who resided on Mt. Tung-shan. The name of the school was derived from combining

the first characters of the name of Hui-neng's residence (Ts'ao-chi) with Mt. Tung-shan. This school became one of the two major currents of Chinese Zen.

4) *Fa-yen (Hōgen) School*
Prospered during the late T'ang under the leadership of Wen-i (885–958), who belonged to Ch'ing-yuan Hsing-szu's tradition of Southern Zen. The school briefly prospered for one hundred years but by mid-Sung had disappeared.

5) *Lin-chi (Rinzai) School*
The second major trend of Chinese Zen that followed the tradition of Nan-yo Huai-jang. This school was founded by Lin-chi I-hsüan. During the Sung dynasty under disciples of the seventh patriarch T'zu-ming (986–1040), it subdivided into two branches:

   a. *Huang-lung (Ōryū) School*
   Founded by Hui-nan (1002–69), who resided on Mt. Huang-lung. The school survived for approximately two hundred years, this was the form of Zen brought to Japan by Eisai.
   b. *Yang-chi (Yōgi) School*
   Founded by Fang-hui (996–1049), who resided on Mt. Yang-chi. This branch became the dominant form of Lin-chi Zen and of the twenty-four transmissions of Zen to Japan, all but four belonged to this tradition.

The philosophies of these so-called 'Five Houses and Seven Schools' did not form solid sectarian lines and one or more frequently were taught simultaneously at the same monastery, just as the great temples would alternate in affiliation depending upon the tradition of the current presiding master. Two of these schools played a dominant role in Japan: the Lin-chi and a modified form of Ts'ao-tung. We will now examine the principal views of the Lin-chi school, most of which they shared in common with the other Zen movements.

3. Discovery of the True Nature and Attainment of Buddhahood
   (*Kenshō Jōbutsu*)

The goal of Zen is to encounter the intrinsic fundamental nature of

Enlightenment existing within each sentient being, which is alternately termed *kenshō* (to discover the true nature) or *satori*. The major difference between the Zen approach and that of other sects, is that being aware of the discriminative nature of human language and all the inherent dangers involved in the attachment to words as well as the intellectualization of the spirit, they sought to transmit the experience of Enlightenment non-verbally (*furyū monji*). This is known as the 'finger pointing at the mind (*jikishi ninshin*),[16] for ultimately, the only way an individual can attain Enlightenment is to awaken his own inner nature. All Buddhist sects employ various *upāya* (means of communicating and attaining Enlightenment), in most cases relying upon scriptures, faith in Buddha, meditation, *vinaya* practice and so on—but each of these, including the teachings themselves, serve merely as guideposts along the way. In the end the individual must either discover or create the awakening within himself. Whether or not he personally takes credit for this discovery is irrelevant, for if he attains true Enlightenment, the wisdom he achieves with that experience will make any form of egotism or spiritual pride impossible. And this is why at the level of Ultimate truth, self-power (*jiriki*) and Other-power (*Tariki*) can be viewed as identical.

The immense danger along the spiritual path is in the attachment to the means or *upāya* and regarding it as a goal in itself—and such a peril is just as implicit for those who venerate the so-called words of the Buddha in the scriptures or Buddhas such as Amida or Dainichi Nyorai, as it is for those who seemingly engage in superstitious folk beliefs. In fact, one of the greatest risks is for the scholar who attempts to discover the highest level of Buddhist truth and reduce it to a simple intellectual formula. The earliest Buddhist masters must have had this problem in mind when they classified actions leading to the psychological state of hell and determined that mental actions had far wider consequences than physical or vocal, since it is more difficult to break free from the intricate snares of one's own mind. Comprehending such hazards, Zen transmission became a subjective experience shared by master and disciple, and expressed by such means as physical action or absurd answers to profound intellectual questions. This is not to say that the Zen sect spurned *upāya*, for meditation, the Rinzai *kōan* and all forms of instruction between master and disciple fall into the general category of *upāya*. But they did reject traditional *upāya* such as reliance upon the scriptures and other paraphernalia of religion, seeking instead to awaken the fundamental Buddha-nature by more direct penetrating methods, breaking through the intellectual *impasse*.

One method employed to jolt the mind out of its normal rut of being, constantly concerned and quibbling over the problem of existence versus non-existence, was the classic answer *Wu* (Jap. *Mu*), perfected by Chaochou, and most commonly associated with the famous *kōan*, 'does a dog have a Buddha-nature?' Just as Nirvana was described in ancient India by *neti, neti* or the denial of what it was not, so the Chinese *Wu* expresses the world of Enlightenment as-it-is in negative terms, transcending all thought of what the common-sense mind believes to be existence—in the form of a permanent entity, or non-existence—as nihilism. By continually facing *Wu*, the mind eventually becomes exhausted of its alternatives and jarred out of its daily pattern in which it simplistically classifies everything it encounters in terms of black and white, and subject versus object. Living with the thought of *Wu* long enough and puzzling over its nature ultimately shocks the mind out of relative value judgements, while shipwrecking logic upon the rocks of the absurd reality that constitutes authentic existence. Only intuitive experience can come to the rescue to harmonize the contradictions that reason is incapable of facing, for the common-sense unenlightened mind is continually attempting to create a fanciful universe centred upon itself and the incurable belief in its own immortality. Like a computer it constantly programs rationalizations to explain change, rebuffs from the real world and calamities—it can even palliate its own final destruction by preparing a pleasant gravesite for future incubation or vicariously dictating the destiny of its heirs in a will. All of these common sense rationalizations are shattered in the experience of *Wu*, the greatest absurdity of all—reality.

Yet the goal of Zen is not merely to shatter or shipwreck the logical common-sense mind—ideally it is to be able to live and act in human life totally free from the crutches of rationalization, facing change, impermanence and above all coming to the basic realization that one's own subjective world is entirely contingent upon the worlds of others. Just as the Confucianists sought to create an ideal man (*chun-tzu*), the Buddhist approach became to *discover* the ideal man. A major difference between the two is that the Confucian ideal man may function perfectly in human society, fulfilling his obligations with polish, whereas the Buddhist ideal man at times in the eyes of the sophisticated world, may well act like a barbarian. The important point for the Buddhist perfect man is his own complete inner equanimity in every situation. And in order to express the necessity for an Enlightened One to participate in normal daily life, which is an inseparable function of Enlightenment, Zen emphasized the concept of the 'natural mind.'

4.   Natural Mind is the Way (*Heijōshin koredō*)

Ma-tsu and his followers revitalized Chinese Zen by bringing it down to the earthy level of daily life and affirming that 'one's everyday mind is the Way.' The ability of the Enlightened One to engage in daily life has been recognized as an inseparable function of Enlightenment in Mahāyāna Buddhism since the time of Nāgārjuna and his threefold classification of the experience of *Śūnyatā* (Emptiness).[17] In fact, even in Early Buddhism there are adequate source materials to demonstrate that the supreme goal was never a complete escape into some form of negative euphoria, such as Nirvana is commonly portrayed in Western-language dictionaries. The ideal was to experience Enlightenment and as the historical Buddha, to return to daily life and function in a normal manner—with the great exception of being freed from the pains of birth-and-death, which ordinary unenlightened individuals constantly experience. Unfortunately, as Buddhism grew more intellectualized, the goal became increasingly less tangible, since it is exceedingly difficult to reconcile the demands of a normal physical body functioning in daily life with spiritual ideals of perfection. On the other hand, to divorce the two was contrary to the spirit of Buddhism. The question thus became to discover the means of perfect balance. And this was accomplished in Zen much in the manner of breaking a wild stallion: first disciplining and negating the ego, while at the same time taxing the reason until it admitted defeat, and then once the fundamental inner nature was awakened and in control, to loosen all restraints.

'Sudden Enlightenment' does not mean awakening is easily attainable, but rather that its arrival cannot be judged in terms of conventional time. Depending upon the individual's psychological state, it might occur upon the first day of religious practice, after long years, or in many cases never. And a distinct problem exists in recognizing true Enlightenment from the multiple pseudo-experiences that plague the lives of beginners. This is why in Zen, the master is to be the judge of the disciple's state of mind. However, as Zen developed institutionally, this recognition often became clouded, as the unworldly master who refused to pass on transmission if he failed to find an awakened disciple, was destined to have his school fade into oblivion—thus, compromises were made. And the pretended Enlightened, to assure their own prosperity, were certain to judge many of their disciples as having experienced *satori*—although in truth they were incapable of determining. Thus just as Pure land followers could slip into a lethargic 'let-Amida-do-it' passivity, so false Zen masters perpetuated the myth that all had attained *satori*, reducing the experience to a level far below Nirvana. The Northern school and later critics rationally perceived the danger of attempting spontaneous living with a simulated notion of Enlightenment—it was an extreme equal to their own intellectualization of the Dharma, that allowed them no time to discover their true nature.

Ma-tsu's concept of everyday life being the way, effectively removed the goal from spurious nihilistic extremes and offered a complete affirmation of human life. But it was a way that could only be embarked upon properly after the attainment of true *kenshō* or *satori*. Then, just as Pure Land devotees could act with perfect spontaneity based upon faith in Amida—Zen followers could engage in any activity, certain they were not being led by blind animal instinct or ego, but by the fundamental nature dwelling within themselves; in the words of Lin-chi, they had attained the status of 'a true man of no rank.'

5. Lin-chi's True Man of No Rank[18]

One day Master Lin-chi delivered a sermon saying: 'Within a lump of red flesh there sits a true man of no rank who is constantly coming in and out of your sense organs. If anyone of you has not yet seen him, look, look!' A monk came forward and asked, 'Who is this true man of no rank?' Immediately Lin-chi rushed down from his seat, seized the monk and said: 'Speak, speak!' But when the monk was about to open his mouth, Lin-chi pushed him away exclaiming, 'What a miserable dung scraper[19] is this man of no rank!' and retired to his chamber.

The moral of this story is that within the body of each of us there exists a true man (fundamental nature), who has no need of ever passing through the fifty-two stages to Enlightenment.[20] This is the spirit and essence of Lin-chi's teachings. And this inherent quality passes in and out of the individual through the senses in the form of awareness of one's subjectivity and so-called objective phenomena. The subjective 'I' believes it is the protagonist in the world of its own creation, but brute reality eventually forces it to realize others too play the leading role in their own private worlds. This jousting for superiority is illustrated in another Lin-chi legend:

Once the master was invited by a bureaucratic patron to deliver a sermon, and just as he was about to preach, an old priest, once a disciple of Ma-tsu by the name of Ma-ku, came forward and asked him: 'The one thousand-armed Kuan-yin has one eye in each of its palms, which is the true eye?' Lin-chi repeated the question and added, 'if you can say it, say it.' Whereupon Ma-ku pulled his sleeve and dragged him down from the platform, climbing up in his place. Lin-chi then stepped forward from the floor below and politely greeted Ma-ku, 'It's a nice day today, how are you?' Ma-ku smiled, at a loss for words, then Lin-chi pulled him down from the platform and resumed his place as Ma-ku returned home.

In this *koan*, by inquiring, 'which is the principal eye of the thousand-armed Kuan-yin,' Ma-ku was asking whether each sentient being can be regarded objectively as equal in existence, or should each man subjectively be viewed as the centre of his own world? Who is the principal figure? Lin-chi's demand that Ma-ku answer his own question demonstrated his refusal to state either view was correct, and in turn Ma-ku's ascendance to the platform silently expressed the equality of both views —alternately man is the hero of his own subjective world, while objectively an equal among other existents.

Lin-chi presented this theory in a more philosophical manner in his 'Fourfold Analysis (Chin. *Ssu-liao-chien*) of the interchangeability of subject and object, the following presents a summary:[21]

1) *Take away the man but not his objectivity*
In other words, the subjectivity of the individual is completely immersed in the objective world, i.e. reading a book, watching a play, enjoying a beautiful view. Lin-chi described this as:

> When the sun rises, it lays embroideries over the earth, the infant's hair hangs white as silk.

meaning that when one is entranced by the beauty and wonder of the world, it is no longer possible to be aware of oneself, like the infant with the long greyish white hair of an old man, totally unaware of what it is.
(Negate the subjectivity but not the objectivity)

2) *Take away the objectivity, but not the man*
To obliterate the objective world by complete submersion within one's own subjectivity. i.e., the artist creating a painting, the poet in his dream—to allow the true man of no rank to come forward, or in Lin-chi's words:

> The Emperor's order has been adopted throughout the land, while the general on the borderland quells the smoke and dust of the battle.

All exterior distractions have been shut out, allowing the subjectivity full control.
(Negate the objectivity but not the subjectivity)

3) *Take away both the man and his objectivity*
The complete serene mind of meditation that permits no movement or ripples upon the poind:

> When communication from Ping and Fen is cut off, one resides isolated in the area.

Neither subjectivity nor objectivity are allowed to function, for the doors of the senses have been closed.

(Negate both subjectivity and objectivity)

4) *Take away neither the man nor his objectivity*

Allowing both subjectivity and objectivity to work freely and interchangeably—coming in an out as the true man of no rank through the sense organs. This is the world of common daily life—but it is also in Zen the world of perfect spontaneity, whereby an Enlightened One carries on the normal tasks of eating, drinking, sleeping, voiding the bladder and defecating. The difference is, that the common ignorant man is aware of no other world than this, while the Enlightened One realizes that this is the ideal balance of four possible realms, or in Lin-chi's definition:

As the Emperor ascends to his throne, the old peasants sing songs.

Peace and prosperity reigns over the land, as both subjectivity and objectivity function contentedly.

(Negate neither subjectivity nor objectivity)

6. The *Kōan*

The rise of Zen in China with its deliberate rejection of faith in the words of the sacred scriptures upset the traditional Buddhist method of study, but at the same time created a new form of literature. Balancing the human weakness to venerate the word itself with the need to preserve the teachings of the great masters and disseminate them among a wider audience than physical and chronological limits might allow, the Zen dialogues came into being. Initially these were records of the lives of the great monks although written very different from the traditional Buddhist biographies or (Jap.) *kōsōden*, that related historical anecdotes in classical language. The Zen records had little interest in history, but sought to record the dialogues between master and disciples in daily language, so filled with contemporary colloquialisms that they are difficult to comprehend today. Certain collections of these dialogues later became known as *kōan*, and consist of laconic riddles with logically absurd anwers.

Initially the term *kōan* (Chin. *kung-an*) signified what authorities variously describe as 'public documents,' 'cases,' or 'laws' that 'established precedents' or 'standards of judgement.' In Zen they became methods of testing an individual's understanding of the teachings, for it was believed that the *kōan* expressed the essence of the Buddha's Enlightenment. And even though the dialogues selected arose out of the subjective relationship between master and disciple, each bore certain universal qualities. Ideally, these would artificially and systematically develop the consciousness of Zen followers into an experience that early masters had produced spontaneously.

Although Zen dialogues date back to the early days of the school, the Rinzai *kōan* began to take form during the late T'ang and through the turmoil leading to the Sung dynasty. Important names during this formative period were the Lin-chi master Fen-yang Shan-chao (947–1024), who established one of the first collections of *kōan* and Hsueh-tou Ch'ung-hsien (980–1052) of the Yun-men school. But one of the most significant influences in establishing a guideline for future Zen collections was the *Ching-te-ch'uan-teng-lu*, an historical collection of the lives of famous monks containing anecdotes and teachings that was compiled in 1004. This work was even incorporated by the Sung government into the *Tripiṭaka*, ranking it equal to the Chinese translation of sutras and commentaries.

The bureaucratic interest in Zen, which demonstrated the growing importance of this school, was not without its detrimental effects. Other records were submitted in the same style as the *Ching-te-ch'uan-teng-lu* and gradually the hand of bureaucracy extended into the Zen temples, in parallel with the establishment of a national system, until the daily routines of the monks became formalized. Just as the spontaneous life styles developed into regulated monastic order, so the earthy and realistic dialogues were reduced to formulae for education or narrow intellectual quibbles, devoid of their dynamic quality. Gradually Sung Neo-Confucian learning, which was greatly indebted to Zen and other forms of Buddhist metaphysics, began to capture of the interest of even the bureaucrats since it offered new vitality, while the *kōan* or dialogues declined to the status of overworked didacticisms.

Under the fifth Lin-chi patriarch Wu-tsu (1024–1104), an effort was made to restore the *kōan* to its original nature as well as to stir the monks lethargized by the formalized routines of their monasteries into the spirit of earlier days. Wu-tsu placed emphasis upon the famous *Wu* of Chao-chou to begin a new phase of *kōan*, culminating in the *Pi-yen-lu* (1125) and *Wu-men-kuan* (1228), the latter composed by Hui-kai (1183–1260) and contained forty-eight concise *kōan* based upon Chao-chou's *Wu*.

Another important restorer of the vitality of the *kōan* was Ta-hui Tsung-kao (1089–1163), who was so opposed to the intellectual approach that he even went so far as to have the *Pi-yen-lu* destroyed, in the belief that its use impaired Zen attainment.

The purpose of the *kōan* in Rinzai Zen is to prod the individual's inner reflections. Although self-reflection is not a quality generally stressed in Zen in the manner of the Pure Land schools, it is a necessary preliminary practice to be discarded once *kenshō* is attained. The first step for the spiritual initiate must consist of intellectual study, reflection, and a desire to transcend oneself. Under the hands of a proper master, these qualities ideally can be developed into *kenshō* and then abandoned as the spontaneous inner nature functions. The *kōan* in the Rinzai sect, is an *upāya* administered in order to provide the catalyst for the first step or transcendence of the outer self into the inner awareness of *kenshō*. It also was used in order to combat two equally dangerous hindrances along the spiritual path: quietism and intellectualization. Quietism is a specific danger arising out of meditation and results in the mind lulling itself into a totally passive state or the temporary suspension of consciousness without any results. In fact this was a criticism, most likely unfairly made, by Shen-hui against the Northern Zen of Shen-hsiu, which appeared to advocate mere tranquillity of mind while approaching the fundamental nature of 'Original Enlightenment.' Later followers of Shen-hui seem to have fallen into the same error he accused his opponents of, but it was a constant danger for any school placing all of its emphasis upon meditation.

The opposite extreme was intellectualism and this was another snare that entrapped Shen-hui's followers in the north, just as it had proven to be a danger for the Northern school patronized by the sophisticated aristocrats of the capital. The vast popularity of Zen with the new classes arising under the Sung dynasty led to the same problem in the south—fashionableness among the ruling classes tended to reduce the dynamic intuitive quality to simple logecisms. Thus the kōan, in an attempt to impede the growth of intellectualism and at the same time prevent the individual from being submerged in quietism, functioned in a twofold manner: 1) ideally to check the intellect either by allowing it to realize its bounds or ideally to shipwreck it, and 2) to affect the maturity of the Zen consciousness.

The kōan checks the intellect by its logical absurdity. It is impossible to solve the problem presented by reason, i.e. Kao-fen Yuan-miao's famous: 'All things return to the One, where does the One return to?' and Chao-chou's reply: 'When I was in the district of Ch'ing, I had a robe that weighed seven chin,' is nonsensical, yet it is capable of producing an inner realization that years of study and reflection might easily fail to achieve.

Ideally, the kōan affects the maturity of the Zen consciousness by producing first a wrought-up state of mind, for as the reasoning is kept in abeyance and proven to be ineffectual, other deeper primordial recesses of the mind are forced to tackle the problem. The kōan can only be properly comprehended and solved when a maturity of consciousness is reached. By giving the mind a problem to work upon, a state similar to the Pure Land reliance upon 'Other-power' is achieved, and perhaps this is one reason why during the fourteenth to fifteenth century of the late Yüan dynasty in China, a merger took place between kōan and nembutsu practice.

With the mind engaged upon a seeming object, self-reflection can be internalized until the self virtually disappears—the mind and body obliterated in existence—and when the object is experienced in fact as one's own fundamental nature, the individual is engulfed in the flood of liberation, while at the same time made aware of his unity with existence—almost as though plunging into the waters of a southern ocean and feeling its all embracing boundless warmth.

Sōtō school critics were to claim the *kōan* to be an artificial contrivance, while others pointed out that if improperly used it could lead to all types of self-delusion or the pseudo-experiences so rampant among spiritual beginners; still it was popularly used among many Sōtō followers as a secondary practice. As a soteriological method the *kōan* is fraught with as many dangers as other forms of *upāya*—be it the Buddhas, sutras, meditation, faith or learning—or even the greatest *upāya* of all Buddhism. All simply point to the way, the final inner discovery *must* ultimately depend upon the individual even though there may be nothing he can take personal credit for accomplishing.

7. Foundation of the Rinzai Order of Zen

Although Eisai was the first to transmit Zen to Japan, the variety he ultimately established was impure in the sense that it composed merely one aspect of the Tendai *Enmitsuzenkai* tradition. The introduction of this form was generally determined by the fact that Japan was not yet ready for Zen and Eisai's own personal background.

It is a popular myth that the Kamakura warriors readily accepted Zen when it arrived in Japan. In truth, at that period the samurai were not capable of accepting such an exotic and highly sophisticated religion from a foreign land.[22] The early Hōjō leaders up to Yasutoki (1183–1242) had virtually no association with pure Zen and the temples they sponsored were all in the mixed tradition, emphasizing esoteric rites. Even after Yasutoki, the understanding of Zen was limited to a small group of elite who believed Zen, as a product of Chinese learning, could place them culturally at par with the Kyoto aristocracy.

A similar situation existed at the capital, where the Court and aristocracy were primarily interested in the benefits of esoteric rituals with only a mild initial curiosity in the strange new practices from Sung China. Thus Eisai, forced to introduce Zen under the guise of esoterism and the presence of the watchful eyes of Mt. Hiei, made *Enmitsuzenkai* the logical compromise. The question is, with his own personal background and inclinations, whether Eisai would have introduced pure Zen practice if the nation had been prepared to receive it?

Eisai's Successors

After the death of Eisai, two of his leading disciples Eichō (d. 1247) and Gyōyū (d. 1241) carried on the tradition of the Ōryū-ha (Huang-lung) Rinzai school in Japan.

Eichō allegedly received the 'Yellow dragon' (Huang-lung) robe Eisai brought from China and became his legitimate successor. However, due to his own strong esoteric background, Eichō even further emphasized the *Enmitsuzen* tradition. He established the Chōrakuji in Kōzuke province of Kantō in 1221 as the centre of his practice and became noted for his famous disciples: Enni Bennen, Muhon Kakushin and Jinshi Eison, who went to China and assisted in the transition to pure Zen. He was succeeded at the Chōrakuji by Zōsō Rōyo (1193–1276) and this temple, officially classified as Tendai, played an important role in Zen development. Ultimately it became the *ujidera* of Tokugawa Ieyasu and given to the prominent Tenkai (1536–1643) to restore, but by late Tokugawa it declined.

Gyōyū, originally an attendant at the Tsuruoka Hachiman shrine, succeeded Eisai at the Jufukuji in Kamakura and was also strongly inclined towards the esoteric tradition. He received the patronage of Minamoto Yoritomo, his wife Masako, and son Sanetomo. After the latter's death, he was invited to found the Kongō Sammai-in (Vajra meditation centre) on Mt. Kōya, where he introduced Zen studies in accompaniment with Shingon. Later, upon the request of Masako and Hōjō Yasutoki, he commuted regularly between Kōyasan and Kamakura. He was succeeded at the Jufukuji by Jyakuan Jōshō (1229–1316). The Ōryū-ha continued its activities through the Kamakura period, with the Kenninji in Kyoto and Jufukuji in Kamakura being the centres of activity.

Bennen and the Shōichi-ha

Enni Bennen (1202–80), a legitimate successor of Eichō, established one of the most prosperous schools of Zen in Japan that received its name from his posthumous title (Shōichi Kokushi) awarded by Emperor Hanazono. Bennen was among the first to successfully form a bridge between pure and mixed Zen. At the age of eighteen he was ordained at the Tendai Onjōji, and subsequently studied under both Eichō and Gyōyū. In 1235 he went to Sung China where he received the *inka* of the Rinzai Yōgi (Yang-chi) school from Wu-chun. He returned to Japan in 1241 and preached at the Sōfukuji, Manjuji and Shōtenji temples in northern Kyūshū but immediately encountered the enmity of the established sects. With the patronage of the influential Kujō family he came to Kyoto and founded the Tōfukuji. Even though this temple was established in the *Enmitsuzenkai* tradition, a marked difference was that Zen was placed in the forefront, with other practices subservient. Bennen was also a persuasive writer on the subjects of *zazen* and *kenshō*, successfully serving to popularize them.

In contrast to other Zen schools, Bennen and his followers encountered more serious oppression from the established sects. But gradually as he instituted his centre in Kyoto and even brought the older Kenninji under his influence, he attracted a large number of aristocratic patrons and finally achieved a certain harmony with the older sects, spending his later years engaged under Imperial request, in the restoration of old temples. In 1257 he was invited by Hōjō Tokiyori to correct Zen discipline at the Jufukuji in Kamakura.

A large number of independent movements arose affiliated with Bennen's Shōichi-ha,[23] and the Tōfukuji developed into the headquarters of a massive nationwide movement embracing more than fifty temples.

Muhon Kakushin

Another important early Japanese Zen master was Muhon Kakushin (1207–98), who had a Shingon background and studied under Eichō and Gyōyū, and even Dōgen prior to visiting China, where he received

Zen transmission from Master Wu-men Hui-kai. Returning to Japan in 1254, he became the founder of the Saihōji (later known as the Kōkokuji), in the vicinity of Wakayama built in memory of Minamoto Sanetomo. Kakushin's movement was extremely esoteric oriented and gained success in the provinces. Since he had once studied under Dōgen, his school had close association with the Sōtō Eiheiji. Also due to its geographical proximity, at the time of Emperor Go-Daigo's secession, it maintained a relationship with the Southern Court at Yoshino. After his death, Kakushin was awarded the title of Hottō Emmyō Kokushi by Emperor Kameyama, and his school became known as the Hottō-ha.

Rise of Pure Zen

Gradually the mixed form of Zen and Tantrism began to gain national acceptance and as the Kamakura warrior class approached the new sect, they quickly realized Zen was not an aristocratic religion, and commenced to feel at ease with the philosophy, seeking to understand it better. This resulted in invitations being extended to leading Chinese Zen masters to visit Japan.

Prior to the introduction of Zen by Chinese masters, certain pure forms of Zen were brought to Japan by Japanese who had studied in China, but the dilemma they faced was either to compromise with mixed practices in order to gain financial patronage, or else retire to seclusion and risk the eventual dissolution of their teachings. Even the most idealistic monks found it nearly impossible to attract disciples and establish any form of institution without a degree of worldly acceptance, that in turn provided the necessities of life for the pursuit of religious study and propagation of the teachings. The invitation by the Kamakura government to leading Chinese Zen masters drastically changed this situation. Unaware in many cases of the *Enmitsuzenkai* tradition, and unwilling in others to accept such mixed practices, the Chinese masters taught Zen as they properly knew it in China, irrespective of the audience. And as the samurai class commenced to appreciate real Zen for both its cultural prestige and teachings, a financial base was established. Thus, just as in the case of all the old established sects of Nara and Kyoto, Zen was first accepted by the ruling classes and imposed upon the nation in a society that was naturally authoritarian. As a result, Zen came to socially and culturally dominate the late Kamakura and Muromachi periods.

Rankei Dōryū (Lan-chi Tao-lung)

In 1246 at the request of Hōjō Tokiyori, Rankei Dōryū (1213–78) arrived in Japan and began to teach Zen at the Jōrakuji in Kamakura. However because of the rapid growth of his disciples, the Jōrakuji soon proved to be too small, and Tokiyori built the Kenchōji in 1253, one of the first of what later became known as the *Gozan* (five mountain) Zen centres. Soon more than two hundred disciples clustered in this temple and it became the mainstream of Kamakura Zen, later known as the Daikaku-ha after Rankei's posthumous title.

Upon the recommendation of the Hōjō family and invitation of Emperor Go-Saga, Rankei moved to the Kenninji in Kyoto in 1259, which had formally been a centre of mixed practice housing Tendai as well as Zen priests. The prior year the temple had been restored by Bennen from a degenerate state with lax discipline, and under Rankei's inflence the Kenninji commenced to practice pure Zen. It would appear that Rankei and Bennen were on good terms and may have worked in cooperation, for although Rankei's master in China was formally Hui-hsing, he had also received instruction from Wu-chun, Bennen's master. Rankei's presence in Japan thus reinforced Bennen's form of Zen teachings and assisted in their propagation.

Rankei's sojourn in Japan was not completely peaceful, for in 1265 he was briefly exiled for slander by his disciple and pardoned later. Tokimune planned to build a great new temple in his honour (which later became the Engakuji), but Rankei died before its completion. The Zen Rankei propagated became very popular among the Kamakura warriors, partially due to his strict emphasis upon discipline. And the Daikaku-ha eventually came close to rivalling Bennen's Shōichi-ha in popularity, however, after the Ashikaga government made its headquarters in Kyoto, the school remained isolated in Kamakura and ceased to develop.

Gottan Funei (Wu-an P'u-ning)

In 1260 upon the invitation of Hōjō Tokiyori, Gottan Funei (1197–1276) arrived in Japan and performed a memorial service for Eisai at the Shōfukuji in Hakata, then proceeded to Kamakura. Gottan was also in the Yōgi (Yang-chi) tradition of Wu-chun, first brought to Japan by Bennen, further transmitted by Mugaku Sogen and indirectly by Rankei.

Gottan's experiences in Japan were disillusioning. Initially he came to Japan in search of a more perfect land to teach Buddhism, since China was then besieged with external threats and internal corruption. But he was sixty-three when he arrived, and at the age where it was no longer easy to adopt to strange customs, let alone the vagaries of the warrior class and aristocratic patrons. By nature, Gottan was an aloof individual not easily understood, and after the death of Tokiyori he became involved in intrigues and accusations that he found intolerable. According to legend, when he arrived at the Kenchōji, he found Jizō bosatsu to be the principal image, and haughtily inquired why, as a Buddha himself, he should be expected to venerate a lower ranking bodhisattva? He is even reported in the Shasekishū to have declared Bennen's disciple Rōyo, too superior for a nation like Japan.

Four years in Japan were all that Gottan was able to endure, and he returned to China in 1263. Still his introduction of pure Zen served as a valuable experience for Japan and although his school, known as the Sōkaku-ha, never developed extensively, it remained in quality an important Zen movement.

Daikyū Shōnen (Ta-hsiu Cheng-nien)

A less spectacular Chinese monk, Daikyū Shōnen (1214–89) arrived six years after Gottan's departure, upon the invitation of Hōjō Tokimune and resided at the Kenchōji and Engakuji in Kamakura; he later became the founder of the Jōchiji. Although his school, known as the Butsugenha, in honour of his posthumous title, was never large, it was exceedingly influential in educating the Kamakura samurai.

Mugaku Sogen (Wu-hsüeh Tsu-yüan)

After the collapse of the Sung dynasty, Tokimune sent two of Rankei's disciples, Tokusen and Sōei, to the Yüan dynasty to invite the distinguished Zen monk Huan-chi Wei-i of Mt. T'ien-t'ung, belonging to Wu-chun tradition. But since Huan-chi had already reached the age of eighty, he suggested his disciple Mugaku (1226–86) come in his place. In 1279 Mugaku arrived in Japan and settled at the Kenchōji, later Tokimune built the Engakuji (1282) and placed him in charge. This movement became known in honour of Mugaku's posthumous title, as the Bukkō-ha.

An important disciple of Mugaku was Kian Soen (1269–1313), who with the patronage of Emperor Kameyama established the Zenrinji in Kyoto. This was later renamed the Nanzenji, and became the most influential Rinzai temple, leading the *Gozan* system.

Another outstanding disciple was Kōhō Kennichi (1241–1316), a son of Emperor Go-Saga, who made a particular contribution to Zen in the eastern provinces or Kantō area, centred at the Unganji in Nasu. Kōhō's background was Tendai, and his teachings of an esoteric nature. Under the leadership of Musō Soseki (1275–1351), a disciple of Kōhō, this form of mixed Zen spread to Kyoto and became exceedingly influential with the Ashikaga government and in the *Gozan* system.

Nanpo Jōmin (1235–1308)

In contrast to the Chinese monks who propagated pure Zen, Nanpo (Daiō Kokushi) was a native Japanese, who began his studies under Rankei at the Kenchōji. In 1259 he went to China and received transmission of the Yōgi-ha (Yang-chi) from the master Hsü-t'ang Chih-yü (a disciple of Yün-an P'u-yen). Upon returning to Japan, Nanpo's activities overlapped those of his former master Rankei, and in popularity nearly equalled the Chinese master Issan Ichinei; his movement became the Daiō-ha.

Nanpo's most illustrious disciple was Shūhō Myōchō (Daitō Kokushi, 1282–1337), who taught in Kyoto and under Emperors Hanazono and Go-Daigo, built the famous Daitokuji temple in 1324. Myōchō was further responsible for the establishment of the Myōshinji in 1337, and entrusted it to his disciple Kanzan Egen. Eventually both the Daitokuji and Myōshinji became independent schools.

Issan Ichinei (I-shan I-ning)

In 1299 Issan Ichinei (1274–1317) came to Japan as an envoy of the Yüan dynasty after their failure to conquer Japan. As a gesture to appease the Japanese, the Mongol court sent one of the most distinguished Zen monks of the day, however, when Issan arrived in Japan, the Hōjō regent Sadatoki first charged him as a spy and banished him to the Shuzenji on Izu peninsula. Later he was pardoned and allowed to reside at the Kenchōji.

As the only distinguished Chinese monk in Japan after the deaths of Mugaku and Daikyū, Issan soon won the favour of Sadatoki and many other prominent samurai leaders. He was invited by Emperor Go-Uda to become the third successor to the Nanzenji temple in Kyoto. Due to his residence in the capital as well as his personal knowledge of Chinese culture and the Confucian classics, he gained considerable popularity among the court aristocracy, and advanced the development of Zen. His movement became known as the Ichizan-ha, in honour of his posthumous title.

Seisetsu Shōchō (Ch'ing-cho Cheng-ch'eng)

Seisetsu (1274–1339) arrived in Japan in 1326 at the invitation of Hōjō Takatoki and resided at the Kenchōji and Engakuji. He later went to Kyoto and taught at both the Kenninji and Nanzenji. He is particularly noted for the transmission of Zen monastic rules and regulations, which, when adopted in conjuction with native Japanese customs became the distinctive Ogasawara-ryū of etiquette, that is still practiced today— Seisetsu's school became the Daikan-ha.

Besides these movements, numerous other Chinese monks came to

Japan who were not successful in establishing independent schools. But with the rapid influx of Chinese masters and Japanese monks returning from China, the quality of Zen swiftly improved. This was accelerated by a general renewed interest among the Japanese populace for things Chinese—thus by late Kamakura, in drastic contrast to when Eisai sought to visit China and was ridiculed, a number of Japanese monks were again leaving for China and spending long periods of study; the most drastic example being Ryūzan Tokken, who spent forty-seven years in China.

In time, the Japanese monks won acceptance even in the Chinese Zen community, which was undergoing multiple political upheavals. And as a result, Japanese Zen came in all respects to equal the glory of Chinese Zen. Contributing determinants to this rapid Japanese growth were undoubtedly the sectarian conflicts in China, as well as the uneasiness resulting from the alien domination under the Yüan dynasty—these factors induced Chinese Zen masters to seek a more fertile and receptive land for their teachings. The last of the Chinese monks arrived around 1351 and after this, with the political turmoil of the Northern and Southern courts in Japan and subsequent unsteadiness of the Ashikaga government, the Chinese monks no longer could be persuaded to take the risk of visiting a nation engulfed in problems equalling those of China. Ashikaga Takauji later unsuccessfully attempted to invite a distinguished Chinese monk, and as Ashikaga control waned the suggestion became even more unthinkable.

8. The *Gozan* (Five Mountain) Temple System

Kamakura Zen can be classified into two categories:
1) Schools founded by Japanese monks who studied in China—i.e. Eisai, Bennen, Kakushin and Nanpo
2) Those founded by visiting Chinese monks—i.e. Rankei, Mugaku, Daikyū, Issan, Seisetsu, etc.

With the exception of Nanpo's Daiō-ha, which spread primarily in the provinces, the shift in the centre of government during the Muromachi period to Kyoto, brought all of these movements under the direct influence of the Ashikaga government. Since schools had blossomed in chaotic profusion around the personalities of the diverse Zen masters, the Ashikaga sought to find some means to systematize them and exert control over the institution as a whole. In Kyoto, the followers of Mugaku, under Musō Soseki cooperated and formed the nucleus of what eventually developed into the five temple ranking system.

After the establishment of the *de facto* Ashikaga government to Kyoto, two major Zen traditions became dominant: Mugaku's Bukkō-ha under the leadership of Musō Soseki, and Bennen's wide-spread Shōichi-ha. These and all Zen schools at the capital and Kamakura, including the Sōtō Wanshi-ha, became part of the *Gozan* temple system. In contrast, the vast network of temples centred in the provinces became known as *Rinka* (lit. 'under the forest'). Included in the latter were the Sōtō Eiheiji founded by Dōgen, the Rinzai Daiō-ha of Nanpo Jōmin (and its later independent branches, the Daitokuji and Myōshinji), and also the Rinzai Genjū-ha transmitted by Onkei Soō (1286–1344) and Fukuan Sōko, with headquarters at the Kōgenji in Tamba province.[24]

From the early to mid-Muromachi period the *Gozan* temples experienced their flowering but by the close of the Muromachi, with the decline and collapse of the central government, which had provided their sponsorship, the *Rinka* temples began to surpass them, since they had become firmly entrenched among the rising local warlords.

The origin of the so-called Five mountain and ten distinguished temples (*gozan jissetsu*) system appears to have begun during the late Kamakura period. The first historical records available imply the Jōchiji was elevated to the status of *Gozan* in 1299. About the same time it is believed that the Kenchōji, Engakuji and Jufukuji also received the same rank, although the early system in unclear. The initial grouping appears to have been limited to the Kamakura area, but after Emperor Go-Daigo's brief restoration, under his patronage the Daitokuji, founded by Shūhō Myōchō, was elevated to that rank in 1333, followed the next year by the Nanzenji being officially classified as the first of the *Gozan* temples; subsequently the Kenninji and Tōfukuji were included. It was not until

1341 that a clear *Gozan* ranking system was established with the following classifications:

First Rank	Kenchōji, Kamakura
	Nanzenji, Kyoto
Second Rank	Engakuji, Kamakura
	Tenryūji, Kyoto
Third Rank	Jufukuji, Kamakura
Fourth Rank	Kenninji, Kyoto
Fifth Rank	Tōfukuji, Kyoto

and as an auxiliary (*jun-gozan*) the Jōchiji, Kamakura.

Whereas the *Gozan* originally must have designated five temples, it now clearly became a temple ranking system.

The origin of the 'ten distinguished temples' (*jissetsu*) is also vague but must have existed as early as the late Kamakura period. In 1358 a new *Gozan* ranking system was established in conjunction with the ten distinguished temples in the following manner:

First Rank	Kenchōji
	Nanzenji
Second Rank	Engakuji
	Tenryūji
Third Rank	Jufukuji
Fourth Rank	Kenninji
Fifth Rank	Tōfukuji
	Jōchiji
	Jōmyōji, Kamakura
	Manjuji, Kyoto

This system shifted and varied as the leaders of the government and Court established favoured new temples and attempted to gain them preferred ranks. But the most influential event in the final establishment of a nationwide *Gozan* system was the development of the *ankokuji*.

Upon the recommendation of Musō Soseki, Ashikaga Takauji and his brother Tadayoshi decided to establish in each province of the land one *ankokuji* (temple for the peace of the nation) and one *rishō-tō* (stupa to benefit all living things), in memory of those who had lost their lives from the time of the Genkō war of 1331–3, when Emperor Go-Daigo overthrew the Hōjō regents. In 1345 Emperor Kōgon officially set forth an edict to inaugurate the system, and between 1362–68 temples and stupas were built or established in sixty-six provinces and two islands. The *ankokuji* temples were strictly limited to powerful Zen temples affiliated with the *Gozan*, having local *shugo* (Ashikaga stewards) as patrons. The basic political motive behind the system was to solidify the shaky authority of the central government in the provinces. Ideally, dedicated in honour of the war dead, the temples would appease the rapidly expanding peasant classes in the provinces, as well as stake out territory under Ashikaga control. In fact, since many of the temples and pagodas had guards, in some cases they acted as military outposts. Traditional historians generally believe that the *ankokuji* were modeled after the *kokubunji* instituted by Emperor Shōmu in 741 during the Tempyō era, but this does not seem to have been the case.[25] Ashikaga Tadayoshi who was in charge, apparently adapted the system after Sung Chinese models, and although the previous existence of the *kokubunji* may have set a certain precedent, the *ankokuji* had a different basis. The *kokubunji*, copies of the *Ta-yün* Chinese model had been established upon Kegon philosophy with the great Dainichi Nyorai of the Tōdaiji as the centre. Politically they strengthened the hegemony of the Emperor, as had their Chinese precedent. In contrast, the *ankokuji* were clustered around the *Gozan* Zen temples and were politically inspired by the *de facto bakufu* government.

Distinct from the *ankokuji*, the *rishō* stupas were built at leading established temples, in particular Shingon, Tendai and Ritsu, with the purpose of assuaging the *shugo* belonging to other sects. Ideally this twin system was to serve as a political enforcement of the *shugo* system and keep recalcitrant war lords in line, but it never had an opportunity to succeed.

Tadayoshi quarreled with retainers of his brother and found himself leading an anti-Takauji faction. In 1351 he fled with his followers to Hokuriku and eventually faced his brother in battle. Overwhelmed,

Tadayoshi capitulated and by 1352 died in confinement at the Jōmyōji, of what the *Taiheiki* describes as jaudice, but actually was poisoning. Not long after his demise, Takauji died in 1358, his son Yoshiakira was occupied pacifying the Southern Court until his death in 1368, and before Ashikaga control was finally established, the power had shifted to the third Shōgun, Yoshimitsu, a ten-year old boy. Thus when the *ankokuji* temples were finally completed, their political rationale had ceased to exist, and the provincial *shugo* were already well advanced towards becoming independent war lords. Neverthless, the *Gozan* system proved to be a practical method of handling the Zen monasteries, and in 1386 after Yoshimitsu built the Shōkokuji, a new order was devised:

	Nanzenji	
	Kyoto	*Kamakura*
First Rank	Tenryūji	Kenchōji
Second Rank	Shōkokuji	Engakuji
Third Rank	Kenninji	Jufukuji
Fourth Rank	Tōfukuji	Jōchiji
Fifth Rank	Manjuji	Jōmyōji

Thus the *Gozan* became equally balanced between Kamakura and Kyoto. In 1401, Yoshimitsu briefly reversed the ranking of the Tenryūji and Shōkokuji, but this was later restored and the list became standardized. However, the 'ten distinguished temples' (*jissetsu*) grew independently, and by 1480–86 forty-six temples were included in this ranking, the number eventually increased to over sixty, and came to form a secondary ranking system beneath the *Gozan*. Finally a third system of 'miscellaneous temples' (*shozan*) was added, and by the late medieval period included two hundred-thirty Zen temples, since the rank had no stringent standards. Thus with the *Gozan* as a nucleus, over three hundred official Zen bureaucratic temples were established.

9. Muromachi Zen Culture

The Muromachi government was unique in Japanese history for its early interest in cultural affairs. Normally new governments do not have time for such concerns, but under the leadership of Ashikaga Tadayoshi, whose political power at times rivalled that of his brother Takauji, the Ashikaga government from the start took an active interest in promoting Zen affairs and culture. Perhaps this is one of the reasons why the Muromachi period became known for its brilliant cultural rather than political success.

Ashikaga Tadayoshi and Musō Soseki

At a time when Zen was still difficult for the samurai to accept due to its foreign ways and strange practices, Ashikaga Tadayoshi received his first Zen ordination before the portrait of Mugaku (Wu-hsüeh) in the Chin-kang Chui-hsia tradition of strictly Chinese Zen and developed an early appreciation for Zen culture as well as a profound understanding of Zen philosophy. Thus when the Ashikaga family rose to political power, the religious policies at the beginning of the Muromachi period were devised by Tadayoshi, and until his disagreement with his brother Takauji, he exerted a dominant influence upon Muromachi culture. Although Tadayoshi's policies ultimately failed—i.e., the *ankokuji* system was finally completed too late to benefit Ashikaga control, the *Gozan* were drastically modified to Japanese taste, and even the Tōjiji estabished by Tadayoshi as the Ashikaga family temple, was lost to the followers of the Chinese Chui-hsia tradition and fell under the 'impure' Zen control of Musō Soseki; still Tadayoshi's influence set a cultural precedent for other members of the Ashikaga family and a tone for future shōguns.

The relationship between Ashikaga Tadayoshi and Musō Soseki was most unusual. It is difficult to understand how Tadayoshi, an adherent of the sophisticated and highly literary Chinese Zen tradition of Chinkang Chui-hsia, could consent to a second ordination in 1349 by Musō Soseki, a somewhat worldly priest engaged in an esoteric mixed form of Japanese Zen. Some historians believe that after his problems with his brother Takauji, Tadayoshi decided to become a follower of Musō in order to placate his brother, who was strongly under Musō's influence.[26] In the *Muchū Mondō*, a record of the lectures and dialogues between Musō and Tadayoshi, some of the barbed questions Tadayoshi directed towards his master indicate that he did not exhibit the usual respect of a disciple.

The figure of Musō Soseki is also enigmatic. Born in Ise in 1275 as a descendent of Emperor Uda, he studied at the Tōdaiji Kaidan-in before turning to Zen and his early background was highly esoteric. This was reinforced by Kōhō Kennichi, his Zen master, who combined esoterism and other practices with Zen, creating a highly assimilated Japanese-form of Zen that Musō further developed and popularized.

It would seem that early in his life Musō sought to flee from honours, for when Kakukai-ni, wife of Hōjō Sadatoki, invited him to Kamakura following the will of Kōhō to become leader of Kōhō's disciples, Musō escaped to Tosa and only reluctantly agreed to return. It was not long before he again fled to become a recluse upon the Miura peninsula, yet in the end he became the most socially active priest in the capital. For some reason, perhaps because of his aristocratic background or great popularity, Musō was sought after by Emperors, shōguns and aristocrats. Not only was he a friend of Emperor Go-Daigo but after the failure of the Kammu Restoration, managed to gain the favour of Go-Daigo's chief foe, Ashikaga Takauji. Yet upon Go-Daigo's death, Musō founded the Tenryūji in his memory, with Takauji's patronage in the face of opposition from Mt. Hiei and even some of the Northern Court aristocrats.

Musō's personality was so dominant and activities so diverse, that it is difficult to assess his character. Allegedly at the time of his death in 1351 (thirtieth day of the ninth month), he left over 10,000 disciples. It is easy to see why Ashikaga Tadayoshi could not completely approve of him, for many of the aristocratic advocates of lofty Chinese Zen objected to the mixed practices and Japanese Zen that Musō advocated. Emperor Hanazono wrote in his diary, that Musō's statements were so common they regrettably failed to reach the profoundity of Zen, yet in the end it was this type of Zen that swept the land, won the allegiance of warriors such as Takauji and came to dominate the *Gozan*.

One of Musō's most beloved disciples was his nephew Shunoku Myōha (1311–88), who became abbot of the Shōkokuji, founded in 1383 as a branch of the Tenryūji, and eventually becoming a high ranking member of the *Gozan*. Other leading disciples of later generations were Gidō Shūshin (1325-88) and Zekkai (d. 1405). These individuals all contributed to the cultural tradition of Muromachi Zen. Musō personally established a reputation in creating landscape gardens and alleged examples existing today are the Tenryūji and famous Saihōji (Kokedera) moss garden. Later *Gozan* scholars were to be known for their role in importing the Neo-Confucian philosophy of Chu-hsi (768-824) and to ultimately have such commitment that they devoted their lives to its study while wearing Zen robes; some even chose to become laymen in order to be independent Confucian scholars.

By the mid-medieval period the *Gozan* Zen scholars dominated domestic policy as well as relations with the Ming dynasty, perhaps modeled after the role of Zen monks during the Sung dynasty in China, which some caustic opponents cited as the reason for the Sung collapse. Their cultural activities extended to the areas of architecture, painting, sculpture, calligraphy, gardening, painting, printing and even medicine. Many today believe that the samurai approached Zen for spirituality, if the truth be known, their spirituality was generally of a superficial nature as they were uneducated, yet they admired the cultural sophistication of Zen. This was one of the reasons why the *Gozan* temples came to devote the major portion of their time to Chinese literature and philosophy, while at the same time including popular Japanese practices such as the *nembutsu*. Although the samurai might admire their seeming-aristocratic nature, others found it intolerable.

Ikkyū Sōjun (1394-1481)

A drastic step further from the polish and sophistication of Musō Soseki, whom some aristocratic Zen followers found too mundane, was the humanity of Ikkyū—a dominant figure in late Muromachi Zen—a man the subject of so many legends that it is difficult to determine his true character and draw a concise line between eccentricity and madness.

Ikkyū, a son of Emperor Go-Komatsu was born in 1394, and received his early education at the *Gozan* although its sophistication failed to impress him. In fact, legend relates that when he departed from the *Gozan*, he left behind his precious *inka* document, and a messenger hurriedly delivered it to him, whereupon Ikkyū threw it in the fire. He engaged in a bitter lifelong quarrel with Yōsō Sōi (1379–1458) of the Daitokuji, continually criticizing the latter for scholarly hypocrisy and selling cheap *kōan* and ordinations to merchants and commoners. In every way Ikkyū opposed the trend of the times—he wore dirty robes, carried a wooden sword and *shakuhachi* flute, ate fish and meat, loved both *sake* and women, and had a son Giō Shōtei. He was known for his advice for sincere monks to leave the monastery, as well as for his beautiful love poems.

In 1474, Ikkyū went to spend his remaining years at the Daitokuji. It is popularly believed that he became abbot of this temple, but that is a position he never held, undoubtedly due to his utter disdain for all forms of conventionality. Although Ikkyū was not a 'holy man' in the common understanding of that term, his honesty and humanism won him a lasting place in Japanese Zen history and placed him in the company of the earthy Hui-neng and Ma-tsu. Ikkyū represented a blunt popular approach to Zen, reflecting the changing times and decay of both the feudal and aristocratic order.

Later Sectarian Developments

By the early Muromachi, in contrast to the prosperity of the *Gozan* at the capitals, the growth of Zen temples in the local prefectures was remarkable. This expansion was not merely the result of individual initiative, for although a number of worthy priests, who despised the aristocratic and bureaucratic attitude of the *Gozan* fled to the provinces, it also reflected a saturation point. So many Zen movements and temples existed in the capitals that the only room for expansion was towards the countryside.

An early example of a popular provincial master was Battai Tokushō (1327–87), a native of Sagami, who gained the patronage of the local warlord Takeda, and in 1380 founded the Kōgakuji in Kai (Yamanashi) province. Battai communicated with the common people by writing *kana hōgo* in simple language, explaining Buddhist doctrines in terms they could comprehend.

In the provinces the Rinzai movement came close to the powerful local Daimyō such as Takeda. And after the Ōnin and Bummei wars, as the *shōen* (estate) system ended and Ashikaga government authority diminished, control shifted to these warlords, who established their own feudal domains, possessing absolute power. During this period the warriors generally turned to Zen, just as the peasants were turning to Shinshū, and urban dwellers to Nichiren. The Daimyō fascination with Zen was based upon various interests; in the first place they found it useful in spiritually unifying their retainers, and thus Zen came to play an important role in the formation of samurai ethics or later code of *bushidō*. The local Zen temples filled the role of *ujidera* or clan temples for the warlords, praying both for their worldly prosperity and spiritual peace during the rapidly changing times. Such a position made the temples dependent upon the fortunes of the Daimyō in war, and they rose and fell sharing the fate of their patrons. Lastly, the Daimyō also had an interest in Zen culture, and by attempting to bring it to their domains managed to diffuse it throughout the nation at the time when the great cultural centres, the *Gozan*, at the capital declined as they shared the fate of their patron—the Ashikaga government.

The final unification of Japan under Tokugawa Ieyasu accelerated the secularization of Rinzai Zen. The interest of the samurai in Zen and Chinese culture had stimulated the *Gozan* monasteries to devote themselves to literature and other cultural pursuits, such as Neo-Confucianism and by the close of the Muromachi period these learned Zen monks dominated the government. Tokugawa Ieyasu to a degree continued the policy by appointing the Nanzenji abbot Sūden (1569–1633) as a political advisor. Despite the growing popularity of Neo-Confucianism, Sūden served three generations of Tokugawa leaders, formulating the Tokugawa religious policies and many of its strict religious controls. Takuan (1573–1645) as the spiritual advisor of Tokugawa Iemitsu, also played an important role in the regime, but of a more religious than political nature.

In the secularization of Rinzai Zen, one of the most important features was the Tokugawa *terauke* system, that required every family in the land to register as members of a local Buddhist temple. The acquisition of large lay congregations and shift in government interest to Neo-Confucianism made relations with the laity a primary concern. *Kana* booklets began in earlier ages, to describe Buddhist doctrine in simple terms increased, also efforts were made to assimilate feudal ethics and present the teachings in a manner that affirmed the feudalistic social structure. Leaders in these areas were Bankei (1622–92) and Hakuin (1685–1768), who both emphasized Zen in daily life and attempted to reinforce the warrior-class morality. Bankei was one of the first Zen masters to pragmatically recognize the limitations of the average man and announce that since everyone has a Buddha-nature by birth, *Zazen* is not necessary for the average man.[27] Hakuin, who is often called the 'Father of modern Zen' attempted to restore Zen purity by avoiding mixed practices, and yet presented the teachings in a manner comprehensive to the laymen. Thus Rinzai Zen moved away from its aristocratic cloisters and approached the common people.

B. Sōtō Zen

In Kamakura Japan, there were two movements of Sōtō Zen: the Wanshi-ha introduced by Tung-ming (1272–1340), that became part of the *Gozan* and declined, and Dōgen's school, historically most significant as it developed into the dominant Zen tradition and second largest school of Japanese Buddhism.

1. Dōgen, the Founder

Dōgen Kigen was born in 1200, on the outskirts of Kyoto the year after the death of Minamoto Yoritomo, and his parentage was a reflection of the social turmoil of the day. His mother was the beautiful Ishi, daughter of Regent Fujiwara Motofusa, who was first given at the age of sixteen to the victorious Yoshinaka of the Minamoto clan in an effort to restore the sagging fortunes of the Fujiwara family. The choice was ill-fated, as Yoshinaka soon parted company with his powerful relative Yoritomo, and met death a few months later. A number of modern historians believe that Ishi is the woman described in the *Heike Monogatari*, to whom Yoshinaka turned when he realized he was about to face defeat, and in her embrace managed to forget the battle.

Disgraced as the mistress of a fallen general, Ishi was again forced to sacrifice herself for her family, when she was given a second time to Koga (Minamoto) Michichika (1149-1202), an elderly poet of minor distinction and well known sensualist, who acted in the capital as a representative of the Kamakura government and served as Minister of the Centre (*Naidaijin*). Dōgen was the issue of this union, but never recognized as a legitimate member of the Koga family. Dōgen was raised by Michichika's son, Michitomo (1170-1227), a poet and editor of the *Shinkokinshū*; however, the two disgraces of his beautiful mother, that undoubtedly kept tongues at the capital wagging, must have made aristocratic life unbearable despite its comforts. Legend recounts that Dōgen's mother desired him to become a priest, and in view of her unhappiness, it would seem quite understandable if she imbued her young son with a strong sense of morality and dislike of worldliness.[28] She died when Dōgen was seven years old, and in his later years at the Eiheiji, Dōgen held two memorial services in her honour, and two for his foster-father (and half-brother) Michitomo. Ostensibly he omitted mention of his father Michichika, and traditional biographers also avoided the name, stating instead that his father was a ninth generation descendent of Emperor Murakami.[29] The circumstances of his birth and ignominious situation of his mother must have influenced the impressionable young Dōgen, and we can imagine that this was a factor in the development of his aloof and austere moralism of later years.

By the spring of 1212, Dōgen decided to abandon his clouded aristocratic life and go to his mother's brother, Ryōkan on Mt. Hiei, for advice upon entering the Tendai order. He was sent to the Senkōbō in Yokawa the same year that Jien became Tendai abbot for the third time, and Dōgen soon learned that the ideal of the monks on Mt. Hiei was attainment of worldly success.

In 1213, Kōen became the seventieth abbot of Tendai, and during the spring of that year, Dōgen received his first ordination, although it is dubious that he received the Tendai bodhisattva *śīla*, since he had not yet reached the required age of twenty. At this time Mt. Hiei was embroiled in a number of worldly disputes. The Enryakuji and Kōfukuji were quarrelling over the ownership of the Kiyomizudera, an event that led to Kōen's resignation and Jien becoming abbot a fourth time. Also in 1214, Mt. Hiei and the Miidera were quarreling over the Hie festival, and this led to the involvement of the Tōdaiji, Kōfukuji and Kongōbuji, as well as numerous *sōhei* night raids. Theology was generally ignored on the mountain, and the common notion was that since man was inherently Enlightened (*hongaku shisō*), there was no need to exert further effort. According to legend, Dōgen questioned this view, wondering why the patriarchs of the past had endeavoured so seriously—and thence decided to leave Mt. Hiei.

After leaving the mountain, Dōgen first went to Kōin of the Miidera, who happened to be a disciple of Hōnen. Supposedly recognizing that Dōgen would not be satisfied with Pure Land teachings, Kōin sent him to the Kenninji temple where he met Eisai.

There is some historical question whether or not Dōgen actually met and studied under Eisai,[30] but if we accept the *Hōkyōki* (Memoirs of Dōgen's study in China), there Dōgen states that he first learned Rinzai under Senkō Zenji (Eisai). And in *Shōbōgenzō Zuimonki*, edited by Ejō, Dōgen repeatedly mentions the example of Eisai. Most scholars believe that Dōgen did have the opportunity to meet Eisai, but at the time, Eisai was over seventy and actively engaged in commuting between Kamakura and Kyoto, and it is most likely that he entrusted the fourteen or fifteen year old Dōgen to his disciple Myōzen. Unlike some of Eisai's earlier disciples, Myōzen was a young man who joined after Eisai's second trip to China and indoctrination in Zen, hence was capable of imparting a relatively pure form of Zen.

Dōgen became a disciple of Myōzen, and in 1223 left for China with his master. Undoubtedly Dōgen's trip was idealistically inspired in the search for true Dharma, but at the same time the aborted uprising of

Emperor Go-Toba during the Shōkyū war of 1221, led to extreme suffering among the aristocracy and remaining members of Dōgen's family. Even in view of his tenuous aristocratic connections, it was a good time to be absent from the capital, as the Hōjō regents carefully purged their enemies.

Upon arriving in China, Dōgen remained aboard ship for the first three months only briefly visiting Zen temples, while his master Myōzen immediately went to Mt. T'ien-Tung in memory of Eisai. Dōgen at first was very disappointed with the Chinese situation as he found the great temples to be bureaucratic and formalistic, lacking the spirit of true Zen. He was even astonished at the masters, for although the Zen rules carefully explained methods of hygiene such as cleaning the teeth, they were generally ignored, and Dōgen found that if he approached within two or three feet of a master, the stench was often unbearable.

One day, however, Dōgen was impressed by an elderly monk from Mt. A-yü-wang, in charge of meals for the monastery who came to the ship to buy dried Japanese mushrooms (shiitake). Since the trip was long, Dōgen invited the monk to spend the night and talk with him, but the monk refused on the grounds that not only did he have duties to perform, but it was contrary to the rule for a monk to spend a night outside the monastery without permission. The young Dōgen was impressed by such conscientiousness, and inquired why one so old chose to do arduous kitchen duties instead of simple meditation or practicing the kōan. To that the old monk replied, that Dōgen did not understand pien-tao (Jap. bendō), meaning ' to make endeavours to practice the way.' Evidently this was Dōgen's first encounter with the idealistic and practical Zen taught by Hui-neng's successors.

Next Dōgen decided to join his master Myōzen at Mt. T'ien-t'ung. At that time this mountain housed one of the greatest Chinese monasteries of the day, the Ching-te-szu, ranking equivalent to the Gozan in Japan. It was a bureaucratic temple, but followed Zen monastic rules on a grand scale. Evidently Dōgen found his treatment at this monastery to be quite humble, and since the monks were ranked in accordance with their *vinaya* ordination as well as seniority, Dōgen found himself at the lowest end of the table at mealtimes. This may have been a result of Chinese ethnocentrism as well as the Chinese Zen emphasis upon Hīnayāna *vinaya*. Dōgen had studied some *vinaya* under his master Myōzen, but in this area he had virtually no seniority. According to legend, Dōgen appealed the situation in a petition to the Emperor and received a responsive hearing, but this is quite dubious, for it seems unlikely that the Emperor of China would have time to listen to a recently arrived young foreign monk's complaints about his ranking at the table and the improper precedence of Hīnayāna *vinaya* in Chinese Zen monasteries.

Soon after Dōgen began to reside at Mt. T'ien-t'ung, he had occasion to meet the old kitchen monk from Mt. A-yü-wang again. At that time he inquired the significance of the Chinese letter *Wu* (Emptiness or Nothingness) and the ancient monk replied " 1, 2, 3, 4, 5." When Dōgen further questioned the nature of *pien-tao*, the old monk answered, 'Everything in the universe has it.' Thus Dōgen came to comprehend the simplicity of truth, or the fact that actual daily life constituted true religious life.

At Mt. T'ien-t'ung, Dōgen began to study under the master Wu-chi Liao-p'ai of the Lin-chi Huang-lung Ta-hui school. And it was now that he finally gained his first glimpse of the secret record of transmission of the master. The desire to see the transmission records of various Zen masters began to absorb Dōgen from shortly after his arrival in China, for he quickly realized that this document, listing the transmission of the Buddha's spirit or Enlightenment, was of fundamental significance and a characteristic of Zen in contrast to other schools of Buddhism. Ordination documents attesting that the master had set his seal of approval (*inka*) upon the Enlightenment of his disciples were also important, but the secret transmission records alone listed the names of the patriarchs and founders of the various schools, thus to transmit a new movement properly, it was essential to have one's name listed among those 'Buddhas.' As Dōgen was later to explain in the *Shōbōgenzō*:

> Only Buddhas transmit the Dharma to Buddhas, the patriarchs to patriarchs, this is the nature of attainment. This is the single

transmission and therefore is Supreme Enlightenment. Unless one is a Buddha, he cannot certify another Buddha, and unless one obtains the certification of a Buddha, he cannot be a Buddha.[31]

Dōgen had already seen the secret transmission records of the Lung-men Fu-yen school as well as the Yün-men school. He had further learned that in China it was even possible for laymen, merchants or women upon occasion, to purchase the right to be listed in succession records by corrupt masters, regardless of their understanding, but the truly great masters were quite scrupulous in their choice of legitimate successors, and it was exceedingly difficult to obtain this honour. Allegedly, Wu-chi later offered Dōgen the privilege to succeed him on several occasions, but according to tradition, the young man was dissatisfied with the worldliness of the Ta-hui school and later in his writings severely criticized this school, although not his early master Wu-chi.

In 1224 when Wu-chi died, Dōgen went on a pilgrimage to various other temples and was about to return to Japan in the belief that there was nothing further to be learned in China, when a monk brought him the news that Ju-ching (1163–1268) had come to Mt. T'ien t'ung as the new abbot. Ju-ching was a Ts'ao-tung master of the Tsu-an Chih-chien tradition and known for the purity of his practice as well as his strict discipline. In Dōgen's Hōkyōki, he relates how unusual it was for Ju-ching to accept disciples or grant interviews, but in the case of Dōgen, the master invited him to come at any time. Perhaps he had an intuitive feeling regarding Dōgen's ability and zeal. Dōgen regularly consulted with him on every detail—even how to properly wear his tabi.

Life at the monastery under Ju-ching was very difficult and the monks were allowed only a couple of hours of sleep a night. During this period Dōgen's former Japanese master Myōzen died at the age of forty-two, and Dōgen performed the funeral service, later taking the ashes back with him to the Kenninji in Japan.

In the fall of 1225, Dōgen attained Enlightenment under Ju-ching and received his inka. Supposedly this happened when Dōgen heard the master reproving a dozing monk asking, 'Why do you sleep? You must drop off the body and the mind !' Modern scholars point out that the idiom 'drop off the body and mind' (Jap. *shinjin datsuraku*) is peculiarly Japanese, and that most likely Ju-ching used 'dust' (Jap. *jin* 塵 Chin. *ch'en*) rather than 'body (Jap. *shin* 身 Chin. *shen*), or in other words, 'drop off the dust of mind,' a typical Zen idiom.[32] Thus Dōgen accidently or deliberately had a 'tremendous misconception' that resulted in the development of a unique depth to his philosophy.[33] In his writings Dōgen implies that *shinjin datsuraku* was one of the most important teachings of his master Ju-ching, however, in the Chinese Zen records of Ju-ching, the phrase is found only once. In the context of 'dropping the dust of the mind to remove the five desires and five hindrances,' it makes perfect sense, although it was a very common statement and can be found even in words attributed to the historical Buddha. But Dōgen uniquely interpreted this as 'to drop the mind and body,' being equivalent to *zazen* (meditation), wherein the devotee engages in mere sitting in place of such physical activities as chanting, incense offering, etc. If this interpretation was a misconception, it was not Dōgen's only one as scholars point out, like Shinran, Dōgen did this frequently, due to either an unfamiliarity with Chinese, or by placing his thoughts in the words of the master or sutra to cloak them with orthodoxy. Such 'misconceptions' successfully added a new dimension to Japanese Buddhism.

In 1227, Dōgen returned to Japan at the age of twenty-seven and announced that unlike other monks, he had 'returned empty-handed,' despite the collection of Zen mementos he carried. While Dōgen had been in China, a few changes had occurred in Japan, Hōjō Yasutoki was now regent, but the violence of the Enryakuji *sōhei* and religious quarrels had not ceased. At first Dōgen settled at the Kenninji temple and there, the year of his return he wrote the *Hukan Zazengi*, which summarizes the essence of *zazen* and announces it to be the sole practice. This work formed the foundation of the new Sōtō sect that he was about to initiate.

In 1230, he left the Kenninji and moved six or seven kilometers south to the Annyōin in Fukakusa. The reasons for his move are uncertain, but it is generally believed he received warning that the monks of Mt. Hiei were about to attack and deport him from the city. It is also possible that he had become dissatisfied with the corruption and stagnation of the Kenninji. The same year Dōgen's famous grandfather Fujiwara Motofusa, died at the age of eighty-six.

While at the Annyōin, Dōgen wrote the *Bendōwa*, the first chapter in his celebrated *Shōbōgenzō*, explaining why Zen was suited for Japan. In this work he set forth eighteen articles to encourage the practice of *zazen*, at the same time, levelling some harsh criticism against the practices of Tendai, Shingon, Kegon and the Pure Land—comparing the constant chanting of the *nembutsu* to the fruitless croaking of a frog day and night in the spring rice-field. He did imply in this work that women and laymen were capable of Enlightenment, an idea he later seemingly set aside in his preoccupation with the monastic life.

In 1233 the nearby Gokurakuji temple was restored by Shōkaku Zenni, Fujiwara Noriie and others, the remaining hall renamed the Kannondōri-in and Dōgen was invited to teach Zen. There he proceeded to set up a Zen monastery with three main buildings:

1) Monks hall (*Sōdō*)—for living quarters and *zazen*
2) Dharma hall (*Hattō*)—place for senior monks to preach
3) Buddha hall (*Butsuden*)—for rituals and considered to be least essential

Upon completion in 1236, the complex was renamed the Kannondōri-in Kōshōhōrinji.

During 1234, Dōgen attracted one of his most important disciples, his future successor Koun Ejō (1198–1280). Two years older than Dōgen, Ejō had initially belonged to Dainichi Nōnin's movement, and upon the death of that master, the majority of his disciples elected to join Dōgen. Thus Dōgen gained the basis of an order, and he commenced to write the first section of his Zen monastic precepts later to be known as the *Eiheiji Shingi*.

In order to defend his fledgling movement, Dōgen submitted a petition to court entitled the *Gokokushōbōgi*, in which he argued that true Zen was the sole Buddhist Dharma to protect the nation. Immediately this stirred up a protest from Mt. Hiei, and they charged Dōgen was actually teaching the interpretation of a *Pratyeka* (Self-Enlightened) Buddha and not true Mahāyāna, therefore his Dharma could only harm the nation. The Court yielded to Tendai pressure in this matter, and Dōgen was placed in a difficult position. In fact, many historians conclude that this was the main reason for his abrupt withdrawal from the capital to Echizen.[34] But at the same time that Dōgen aroused the enmity of Mt. Hiei, he also encountered a severe form of competition from Bennen, who had just returned from China with the popular Zen teachings of Wu-chun, the forceful patronage of Kujō Michiie, and settled practically next door to Dōgen to build the prestigious Tōfukuji. Bennen's group, in the *Enmitsuzenkai* tradition, after some struggle eventually managed to establish friendly relations with the older established temples. It also won the patronage of the Fujiwara family and other aristocrats, since it freely used the esoteric rituals so popular with the aristocracy. This competition must have posed a major threat to Dōgen in his attempt to propagate pure Zen. And at nearly the same time, Dōgen received from China a text from his master Ju-ching, and was reminded of his master's parting admonition 'that he should retire deep into the forest and educate only a few elect disciples,' this advice Dōgen chose to follow.

Dōgen's move to Echizen removed his school for the remainder of his lifetime from the mainstream of Kamakura Buddhism. For whereas the other new sects all stressed *mappō shisō* and advocated universal Enlightenment; Dōgen rejected *mappō* and now seemingly repudiated the idea that laymen or women were capable of attaining Enlightenment by centering all his efforts upon monks (*shukke*), and even here his ideal became 'to educate one, or even a portion of one follower' (*ikko hanko*) perfectly in the pure Dharma rather than having a large group of disciples. Perhaps this attitude, as critics imply, was the result of failure in Kyoto to meet Bennen's competition and thus he retreated.[35] In one area however, Dōgen's school was similar to all the other new Kamakura Buddhist movements—the emphasis upon a single practice, in his case the sole practice of *zazen* (*shikan taza*). And unlike the Pure Land advocates who sought to include other practices *within* the *nembutsu*, Dōgen saw no compromise and believed that his Dharma *alone* represented Absolute Truth. *Zazen* was *the* path to Enlightenment and all others *upāya*, which he chose to regard as inferior. In fact, he even objected to calling his school the Zen-*shū* or Sōtō-*shū*, since this intimated it was merely one sect of Buddhism; he believed it *was* Buddhism. Such an uncompromising attitude was unlikely to win Dōgen popularity—hence his move to Echizen cut him off almost completely from the affairs of the Court and the government at Kamakura.

The layman Hatano Yoshishige invited Dōgen to Echizen and at first he stayed at the old Yoshiminedera until Hatano completed the Daibutsuji. This was later renamed the Eiheiji in honour of the tenth year of the Eihei era (67 A.D.), when Buddhism allegedly was transmitted to China. There may have been reasons other than Hatano's patronage for Dōgen's choice of location at Echizen, as it seems a number of the former disciples of Nōnin came from the area, and we can imagine that they influenced Dōgen's choice.

During his peaceful sojourn at the Eiheiji, Dōgen was invited to Kamakura by Hōjō Tokiyori during the winter of 1247 and spent some months at the centre of government. But it seems that this was not a happy or successful experience and Dōgen was relieved to return back to his peaceful solitude.

In the summer of 1252, Dōgen's health began to fail and the preaching record of the temple indicates that year he drastically reduced the number of his sermons. By the new year of 1253 he realized that he was about to die and wrote a draft of the *Hachidainingaku* (Eight Teachings of the Superior Man). This was based upon the *Yuikyōkyō* (*I-chiao-ching sutra*) allegedly setting forth the essence of Śākyamuni's teaching just prior to his death, which Dōgen interpreted in eight points:

1) to reduce desire
2) to attain satisfaction
3) to enjoy (seek) serenity
4) to make efforts
5) not to engage in improper thought (to maintain concentration)
6) to practice meditation

7) to practice wisdom

8) not to engage in improper discussion (useless debate, etc.)

One day as Dōgen lay seriously ill, he called his disciple Tettsū Gikai (1232-1309) to his bedside and imparted instructions for the future of his order. Why he particularly chose this monk or the nature of his instructions are uncertain—it is possible he felt close to death, but this event later had far reaching implications in the division of Dōgen's order.

Persuaded by his friend and patron Hatano, Dōgen decided to go to Kyoto for treatment on the fifth day of the eighth month in 1253, accompanied by his trusted disciple Ejō. There on the twentieth day of the same month, Dōgen died at the age of fifty-four. He was cremated at Higashiyama, and Ejō returned to the Eiheiji with his ashes and performed the funeral service. In 1854 Emperor Kōmei granted Dōgen the posthumous title of Busshō Dentō Kokushi, and in 1879, Emperor Meiji elevated him to become Jōyō Daishi.

2. Dōgen's Interpretation of 'Transmission Outside the Scriptures' (*Kyōgebetsuden*)

A characteristic of Zen thought is the belief in an intuitive means of transmitting the experience of the Buddha's Enlightenment. Recognizing language incapable of communicating even ordinary human experience without severe distortion, they reject the possibility that language can ever convey a spiritual experience as profound as Enlightenment. In this respect, they follow closely in the footsteps of the Mādhyamika tradition, although their denial of human language in favour of intuition is presented in an earthy and practical fashion rather than as a dialectic philosophy.

Symbolically, Zen traces its origin to the time when the historical Buddha held a flower up to his audience and its significance was grasped only by Mahākāśyapa, who quietly smiled. This flower and smile (*nenge mishō*), have always represented the ideal Zen approach, uncluttered by the half truths and false conceptualizations inherent within traditional forms of communication. For some, the intuitive approach must first be achieved by a shock and jar to the reason in order to create a receptive ground, but ultimately it reflects the simple and direct interpenetration or transmission from mind to mind (*ishin denshin*) without the use of words (*furyū monji*).

Dōgen sought to express the significance of this dynamic intuitive communication in the title of his major work. Literally, *Shōbōgenzō* denotes 'storehouse (*zō*) of the eye (*gen*) of the true dharma (*shobō*).' And in it he sought to clarify the nature of the intuitive experience as well as the essential form of its transmission. A major criticism he directed against the entire notion of 'transmission outside the scriptures' (*kyō-gebetsuden*), was that he believed such a concept implied the existence of an actual 'teaching' beside the scriptures, and thus managed to convey two false impressions: first, that a body of *doctrine* was being transmitted rather than an intuitive experience, and secondly, that the scriptures themselves could not be conducive to Enlightenment.[36] As he reasoned, if it be possible for individuals to receive the intuitive experience of Enlightenment by observing the serenity of nature and thereby 'hearing' the Buddha's preaching in the whispering of the wind or the bubbling of a mountain stream, then it also must be possible to penetrate the symbolic language of the scriptures and receive the same experience.[37] Although Dōgen rejected the traditional paraphernalia of religion such as incense offering, sutra chanting, veneration of the Buddha, etc. as secondary or inferior practices, he was not insensitive to the fact that if an individual be spiritually receptive, the scriptures were capable of exerting the same soteriological effect as the observance of nature—it all depended upon the attitude of mind. Similarly he did not believe that the popular Zen concept of 'no-words' (*furyū monji*) actually was a prohibition against human language, as he was aware of the potentiality of language to stir the receptive mind.[38] In this manner, Dōgen sought to balance some of the extreme views found among contemporary Zen followers. Although he personally set forth sitting in meditation alone (*shikan taza*) as the ideal practice, he did not completely disprove of the benefits of other forms of devotion.

A prime consideration for Dōgen after emphasizing the intuitive nature of the communication of Enlightenment, was the method of transmission. He summarily rejected such appelations as Zen or Sōtō for his movement, since he had complete confidence that he was transmitting *Buddhism* itself, and in this respect he had a confidence not unlike Nichiren, of being orthodox among the orthodox.[39]

In his particular emphasis upon transmission as the essence of Zen life, like all other Zen masters, Dōgen placed the burden of finding the proper master upon the disciple. In fact he viewed the encounter between a disciple and his true master just short of destiny.[40] This is one characteristic of Zen that has met modern criticism, since it would seem in the Mahāyāna spirit that the master should seek disciples, whereas the Zen attitude has always been for the master to engage in an extremely passive, at times even hostile attitude towards potential disciples. When urged to go to the Kamakura area to teach Zen, Dōgen replied:

> If anyone wants to study Buddhism, he will come here, even if he has to cross mountains, rivers and seas. If I take my teaching to people who do not have the desire to study, I don't know whether they will listen to me. Might I not just be leading people astray for the sake of my own livelihood or because I want material wealth? This would just wear me out, I can't see the point in going.
>
> *Shōbōgenzō Zuimonki*[41]

Such a haughty attitude appears to contrast with the life of the historical Buddha or spirit of Mahāyāna, and perhaps encourages the tendency to regard Zen, with its emphasis upon *vinaya* practice and monasticism, as representing the Hīnayāna spirit. Dōgen's Zen was essentially a religion to seek the way (*kyūdō*) and not to progagate the teachings (*fukyō*).[42]

The main priority in Dōgen's teaching was the way of learning (*gakudō*), in which he included the self-reflection that leads to 'dropping the body and the mind.' And it is clear that although he makes certain mention in his writings of working to benefit others, his chief concern was with the dedicated disciple, whose karma led him to the proper Zen master with whom he could engage in the single practice of sitting-meditation (*shikan taza*). Virtually he offered no solution for those who were disinclined to embark upon a stern monastic life, or for women, who were not allowed the privilege of becoming proper disciples. Although on occasion he speaks of the potentiality for laymen and women to attain Enlightenment,[43] his writings imply that monks alone are the chosen few who will attain Buddhahood.

Some critics view Dōgen's attitude as aristocratic,[44] however, those familiar with the monastic life will quickly recognize it as a common attitude shared among monastics, that makes the abrasiveness of living in close contact with imperfect humans bearable. For as long as an outer world of hopeless sinful creatures destined to future misery can be imagined, the harsh, boring daily discipline, accompanied by constant observation of one's own failing can be endured—if the 'chosen' are weak, how much more deplorable must the rest of mankind be? Their attitude towards laity and women—or the entire non-monastic society, was therefore paternalistic, for they had no reason to imagine equality. The elect who were chosen to join their ranks and attain Buddhahood would feel the call to come in search of the perfect master—as for the rest, they could merely hope to benefit from the virtues acquired by the monks.

3. Practice Equals Attainment

One of the key concepts in Dōgen's philosophy was his unique notion of practice (gyōji). Although ultimately he defined it as equivalent to zazen (meditation), in its broadest sense, he also interpreted practice as encompassing every action in life.[45] This can be compared with the popular Zen notion of 'Natural Mind is the Way' (heijōshin koredō), with the exception that Dōgen carefully avoided expressing daily actions in the terminology of Ma-tsu and his followers; such vulgar items as the dung-scraper were abhorrent to him.

Dōgen's concept of every action being equivalent to practice was based upon the philosophy of Original Enlightenment (hongaku shisō), wherein all human actions basically are viewed as the actions of the Buddha—but one important point he stressed was the fact that such actions comprise *perpetual* endeavour. This was the answer to the question he posed early in his religious life,—if one engages in practice in the hope of attaining Enlightenment, then after achieving that goal, why continue to practice? Dōgen's final answer was that practice (which he primarily identified with *zazen*) and attainment, were in fact identical (*shūshō ichinyo*).[46] Enlightenment was not an abstract entity to be sought and acquired, but rather an instrinsic part of the so-called means in itself. This was Dōgen's solution to the age-old problem in Buddhism of contrasting the means with the goal, and in many cases of falsely accepting either one or the other as a final resting place. Just as the historical Buddha during his lifetime emphasized the need for continuous practice after Enlightenment, and Nāgārjuna in his Mādhyamika philosophy set forth the notion of *Sūnyatā artha* (practice of Enlightenment), in order to demonstrate the actions of the Enlightened One in the everyday world, so Dōgen also felt the need to resolve this misunderstood dichotomy.

In a manner not unlike Shinran's concept of repeated chantings of the *nembutsu* for the purpose of thanksgiving, Dōgen believed this continual practice after attainment was a form of returning virtue or one's obligations (*hōon*). In other words dedicating one's body and actions as a form of gratitude to the manifestation of Reality or *Dharmadhātu*, in which we all participate.

4. The Manifestation and Attainment of Ultimate Reality as *Genjō Kōan*

As we have earlier noted the *kōan* was a major practice of Rinzai Zen, and although Dōgen acknowledged its usage as beneficial, he in no way granted it equality with his single practice of sitting-meditation (*shikan taza*). Yet the first chapter of his own arrangement of the *Shōbōgenzō* (the modern chronological edition places it third), is entitled *Genjō kōan*. Many Zen scholars even believe he considered this particular chapter to represent the essence of his teachings.[47]

Dōgen viewed the *genjō kōan* in a very different manner than the traditional Zen *kōan*. *Genjō* literally means 'to manifest and achieve,' while Dōgen considered *kōan*, as a 'public document' or 'standard of judgement,' to be synonymous with truth. In his view, *genjō kōan* denoted the 'manifestation and achievement of truth'—further interpreted in terms of Kegon philosophy as the 'manifestation of the *Dharmadhātu* (Ultimate Reality) and attainment of Enlightenment.' Dōgen's definition is as follows:

> The fish swims in water without ever mastering the water, the bird flies in the air without ever mastering the air . . . and if the bird is placed outside of air it will surely die, as the fish will surely die placed outside water. One must realize that water is life and air is life . . . Considering this fact, if there should be birds and fish who try to fly or swim only after they have mastered the air and water, then they will never find a path (to fly) nor a place (to swim) in either the air or water. When one realizes this in accord with his own actions, then that is *genjō kōan*.[48]

What he meant is that reality cannot be separated from the individual's present actions and experience. If we stop and refuse to act until we thoroughly understand the nature of life and our future goal, we will wither away from atrophy. Our finite minds can never comprehend the infinite, just as the bird is incapable of objectively meditating upon the nature of flight and its course. Although the bird may spend its life flying, it can never begin to fathom the limitless bounds of the sky, nor can a single fish ever hope to touch all the depths and breadths of the oceans and seas. The only reality for the bird is its present flight, and for the fish its momentary place in the sea. In the same way, the only reality for man is his present action, beyond this there is nothing more, nothing less. There is no transcendent goal to seek to be Enlightened, for Enlightenment (the manifestation of Reality) consists in merely living, acting and being at the present moment.

In a slightly different manner, Dōgen explained *genjō kōan* as follows:

> To master the Buddha way is to master oneself,
> To master oneself is to forget oneself,
> To forget oneself is to realize the myriads of dharmas,
> To realize the myriads of dharmas is to drop one's body and mind, and the body and mind of others.[49]

Just as the bird cannot find a path in the sky by any other means than soaring into the sky and uniting with it in flight, so man must drop all his dualistic differentiation and clinging to self to merge with Ultimate Reality or the Manifestation of existence—thus practice and attainment become identical. And it was upon such a conception that Dōgen formulated his theory of the Buddha nature and time.

5. All Existents are the Buddha Nature

Deliberately misreading the famous quotation in the *Nehangyō:* (lit.) "Everywhere exists the Buddha nature," (悉有佛性) as "all existents are the Buddha nature," Dōgen attempted to destroy the misconception that the Buddha nature eternally existed as some form of entity or Being.

The endless human longing for a lasting permanence (Skt. *ātman*) within either the individual or in the universe plagued Buddhism from its inception. Although the *anātman* theory was endlessly repeated in Early Buddhism, the growth of Mahāyāna philosophy with new concepts such as the 'Buddha nature', once again allowed the *ātman* to slip in again in a new form. There were always those who forgot that the 'Buddha nature' simply meant the 'quality of Enlightenment' and attempted to transform it into some form of individual soul or monistic Being. To such people, the notion of impermanence (Jap. *mujō*) was repugnant, since their aim was to find something durable and abiding to cling to in the face of the change they constantly saw reflected in the world about them, which frightened and intimidated them. To make such individuals aware of the misguided nature of their hopes, Dōgen was fond of quoting Hui-neng's phrase: "impermanence is the Buddha nature,"[50] for he believed that the mountains, trees, water and all the manifestations of Reality (*genjō kōan*), including human beings, were the Buddha nature. This is why he so specifically read the quotation as (noun) 'all existents', rather than (verb) 'everywhere exists.' There was nothing solid to grasp or cling to—no self or Being. The Buddha might be eternal, but an eternal impermanence consisting of the constant rise and fall of transitory existents.

After first demolishing the myth of the Buddha nature as representing an eternal Being, Dōgen secondly wished to make certain that his followers did not cling to the belief that the Buddha nature might represent some form of entity or essence (*ātman*) within themselves. One way he did this was to severely attack the Zen concept of *kenshō* (to discover the 'true nature') on the grounds that it gave the false impression that a 'true nature' or other form of solid essence existed within the individual. Here he even went so far as to declare the *Platform Sutra of the Sixth Patriarch* a forgery, since it used the term 'discover the true nature.'[51] A second method was his interpretation of the 'mind is the Buddha.'

Sokushinzebutsu (*Mind is the Buddha*)

Man's first pitfall was to translate his human longing for permanence into an eternal Being, but second, and closely related was the attempt to find a source of permanence within himself, thus in order to use the term 'mind is the Buddha' (*sokushinzebutsu*), Dōgen first had to be certain that neither the 'mind' nor the 'Buddha' would be regarded as permanent entities.[52] He then interpreted *sokushinzebutsu* as 'the mind commenced upon the way' (*hosshin shugyō bodai nehan*), or literally, 'the raised mind practicing to attain Bodhi and Nirvana.'[53] This definition was aimed at eliminating a third misconception—namely, that all the base functions of the ignorant mind could be equated with Buddhahood. In keeping with his earlier identification of practice and attainment, Dōgen in this instance equated the mind *dedicated* to the pursuit of Enlightenment or acting in an authentic manner, with Buddhahood. In his view, "all existents (the manifestation of Reality or *genjō kōan*) of which sentient beings form a part, is the Buddha nature.[54] This nature cannot be 'sought' after, as there is nothing substantial to seek. Man cannot stop living and acting to discover the nature of the Reality in which he participates, anymore than the bird can stop flying in order to trace its path in the air. The present moment and present action constitute Reality, this is why they are to be called the 'actions of the Buddha' (*gyōbutsu*). And the functions of the mind of one who lives in an authentic manner (seeking the way), be they love or hate (more properly stated as attraction and repulsion), become the *bodhi* mind or 'mind of the Buddha' (*sokushinzebutsu*).

In this instance, 'mind' is not artificially separated from 'body' anymore than 'practice' can be separated from 'attainment,' thus *sokushinzebutsu* means the individual who attains Enlightenment, and achieves a mind free from discrimination following the sole practice of meditation (*shikan taza*).[55] Since in Zen, the quality of Enlightenment is directly transmitted, the experience of that person becomes identical to the Enlightenment of the historical Buddha Śākyamuni and all the Buddhas of the past, or in Dōgen's words:

> Various Buddhas symbolize Śākyamuni Buddha, and Śākyamuni Buddha symbolizes the 'mind is the Buddha' (*sokushinzebutsu*) . . . When one becomes an Enlightened Buddha, together with the various Buddhas of the past, present and future, certainly one will become Śākyamuni Buddha, this is precisely *sokushinzebutsu*.[56]

The Absolute Now or Totality of the Moment

The basis of the Buddhist doctrine of impermanence is the law of Interdependent Origination (Skt. *Pratītya-samutpāda*), wherein all existents are believed to rise and fall in accord with interrelated conditions. Dōgen's notion of the *genjō kōan* was in effect another expression of the dynamic functioning of Interdependent Origination, and it was natural with his concern for the temporary manifestations of Reality, that he would be interested in exploring the significance of time. In his *Shōbōgenzō*, he has one chapter (*U-ji*) devoted to 'existence is time" as well as numerous other references. His views closely follow the Buddhist tradition, but there is a uniqueness in his method of presentation, as well as the manner in which it leads to the sole practice of meditation (*shikan taza*). Basically, following his thought, time can be classified into six categories:[57]

a. Self-identity of Existence and Time

In Buddhism, time cannot be regarded as an empty hollow concept for it is inseparably related with existence. 'Existence is not placed within the framework of time, but existence itself is time.'[58] For example, when we think of morning, a number of sensory phenomenal characteristics come to mind, such as the rising of the sun, the crowing of a rooster, the smell of breakfast cooking, the sound of the school bus, etc. All of these things immediately conjure up the picture of morning even without the verification of a clock. Time has no significance without existence, for time must always be considered in relation to some-*thing*. Even such a prosaic hour as four o'clock in the afternoon can only derive its meaning in terms of existence—besides its point on the clock or watch, which separates it from other hours, it must be thought of in reference to some-*thing*—i.e., an appointment, the end of class, the waning sun, two hours before dinner, time in summer for a swim but in winter for hot tea, etc. Time on an empty planet lacking even a change in light or darkness would be utterly without significance—thus time and existence must be viewed as inseparably related.

b. Specific Time

Each single moment is captured and isolated in the midst of the infinite continuity of time. This is common man's view of time, he isolates the moments, names them and builds upon them to create the day, week, month or year. In the Buddhist view, Dōgen took this notion of time one step further by seeing the position of each existent during the isolated moment—its temporary condition and the space it occupies. For example, at this specific moment of time, a dog is stretched out on the study floor before the fire with its head resting upon a book—a few minutes from now the dog may be outside playing with its mates, the book back upon the shelf, the fire dying out and the lights off in an empty study. Each moment contains a similar multitude of relationships. Dōgen could even imagine the condition of the peak of a mountain or depth of an ocean in a moment of time[59]—for from the far reaches of the stars to each individual spot on earth, the single isolated moment holds an infinite number of happenings and captures numberless existents.

c. Basic Time

Beneath all the separate moments that man accepts, is an endless un-fathomable form of time, contrary in every respect to the isolated frag-ments we know. For if the progressive moments of time were the only real time, Nirvana would be such a moment, briefly passing from future to present—yet Nirvana is far more than that. Although this time cannot be regarded as substantial, for it too is interdependent, it engulfs all that the senses cannot discern and transcends the phenomenal world, running as a basic original time.

d. Principle of Continuity in Time

The ceaseless continuity of the moment in an endless system that be-comes equivalent to the process of human experience—continually flowing from past to future and vice versa.

e. Absolute Present

Dōgen, in typical Zen manner, enigmatically defined the Absolute present as, 'the continuity of non-continuity.'[60] Here he takes into con-sideration the isolated fraction of a second (non-continuity) that common man grasps, as well as the constant eternal manifestation of each moment of time (continuity). He explains this in the following manner:

> Firewood becomes ash and cannot revert back to firewood, however, one should not cling to the idea that firewood pre-cedes and ash follows. We must realize that firewood is at the state of firewood existence, and even though we may con-sider its future and past, before and after, these are separate. Ash is at the state of ash existence, and has its own before and after. Just as once firewood becomes ash, it can never revert back to firewood, so after death, one can never revert back to birth. It is the tradition of Buddhist Dharma not to consider that birth becomes death, thus it is called non-birth. The fact that death will not become birth is due to the Buddha's turning of the wheel of the Dharma, therefore it is called non-extinction. Birth is a single state of existence and death

is a single state of existence. It is like winter and spring, one should not think that winter can become spring nor does spring become winter.[61]

Since there is no underlying 'essence' in the first place, winter is not some-*thing* that can change into spring, nor birth into death. Nāgārjuna denied in his famous Eightfold Negation that there could be 'birth or extinction, annihilation or permanence, identity or diversity, coming or departure,' for all such notions imply the coming or going of some-*thing*. In a like manner, Dōgen believed the quality of the present practice cannot be *transformed* into Enlightenment, since no-*thing* exists to transform. Total reality is the existential here and now; the practice of the moment *is* Enlightenment.

The Absolute Eternal Now is timeless, without beginning or end, self-contained, yet perpetually dynamic. This is the paradoxical moment that defies man's logical attempts to capture it and reduce it to either a building block for the future, or consummation of the past. Dōgen defined this vitality as, 'from today continues today,'[62] meaning in ef-fect, that 'today is always today'—for time flows from the present of this moment to the present of the next 'this moment', and thus embraces past and future in the eternal moving present.

f. Applied Time or Time in Practice

Briefly can be defined as the soteriological role of time. Dōgen's view was that time cannot exist without practice (*gyōji*), and this is in keeping with the Zen notion that 'everyday is a good day, every time a good time' for practice—or that one hundred years of living can be achieved within one day,—depending upon the profound realization of the true meaning of life.[63] Just as Dōgen could visualize the dynamically chang-ing moment (=existent), transitory in nature to be the Buddha nature, so he believed that each moment of practice formed a totality within itself. One must live each moment for itself and within itself—thus it is improper to say 'birth leads to death', for birth is a moment totally unique in itself:

Merely considering birth and death are Nirvana, one should neither avoid birth and death nor seek Nirvana; only at such a moment can one become free of birth and death. It is improper to consider that birth leads to death, for birth is a temporary state separate from future and past, therefore in Buddhist Dharma birth is called non-birth. Extinction is also a temporary state separate from past and future, therefore extinction is called non-extinction. So when we speak of birth, there is nothing other than birth, and when we say extinction, there is nothing other than extinction.[64]

Since each moment is a totality within itself, the ultimate time becomes sitting-meditation (*shikan-taza*). For although by itself the hour possesses no meaning—if the individual occupies it with meditation, he is capable of condensing the experience and wisdom of a hundred years within the moment.

As Dōgen's philosophy was exceedingly abstract and experiential, designed for those wholly committed to the discovery of religious truth, it offered meagre fare for the layman with little time to devote to meditation; yet Dōgen's Sōtō Zen was able to develop into a mass lay movement, while the popular Rinzai of the capital failed to do so. In order to understand how Dōgen's monastic community based upon the single-practice of *zazen* managed to evolve into the largest Zen following in present day Japan, we will turn to examine the evolution of the Sōtō order.

6. Foundation of the Sōtō Sect

After Dōgen's death, he was succeeded at the Eiheiji, first by Koun Ejō (1198–1280), editor of the *Shōbōgenzō*, and secondly, by Tettsū Gikai (1219–1309). But at the time of the latter's succession, a dispute arose that divided the order. This argument, which superficially dealt with the problem of rank and seniority between Tettsū and the disciple Gien, represented a very complex problem.

From its origin, Dōgen's Sōtō order, unlike other Buddhist sects, was composed not only of direct disciples, but also of groups with similar views that chose to affiliate with his movement, such as the followers of Dainichibō Nōnin, who joined Dōgen prior to his move to the Eihei-ji. An order built upon such a loose federation rather than the strong ties of master-disciple loyalty, stood upon extremely tenuous ground. Although personal loyalty to the founder was not sufficient to prevent doctrinal divisions, as in the case of the Nichiren sect, it did provide a cohesiveness. This was a characteristic Japanese Zen lacked, for despite the emphasis upon orthodoxy of transmission, temple independence allowed a free choice in the change of affiliation. The Zen patriarchs may have possessed strong personalities, yet as they were mythologized, loyalty to them became spiritual rather than personal. The Rinzai school was never to attain unity as an order, and Dōgen's following would probably have shared the same fate if it had not become a popular mass movement with a necessity to focus upon the personality of the founder.

Some followers, like the Chinese monk Jakuen (Chin. Chi-yüan, d. 1299), who established a following at the Hōkyōji in Echizen, joined Dōgen because they believed he represented the pure Zen tradition of Sung China with its emphasis upon monastic life. However, certain direct disciples such as Tettsū, who had converted the Shingon Daijōji of Kaga into a Zen centre, were vitally aware of the popular movement of other Japanese sects towards the rural massess and anxious to emulate it. Although the influence of the Eiheiji did gradually spread through Echizen, Kaga and Noto provinces and even down to Kyūshū, expansion was hindered by the Zen monastic attitude. Perhaps if Dōgen's disciples had resided in the capital or centres of culture, they might not have noticed this disparity between the success of their order and popular movements, but living in the heart of the countryside among the rural population, it was nearly impossible to overlook the inroads of the early nembutsu and Shugen followers to fill the religious void in the lives of the masses.

The basis of the dispute between Tettsū and Gien was actually a clash between the conservative monastic followers, who sought to preserve Dōgen's simple and pure tradition of Zen—as represented by Gien;

and the progressives, led by Tettsū, concerned in making the Sōtō sect a mass movement.[65] The result was that Tettsū and his group permanently left the Eiheiji and made the Daijōji in Kaga their headquarters, having no further association with the Eiheiji until the late Muromachi when they came back to control the temple. The success of their movement was largely due to the efforts of one man, Keizan Jōkin.

7. Keizan Jōkin (1268-1325), the 'Second Patriarch'

Born in Echizen fifteen years after the death of Dōgen, Keizan is figuratively regarded by modern Sōtō followers as the 'second patriarch,'[66] since he is considered responsible for the evolution of the Sōtō mass movement. A disciple of Tettsū, during his youth Keizan studied under diverse Zen masters such as Ejō and Jakuen, leading Rinzai scholars, and even under some of the masters of the older traditions as well as Pure Land. As a result of this wide background, he was to assimilate teachings of the other schools into the Sōtō sect.

In converting the Daijōji temple from Shingon to Zen, Tettsū was the first to establish close relations with followers of the older sects; Keizan continued this policy. Gifted with rare leadership abilities and a willingness to assimilate, Keizan won further adherents from the older schools. He transformed the former Shingon Yōkōji into a leading centre of Zen studies, and also converted Jōken, the Ritsu master of the Shogakuji, making that temple into the prestigious Sōjiji, which later became the second headquarters of the Sōtō school.

Many of the older sects of Buddhism were in the process of expanding into the rural communities but, generally, they still considered themselves too aristocratic to be concerned with basic problems of the masses such as funerals. This was one area the followers of Keizan entered, assimilating popular esoteric rites of the older sects, as well as Shungendō, and devising simple funeral and memorial services that featured sermons on Buddhist teachings for warriors and commoners alike. At the same time, they also used popular esoteric rituals and prayers for worldly benefits (kajikitō), particularly during times of social unrest and natural calamities. Sōtō priests became leaders of causes for social action and engaged in projects such as constructing bridges, irrigation systems and forms of medical treatment. In this manner their activities came to sharply contrast with the Rinzai *Gozan* monasteries, that stood aloof from the peasants and were absorbed in foreign Chinese culture. Muromachi followers of Keizan even began to use Dōgen's quotations on faith as the nucleus of a mass movement. *Zazen* was not abandoned, but it was recognized as a difficult daily practice for the layman, and often replaced by the simple notion of taking refuge in the Buddha (*Namu kiebutsu*), a faith based upon the belief in the 'mind is the Buddha' (*sokushinzebutsu*).

By these means, the Sōtō sect was able to attract the masses, whereas Rinzai Zen failed to do so, largely because Sōtō followers were not restricted by the aristocratic *Gozan* framework. Isolated in the country-side, Sōtō priests felt a natural familiarity with the peasants. Few of them had the opportunity to visit Sung China, and this foreign cultural in-fluence that tended to alienate and create a disregard for the common people, was kept to a minimum. Finally, since the masses formed their audience, they made efforts to create popular events such as *jukai* (trans-mission of the *śīla*), in which large numbers could participate. In this manner, under the ideals of Keizan, the Sōtō order evolved into a mass movement.

Keizan died at the Yōkōji during the eighth month in 1325, at the age of fifty-eight, and in 1909 was granted the posthumous title of Jōsai Daishi by Emperor Meiji. Two outstanding successors continued his tradition: Meihō Sotetsu (1277-1350), third master of the Daijōji, and Gazan Shōseki (1275-1365), who resided at the Yōkōji and Sōjiji. Gazan proved to be the most successful of Keizan's disciples, due to his long life and outstanding ability to educate numbers of brilliant disciples who spread throughout Japan. One of the most remarkable examples was Tsūgen (1323-1391), founder of the Yōtakuji in Tamba province, a former well-known centre of Shugen practice. Ultimately the disciples of Gazan at the Sōjiji became the most prosperous congregation of Sōtō Zen and that temple came to exert a dominant role in Sōtō affairs.

8. Reunification of the Sōtō Order

Although the Eiheiji was not able to match the remarkable expansion of Gazan's Sōjiji, nor even of the Daijōji and Yōkōji, belonging to Meihō's followers, they did continue to steadily grow and never lost the prestige of being the original headquarters founded by Dōgen. And with the development of a mass movement, the role and personality of the founder and his original temple came to be more important to those working among the masses than to the monks engaged in simple Zen practice.

By the late Muromachi, with the rise of the great Daimyō, a movement occurred to bring all religious institutions in the various domains under central control. For the first time this created, at least within the domains of each single Daimyō, a horizontal association among previously isolated Zen temples, and eventually formed the nucleus for the gradual nationwide unification of the Sōtō congregation. As it picked up momentum, the rallying cry became, 'return to the ancient way,' which in effect meant establishing the personality of the founder Dōgen as a centre of unification for the mass movement. Such an effort naturally focused upon the Eiheiji temple, and would never have succeeded if by the mid-Muromachi, a number of monks belonging to the various temples of Keizan's tradition had not already begun to take up residence at the Eiheiji. In time they gained control, and it became quite simple to encourage nationwide unification under the Eiheiji, since followers of Keizan all over the country now felt welcome there.

By the year 1507, Emperor Go-Kashiwabara presented a plaque to the Eiheiji announcing that it was the foremost temple of the Sōtō school in the land, and in 1539 it received the official title of *Chokuganji* (Temple of the Imperial Vow). The prestige of the Eiheiji developed so rapidly that in order for lesser groups to establish proper lines of transmission, it became possible to purchase succession to the Eiheiji for a single night; thus the followers of obscure masters could claim that they were directly established by a former successor of the Eiheiji, headquarters of the Sōtō sect.

In 1589 the Sōjiji was recognized as the second principal temple of the Sōtō sect in honour of Keizan, and together these two headquarters temples have remained the centre of Sōtō activities up to modern day. A significant culmination in the development of Sōtō faith occurred in 1890, when Baisen (d. 1901) of the Sōjiji and Takushū (d. 1897) of the Eiheiji selected excerpts from the Shōbōgenzō and compiled the essence of Dōgen's teachings for the benefit of the laity. This became the Sōtō Kyōkai Shūshōgi (Teachings of Practice and Attainment in the Sōtō sect). The brief work contains a total of 3,704 Chinese and Japanese characters and is divided into five chapters dealing with: 1) the discovery of oneself in order to achieve a happy and significant life, 2) repentance, 3) acceptance of the śīla, 4) benefitting others, and 5) the practice of returning virtue in thanksgiving. The views presented are Dōgen's, with a slight change in arrangement that effectively provides a modern interpretation emphasizing faith. The Shūshōgi became the principal scripture of the modern Sōtō sect and is recited daily at all important functions. Its completion symbolized the Sōtō evolution from a monastic order to the second largest Buddhist congregation in modern day Japan.

C. Other Zen Movements

Besides the Sōtō and Rinzai schools, a number of independent Zen movements flourished during the Kamakura and Muromachi periods. Many of these formed loose affiliations with the dominant schools, but three deserve special mention for their unique character:

1. Wanshi-ha (Chin. Hung-chih school)

An offspring of the Chinese Sōtō school brought to Japan in 1309 by Tonmin Enichi (Chin. Tung-ming Hui-jih, 1272–1340), the fifth successor of Hung-chih Cheng-chio. Tonmin came upon the invitation of Hōjō Sadatoki and resided at the Engakuji and Kenchōji in Kamakura. In 1351 he was joined by Eiyo (Chin. Yung-yü), a disciple of one of his senior colleagues. Eiyo was one of the last Chinese monks to arrive in

Japan, he became a close friend of Musō Soseki and resided at the Tenryūji and Nanzenji in Kyoto.

Although the Wanshi-ha officially belonged to Sōtō Zen, it was quite different from Dōgen's movement. In China it had been strongly influenced by the Chin-kang Chu-hsia tradition and thus tended to be extremely artistic and literary, fitting well into the Rinzai milieu in Japan. In fact, its followers later moved to various *Gozan* temples and became the only Sōtō school to be included within the system. However, it was not always lacking opposition, Tonmin believed in the Sōtō theory of Five Ranks and at times, particularly early in his career, was a quite enthusiastic exponent of Sōtō philosophy.

The Wanshi-ha exhibited strong Chinese characteristics, as a majority of its disciples had visited China and were expert in Chinese culture. At the early stages, it received its primary support from the Hōjō regents, but later its benefactors numbered among the most distinguished aristocrats. During the late Muromachi period however, its main patron became the Asakura family and when those warlords were defeated by Oda Nobunaga in his drive to reunify Japan, the sect shared the fate of its sponsors and rapidly declined, hastened no doubt by pressure from the Rinzai Musō-ha.

2. Fuke-shū

The origin of this school is believed to date back to a T'ang Chinese priest named Fuke Zenji (Chin. Pu-hua), who lived a simple life wandering through the countryside to the accompaniment of bells and chanting. The school was brought to Japan during the mid-thirteenth century by Shinji Muhon Kakushin (posthumous, Hottō Kokushi), who built the Kōkokuji temple in Kii province. Kinsen, a disciple was legendarily believed to have been expert at the flute and invited to court.

During the early medieval period this group had not yet formed a sect, but constituted an important movement of half-monk half-layman beggar priests. They were alternately called such names as 'boro-boro,' 'uma (horse) hijiri,' or 'komosō' (monk of a straw mattress). They travelled as transients throughout the countryside chanting the *nembutsu*, playing the *shakuhachi* flute and begging for alms. Their popularity stemmed half from the entertainment they provided to the masses. During the Warring States and early Tokugawa, the movement unified into a religious congregation. Their evolution is difficult to trace and it is uncertain when they began to take the name *komusō* (monk of Emptiness). Some theories ascribe this new name to the seventh successor Komu,[67] while others believe the early followers merged with existing door to door flute players known as the '*komusō*'. Still another theory attributes the new name to the philosophical interpretation of the *shakushachi* flute as an instrument of the Dharma symbolizing the pure mind of Enlightenment.[68]

During the late Muromachi and early Tokugawa, as the movement grew, it gradually became a sanctuary for *rōnin* (masterless samurai) and other social outcasts. The philosophy advocated no members, no patrons, and no fixed income. Their life was devoted to alms begging, although some were known to engage in making tea kettles and teaching the *shakuhachi* flute. The group recognized no scriptures, but rather believed the flute was a method of controlling the mind and art of breathing, leading to spiritual awareness. For those dissatisfied with the feudal system, it offered a natural sanctuary, yet as is so necessary in Japanese society, provided a social group or proper rationale for retreat.

In 1677 the Tokugawa government made its first attempt to regulate the various Komusō schools and at that time the main headquarter temples were regarded as the Ryōhōji of Musashi, Ichigatsuji of Shimofusa and Myōanji of Kyoto. Ultimately during the declining era of Tokugawa control the movement was regarded as a possible threat to the government and breeding ground for undesirables. In 1847 it was officially placed under the jurisdiction of the Rinzai sect and in 1871, shortly after the Meiji Restoration was banned.

3. Ōbaku Zen

Although the Ōbaku-shū formally belongs to the Tokugawa period, it characteristics are comparable to the earlier Zen schools, and, since it became the 'third' sect of Japanese Zen, we briefly mention it here.

Ōbaku Zen was first brought to Japan in 1654 by Ingen (Chin. Yin-yüan, 1592–1673) during the decline of the Ming dynasty, perhaps as an escape from contemporary political turmoil as well as an answer to the request of the affluent Chinese colony in the Nagasaki area. After residing for a time at the Kōfukuji in Nagasaki, in 1661 Ingen received government permission to restore a former Genjū-ha Zen temple in Uji, and this he made a replica of the Mampukuji (Chin. Wan-fu-szu) on Mt. Ōbaku (Chin. Huang-po), even giving it the same Chinese character name. It would seem that Tokugawa interest in Ingen was not centred in importing a new form of Zen to Japan, but rather as a means of revitalizing the Rinzai order, which by late Muromachi had declined to the practice of the arts of painting, tea ceremony and calligraphy rather than Zen. The Tokugawa hope was that a form of pure Chinese Zen would incite new interest, as well as possibly correct the influence of Shingon, Kegon and other forms of Japanese Zen assimilation.

Although Ingen's Zen was purely Chinese, it could scarcely be called 'pure' Zen, since it incorporated the practice of the *nembutsu* and even certain Tantric *mantra* and *dhāraṇī*, which in China had come to dominate Zen after the Sung dynasty. This form of Zen *nembutsu* was not used in the sense of 'Other-power', but rather as a means of raising the individual level of spiritual awareness. In China, what is popularly known as *Nembutsu kōan* Zen (*Nien-fo-kung-an* Ch'an). was introduced by such Zen masters as Yun-ming Yen-shou (904–75). The Pure Land in this instance was considered as a psychological state of mind to be achieved.

The Ōbaku sect was noted in Japan for its distinct Chinese character, in fact all the major posts of the monastery were held by native Chinese. The temple masters up to and including the thirteenth successor were Chinese by birth, and the language, customs, food, etc. of the monastery were all Chinese. In fact, many Japanese who visited the temple during its early generations compared the experience to an actual visit to China. The first native Japanese temple master was the fourteenth successor but even after this, his successor as well as the twentieth and twenty-first masters were native Chinese.

The temple attracted immediate attention in Japan and quickly became a major centre of Chinese culture, drawing monks and laymen alike. Eventually a number of Japanese monks constructed residences on the periphery where they remain today as small temples. Both Sōtō and Rinzai Japanese monks joined in Ingen's group to study the exotic Chinese culture and calligraphy, but the movement was not without its critics. Several Rinzai theses were written challenging the sect's eclectic philosophy, and Sōtō critics cited Ōbaku as a reason for their 'restore the ancient order' (of Dōgen) movement. In 1876 the Ōbaku was officially recognized as an independent sect of Buddhism, today it still maintains over five-hundred affiliated temples.

CHAPTER V

ROLE OF THE OLDER SECTS DURING
THE KAMAKURA AND MUROMACHI PERIODS

A. Nara Buddhism

There is a tendency in discussing the mass movements of the Kamakura period to portray the older sects in the role of reaction or even as 'anti-religious,' as though their only function was to preserve and cling to the corruption the new schools rejected.[1] This is not an accurate picture, since the Nara sects did more than react and were not devoid of their own idealistic reformers.

If we characterize the new Kamakura Buddhist movements as 'single-practice' oriented, then the contemporary direction of the old Nara sects can only be described as eclectic and 'multi-practice,' both were strongly influenced by the spirit of *mappō*. The ancient capital perhaps experienced the effects of *mappō* more acutely than the rest of the nation, since the Taira attack of 1180 destroyed its most famous temples, the Tōdaiji and Kōfukuji, and even Kujō Kanezane despaired whether they could ever be restored. But restoration became a political project and nationwide campaign in which the war victor and leader of the new Kamakura government, Minamoto Yoritomo participated, in hopes of furthering national harmony, as well as an excuse to cast his former Taira enemies into an unfavourable light. The physical restoration of Nara, expressed in a renaissance of Buddhist art and iconography, as well as the actual physical reconstruction of the temples, was joined by a desperate attempt to create a spiritual regeneration among the old sects, who felt threatened in their very existence by the vitality and popularity of the new Kamakura movements.

Reaction and Counter-Reaction

If we classify the various types of reaction to the Buddhist institutional corruption of the late Heian period and the influence of *mappō* thought, we will encounter the following varieties:

1) Rejection of Heian esoteric rituals, prayers for worldly benefits and corruption in general, that brought about a restoration of individual faith, with a deep feeling of introspection—Jōdo and Jōdo Shinshū.

2) Rejection of esoteric rituals and corruption joined with the ideal of restoring the golden days of Śākyamuni and the Tendai order through individual faith—Nichiren.

3) Rejection of Heian corruption inspired by Chinese influence and emphasis upon a restoration of the *vinaya* and monastic life—Zen.

4) Reaction to Heian corruption combined with a counter-reaction to the new Kamakura schools, leading to a 'return to the ancient way' and revival of Nara Buddhism through emphasis upon *vinaya* and restoration of the monastic life—the Nara sects.

Among these groups, the Pure Land alone followed the way of 'Other-power' and had the least in common with the Nara schools. Together with the Nichiren, they included everyone in their appeal without singling out a special group, and they rejected esoteric rituals. In contrast, the Zen concern for restoring the *vinaya* and monastic life, narrowed their appeal to a select audience, and this combined with their rather ambivalent attitude towards esoteric rituals, placed them the closest to the Nara position.

The obvious Nara counter-reaction to the Kamakura schools resulted in attempts to influence the government to suppress the new movements and punish their leaders. But the combination of reaction and counter-reaction created a new ideology—for if this was indeed the age of *mappō* (Degeneration of the Dharma), then the ideal should be to turn back and restore the days of *shōbō* (True Dharma), that existed during the lifetime of Śākyamuni through study and devotion to the historical

Buddha. At the same time, the *vinaya* or the precepts of the Buddhist order left by Śākyamuni had to be restored.

If we compare the Kamakura development of the Nara sects with the new schools of Buddhism, we will note a number of interesting contrasts—one of which is the fact that whereas each of the new sects evolved in some manner from the Tendai order, the transformation of the older schools was made under the influence of Shingon esoterism.

The link between the Six sects of Nara and Shingon was first established by Kūkai, who maintained a harmonious relationship with the southern capital, in contrast to Saichō's position of no-compromise and struggle for an independent Mahāyāna *kaidan*. Kūkai's attitude, plus the general interest in the new esoteric philosophy introduced from China, and aristocratic pressure, quickly spread Tantric influence among the old sects, but a major factor was the effort of Shingon monks to study and restore the older schools.

As early as the tenth century, Shōbō (839–909),[2] founder of the Shingon Onoryū, established the Tōnan-in of the Tōdaiji as a centre of Sanron studies. This led to an intensified interest among the Nara monks in esoterism, as well as a revival of Sanron. The combination of Sanron and Shingon studies became known as *Ronmitsu*, and it was developed during the late Heian period by leading Sanron scholars such as Yōkan (1033–1111) and Chinkai (1087–1165). And if we examine the list of abbots of the Tōdaiji between 924–1183, with few exceptions, the majority were Sanron and Shingon monks. At this time even the Hossō Kōfukuji temple contained many Shingon followers and the abbot Jōshō (911–983) professed to be a Hossō-Shingon monk. The Shingon influence formed the basis of Nara Buddhist development from the close of the Heian through the Muromachi periods.

1. Transformation to Faith

The Six Sects of Nara during their period of dominance are generally regarded as an academic form of Buddhism, since their interest was scholarly rather than devotional. This does not mean that Nara Buddhism was completely lacking in faith, for it is obvious a number of popular devotions to Yakushi, Śākyamuni, Amida, Kannon were present, as well as chanting of various sutras for the protection of the nation and even a growing belief in the *Lotus Sutra;* however, faith and theology were separate domains. The monks spent their time in the study of topics that afforded scarcely any visible practical application, while using separate devotions in their personal lives, as well as in dealing with the aristocratic laity; faith and theology were both present but kept quite distinct.

The Heian period began upon such a note, but gradually under Tendai and Shingon influence, faith and theology were slowly drawn together, and this was one of their greatest contributions to Japanese Buddhism. Tendai *shikan* meditation led to various devotions, in particular the development of Pure Land faith in Amida, while in Shingon, although Dainichi Nyorai was the principal image (as in the Nara Kegon school), this Buddha was too abstract and intangible to become a devotional object, thus Shingon multi-practices encouraged other Buddhas and bodhisattvas to fill that role; this trend strongly influenced the Nara sects.

Varieties of Faith

If we were to divide the Kamakura sects in terms of principal Buddha images, we would have two distinctions: the Pure Land schools, in search of a teaching suitable for the days of *mappō* who turned to Amida, and in contrast, Nichiren and Zen, both seeking to restore a past order, who placed confidence in Śākyamuni. The old Nara schools shared the latter view and were dominantly oriented towards faith in Śākyamuni, although they also had a number of related devotions that we will briefly analyze:

Shaka (Śākyamuni) Faith

The popularity of devotion to Shaka among the leaders of Nara Buddhism during the Kamakura period, was in large part a reaction to *nembutsu* faith in Amida.[3] It was therefore particularly important to figures such as Jōkei, a leading Pure Land critic, and exponent of *vinaya* reform. One of the major charges in the Kōfukuji petition, which he allegedly composed, was the fact that Hōnen's *nembutsu* movement neglected and mistreated the founder of Buddhism.

Shaka devotion became a natural reflection of the desire to return to the days of 'True Dharma' prior to the degeneration of *mappō*. To stem the tide of the seemingly radical Buddhism, that ignored the established Japanese Buddhist tradition of catering to the aristocracy and ruling classes by carrying its message to peasants and commoners; of the movement that surrendered all self-efforts to attain Enlightenment and openly supported the abolition of the monastic life by allowing its clergy to marry, eat fish and meat, and act like laymen. In their reaction to the unmistakable 'degeneration' of this new Buddhism, which they considered to be the very symbol of *mappō*, the Nara Buddhist leaders combined faith in Shaka with efforts to restore *vinaya* monastic practice. But the popularity of Shaka faith was not totally a reaction against the *nembutsu* movement, for the omnipresent spirit of *mappō* made a return to the purity of the 'ancient way' as likely a solution as the search for a new order.

Shaka faith was strongest among those who advocated *vinaya* reform, such as Eison and Ninshō, leaders of the Shingon-Ritsu. They used the *Hikekyō* (*Karuṇā-puṇḍarīka-sūtra*), which served as a popular basis of Shaka faith among Nara Buddhists.[4] This sutra describes Śākyamuni as a white lotus flower of compassion, born in the polluted world to aid sentient beings. In company with devotion to Mañjuśrī, the *Hikekyō* was used as a theological justification for social work among the sick and poor by those following in the footsteps of Prince Shōtoku, Gyōgi bosatsu and Kūkai.

A further inducement for Shaka faith was the relationship between Shaka and the popular esoteric cult to Zaō Gongen that had commenced in the Heian period and reached its peak during the Kamakura.[5] According to this belief, Zaō Gongen was an *upāya*-body or manifestation of Shaka, designed to frighten the perverse into an acceptance of Buddhist teachings.

The style of Shaka images was profoundly influenced by the visit of

the Tōdaiji monk Chōnen (d. 1016) to Sung China and his return with
the Shaka image housed in the Shaka-dō of the Shōryōji temple. This
image, believed for centuries to have been transmitted from India due to
its distinct Indian character, became the basis of what is known as the
Shōryōji style. It was widely imitated throughout the country and even
associated with a form of Shaka *nembutsu*. One of the most popular festivals in honour of Shaka was the *Nehan-e*, held annually on the fifteenth
day of the second month.

Amida

Although faith in Amida during the Kamakura period is generally
associated with the Pure Land schools, these were not the sole sources
of the devotion. In the southern capital, Amida faith became more
popular than ever, undoubtedly stimulated by the mass movement and
a few Nara monks, such as Myōhen, became affiliated with the Jōdo
sect. However, although Myōhen is regarded by the Jōdo tradition as
a disciple of Hōnen, his *nembutsu* practice was within the Nara tradition
combining *vinaya*, Shingon and the *yūzū nembutsu*.

To venerate Amida, most of the Nara temples constructed either
Jōgyō-dō or Amida-dō halls and kept *dōsō* monks engaged in the perpetual practice of the *nembutsu*. Despite certain influence from the Pure
Land schools, on the whole, the Nara sects practiced the Shingon esoteric
nembutsu. It was regarded as a means of accumulating virtue and emphasis
was placed upon the quantity of chantings.

Miroku (Maitreya)

Miroku, the Buddha to come, believed to reside in the Tuṣita heaven,
was also a focus of popular devotion. This cult was actually an extentua-
tion of Shaka veneration and frequently combined with it, since Shaka
was regarded as the Buddha who had already departed from this world.
For example, Myōe Kōben, a famous Kegon monk known for his
devotion to Shaka, turned at the time of death to Miroku in hope of
reaching the Tuṣita heaven.

In Japan, Miroku faith was of ancient origin, dating back to the Asuka era. Heian aristocrats such as Fujiwara Michinaga were known to have buried sutras in honour of the future Buddha and in longing to attain his Tuṣita heaven. During the Kamakura period, Miroku faith was popular among followers of the Hossō school, in particular at the Kōfukuji where Jōkei was a leading advocate, and Mt. Kasagi was regarded as representing the Pure Land of Miroku. The devotion was also widespread among Shingon followers. Shūshō, a Kegon-Mikkyō follower at the Tōdaiji, completed a five volume biography of prominent Miroku believers, which served to stimulate interest in the faith.

Monjushiri (Mañjuśrī)

Another popular bodhisattva was Monjushiri, an attendant in the Shaka triad representing 'wisdom; in contrast to Fugen (Samantabhadra), the symbol of 'compassion.' Faith in Monju advanced during the early Heian period based upon the *Monjushiri Hatsu-nehangyō* (*Mañjuśrī-parinirvāṇa-sūtra*). This became one of the bases for social work among the poor and needy advocated by the Shingon-Ritsu followers. Monju-e gatherings were also popular in the provinces. The cult to Fugen failed to ever attract a large following in Japan.

Kannon (Avalokiteśvara)

From earliest times a large devotion to Kannon existed in Japan. Besides appearing in the *Larger Sukhāvatī-vyūha* and *Dainichikyō* sutras, an entire chapter of the *Lotus Sutra* dealt with the worldly benefits of this bodhisattva, who was also known as an attendant of Amida representing 'compassion' in company with Seishi (Mahāsthāmaprāpta) as 'wisdom.' Although Seishi was often portrayed in Pure Land iconography, the bodhisattva failed to ever develop popularity in Japan.

Kannon faith was disseminated by the older sects as a counterpart of Amida faith among the rural masses. Kannon-kō meetings were held monthly and even the *Fudaraku* (Potalaka) Pure Land of Kannon was presented as superior to Amida's Pure Land, but the devotion failed to gain the popularity its sponsors had anticipated.

Jizō (Kṣitigarbha)

Another devotion propagated by the older sects among the masses during the Kamakura period was belief in Jizō. This bodhisattva, considered as an earth guardian, became the protector of good harvests and was venerated quite similar to the indigenous Shintō earth god. In later times, Jizō was associated with the suffering dead in hell. The *Shasekishū* extolled the merits of Jizō by pointing out that while Shaka abandoned the land and Amida resides in the Western Pure Land, only Jizō can be found among the suffering existences.

During the Muromachi period a further development in Jizō devotion made the bodhisattva the master of Sai-no-kawara, the place of children's sufferings and Jizō became a popular patron of children. Numerous countryside festivals such as the Jizō-bon are still observed today.

Shōtoku Taishi

Closely related to faith in Kannon, considered from early periods to represent the *honji* (true nature) of Prince Shōtoku, this cult was popular in Nara during the Kamakura period. To a certain degree, as the 'Father of Japanese Buddhism', Prince Shōtoku epitomized the 'return to the ancient way' and he had set a precedent for the combination of theology, practice and social work. During the Kamakura period new *honji* Buddhas such as Shōbōmyō Nyorai and Dainichi Nyorai were assigned to the Prince. But Eison, the most well-known exponent of Shōtoku faith, considered Shaka to be the true *honji*.[6] Eison related Shingon-Ritsu *vinaya* practice, injunctions against the taking of life and medical-social work all to his faith in Shōtoku, who was known as the first in Japan to established an asylum, infirmary and dispensary at the Shitennōji. As a manifestation of Shaka, it was believed that Shōtoku possessed an eternal body that would appear whenever the conditions were proper.

In keeping with the emphasis upon 'returning to the ancient way', besides the foregoing, veneration of the Buddha's relics (*śarīra*) and Ganjin, the transmitter of the Buddhist *vinaya* to Japan, also became important. Such forms of devotion not only served as objects of faith among the Nara monks and means of approaching lay patrons, but also at this time became the subjects of theological study within the individual sects.

2. Activities Among the Nara Sects

The Nara leaders were as profoundly disturbed by the notion of *mappō* (Degeneration of the Dharma), accompanied by the war and calamities befalling the nation at the close of the Heian period as the new Buddhist movements, but their reaction assumed a different perspective. If *mappō* signified the period when 'only the teaching remained while practice and attainment were impossible,' then they wanted to find a way to restore the latter. They sensed a severe crisis within the old order, for it was obvious that during such rapid social change, academic Buddhism and the Buddhism of esoteric rituals were inadequate. This feeling of crisis and grief over the Buddhist degeneration they witnessed about them, led to reflection and the search for a solution *within* their traditions, rather than joining the surging new movements that threatened to sweep away the past in an effort to establish a new order.

The majority of Nara leaders were firmly convinced that regardless of the time, one should strive and endeavour, this was ingrained within their traditional mode of thought. Thus when they viewed the obvious corruption within the Buddhist institution, they left and established hermitages on the peaceful neighboring mountains, where they could devote themselves to study and practice; such a lifestyle had by now become respectable through the influence of Mikkyō and Shugendō. With a sense of urgency they sought to discover the proper teaching and practice to restore the possibility of Enlightenment and thus reverse *mappō*. To a certain degree these individuals possessed a theological freedom that their spiritual ancestors had lacked, for Japan had gained self-confidence and they were no longer strictly bound by the restrictions of Chinese and Indian Buddhism. They now realized that theology and philosophical study must be related to religious experience, and all of their efforts to systematize the doctrines of their various schools were closely related to practical application. To view their methods, we will now briefly examine the activities of each of the four active schools of Nara Buddhism.

Sanron

Under the leadership of the Tōnan-in of the Tōdaiji, the major interest of the Sanron school was devoted to *Ronmitsu*, combining Sanron and Shingon teachings. One of the most distinguished scholars of this tradition was Myōhen (1142–1224), who later became a recluse upon Mt. Kōmyō and in 1195 moved to Kōyasan, where he entered *nembutsu* practice and took the name of Kū Amida Butsu.

Other leading scholars were Chūdōbō Shōshu (d. 1291) of the Tōdaiji Shingon-in, who theologically attempted to harmonize Mikkyō-Ritsu and Sanron, and Chōzen (d. 1307) of the Kōryūji Keigū-in of Kyoto, also interested in the assimilation of Sanron and Ritsu. The centres of Sanron activity through the later Muromachi period were these two temples and the Shinzen-in of the Tōdaiji. The Sanron did not develop a congregation and in time it joined the Kusha and Jōjitsu, becoming merely a subject of academic study.

Hossō

As the main stream of Buddhism shifted from Nara to Kyoto during the early Heian period, the Hossō school alone among the Nara sects continued to exhibit vitality. Near the close of the tenth century, Jōshō (911–983), the seventeenth successor of the Kōfukuji, established both an Ichijō (Ekayāna)-in and Daijō (Mahāyāna)-in; these two Kōfukuji sub-temples became the major centres of Hossō studies during succeeding generations.

Just as the Hossō vitality was the last among the Nara schools to decline, they can also be credited with early attempts to revive the Nara spirit. In 1094 Eichō submitted a catalogue of scriptures belonging to the various Buddhist sects and commentaries to the Shōren-in in Kyoto, representing one of the first efforts to compile and organize the knowledge of the past. Although it took several generations for more work to be done in this area, the gradual revival of interest in classical scriptures and Buddhist history spearheaded the Nara restoration movement. In 1176 Zōshun of the Kōfukuji, under the sponsorship of the Retired Emperor Go-Shirakawa, completed a catalogue of Hossō commentaries, and his disciple Kakuken (1131–1212) wrote the *Sangoku Dentōki* (Record of the Transmission of Buddhism in Three Countries) in 1173. To a certain degree, the Nara Buddhist interest in classical scriptures and history of the past is comparable to the later Tokugawa political movement of National Learning (Kokugaku), that ultimately through emphasis upon classical literature and Japanese history led to the restoration of Imperial rule. As one of the first to study the Buddhist historical tradition, Kakuken's work must have stimulated later monks such as Sōshō and Gyōnen of the Kegon school. Kakuken's family ties also served to extend his influence; his younger brothers were Myōhen of Mt. Kōya and the popular preacher, Chōken, while Shōkaku of the Ango-in and Jōkei, the mid-restorer of Hossō, were among his nephews.

After the mid-Heian period the Hossō school became exceedingly esoteric. Influence of the Kōfukuji rapidly expanded and such temples as the Yakushiji, Hōryūji, Saidaiji, Daianji and Kiyomizudera came under its control, as well as a number of Shintō shrines.

The most distinguished Hossō scholar of the Kamakura period was Jōkei (1155–1213) or Gedatsu Shōnin, a grandon of Fujiwara Michinori. He entered the Kōfukuji at the age of eight and had spent thirty years there when in 1192, he attended a service at the palace and became disillusioned by the monks who wore grand robes and scorned his simplicity. He then decided to give up his life at the Kōfukuji and become a recluse on Mt. Kasagi, then generally believed to be the Pure Land of Miroku. The remainder of his life was devoted to Miroku veneration, *vinaya* practice and Hossō study. Not only did he attempt to systematize Yuishiki (Vijñānavāda) philosophy, but he also tried to assimilate Mikkyō, Zen and the *nembutsu* within it. He was particularly interested in visualization meditation and made an effort to interpret the Miroku *nembutsu* in terms of Yuishiki doctrine.

Jōkei is generally believed to be the author of the Kōfukuji petition that attempted to ban Hōnen's *nembutsu* movement, this was written after his retreat to Mt. Kasagi. Jōkei was one of the strongest critics of Hōnen, for in his dedication to restore *vinaya*, he considered that those who abandoned the discipline and denied the efficacy of self-power to be a major cause of *mappō*. Ironically, Hōnen's foremost patron, Kujō Kanezane, was very fond of Jōkei, and considered him to be one of the outstanding monks of the era. But the question arises, why a recluse would compose such a worldly document, primarily concerned with accusations of a political rather than theological nature? In this respect, the petition appears to represent a sectarian reaction rather than a true idealistic concern.

In 1208 Jōkei moved west to the Kaijūsenji, and died there five years later at the age of fifty-nine. His most important theological work was the *Yuishiki Dōgakushō* (Treatise on the Study of Vijñānavāda). Jōkei is particularly noted for his influence upon the development of Kamakura *vinaya* practice and his disciples Kainyo, Kakushin, and Ryōsan, all contributed to *vinaya* restoration.

Ryōhen (1192–1252), a disciple of Kakuhen, was also an important follower in Jōkei's tradition. He became disillusioned with the worldly goals of the Buddhist community and at the age of forty-nine became a recluse at the Chikurinji on Mt. Ikoma. Like Jōkei, Ryōhen was devoted to Shaka, Miroku and Jizō, but he also had a particular belief in Amida. In his attempt to systematize Hossō teachings, Ryōhen assimilated Kegon, Tendai, and Sanron, as well as the Pure Land *nembutsu*; after his period Hossō activities declined.

In 1892 the Hōryūji, Kōfukuji and Yakushiji were made the three main headquarters of the Hossō sect under a single abbot. The congregation included forty some branch temples.

Kegon

During the early tenth century, Kōchi (897–979) established the Sonshō-in at the Tōdaiji, making it a centre of Kegon studies. His direct disciples Kanshin and Matsubashi founded traditions that ultimately led to the medieval restoration movements of Myōe and Gyōnen. But before

the Kegon sect was able to experience its first revival, it underwent a serious decline as its teachings were absorbed into the Tendai
sect. The first Kegon restorer was Myōe Kōben (1173–1282). Born of a
socially prominent family in Kii province, when Myōe was eight, his
father was killed by the Minamoto, and a year later his mother died.
He then went to study Mikkyō under his uncle Jōkakubō Gyōji at the
Jingoji on Mt. Takao; he later studied Kegon and was ordained at the
Tōdaiji. Finally becoming dissatisfied with the worldly life at both
temples, Myōe became a hermit at Shiragami no mine in Kii province
for a time, prior to establishing a centre of Kegon studies at the Kōzanji
on Mt. Toganoo.

More than perhaps any other Nara priest, Myōe grieved over the fact
that he had not been born during the lifetime of Shaka, and in his expression of this grief, he decided to make a pilgrimage to India. His
plans were so complete that not only did he decide upon matters such as
food and clothing, but even calculated the exact number of years required
to walk from Ch'ang-an to India. Unfortunately health and circumstances
did not permit such a journey, although his travel plans have been preserved at the Kōzanji.

Myōe was influenced by the Pure Land chanting of the *nembutsu* and
in imitation, devised a form of devotion to the Three Treasures (Buddha,
Dharma and Sangha). Supposedly he respected Hōnen during his lifetime, but after Hōnen's death, upon reading the *Senjakushū* for the first
time, Myōe became a strong critic of the Pure Land movement and wrote
the *Saijarin* (Wheel to Smash the False Doctrine) as a refutation, as well
as further supplements. Although Myōe attracted many aristocrats such
as Emperor Go-Toba and Hōjō Yasutoki by the purity of his life and his
strong faith in Shaka, his following at the Kōzanji did not increase after
his death in 1232.

The 'Middle-Restoration' of the Kegon sect occurred at the Tōdaiji
under the leadership of Sōshō (1202–92) and his disciple Gyōnen. Sōshō
(or Shūshō), was of Fujiwara descent and studied Kegon as well as Hossō
and Kusha at the Tōdaiji. During his youth he was devoted to Amida,

but in 1230 he converted to Miroku faith and went to Mt. Kasagi to engage in practice, where he came under the influence of Jōkei's disciples.

Sōshō was a prolific writer and his most noteworthy works were on the subject of Miroku faith, over four hundred items are still preserved at the Tōdaiji. In his writings he was strongly aware of competition with Amida devotion.[7] Sōshō attempted to stimulate the 'restoration of the ancient order' by composing a multi-volume biography viewing the accomplishments of venerable monks of the past; this served as his method of unity practice and theological study.

Gyōnen (d. 1321), a disciple of Sōshō, became one of the most outstanding Nara scholars of the Kamakura period. He managed faithfully to study the doctrine of every sect of Buddhism, including Zen and Pure Land. Under the patronage of Emperor Go-Uda, he resided at the Kaidan-in of the Tōdaiji and devoted his life to writing, in which he was unequalled producing some 1,200 works. One of his most famous studies is the *Hasshū kōyō* (Essentials of Eight Sects), which even today provides contemporary scholars with one of the most comprehensive accounts of the doctrine and philosophies of the older schools. Gyōnen also composed a number of historical studies.

After its brief revival, the Kegon sect failed to prosper as a congregation. Its permanent headquarters became the Tōdaiji temple with over thirty branches.

Ritsu and Shingon Ritsu

After the transmission of *vinaya* to Japan by Ganjin in 736, national *kaidan* (ordination platforms) were constructed at the Tōdaiji, Kanzeonji in Dazaifu and Yakushiji of Shimotsuke. Later, joined by Ganjin's own Tōshōdaiji, these temples controlled the ordination of all Buddhist priests in Japan up until the Heian period, when Saichō finally won the right to construct a Tendai Mahāyāna *kaidan* on Mt. Hiei in 822. Ironically, after the establishment of a Tendai *kaidan* the old Ritsu sect of Nara began to decline. This was because the ordination platform had become an integral part of the Nara Ritsuryō government, and as that system began to disintegrate, the official temples housing the *kaidan* lost financial support. The Tendai victory as well, had largely deprived them of their rationale for existence.

In Early Buddhism, *vinaya* (the rules and regulations for the clergy), formed an inherent part of each sect of Buddhism and was not transmitted as an independent sect. The Ritsushū had its origin in China but did not attract a large following. Its quick rise to prominence in Japan was partially due to the Japanese sense of inferiority in confronting Chinese Buddhism, as well as a means of meeting the intense need to establish proper criteria for being Buddhist. The Ritsu also served as a convenient method of government regulation, since control of ordination exposed the heart of the Buddhist institution to government control. This last important reason for the Ritsu rise to prominence contained the germs of its decline. By 938, the Ritsu sect had reached such a state that its line of succession nearly ended.

The arrival of the *mappō* era, general institutional corruption and the popularity of the *nembutsu* were all factors intensifying the neglect of the *vinaya*. Pure Land advocates stressed that man was too weak to ever attain perfection by his own efforts, and the obvious neglect of *vinaya* among the monks of the established sects appeared to substantiate their claims. Furthermore, the endless, often petty, regulations for monks and nuns appeared to have little relevance to real life and the search for Enlightenment. Thus a number of diverse views arose such as: "why bother to observe meaningless rules?" or the further extreme, "in view of man's hopeless state, why bother at all?" Young aspiring monks only had to observe the conduct of their elders to become quickly disillusioned with observance, and the pure monk who maintained the *śīla* became a rare creature.

The Pure Land idealistically led in one direction—their leaders did not renounce proper *vinaya* as such, but merely questioned whether human beings were capable of perfection despite innumerable rules of conduct, and pointed to the existing clergy as an example of self-power *vinaya* failure. They did not totally abandon Buddhist morality, but placed it in a secondary role, believing that perfection of faith was capable of leading to a spontaneous moral life. However, not a few clerical followers joined Hōnen with the notion that this was one means of forever being rid of useless rules and prohibitions. Such an attitude combined with the sectarian Nara interpretation of Hōnen's teachings created a natural reaction. In the southern capital a strong movement arose to restore *vinaya* and return to the golden way of proper Buddhist observance prior to *mappō*, this naturally brought the Ritsu sect back to light.

One of the first to note and regret the decline of *vinaya*, was Jitsuhan (d. 1144), of the Nakanokawadera temple. According to legend, in the dream of restoring the *vinaya* tradition he went to the famous Tōshōdaiji kaidan-in to receive the *śīla*. There instead of encountering a community of monks engaged in practice, he found the temple grounds converted into agricultural fields and a single maintenance layman plowing with an ox. Undaunted, Jitsuhan received the *śīla* from this layman in Ganjin's memorial hall and commenced upon his career of teaching the *vinaya*. He is known to have completed formal studies of Hossō at the Kōfukuji, Mikkyō at the Daigoji, and Tendai at Yokawa on Mt. Hiei, and he used a combination of those disciplines in his teachings. Jitsuhan's tradition of *vinaya* became associated with the Hossō *vinaya* transmitted by Jōkei, and the latter's disciples, Kainyo and Kakushin, who established a special centre of *vinaya* studies at the Jōki-in of the Kōfukuji.[8] Kakujō (1194–1249) also known as Gūjō, was a distinguished successor of this tradition.[9] He restored the Tōshōdaiji and was considered by many to represent a second coming of Ganjin. Kakujō died in 1249 at the age of fifty-six, and in 1330 received the posthumous title of Daihi bosatsu from Emperor Go-Daigo, but after his death his tradition declined.

In contrast, a new movement known as Shingon-Ritsu was initiated by Eison (1201–90). Eison began his studies in Mikkyō at the Daigoji and later went to Mt. Kōya before deciding to devote his life to *vinaya*. Becoming a disciple of Kainyo in 1236, together with Kakujō and several others, he went to the Tōdaiji and performed his own 'self-pledge ordination' (*jiseijukai*). This idea was based upon the *Senzatsu zenaku gōhōkyō* (which permitted Mahāyāna self-ordination to be performed before a Buddha image at times when a proper *vinaya* master did not exist) and the *Yugaron* (*Yogācāra bhūmi*). Although this form of ordination met with certain criticism, it seemed an appropriate solution in a day when it was impossible to find ten necessary *vinaya* masters for proper Ritsu ordination.

According to Shingon-Ritsu teaching, *vinaya* was interpreted based upon Shingon doctrine. In contrast to early Ritsu, religious activities were now extended to the masses, and Eison travelled through the countryside granting a form of ordination to the laity as well as monks. By the time of his death in 1290 at the age of ninety, it is believed that 97,710 had received Ritsu *śīla* from him. Another important aspect of his teaching was directed against the taking of life. He established animal sanctuaries, on some occasions even destroyed fishing and hunting gear, and extended his campaign to 1,356 places of *hōjō* (release of life) practice, even including the untouchable *hinin* class—so closely associated with the taking of life, in his social work.

Eison was responsible for making the Saidaiji one of the most important contemporary centres of *vinaya* studies. Although this temple had originally been under the jurisdiction of the Kōfukuji, it gradually became independent and the principal temple of Shingon-Ritsu activities.

In 1265 at the age of sixty-two, Eison went to Kamakura at the request of the former regent Hōjō Tokiyori and spent six months there working with his disciple Ninshō. He was so successful in propagating Ritsu, that by the time of his death, the Saidaiji had 1,500 branch temples. In the year 1300 Eison was granted the posthumous title of Kōshō bosatsu by the Retired Emperor Kameyama. Although Eison was succeeded at the Saidaiji by Shinkū, his most illustrious disciple was Ninshō of the Gokurakuji in Kamakura.

Ninshō (1217–1303), also known as Ryōkan, was a major object of Nichiren attack and a controversial personality. In 1261 he went to Kamakura and with the support of the Hōjō Regents restored the Gokurakuji, making a Shaka figure in the Shōryōji style the principal image. Exteriorally Ninshō had a reputation of great sanctity as he was known to wear poor robes, eat simple food and engage in social work. However, his use of Hōjō patronage and apparent eagerness to seize honours, led many to criticize him, even pointing out the possible material profits he gained from his social work. There is no question that he was a brilliant and capable man, as is evinced by his management of the Gokurakuji, and it is difficult to be certain whether his detractors were sincere or motivated by jealousy. But unlike his master Eison, Ninshō was willing to accept reward for the successful performance of Shingon rituals to overcome calamities and protect the nation.

Ninshō became the undisputed leader of the Kamakura religious community. He also accepted posts of honour throughout the country. His social works entailed the construction of hospitals, bridges and assistance to the needy, in 1298 he is even known to have built a horse hospital in Kamakura. He died in that city in 1303 at the age of eighty-seven and in 1328, Emperor Go-Daigo granted him the posthumous title of Ninshō bosatsu.

The Shingon-Ritsu movement was completed by Onkō (1718–1804) during the Tokugawa period. Its religious activities included the propagation of faith in Monju and the Shaka *nembutsu* among the masses, in company with the prohibition of killing and teaching of the eight *śīla*[10] as a means of cleansing sin and accumulating virtue. During the Meiji era the Saidaiji became independent as the official Shingon-Ritsu shū, the Tōshōdaiji also developed its own independent form of *vinaya*.

Beside the various Ritsu revivals of the southern capital, a new form of *vinaya* was introduced from China by Shunjō and Donshō in Kyoto. This became popularly known as northern capital Ritsu.

Shunjō (1166–1227) returned to Japan in 1211 after a twelve year period of study in China and under the patronage of leading aristocrats and the Hōjō family, established the Sennyūji in the Higashiyama area. This temple became the centre of Kyoto *vinaya* as well as a popular burial site for Emperors. As Shunjō had studied Tendai and Mikkyō besides *vinaya*, his new form of Ritsu was extremely eclectic, and included even Zen and Pure Land devotions. Many of Shunjō's disciples went to Sung China to study.

Donshō (d. 1239) was a contemporary of Shunjō, who spent two periods in China totally twenty-two years. He established the Kaikōji in Kyoto after his first return in 1228, and after a second return in 1240 made the Sairinji of Dazaifu and Tōrinji in Kyoto centres of *vinaya* practice. Although it gained a brief popularity, this northern form of Ritsu never acquired a large following.

From this brief survey, the eclectic multi-practice nature of Nara Buddhist activities during the Kamakura period is apparent. From the earliest days in Nara, the study of all Six Sects had been combined at the large temples such as the Tōdaiji, and this created a natural tendency to unify and assimilate doctrine and practices.

But despite their multi-practice tendency, most Nara Buddhit leaders were strongly opposed to new Kamakura Buddhism, in particular Hōnen's Pure Land movement. A great deal of their hostility stemmed from a sectarian inability to appreciate the true meaning of the 'Other-power' single-practice *nembutsu;* the Kōfukuji petition of 1205 composed by Jōkei and Myōe's *Saijarin*[11] present examples of such sectarian bias. Not all of the Nara leaders were caught in such a pitfall, and some such as Myōhen and Gyōnen, were able to rise above sectarian fears for vested interests and establish close contacts with the new sects, yet even they failed to create a lasting tradition.

The greatest stumbling block for members of the old Nara sects was their failure to transcend a traditional pattern of thinking that considered Buddhism as a subject of academic study, and religion for the aristocracy and protection of the nation, rather than a means of personal salvation. Even though they came to recognize the need to combine theological study and practice, they were uncertain of a proper direction to assume. To a certain degree multi-practice represented indecision, and ultimately led to hodge-podge. No concerted effort ever arose, besides the limited Shingon-Ritsu movement, to present a form of devotion capable of practice by the masses. In this respect the Nara leaders were handicapped by their own inbred intellectual and aristocratic tradition and a Hīnayāna spirit; they were unable to understand or appreciate the needs of the masses. Even their reaction to *mappō* thought represented more of an adoption and reaction to the Pure Land view than a true individual awareness.

The various Nara restorers and scholars appear like fire sparks throughout the Kamakura and Muromachi periods, yet they were never capable of kindling sufficient flame to expand—or in most cases, even to insure continuity, whereas the new Kamakura sects spread like wildfire. Perhaps the historical moment for Nara Buddhism had passed, and time and place weighed against their success—to a certain degree their later Kyoto counterparts faced the same handicaps.

B. Medieval Tendai

Tendai was placed in even more of a reactionary role than the Nara sects during the Kamakura period. Although it is popularly considered to be the 'mother' of all the new Kamakura Buddhist movements, it gave birth unwillingly, and in the belief that its young would devour it, fought them every step of the way.

1. *Sōhei* Violence

The history of Mt. Hiei from its golden age until its destruction by Oda Nobunaga in 1571, is a recurrent cycle of violence and conflict balanced with sporadic attempts at restoration. It was during the term of the abbot Ryōgen (912–985), credited as middle-restorer, that the priest-soldiers (*sōhei*), first came to prominence. These individuals were generally recruited from among the low-ranking priests, who served in menial maintenance roles (*dōshū*), such as cooking and cleaning upon the mountain, a counterpart of the lay brother in western monasticism. Socially they were quite different from the scholar-monks (*gakuto* or *gakushō*), mainly from aristocratic backgrounds, and the sore festering wound of class distinction became a major source of conflict.

One of the most severe battles between lay monks (*dōshū*) and scholar-monks (*gakuto*), occurred during 1178–9. This was incited by an attack of the *gakuto* upon the living quarters of the *dōshū* in the eighth month of 1178, destroying their dormitory and seizing possessions, allegedly to right an earlier grievance. The *dōshū* responded by going into the local provinces to recruit bandit mercenaries to assist them and won the first battle. The *gakuto* then appealed to the Court, and Retired Emperor

Go-Shirakawa ordered Taira Kiyomori to send troops to their aid, but when this attempt failed, *dōshū* power further increased. Continual skirmishes occurred over the following months and finally in the seventh month of 1179, the government sent a massive number of troops to thoroughly seek out and attack all *dōshū* hiding in the hills and canyons of Mt. Hiei, as well as in local provinces, but again failed. Peace was finally attained during the eleventh month, when the *gakuto* of the Western Pagoda severely defeated the *dōshū* of Yokawa, and negotiations led to a cessation of hostilities. But by 1203 another massive outbreak occurred, this time the issue involved *gakuto* precedence in the bath house, which the *dōshū* chose to ignore. A minor skirmish developed into a full scale war, leading to the intervention of the cloistered Emperor and forced resignation of the current abbot, but that did not quell matters, and in a gigantic conflict between *dōshū* and government troops, over three hundred died. The issue was only resolved when Emperor Go-Toba granted the *dōshū* amnesty as part of his plan to use their services in his conspiracy against the Hōjō regents in Kamakura. But peace on Mt. Hiei was not lasting, and by 1226 another major encounter erupted in a border dispute between the estates of the Eastern pagoda and Yokawa.

Generally the internal disputes on Mt. Hiei involved either confrontations between the *dōshū* and *gakuto* monks, or else contests between the three powerful sections of the Enryakuji complex: the Eastern Pagoda, the Western Pagoda and Yokawa.[12] From the late Heian period until the destruction of Mt. Hiei in 1571, these disputes were so frequent that they virtually defy description. But they were not the only battles waged by the Mt. Hiei *sōhei*. *Gakuto* and *dōshū* frequently combined in feuds with other powerful temples, as well as to oppose the new Kamakura sects. One of the most dominant long-lasting quarrels was between Mt. Hiei and the Jimon of the Miidera.

The Sanmon-Jimon bitterness began in 993, when Enchin's disciples fled Mt. Hiei and established the Onjōji or Miidera temple. This feud between the followers of Ennin and Enchin was actively carried on until 1571, and in the long struggle, the Jimon consistently played the role of underdog—but after each defeat, they received support from both the Kyoto aristocracy and Kamakura government to finance the rebuilding of their temple complex after Sanmon devastation. The Miidera was fortunate to have established early ties with the Minamoto family, and when Minamoto Yoritomo came to power, became one of his favoured temples. But even later Kamakura leaders, as well as Kyoto aristocracy, supported the Miidera, partially as a means of checking the power of the Sanmon monks and partially due to personal respect. The Retired Emperor Go-Shirakawa even proclaimed himself to be a Jimon monk.

In the long conflict with Mt. Hiei, the Sanmon monks periodically raided and destroyed the Miidera. For example, in 1214 over what had began as a minor personality dispute, the Sanmon *sōhei* burnt the Miidera to ashes for the fifth time. In this instance, although the Kamakura government and Kyoto aristocracy aided in restoration, the Jimon monks were not satisfied without exacting some form of revenge against Mt. Hiei. They turned to the powerful Tōdaiji and Kōfukuji for assistance, and in union staged an attack against the Sanmon *shōen* in the foothill areas, but in retaliation the Mt. Hiei *sōhei* burnt down the Miidera another time. If there is a moral involved, it must relate either to the undying nature of the human ego among religious, or else to the nature of an institution to reflect the psychological maturity of its members.

One of the greatest sources of conflict between the Sanmon and Jimon, was the Miidera desire to establish its own *kaidan* rather than being forced to send its monks to Mt. Hiei for ordination. As early as 1039, they made their first request to the court and appealed annually thereafter, but were constantly opposed by Mt. Hiei. Finally in 1260 they received permission to establish a *sammaya kaidan*, but this led to such a massive Mt. Hiei protest that the government revoked permission. In turn the monks of Miidera were so angered that they abandoned the temple in a body. To make amends the government granted the Miidera control of the prestigious Shitennōji, but after the Jimon monks agreed to return to their temple, the Sanmon then protested the award, and a new quarrel commenced.

Besides the constant round of warfare with the Miidera, the Sanmon monks frequently clashed with the great Nara temples, in particular the Kōfukuji. And in combat against the new Kamakura sects, they are most well-known for destroying Hōnen's tomb, the burning of the Higashi Honganji at Ōtani in 1465, and the destruction of the twenty-one Nichiren headquarters temples in 1536. But the continual belligerance of the Sanmon monks eventually proved to be self-destructive. Their participation in the Kemmu Restoration and subsequent granting of refuge to Emperor Go-Daigo at the time of his downfall, incurred the enmity of the Ashikaga government, while continual Sanmon interference in other political affairs created enemies among the local warlords, who began to encroach upon the shōen of Mt. Hiei.

The greatest Sanmon misjudgement was in arousing the anger of Oda Nobunaga by conspiring against him and supporting his enemies, the Daimyō Asakura and Asai. This led during the ninth month of 1571 to a massive attack upon Mt. Hiei of 25,000 samurai led by Nobunaga. Contemporary accounts relate the death of over three thousand monks and laymen in the assault, among whom there was no differentiation between abbot, distinguished scholar or priest-soldier—as well as the destruction of every temple, building and shrine upon the mountain until not a single tree nor blade of grass remained.[13]

This devastation became a tremendous blow for the nation, for Mt. Hiei represented one of the oldest centres of Buddhist Dharma in Japan, as well as the site of rites for the peace of the nation and prosperity of the Imperial family—its destruction appeared nothing short of sacrilegious. In the past although the activities of the Mt. Hiei sōhei had often been resented by Shōgun and Emperor alike, no one had ever entertained the drastic notion of destroying a place so sacred to Japanese tradition. And to compound matters, there was no way the mountain could be restored as long as Nobunaga lived. Thus on the second day of the sixth month in 1582, when Nobunaga was assassinated at the Honnōji temple, an immediate plan surfaced to restore Mt. Hiei. Emperor Ōgimachi began an offical project in which the new warlord leader of Japan, Toyotomi Hideyoshi participated, as well as the lesser known

Tokugawa Ieyasu. In 1585, the *Konponchūdō* (main hall), was roughly completed. The project took many years, and it was not until the period of Tokugawa Iemitsu that activities on Mt. Hiei returned to a normal state.

2. Theological Developments

The influential Eshin-ryū of Tendai that moved to the Kantō area and became known as Inaka (countryside) Eshin, or Inaka Tendai, was primarily responsible for the theological restoration of Mt. Hiei after Nobunaga's attack. To briefly summarize its background, Ryōgen, the middle-restorer of Tendai had two outstanding disciples: Genshin (942–1017) and Kakuun (953–1007), regarded respectively as the founders of the Eshin-ryū and Danna-ryū. Although these two schools developed more along personal rather than theological differences, they formed the main stream of Tendai theological study (*engyō*, in contrast to Tai-mitsu) during the medieval ages.

The tradition claiming Genshin as founder, settled in the Yokawa area of Mt. Hiei and subdivided into four schools: the Sugiu, Gyōsenbō, Tsuchimikado-monzeki and Hōchibō. The Danna-ryū with its centre in the Eastern Pagoda also subdivided into four schools: the Ekōbō, Chikurinbō, Bishamondō and Inokuma. [See Appendix chart I] Together these were commonly known as the *Edan hachi-ryū* (Eight schools of E and *Dan*). The Danna-ryū did not spread to the provinces and became extinct at the time of the Mt. Hiei destruction. In contrast, the Eshin-ryū was transmitted to the Kantō area by the monks Shinga, (under whom it is popularly believed that Nichiren studied Tendai while in Kamakura) and Shinson. This tradition thrived in the Kamakura area and produced a number of distinguished scholars, such as Sonshun (1451–1514) fourth abbot of the Getsusanji. Upon the destruction of Mt. Hiei, the Inaka Eshin-ryū was reintroduced as part of the restoration and became the basis of modern Tendai theology.

Nankōbō Tenkai (1536–1643) was one of the most outstanding exponents of the Inaka Eshin-ryū. In 1625 under Tokugawa sponsorship, he established the Kaneiji, also known as the Tōeizan (Eastern Mt. Hiei,) in Edo, modeled after the Enryakuji to guard the evil northeastern corner of Edo castle. Tenkai was also responsible for founding the Rinnōji, which was placed in charge of the Tōshōgū shrine, the mausoleum of Tokugawa Ieyasu. In keeping with Tokugawa policy, Tenkai planned to use these two temples to balance the power of Mt. Hiei, and to make Edo a centre of cultural activities. It was not until 1659, sixteen years after Tenkai's death, that his plan was realized. That year the third son of Emperor Go-Mizunoo combined the abbotship of the Tōeizan, Rinnōji and Enryakuji, and chose to reside in Edo at the Tōeizan. This completely shifted Tendai power to Edo, however, the victory was not lasting. During the Meiji Restoration the Tōeizan was destroyed, and since it had represented a bastion of the defunct shōgunal power, no attempt was made to restore it; the site became Ueno park.

The main theological characteristics of the Inaka Eshin-ryū were: the belief in the *Lotus Sutra* as supreme, with all other sutras viewed as *upāya* (accomodated teachings), the Absolute transcendence of *shikan* (meditation) over the relativity of both the *honmon* and *shakumon* sections of the *Lotus Sutra*,[14] and one thought of faith (*ichinen shinge*) as the starting point of meditation.[15] The school also became interested in developing oral transmission.

Kuden (Oral Transmission)

From the time Saichō first introduced esoterism into orthodox Tendai philosophy, a problem arose regarding how to harmonize the distinct exoteric and esoteric teachings. Later successors such as Ennin and Enchin elevated esoteric Taimitsu at the expense of traditional Tendai *Lotus* belief, but in time a certain synthesis developed among the moderates of both traditions. One of the theological means of achieving unity was use of the concept of Original Enlightenment (*hongaku shisō*), and in place of following the orthodox manner of justifying this theological view on the basis of scriptural authority, oral transmission (*kuden*) was used in the esoteric style.

According to this method, a master would communicate his doctrine secretly to a single disciple. The teachings themselves consisted of general

Tendai doctrines, although in many cases so-called 'secret transmissions' of Saichō, Ennin and Enchin were passed on that were not authentic. The Eshin and Danna schools used both scriptural and oral transmission in their development. By the close of the Heian period, the oral transmissions were gradually committed to writing in the form of 'Records of Oral Transmission' (kudensho). Throughout the Kamakura and Muromachi periods, oral transmission became one of the most significant Tendai theological occupations.

Despite the activities of the Eshin-ryū, and flourishing practice of oral transmission, Tendai theology made little contribution to the Kamakura mass movement, except in its role as an inspiration for the rise of new sects. The subtle interpretations and arguments of Tendai theology might be considered superior to the at times ill-defined views of the founders of the new schools, but this philosophy could only be appreciated by a handful of individuals possessing ample leisure time. The changing social and political conditions of the day mitigated against such intellectual pastimes and the unsettled violent atmosphere of Mt. Hiei made it imperative for those who sought to quietly engage in practice to either isolate themselves in hermitages or flee the mountain.

3. Taimitsu

In contrast to the intellectual nature of Tendai theology, developments in Taimitsu during the Kamakura period were predominantly related to the systematization of practice. The schools split up into a confusing disarray as Appendix chart II indicates; personalities were the major causes of differences.

At the Miidera, the Chishō Daishi (Enchin) tradition of Taimitsu was the major study and became popularly known as the Mii-ryū. Nichiin was a leading esoteric master and favourite of Minamoto Yoritomo.

The uniqueness of each Taimitsu school was derived from its varieties of secret ritual and magical prayers. These were primarily devoted to serving the needs of the aristocracy and Kamakura leaders. During the late Muromachi, both Sanmon and Jimon schools of Taimitsu entered into a period of decline that was culminated in the 1571 destruction of

Mt. Hiei. Prior to this however, the Hōman-ryū had managed to become established at both the Rinnōji and Tōeizan in the Kantō area. With the restoration of Mt. Hiei the Taimitsu schools experienced a brief revival but once again declined during the Meiji Restoration.

Shinzei-ha

The independence of the *nembutsu* movement created a certain void within the Tendai sect, those interested in *nembutsu* practice generally chose to follow the new schools, while the Tendai *nembutsu* declined. During the fifteenth century Shinzei changed this situation.

Born in Ise in 1443, Shinzei studied twenty years at the Western Pagoda on Mt. Hiei before becoming a recluse at Kurodani, where he recited 50,000 *nembutsu* daily and studied the *Tripiṭaka*. He then began popular (*shōdō*) style preaching. He received tremendous respect at Court, where he lectured on the *Ōjōyōshū*, and was noted for refusing gifts at the end of his lectures. Many Court ladies and members of the aristocracy received the *śīla* from him, and he gradually developed a sizeable following.

In 1486, Shinzei restored the Saikyōji in Ōmi and made it the headquarters of his movement. Originally this temple had been founded by the abbot Ryōgen, and it became closely associated with Genshin's Yokawa *nembutsu* followers. In 1325, it was restored by Echin (d. 1356), who attempted to make it a special temple for the practice of Tendai Mahāyāna *śīla* (*endonkai*). With such a history, it was a logical place for Shinzei to begin a movement unifying 'nembutsu practice and Mahāyāna *śīla*' (*kaishōitchi*). As a continuation of Genshin's Tendai *nembutsu* tradition, Shinzei's movement represented both a reaction against the neglect of the *śīla* by the Kamakura Pure Land schools, as well as competition with them to attract the masses; it also formed a medieval counterpart to the *nembutsu hijiri* of Kōyasan.

Shinzei won the support of Ashikaga Shōgun Yoshimasa, and in 1492 Emperor Go-Tsuchi-mikado received the *endonkai* from him in company with a number of aristocrats. When Shinzei died in 1495 at the Sairenji in Iga, he left five-hundred disciples. In 1883 he was granted the posthumous title of Jishō Daishi. Shinzei was succeeded at the Sai-kyōji by his disciple Seizen.

In 1872 the Meiji government briefly attempted to unite both the Jimon and Shinzei-ha under the abbot of Mt. Hiei, but in 1878 the plan was abandoned and both were recognized as independent. Today the Shinzei-ha with headquarters at the Saikyōji forms the third largest sub-sect of Tendai, with approximately 430 branch temples in Ōmi, Ise and Echizen regions.

Shinzei's movement represented one attempt to popularize Tendai and keep it abreast of the new Kamakura schools. Seemingly their exodus drained Tendai vitality as they took with them many of the idealistic Tendai monks who were unwilling to tolerate the corruption of Mt. Hiei or the constant warfare that disrupted normal life. But all the Tendai idealists did not desert—many who remained withdrew from the worldly affairs of the mountain into peaceful isolation, ap-plying themselves to study or practice, and among the latter, new Tendai devotional developments such as Shōmyō-dō, Shugendō, and Ichijitsu Shintō evolved.

Shōmyō-dō

The special melody used in Buddhist services known as *bonbai*, was introduced on Mt. Hiei by Ennin from China during the ninth century. Later it was transmitted to Ryōgen, Genshin and ultimately system-atized by Ryōnin, founder of the Yūzū Nembutsu, to a distinct style of melody that influenced Japanese music in general.

During the Kamakura period, in parallel with the popularity of esoteric Buddhism, which placed emphasis upon chanting, ritual and *mudrā* to attain Enlightenment, a new devotion evolved known as *shōmyō jōbutsu* (chant the sutra and become Buddha). According to this belief, the melodic chanting of the sutra, which required concen-tration and effort, was no longer just a ritual supplement, but regarded in itself as a practice capable of leading to Enlightenment. This was an expression, not unlike the *nembutsu*, that allowed emphasis to be trans-ferred from ritual for the sake of worldly benefits or aristocratic pleasure, to an intensification of individual faith. For idealists who chose to remain within the Tendai sect, Shungendō and pilgrimages through the mountains (*kaihōgyō*) also filled such needs.

Honzan-ha of Shugendō

During the Kamakura period, the major Tendai centre of Shungendō was the Shōgo-in Honzan-ha. This tradition traced its historical origin back to 1090, when Emperor Shirakawa made a pilgrimage to Kumano and decided to make Zōyo (1032–1116), who accompanied him, the overseer of the entire Kumano *sanzan* (triad of mountains). Subsequently, when Zōyo became abbot of the Onjōji in 1100, Kumano Shugendō became permanently associated with the Jimon Miidera; a number of events contributed to their lasting relationship. For instance, Zōyo established the Shōgo-in in Kyoto as a branch of the Miidera, and when the Retired Emperor Go-Shirakawa's son became a monk there, he brought with him substantial *shōen* (estates) in the Kumano area. Furthermore, the frequent Sanmon attacks on the Miidera forced the monks of that temple to flee to the mountains and stay for long periods while their temple was being restored, this afforded them natural ties and a close feeling of familiarity with Shugendō followers.

Shugendō practice also managed to provide the Jimon monks with an edge of superiority over their Sanmon competitors, not only did the Miidera combine Tendai exoteric teachings and Mikkyō, but they were one of the few institutions to boast of Shugen ability; this naturally attracted the aristocracy and some, such as the son of Emperor Juntoku, joined the Miidera. Also the hitherto unaffiliated *yamabushi* in the mountains decided to join the Miidera. After it became a practice for the Jimon monzeki abbot to make a pilgrimage to Kumano during the early thirteenth century, monks practicing Shugen began to organize into the Honzan school.

By the Muromachi period as Shugen followers settled into permanent temple-hostels (*shukubō*), and pilgrimage routes established in fixed patterns, the individualistic *yamabushi* lifestyle began to disappear.[16] Shugen followers were regarded as adept in magico-esoteric practices and incorporated into the domains of the local Daimyō. Thus institutionalism destroyed the early Shugen individualistic religious experience, but at the same time, the type of naturalistic belief that had inspired Shugen, found its niche within the religious institutions.

Idealistic Sanmon monks on Mt. Hiei also practiced mountain pilgrimages (*kaihōgyō*) as instituted by Sō-ō (831–91). By the Kamakura period they were considering the entire Mt. Hiei to be a manifestation of the Buddha-body and making pilgrimages through the peaks and canyons a form of religious veneration. As a means of revolting against scholastic Tendai philosophy, which tended to neglect practice, mountain veneration and pilgrimages were closely related to the belief in the indigenous Shintō gods.

4. Sannō Ichijitsu Shintō

The Tendai movement to assimilate the gods of the indigenous Shintō faith within its fold, in keeping with the popular *honji-suijaku* theory, was known as Sannō Ichijitsu Shintō. This was closely related to the withdrawal of idealistic Tendai monks into mountain retreats and practicing Shugen, for the native gods were intimately connected with nature and the mountains steeped in their tradition. But the Tendai assimilation was not totally idealistic, for Ichijitsu Shintō also represented a very worldly attempt to expand Tendai hegemony among the rural masses, particularly to the residents of the vast Tendai *shōen*, to insure their peace and loyalty. The peasants were unable to appreciate either the subtleties of Tendai philosophy or the aesthetic qualities of its esoteric rituals, yet they did have intense faith in the indigenous gods, who represented for them the very earth they tilled, and exerted an influence over nearly every aspect of their agrarian lives. To gain the cooperation of such workers, as well as to extend Tendai influence in the provinces, the incorporation of Shintō deities played a important role.

Followers of Sannō Ichijitsu Shintō claimed Saichō or Ennin as founder to gain orthodoxy, and a number of forged writings were created. There is no question today that the basic works describing Sannō Ichijitsu Shintō are products of the Kamakura era,[17] and the origin of the thought is usually placed from the end of the Kamakura through the Northern and Southern Court periods.

Ichijitsu Shintō rose from devotion to Sannō, the name given to the indigenous gods of Mt. Hiei in imitation of Mt. T'ien T'ai in China, it was also the Japanese transliteration of 'King of the Mountain,' one of the titles of Vulture Peak (Gṛdhrakūṭa) found in the Lotus Sutra. Sannō was first applied to the Mt. Hiei gods during the lifetime of Saichō, and in 887 Ennin requested the court to appoint a nembundosha (annual priest) for them, explaining their origin and role.

Faith in the gods as protectors of Mt. Hiei gradually grew, and by the late Heian period with the development of honji-suijaku thought, the three shrines on the foothills of Mt. Hiei were linked to the three major pagodas and images on top of the mountain in the following manner:

Suijaku (Manifestation)	Honji (True-nature)
Ōmiya	Shaka
Ninomiya	Yakushi
Shōshinshi	Amida

A number of theories arose to connect the gods with Tendai doctrine, the most popular is attributed to Gyōen (d. 1047), who is mentioned in the late Kamakura Genkō Shakusho as having frequent communion with Sannō. Gyōen interpreted the two similar characters composing the name Sannō (山王) as 'three strokes signifying the three Tendai truths (Emptiness, temporary and middle) and an underlying stroke denoting oneness.'[18] The combination of 'three and one' also signified that 'all the underlying truths exist within one mind, and three thousand worlds are contained within one mind; thus the name Sannō, and by extenuation the body of Sannō, is identical to the Buddhist Dharma.'[19]

The final systematization of Sannō-Ichijitsu Shintō is usually believed to have been completed by Nankōbō Tenkai during the Tokugawa period. Although a number of developments such as the Nichiren adaptation of thirty-protector Shintō gods did develop out of Tendai Ichijitsu Shintō, the movement failed to attain the popular appeal of Shingon Ryōbu Shintō.

In summary, Tendai activities during the Kamakura-Muromachi periods can be divided into three general areas: first—the worldly enterprises that were concerned with extending Mt. Hiei's political influence, protecting its vast *shōen* and the private interests of certain factions of monks, these led to the constant outbreaks of violence; second—engagement in the complexities of Tendai theology or Taimitsu rituals; third—entering the solitude of mountain temples or retreats and practising private devotions. These activities were not necessarily exclusive, as some scholars chose to work in seclusion, but often those who chose to become recluses or pursue devotion were escaping as much from the over-intellectualization of Tendai theology as from the violence and corruption of the worldly monks.

C. Shingon Developments

At the close of the Heian period, aristocratic Buddhism was dominated by two trends: 1) Shingon-esoterism, in particular the use of *kajikitō* or esoteric rituals for worldly benefits, and 2) the early form of *nembutsu* belief that looked for an after-life in the Pure Land symbolized by the Byōdōin of Uji. Although the role of the court aristocracy eventually began to diminish, the new samurai ruling class that replaced them carried on an interest in esoteric rituals.

1. Esoteric Centres

During the early Kamakura, besides the growing influence of Tantrism among the Nara sects, two important centres of esoteric activities influenced the court aristocracy: The Ninnaji, in particular under the leadership of Shukaku (1150-1202), a son of Emperor Go-Shirakawa, and the Daigoji. All of the so-called thirty-six schools[20] of Tōmitsu evolved from these two temples, and among their offspring, a number of interesting developments arose such as Ryōbu Shintō and Shugendō. The Daigoji for example was responsible for the evolution of the Miwa-ryū of Ryōbu Shintō, as well as the Tōzan-ha of Shungendō. The latter, allegedly founded by Shōbō (832-909), and based at the Sambō-in sub-temple, became so powerful, that in 1275 Dōchō, a monk supported by Shugen followers, became abbot of the entire Daigoji complex. And during the close of the thirteenth century under Kenshun, and his disciple Manzei (1378–1435), the Sambō-in began to dominate Daigoji activities. In contrast to the popularity of these two temples, the Tōji, previous heart of the Shingon order began the early Kamakura in a state of decline, and was only gradually restored with the support of Retired Emperor Go-Uda.

Shingi-Shingon

Mt. Kōya remained too distant from the capital to exert influence upon political activities. In many respects this was an advantage, as it kept the monks relatively free from the intrigues and violence of *sōhei* activities—but Kōyasan's internal problems rivalled those of Mt. Hiei.

The dispute between the Kongōbuji, the main temple on the mountain, and the newly developed Daidenpō-in of Kakuban began during the early twelfth century, when followers of the latter were forced to flee to Mt. Negoro;[21] in total the quarrel lasted over one hundred and forty years. After periodic skirmishes in which the Daidenpō-in repeatedly attempted to return to Mt. Kōya, the most serious battle occurred in 1243, resulting in the exile of twenty-six Kongōbuji monks by the Court. But despite continual Court intervention, Kongōbuji monks were adamant in their refusal to allow the Daidenpō-in followers to ever return to Mt. Kōya. In fact in 1286, when an appeal was made by the Daidenpō-in to the Court, monks of the Kongōbuji threatened to abandon that temple in a body if the petition was granted. It was then that Raiyu (1226–1304) head of Daidenpō-in Academic affairs, conferred with the Kōyasan abbot and decided to permanently move both the Daidenpō-in and Mitsugon-in to Mt. Negoro and establish a new sect of Shingon—the 'Shingi-Shingon.'

One serious theological development occurring in the rise of Shingi-Shingon was Raiyu's advancement of the *kajishin* theory. Traditionally in Shingon, the Buddha who preached both the *Dainichikyō* and *Kongōchōkyō* was believed to be the Eternal *Dharma-kāya* (*honjishin*) rather than the historical Śākyamuni. But Raiyu opposed this interpretation on the grounds that the Absolute *Dharma-kāya* was formless and eternal, hence could not enter the world to preach. In his view, the manifestation-body (*kajishin*) was responsible for preaching the two sutras. This theory, completed by the fourth successor Shōken (1307–92), became the essence of Shingi-Shingon, Raiyu's disciples formed the Chūshōin-ryū.

Theological Activities

Despite the division in the order, Mt. Kōya continued to enjoy prosperity. A popular practice, that has been continued to modern day, became the construction of memorial *stūpa* upon the mountain. In 1213 a stone memorial tablet was erected in memory of Hōnen, and in 1285 a special service was held upon the completion of a twenty year project to build stone *stūpa* to mark every *chō* (one *chō*=109 metres) along the roadway up the mountain. Each *stūpa* was carved with a Sanskrit *bīja* (seed-syllable), symbolizing the various deities of the *mandara*, as well as the name of its donor, among whom appeared major figures of the Kamakura government and commoners; many of these can still be seen today. Another activity, in keeping with the cultural development of the period, was the printing of Buddhist texts. In 1253 Kūkai's *Sangōshiki* (Indications of the Goals of the Three Teachings) was printed for the first time, followed by the *Jūjūshin-ron* (Ten Stages of Development of Mind); this practice was continued during the Muromachi period.

A major religious development was the growth and popularity of the Shingon *nembutsu*. Leaders in this movement were Myōhen Shōnin, whose eight *hijiri* became the nucleus of Shingon *nembutsu* faith, and Chōgen, the monk in charge of restoring the Tōdaiji, who established one of his seven perpetual *nembutsu* halls on Mt. Kōya. Another active group was an offspring of Genshin's Yokawa *nembutsu* followers practicing the twenty-five *nembutsu* meditations, and in 1275, Ippen visited the mountain. All varieties of *nembutsu* devotion including such mixed practices as dancing and beating the drum existed, and certain Shingon scholars became disillusioned with such conduct. A movement to restore the theology of Kūkai and set aside the overemphasis upon rituals and *nembutsu* practice arose, led by Nanshōbō Kakukai (1142–1223).

Born in Tajima in 1142, Kakukai was educated in the Onoryū tradition of Shingon by Jōkai (1074–1149) at the Daigoji. He later resided at the Keōin on Mt. Kōya, and became known for his belief that 'the Pure Land did not necessarily exist in the West, for all one needed to do was to purify his own mind and it would become a Pure Land.' Kakukai quit this life in 1223 at the age of eighty-two, when according to tradition, he chose to fly away with evil spirits to save them from their unhappy existence. His most outstanding disciples were Hosshō (d. 1245) and Dōhan (1184–1252), who established major centres of study and popularized the practice of theological discussions (*rongi*).

Except for a brief lull during the Northern-Southern Court period, theological activities prospered on Kōyasan. Two important Muromachi scholars were: Yūkai (1385–1416), famous for the *Hōkyōshō* (Gem Mirror Treatise), a work on pure Tantrism, as well as his denunciation of the degenerate Tachikawa-ryū, and Chōkaku (1340–1416). Together they completed Shingon systematization, however, although they were succeeded by a number of capable disciples, their tradition ultimately lost its vitality and bogged down into philosophical quibbling.

A different form of Shingon advancement during the medieval period was among the masses. Undoubtedly Shingon also felt pressure from the new Kamakura sects, but their response was less reactionary and of a more positive nature than the other established sects. Hōnen's disciples maintained close relations with both Kōyasan and the Shingi-Shingon of Mt. Negoro.

Shingon influence spread among the masses during the Kamakura period mainly through popular prayers for worldly benefits (*kajikitō*), combined with the Shingon theurgic form of *nembutsu* and the cult to Kūkai. In the 1270's the threat of the Mongol invasion led to rituals for the protection of the nation held throughout the land, and these were generally credited with staving off the Mongol attacks.

During the Muromachi period, the downfall of the court aristocracy led to a decline of the Tōji and Ninnaji temples and Kōyasan began to play an increasing role, due to the activities of its popular *hijiri* among the masses; eventually it became the centre of Shingon activities. The isolation of the mountain allowed its priests to continue activities after the Ōnin war, when other great temples were caught in the wars between the various Daimyō; Inyū (d. 1517) was one of the foremost theologians of this period. However, during the Tokugawa period, Shingon theology prospered only under the Chizan and Buzan branches of Shingi-Shingon.

2. Ryōbu Shūgō Shintō

Symbolic of the success of Shingon among the masses, was the popular development and growth of the movement known as Ryōbu Shintō. The title was derived from the belief that the Inner and Outer shrines of Ise respectively represented the *Taizōkai* (Garbhadhātu) and *Kongōkai* (Vajradhātu) *mandaras*. Amaterasu Ō Mikami enshrined within the Inner Ise shrine was identified with Dainichi Nyorai of the *Taizōkai*, while Toyouke no Mikami of the Outer Shrine was symbolized by the Dainichi of the *Kongōkai*.[22]

Ryōbu Shintō was strongly influenced by vocal transmission, which allegedly established its orthodoxy. The textual basis was the *Tenchireiki-ki* attributed to Kūkai, actually a much later forgery. Two dominant schools developed: the Miwa and Ninnaji, each with their unique theological interpretations.

Miwa Shintō is believed to be the earliest form of Shingon Shintō, advocated by the Jingūji (shrine-temple) of the Ōmiwa Shrine, which considered Mt. Miwa of Yamato as its divine body. Its theology was derived from a revelation during which the Miwa Myōjin announced its proper name to be *Ten Konrin Ō Kōmyō Henshō Dainichi Son*. By a somewhat tortuous explanation, three characters were selected from this title and given the following symbolism:

> *Ten—Nirmaṇa-kāya*—compassion (*hi*)
> *Shō—Saṃbhogha-kāya*—wisdom (*chi*)
> *Son—Dharma-kāya*—principle (*ri*)

These three bodies were considered to be unified within Dainichi Nyorai and also represented the three manifestations of that Buddha in the form of:

1) Amaterasu Ō Mikami
2) Miwa Daimyōjin
3) Ise Jingū

In this relationship, the Ise Jingū was considered to be the manifestation (*suijaku*) of the Miwa Daimyōjin, since Miwa antedated the Ise Shrine and considered itself superior as a proper place of Shintō origin. The twin peaks of Mt. Miwa were also believed to represent the *Taizōkai* (northern peak) and *Kongōkai* (southern peak) *mandaras*, while the canyons and other geographical features of the mountain were likened to Tantric ritual instruments.

The theological systematization of this school was completed by Jitsukyō, a disciple of Jitsugen (1180–1249) of the Daigoji Onoryū. In this respect, the Miwa-ryū can be regarded as an offspring of the Onoryū, although it independently became one of the thirty-six schools of Shingon Tōmitsu.

Somewhat later in development, the Ninnaji school traces its origin to the legend of Emperor Saga granting Kūkai the Shintō *kanjō* (*abhiṣeka*) ordination in exchange for the Shingon *kanjō*. It can be regarded as an offspring of the Tōmitsu Hirosawa-ryū. Two later known schools of Ryōbu Shintō were the Bosatsu-ryū and Unden-ryū. During the Tokugawa period, Jiun Onkō (1718–1804) attempted to restore Ryōbu-Shintō and correct improper interpretations. After the Meiji separation of Buddhism and Shintō, with the exception of Onkō's tradition, all forms of Ryōbu-Shintō virtually became extinct.

CONCLUSION

The new movements of the Kamakura period represented an attempt to overcome the Nara and Heian scholastic-aristocratic Buddhism —the established religion dedicated to the peace and prosperity of the nation and welfare of the ruling class. Although using the theology of the older sects as a foundation, the leaders of the new Kamakura schools all turned to the purity of a single-practice, through which they linked their explicit philosophies to daily life and broadened the appeal of Buddhism to every Japanese. And their success was highly contingent upon correct assessment of the dramatic social upheaval occurring in medieval Japan.

Social Upheaval—a time for personal introspection

The end of the Heian period climaxed the golden days of the aristocracy and rise of a new social order in which the middle and lower-middle class became actively involved. For contemporary religious leaders, it was a time of walking upon shifting sands—the wrong choice of audience, patron or allegiance would suddenly find them engulfed and lost. Even the old established temples were forced to realize that their security was in jeopardy as the traditional class structure collapsed. The Warring States era most clearly brought this to light, when overnight a great Daimyō patron could fall, to be replaced by a new leader from the lower-classes—it indeed appeared to be a time when the 'inferior overcame the superior' (*gekokujō*), as power became the determinant of social status.

Such social fluidity and political chaos made it easy for religious to escape from the bonds of tradition. Even the ingrained aristocratic monks of Nara such as Jōkei and Myōe, could turn their backs on life at the affluent temples and openly choose to live in the mountains as recluses— a practice that back in the days of Nara Buddhist ascendancy was once considered unacceptable, and that even during the Kamakura period must have represented unconventional conduct.

In such an unsettled age, it was better to take an individual stance and select one's own sponsors and patrons rather than throw in lot with the great temples, whose politics were dedicated to the interests of their great *shōen* estates. Security could be found nowhere except in the right personal choice—this historical moment made individualism a religious necessity, and the introspection of *mappō* thought further enforced it. For in the time of earthquakes, drought, pestilence and war, every man faces the possibility of death as acutely as upon his own deathbed—it is then that he comes to realize his 'aloneness' and the significance of the actions or *karma* that make him unique.

The Rising Role of Women

When traditional scholars view the social fluidity of the Kamakura and Muromachi periods, they quickly note the rise of the lower and middle classes, but tend to overlook the role of women, except negatively pointing out the frequent moral charges raised against the new movements.[1] Yet the appeal of the new Kamakura leaders to women was a major reason for their success.

During the Heian period both Mt. Hiei and Kōyasan prohibited women from even entering their sacred precincts, and the general thought was that women were incapable of attaining Enlightenment. But in Japanese history a certain change can be observed in the role of women from the late Heian up to the Warring states era, the status of women rose in company with the general mood of social awareness, and it abruptly declined again as the sword became the measure of social status. The new Kamakura leaders were keenly aware of this change, and in some manner each responded to it:

Hōnen was the first to develop a large female lay following, and although it created problems for some of his disciples, as in the case of Jūren and Anraku, Hōnen personally never faced any moral accusations. The Pure Land emphasis upon the weakness and limitations of man, encouraged its followers to welcome people of all classes and even women engaged in the most demeaning professions. In turn, Hōnen was assisted by women during his exile, and six attended his death. Also in the Pure Land tradition, Shinran's marriage and the subsequent blood-succession of his order created a drastic change in the overall view of laity and women, setting a future precedent for all Buddhist sects.

Nichiren also made an appeal to women, including them as an important part of his order. And even Dōgen, who advocated the monastic life, was known to state that women were not necessarily inferior to men, since intrinsic worth was determined by the harmony of one's life with the way, and of one's body with the right law.[2] His school, as it became a mass movement, received strong support from its female followers. And finally, despite the criticisms of the older sects regarding the morality of the affiliation of women with the Pure Land movement, we find great Kyoto and Nara leaders such as Jien, Myōe and Eison responding to the needs of the time by working to educate women.

Kamakura Buddhist leaders provided women with spiritual support, but in return, they received an important financial basis for their institutions. After their long alienation, Japanese women made zealous religious followers, they were instrumental in converting their husbands, particularly in the Nichiren sect, and provided a means of perpetuation by instilling religious values in their children. In effect, women provided the understructure of the mass movement, just as they still continue to do today.

Problems of the Mass Movement

For the first time in Japanese Buddhist history, the simplicity of clear down-to-earth teachings became the religion of the masses, yet this conversion did not automatically solve Buddhist problems, in fact it created new ones.

In the first place, whenever a religion, despite its initial purity, becomes involved with classes of people at every level, its teachings cannot remain pure, for the mentality of the individuals involved and different levels of understanding, invariably create degrees of compromise. Even though the Kamakura sects were anxiously striving to overcome the extremes of the Heian assimilation of folk-beliefs and impure practices, they ended up creating their own. Medieval Shinshū priests were using *dangibon* to incorporate Shintō beliefs, the *Gozan* Zen temples established in the tradition of pure Chinese Zen, yielded to popular pressure to include esoterism and mixed practices, while the Nichiren found that the masses preferred worldly benefits as an 'end' rather than merely as a 'means.' And the continual struggle to maintain purity versus the weight of popular interest, caused divisions and dissensions within the new sects.

Furthermore, the new Kamakura Buddhist movements were centred around the personalities of their founders. As these movements became established and the actual personalities of the founders grew dim—multiple interpretations arose among later successors purporting to be their true ideals. Thus if a number of Kamakura leaders could have returned to their sects four or five centuries later, we can only wonder what their reactions would have been? Mass movements required devotion to the founder—yet the competition in that area among disciples and successors led to diverse interpretations and schisms.

Finally, as the new Buddhist movements attained success, recognition and establishment, they inherited all the problems of the older sects. The institution became a social-political entity concerned with its own preservation and its institutional ego.

The Kamakura and Muromachi periods created one of the most exciting times in Japanese Buddhist history—yet as the new movements succeeded, the ancient spectre of corruption and decay began to cast its shadow over them. Institutional problems and sectarian divisions quickened the age-old cycle leading to decline. And when Japanese society finally regained political stability under the iron hand of the Tokugawa government, the new Buddhist institutions became part of the establishment, but the price they paid for security was stagnation. The bold innovation of their founders, who had managed to establish a well-digested theological system for man's salvation applicable to the daily life of every Japanese, was set aside as petty individual concerns ruled the day—simply taking for granted the allegiance of the masses, as the Nara and Heian sects had once taken for granted the perpetual patronage of the aristocracy.

The Meiji period witnessed a new struggle and attempt at reform—this in itself would comprise an entire volume of study. But today Japanese Buddhism once again is experiencing stagnation and the problems of a modern age, in company with all the great world religions. Perhaps the past history presented within these two volumes offers some clue to a future direction. Modern literate and sophisticated masses are becoming dissatisfied with religions that look backward to days of glory—the present is always more exciting than the past—and it is time to realize that the foundation of Japanese Buddhism never was and never will be a one time endeavour—step by step, and day by day, it must undergo perpetual renewal.

ABBREVIATIONS

T.   Taishō Shinshū Daizōkyō 55 vol. (1922–33)

Pāli Text Society Series (London)

AN   Aṅguttara Nikāya 5 vol. (1885–1900)
DN   Dīgha Nikāya 3 vol. (1960, 66, 67 reprints)
MN   Majjhima Nikāya 3 vol. (1887–1902)
SN   Saṃyutta Nikāya 5 vol. (1885–1900)

Journals

IBK   Indogaku Bukkyōgaku Kenkyū (Tokyo)
MN   Monumenta Nipponica (Tokyo)

Note on languages:

Diacritical marks are omitted on frequently used Japanese proper nouns (i.e. Tokyo, Kyoto) and Sanskrit terms that have become part of the English language (i.e. Nirvana, sutra). Chinese pronunciations are derived from *Mathews' Chinese-English Dictionary* (Cambridge, 1966 ed).

Note on ages:

Japanese ages are presented in the traditional method of counting, whereby an individual is considered one year old at the date of birth.

FOOTNOTES

CHAPTER II—PURE LAND SECTS, THE PATH OF FAITH

1 The Kangaku-e (Meetings to Encourage Learning) were composed of twenty Tendai priests and twenty scholars of the Kangaku-in, who gathered together on the 14th and 15th days of the third and ninth months to listen to lectures on the *Lotus Sutra*, after which they composed poems on topics selected from the sutra. The *nembutsu* was chanted at these meetings for the purpose of attaining spiritual purification. The movement was not long lasting, although a revival was attempted during the Tokugawa period. Its founder Yasutane later became a Tendai priest with the name of Jakushin.

2 The historical Buddha had not allowed his monks to use the Brahmanic chants but did encourage music as a means of spiritual stimulation, as well as serving as a mnemonic aid in memorizing the teachings. The chanting of sutras to music was popular in China and introduced to Japan during the Nara period. Both Shingon and Tendai developed their own varieties, Shingon chanting was known as Shinryū, and the Tendai form, considered to have been restored by Ryōnin, was called Ōhararyū. The latter is still used on the occasion of special services.

3 The Tendai view is properly known as *ichinen sanzen* (one thought equals three thousand worlds). The hyperbolic figure of three thousand is arrived at by the belief that each of the ten worlds (hells, *preta*, animal, *asura*, human, *deva*, Śrāvaka, Pratyeka Buddha, bodhisattva and Buddha) are mutually inclusive embracing the other nine within them, creating a total of one thousand realms. These in turn are further subdivided into: 1) subjective entity, 2) the five psycho-physical constituents, and 3) the container world, making a grand total of three thousand realms. By stating the ten worlds are contained in one thought, Ryōnin set forth the concept in its essence.

4 also known as Yūkan or Ninkō.

5 Tsukamoto Zenryū and Umebara Takeshi, *"Fuan to Gongu"* in *Bukkyō no Shisō* vol. 8 (Tokyo: Kadokawa, 1971) p. 48.

6 DN III p. 169 ff.

7 See Fujita Kōtatsu, *Genshi Jōdoshisō no Kenkyū* (Tokyo: Iwanami, 1970) p. 502 ff.

8   Cf. Edward Conze, *Buddhism: Its Essence and Development* (New York: Philosophical Library, 1951) p. 147; Sir Charles Eliot, *Japanese Buddhism* (New York: Barnes and Noble, 1969) p. 104.

9   See Lalta Prasad Pandey, *Sun Worship in Ancient India* (Delhi: Motilal Banarsidass, 1971), in particular his chapter entitled "The Problem of Foreign Elements in Indian Sun Worship" pp. 177–90.

10 For an English discussion of some of the dominant theories see "Amita" in *Encyclopaedia of Buddhism* Vol. I p. 443 ff. The Viṣṇu theory set forth by Prof. Ogiwara Unrai should be considered in accompaniment with J. Gonda, *Aspects of Early Viṣṇuism* (Delhi: Motilal Banarsidass, 1969).

11 DN II, 103. The same story is repeated in AN I, 309 and SN V, 259.

12 For a full discussion of the philosophical precedents for these terms see Fujita, *op. cit.* pp. 322–35.

13 SN I 15, 47 describes the four varieties of light in the world as sun, moon, fire and the Enlightenment of the Buddha, which is supreme. A slightly different version in SN II, 284 presents five varieties of light: sun, moon, the warrior, the Brahmin and the Buddha. In AN I, 227–8 the Buddha is spoken of as suffusing the three thousand worlds with radiance, and in AN II, 130–1 and MN III, 120, 123–4, the infinite radiance of the Buddha is discussed.

14 Their list of the Buddha's attributes in which infinite life and light are listed consecutively is found in the *Samaya-bhedoparacana cakra* T. Vol. 29 p. 15 ff.

15 SN II, 105. Yūki Reimon, "Indo ni okeru Shoki Jōdokyō no Itosuru Mono" in *IBK*, vol. III no. 1 (September 1954) pp. 44–8 sets forth the interesting theory that Amida faith in India was perhaps a lay Buddhist reaction to the Sarvāstivādin tendency to interpret Śākyamuni's *Mahāparinirvāṇa* as near extinction and that the possible intention of the author of the *Daimuryōjukyō* was to prove the eternal lifespan of Śākyamuni using the figure of Amida as a typical method of Buddhist expression. He cites the *Lotus Sutra* as another possible example of reaction against the devotional neglect of Śākyamuni by Abhidharma scholastics.

16 Amitābha, Akṣobhya, Vairocana, Amoghasiddhi and Ratnasambhava. For a description see Benoytosh Bhattacharrya, *The Indian Buddhist Iconography* (Calcutta: K. L. Mukhopadhyay, 1958) pp. 49–50.

17 The Jōdo system of eight patriarchs includes: Aśvaghosa, Nāgārjuna, Vasubandhu, Bodhiruci, T'an-luan, Tao-ch'o, Shan-tao and Hōnen. Another system of six patriarchs lists: Vasubandhu, Bodhiruci, T'an-luan, Tao-ch'o, Shan-tao, Huai-kan and Shao-k'ang. This was obviously one area in which Hōnen's doctrine was not completely systematized.

18 cf. Kaneko Daiei, *Shinshū no Kyōgi to Sono Rekishi* (Kyoto: Hyakkaen, 1965) p. 244.

19 Hui-yüan (523-92) of the Sui dynasty, a student of the Tendai patriarch Hui-szu, who is known for his commentaries on the Pure Land sutras, and Chi-ts'ang (549-623), the reviver of the San-lun sect, known for his interest in Pure Land teachings, also fell into this category.

20 T. vol. 40 p. 838

21 T. vol. 47 p. 12

22 T. vol. 47 p. 8

23 T. vol. 37 p. 24

24 Other important Chinese Pure Land devotees were Tz'u-min, also known as Hui-jih (680-748), who combined Pure Land and Ch'an meditation and Fa-chao (ca. 822), who was interested in harmonizing Pure Land tenets with other schools.

25 Kaneko, *Shinshū no Kyōgi to Sono Rekishi* p. 297. Shigaraki Takamaro, "Hōnen ni Itaru Senju Shisō no Keifu" in *IBK* Vol. XXII no. 1 (December 1973) pp. 78-83, traces the origin of Hōnen's single-practice to Shan-tao, Genshin, Yōkan and Chinkai.

26 The traditional view maintains that there were originally twelve translations, but modern studies consider the existence of seven of the non-extant translations to be quite doubtful. See Fujita *op. cit.* p. 29. There is also considerable confusion regarding the original Sanskrit titles of the existing translations.

27 For a full discussion see Fujita *op. cit.* pp. 37-50.

28 *Ibid.* p. 75.

29 There is quite a discrepancy in the number of vows from the time of the earliest existing texts:

Han and Wu versions . . . . 24 vows
Sung . . . . 36 vows
Wei and T'ang versions . . . 48 vows
Sanskrit . . . . 46 vows
Tibetan . . . . 49 vows

30 Implying that all will attain enlightenment as *Śrāvaka* (hearers) of the Buddhas teachings and none will be *Pratyeka* (Self-Enlightened) Buddhas.

31 The five cardinal crimes in Buddhism are:
   1) Premeditated murder of one's natural mother.
   2) Premeditated murder of one's natural father.
   3) Premeditated harm of an Enlightened One.
   4) Premeditated destruction of the Buddhist community.
   5) Premeditated murder of Arhats.

32 The thirty-two marks of a superior man are as follows:
   1) protuberance on the head
   2) hair of head to be dark blue in colouring and curling towards the right

3) even and broad forehead
4) twist of hair between the eyebrows
5) dark blue eyes
6) forty teeth
7) even and orderly teeth
8) teeth closely joined to each other
9) very white teeth
10) ability to taste the unique quality of every food
11) an excellent jaw like the lion's
12) a long and thin tongue
13) a voice like the Brahman's
14) well-framed shoulders
15) seven prominences on the body (on both hands, on both feet, on both shoulders, and on the back)
16) both shoulders well-filled
17) fine golden skin
18) arms reaching to the knees when standing upright
19) upper half of body majestic, like a lion
20) body as wide as a Nyagrodha tree in circumference
21) hair growing from each pore
22) hair bending upwards with the points curling towards the right
23) male organs ensheathed in a membranous cover (like a horse or elephant)
24) well-rounded thighs
25) deep-seated ankle bones
26) soft and tender hands and feet
27) hands and feet with webs between the fingers and toes
28) long fingers
29) soles bearing the mark of a wheel (with 1,000 spokes)
30) both feet standing erect
31) broad long heels
32) calves like the shanks of a black antelope

33　This vow in effect grants equality only to the bodhisattvas of other lands who have actively engaged in the work of salvation. Those who have not are required to experience 'one-birth,' or to spend some time actively engaged in helping others attain Enlightenment.

34　We must note here that the text clearly states 'hates her female body,' which does not necessarily imply any form of discrimination. On the other hand, if we consider the fourth vow which states that the beings will have no difference in appearance, then we will have to wonder whether male or female is the ideal appearance.

35 These three degrees of Dharma represent the three varieties of peace of mind
through the realization of the truth:

    1) Response to sound—by listening to the voice of the preaching
    Buddha and becoming aware of truth.

    2) Intellectual response—entering the truth through one's own com-
    prehension.

    3) Intuitive response—attaining the truth without attachment to ap-
    pearance, sound or intellectualization.

36 AN III, 184; IV, 186, 209, 213; DN I, 110; II, 41; MN II, 145. Occasionally
these are described as the four *kathā: Dāna, Śīla, Sagga* and *Magga* (the way).

37 Purification (Skt. *vyavadāna*) and pollution (*saṃkleśa*) form a regularly contrasting pair of antonyms from the early Nikāyas through the development
of Mahāyāna. cf. SN III, 151. We can also note the emphasis upon ethical
purity (*visuddhi*) in MN I, 147–50 and DN III, 288, which became the basis
for Buddhaghosa's systematization in the *Visuddhi-magga*. Earlier writers on
the subject were Buddhadatta in his *Abhidhammāvatāra* and Upatissa in the
Vimutti-magga.

38 In the cases of Godhika and Vakkali, which appear to be based upon a single
legend, the historical Buddha determined their action to be non-worldly.
SN I, 121–3, SN III, 124.

39 MN I, 508; DhA III, 267 etc.

40 Later Pāli writers were to classify the *deva* into three categories: *sammuti deva*
(conventional deities in public opinion such as kings and princes); *visuddhi-
deva* (divine by having attained purity or merit, i.e. Arahants and Buddhas);
upapatti-deva (beings born divine). cf. PTSD p. 329. The *visuddhi-deva* were
considered to represent the highest stage of spiritual development.

41 See Kaneko Daiei, *Fuhen no Hō, Tokushu no Ki* (Kyoto: Kaneko Daiei
Sensei Beiju Kinenkai, 1968).

42 T. Vol. 47 p. 8. For a study of the transcendence of the Pure Land over the
Three Worlds see Kaneko Shimpo, "Jōdo no Sangai Shō Fushō ni tsuite"
in *IBK* Vol. XXI no. 1 (December 1972) pp. 351–4.

43 See *Foundation of Japanese Buddhism* Vol. I p. 235 ff.

44 *Ibid.* pp. 80–4.

45 The Sanskrit original for these terms is not certain, however, Yamaguchi
Susumu in his *Seshin no Jōdoron* (Kyoto: Hōzōkan, 1963) p. 101 has recon-
structed them from the Chinese translation in the following manner:

    Realm of Pollution . . . . .*saṃkleśa*
    Realm of Purification . . .*vyavadāna*

46 T. vol. 26 p. 232

47 Yamaguchi, *op. cit.* p. 118.

48 This view is partially based upon the opinion of Satō Kenju in *Bukkyō no*

Shisō, Kōza Bukkyō vol. 2 p. 234–47. See also Tao-ch'o's description T. vol. 47 p. 7.

49 T. vol. 47 p. 9.

50 Pure Land theologians prefer to consider Amida in this respect by the title of Tathāgata (Jap. *Nyorai*) rather than 'Buddha' to emphasize the coming from 'as-it-isness.'

51 The three pillars of practice of so-called 'three learnings' consist of *śīla*, *samādhi* and *prajñā*. It was believed that after the body had been controlled by *śīla* (discipline) and the mind by *samādhi* (meditation), it was then possible to comprehend reality as-it-is. DN I, 62–85. In his *Visuddhi-magga*, chapter one, Buddhaghosa clearly makes these three the cornerstone of his 'path of purity' (lit. *visuddhi-magga*).

52 T. vol. 25 p. 190.

53 For a study of the diverse implications of this crucial term, see Daigan and Alicia Matsunaga, "The Concept of *Upāya* in Mahāyāna Buddhist Philosophy" *Japanese Journal of Religious Studies* Vol. 1 no. 1 (March 1974) pp. 51–72.

54 Due to the rise of sectarianism and constant endeavour of each new sect to present a more direct means to reach Absolute Truth, the term *upāya* (Jap. *hōben*) has been frequently used to denigrate the teachings of other sects with the implication that only one's own doctrines directly convey Absolute Truth. Insofar as theologically, Absolute Truth can never be expressed in human language nor perfectly revealed at the mundane level, such arguments merely represent sectarian quibbling. But as a result, in modern Japanese the term *hōben* has come to denote a 'falsehood.'

55 Kaneko Daiei ed. *Kyōgyōshishō* in *Shinshū Seiten* (Kyoto: Hōzōkan, 1960) p. 308–9.

56 T. vol. 14, p. 549.

57 Shinran's *Yuishinshōmoni* contained in Kaneko, *Shinshū Seiten* p. 660–61.

58 T. vol. 40 p. 841. This appears to be an elaboration of the earlier Yogācāra concept of *para-sambhoghakāya* and *sva-sambhoghakāya*.

59 *Kyōgyōshinshō* in Kaneko, *Shinshū Seiten* p. 286.

60 cf. DN III, 1 ff.

61 The problems of such an interpretation are clearly evident in Har Dayal, *The Bodhisattva Doctrine in Buddhist Sanskrit Literature* (Delhi: Motilal Banarsidass, 1970) p. 65, when he interprets Amida's 'earnest wishes' in the following manner: '*May* all beings be of golden complexion,' etc. which implies either the possibility that the aspirations will not be fulfilled or else some type of divine mandate.

62 giving (*dāna*), discipline (*śīla*), patience (*kṣanti*), diligence (*vīrya*), meditation (*dhyāna*) and wisdom (*prajñā*).

63 This is the opinion of Tamura Enchō in *Hōnen* (Tokyo: Yoshikawa Kōbunkan 1964), who theorizes that she was either killed during the raid or committed suicide as a result of it. The most obviously contrived example to
demonstrate Hōnen's filial piety is found in the letter allegedly written by
the young Hōnen requesting his mother's permission to enter Mt. Hiei, cf.
Hōnen Shōnin Zenshū (Kyoto: Heirakuji, 1974) p. 819 for its complete context. Shunjō's biography composed nearly two centuries later also mentions
that Hōnen's mother granted permission for his entrance to Mt. Hiei, cf.
Harper Coates and R. Ishizuka tr. *Honen the Buddhist Saint* (Kyoto: Society
for Publication of Sacred Books of the World, 1949) pp. 124-5.

64 There is no certain record of either Hōnen's worldly name nor the name
he received upon his first ordination on Mt. Hiei. Genkū was derived from
the first character of Genkō (源光), Hōnen's first master on Mt. Hiei, and
the second character from Eikū (叡空), his second master.

65 The twenty-five meditations are designed to overcome the twenty-five
stages of existence consisting of:
    four evil existences
    four continents
    six *kāma dhātu*
    seven *rūpa dhātu*
    four *arūpa dhātu*

66 Ishii Kyōdō, *Nihon Bukkyō no Shūha* in *Kōza Bukkyō* vol. VII (Tokyo:
Daitō Shuppansha, 1958) p. 49.

67 Chikai was founder of the Bishamondō-ryū, a sub-sect of Tendai Danna-
ryū. Sōshin, also known as Hōchibō was a leading Tendai scholar affiliated
with both the Danna-ryū and Eshin-ryū. Myōhen (1141-1224) was a Sanron-
Shingon scholar who spent his latter years as a *nembutsu* recluse upon Kōyasan. Jōkei of Kasagi (1155-1213) a famous Hossō scholar was one of Hōnen's
most serious detractors and is believed to have composed the Kōfukuji
petition of 1205 to ban the *nembutsu* sect.

68 For a description see *Hōnen Shōnin Zenshū* p. 473-4; also Tamura, *Hōnen* p.
76-86.

69 Akamatsu Toshihide ed. *Bukkyōshi* vol. 2 (Kyoto: Hōzōkan, 1968) p. 34.

70 Ishida Mizumaro, *Jōdokyō no Tenkai* (Tokyo: Shunjūsha, 1967) p. 265. In
his Tendai ordination rites, Hōnen linked the recitation of the *nembutsu*
with the keeping of the ten cardinal precepts of the *Bommōkyō sūtra* and the
observance of the forty-eight lesser precepts with reliance upon Amida's
forty-eight vows. Some scholars point out however, that Hōnen had no
single-practice precedents to follow and that in dealing with other sects was
forced to establish his own example. cf. Itō Shintetsu, "Hōnen Shōnin no
Tōdaiji Kōsetsu ni tsuite" in *IBK* vol. X no. 1 (January 1962) pp. 88-93.

71 contained in *Hōnen Shōnin Zenshū* p. 865–7. For a discussion of these experiences see Fujiyoshi Jikai, "Bannen no Hōnen Shōnin", *IBK* vol. XX no. 1 (December 1971) pp. 121–7.

72 *Hōnen Shōnin Zenshū* p. 681.

73 "*Jūnimondō*" in *Hōnen Shōnin Zenshū* p. 634.

74 For a discussion see Furuta Shōkin, "Kamakura Bukkyō ni okeru Jikaishugi to Han Jikaishugi" *IBK* Vol. VI no. 1 (January 1958) pp. 94–103.

75 Tamura, *Hōnen* p. 147–8.

76 Coates, *Honen* p. 395; *Hōnen Shōnin Zenshū*, p. 1166–7.

77 Coates, *Honen* p. 405.

78 *Senjakushū* in *Hōnen Shōnin Zenshū* p. 393 ff.

79 Akamatsu ed. *Nippon Bukkyōshi* Vol. 2 p. 73.

80 This is the opinion expressed in Shunjō's biography. cf. Coates, *Honen* p. 784.

81 Ishida, *Jōdokyō no Tenkai* p. 275.

82 Coates, *Honen* p. 784.

83 This is alternately known as the Karoku or Antei persecution. The year 1227 coincided with the third year of Karoku and first year of Antei. There is some dispute regarding what month marked the beginning of Antei, current calendars place it as the tenth month.

84 Ryōkai was only abbot for the period of one year, he later became a *nembutsu* follower.

85 cf. Akamatsu Toshihide, *Shinran* (Tokyo: Yoshikawa Kōbunkan, 1961) p. 47.

86 Kyōgaku Kenkyūsho, *Shinran Shōnin Gyōjitsu* (Kyoto: Kyōgaku Kenkyūsho, 1961) p. 121.

87 Akamatsu, *Shinran* p. 60 ff.

88 The geneologies of the Hino family and Honganji list the offspring of this marriage, cf. Ienaga Saburō, *Shinran Shōnin Gyōjitsu* (Kyoto: Hōzōkan, 1969). We can only imagine that later followers might have fictionalized this first marriage for Shinran in order to disguise the fact that Eshin-ni was not of noble birth.

89 There has long been a dispute over the English usage of 'priest' in reference to a member of the Buddhist clergy. We have previously in other works, expressed our preference for 'priest' in keeping with its definition as "one who performs sacrificial, ritualistic, mediatorial, interpretative or ministerial functions, esp. as an authorized or ordained religious functionary or official minister of a particular religion." *Webster's Third International Dictionary* (1966 ed.) p. 1800. The same dictionary (p. 1460) defines 'monk' as 'a man who is a member of a monastic order; also a man who has retired from the world to devote himself to asceticism as a solitary or cenobite.' Here we

generally use the term 'monk' when referring to those who dwell isolated in temples and 'priest' for those who work among the people. In some cases the usage necessarily overlaps.

90 There are some ten letters written to Kakushin-ni between the years 1256–68 that prove to be a most important source of biographical information. For the original and modern Japanese version see Ishida Mizumaro, *Shinran to Sono Tsuma no Tegami* (Tokyo: Shunjūsha, 1968), pp. 207–55.

91 Ishida, *Shinran to Sono Tsuma no Tegami* p. 200–1.

92 *Ibid.*

93 When Shinran's great grandson Kakunyo wrote the *Kudenshō*, he cites that Eshin-ni was the mother of six children, which agrees with the Honganji geneology. cf. *Kudenshō* in Kaneko ed. *Shinshū Seiten* p. 831.

94 Akamatsu, *Shinran* p. 75 maintains Shinran married Eshin-ni in 1205.

95 *Tendaishū Seiten* in *Kokuyaku Daizōkyō* (Tokyo: Tōhōshoin, 1930) p. 2.

96 Miyazaki Enjun, "Shinran to Sono Kyōdan" in *Bukkyō no Shisō* of *Kōza Bukkyō* vol. 5 p. 165. This theory is still in doubt since the migration might have occurred at a later date.

97 This is recorded in Eshin-ni's letter of 1263. cf. Ishida, *Shinran to Sono Tsuma no Tegami* p. 224–5.

98 Shinran Shōnin Zensho Kankōkai, *Shinran Shōnin Zenshū. Gengyōhen*, vol. 1 p. 33. See also *Tannishō* in *Shinshū Seiten* p. 802.

99 Ishida, *Shinran to Sono Tsuma no Tegami* pp. 195–7. The actual letter requests this for "*Imagozen no Haha*," which contemporary scholars interpret to be Shinran's daughter Kakushin-ni. cf. Akamatsu, *Shinran* p. 330–3.

100 *Tannishō* in *Shinshū Seiten* p. 786.

101 A very similar form of three minds is found in the *Meditation Sutra:*
   1) The mind that is true and sincere
   2) the profound mind.
   3) the mind desiring to be born in the Realm of Purification by means of the transference of Amida's practice.

These are considered to be the three aspects of mind of sentient beings granted by Amida, in contrast to the three qualities of mind of Amida found in the Eighteenth vow. Since the mind of Amida becomes the mind of sentient beings, both in effect are identical.

102 *Kyōgyōshinshō* in *Shinshū Seiten* p. 228.

103 *Ibid.*

104 *Larger Sukhāvatī-vyūha* vol. 2 quoted in *Kyōgyōshinshō* p. 233.

105 Kaneko, *Shinshū no Kyōgi to Sono Rekishi* p. 54.

106 T. vol. 37 p. 271.

107 *Kyōgyōshinshō* p. 254–5.

108 Kaneko, *Fuhen no Hō, Tokushu no Ki* pp. 33–6; see also *Tannishō* chap. XV

in *Seiten* pp. 798–800.

109 The irreversible state (*avinivartanīya*).

110 *Kyōgyōshinhō* in *Seiten* p. 190.

111 *Tannishō* Chap. XVI in *Seiten* p. 801.

112 Shinran's letter, fourteenth day, twelfth month, second year of Shōka (1258) contained in *Mattōshō* 5, *Seiten* pp. 697–8.

113 *Kyōgyōshinshō*, *Seiten* p. 412.

114 *Seiten* p. 529–31.

115 *Goshōsokushū* 4 in *Seiten* p. 735–7.

116 DN I, 9.

117 Kaneko Daiei, *Kōgoyaku Kyōgyōshinshō* (Kyoto: Hōzōkan, 1959) pp. 523–4.

118 Yuizen did not retire gracefully from the scene, for in 1309 he absconded to Kamakura with the head of Shinran's image from the mausoleum and proceeded to have a body carved for it. He died in 1317 at the age of sixty-five, and the image-head was restored.

119 The Izumoji-ha still considers Zenran to be Shinran's first successor, all other Jōdo Shinshū sects recognize Nyoshin as first. For an interesting article on the character of Zenran see Miyaji Kakue, "Zenran no Igi ni tsuite" in *IBK* Vol. IV no. 1 (January 1956) pp. 252–6.

120 Certain old temples do claim Shinran as founder, in the sense that they existed during his lifetime and his presence built their Shinshū congregations.

121 *Tannishō* chap VI, *Seiten* p. 787–8.

122 Kyōgaku Kenkyūjo, *Shinran Shōnin Gyōjitsu* (Kyoto: Higashi Honganji, 1961) pp. 176–206.

123 The Kibe-ha is the only Jōdo Shinshū sect to recognize Zonkaku as fourth successor.

124 *Ippen Hijirie* in *Jishū zensho* (Kamakura: Geirinsha, 1974) p. 8.

125 *Ippen Shōnin Goroku* in *Jishū Zensho* p. 12. Literally, the title of this verse means 600,000 people, although it was intended to refer to the beginning of each line.

六字名号一遍法
十界依正一遍体
万行離念一遍証
人中上々妙好華

126 *Jishū Zensho* p. 6.

127 *Ibid.* p. 23.

128 For a discussion of this probability see Gorai Shigeru "Ippen Shōnin to Hottō Kokushi" in *IBK* Vol. IX no. 2 (March 1961) pp. 508–15.

129 *Jishū Zensho* p. 34.

130 Akamatsu ed. *Nippon Bukkyōshi* vol. II p. 149.

CHAPTER III—NICHIRENSHŪ, FOLLOWERS OF THE LOTUS

1 *Nichirenshū Seiten* in *Kokuyaku Daizōkyō* (Tokyo: Tōhōshoin, 1928) p. 523.

2 letters sixteenth day, second month 1275, found in *Seiten* p. 537–8.

3 *Hōonshō* in *Seiten* pp. 171–2.

4 *Nanjō Hyōehichirōdono Gosho* in *Seiten* p. 510.

5 Nichiren's master Shunban belonged to the Eshin-ryū, however, Mochizuki Kankō, *Nichiren Kyōgaku no Kenkyū* (Kyoto: Heirakuji, 1968) p. 53, maintains that Nichiren transcended the theological quarrels between the two schools.

6 *Kanshin Honzonshō* in *Seiten* p. 10. He also frequently expressed this view by the term *sangoku shishi* (three countries, four masters). cf. *Shōgumondōshō* in *Seiten* p. 267.

7 quoted in Ōno Tatsunosuke, *Nichiren* (Tokyo: Yoshikawa Kōbunkan, 1972) p. 44.

8 cf. *Akimoto Gosho* in *Seiten* p. 424.

9 *Ibid.*

10 Kino Kazuyoshi and Umebara Takeshi, *Eien no Inochi, Bukkyō no Shishō* vol. 12 (Tokyo: Kadokawa, 1973) p. 35.

11 *Risshō Ankokuron* in *Seiten* p. 113–6.

12 *Seiten* pp. 474–5.

13 Kino, *Eien no Inochi* p. 72.

14 Ōno, *Nichiren* p. 125.

15 *Kaimokushō* in *Seiten* p. 88.

16 *Shimoyamashō* in *Seiten* p. 485.

17 For a discussion of Nichiren's life on Mt. Minobu see Suzuki Jogen, "Minobu ni okeru Nichiren no Seikatsu" in *IBK* Vol. XIII no. 1 (January 1965) pp. 317–20.

18 quoted in Ōno, *Nichiren* p. 216.

19 See Tamura Yoshirō, "Nippon Chūsei shisō to Tendai Hongakushisō" in *IBK* Vol. XVI no. 2 (March 1968) pp. 554–60.

20 The first sutra to be translated mentioning this concept was the *Kongō sammaikyō* rendered into Chinese prior to 385 A.D. The *Awakening of Faith* was not translated until the sixth century. For an English version of this section in the latter, see Yoshito Hakeda, *The Awakening of Faith Attributed to Aśvaghosa* (New York: Columbia Univ., 1967) p. 37 ff.

21 See Mochizuki, *Nichiren Kyōgaku no Kenkyū* p. 39.

22 Prof. Mochizuki does not believe the difference between the two schools to be as great as later critics assume. cf. *op. cit.* p. 48. Even the notion of 'gradual Enlightenment' necessarily involves an innate potentiality within the individual.

23 Some scholars find a similarity in approach between Nichiren and Shinran. cf. Tamura Yoshirō, "Shinran Nichiren Ryōshi ni okeru Kuonbutsu Shisō no Taihi" in *IBK* Vol. V no. 2 (March 1957) pp. 584–87.

24 *Hsüan-i*, I, T. Vol. 33 p. 682.

25 *Seiten* p. 118 ff.

26 *Seiten* pp. 223–6. See also Pier Del Campana. "*Sandaihihō-shō*" in *MN* Vol. XXVI no. 1–2 (1971) pp. 205–24.

27 Mochizuki, *Nichiren Kyōgaku no Kenkyū* p. 128.

28 cf. *Senjishō* in *Seiten* p. 132.

29 *Seiten* p. 108. In fact some scholars believe the *Senjakushū* greatly influenced the writing of the *Risshō Ankokuron*. See Asai Endō, "Nichiren Shōnin no Gogihan no Seiritsu ni tsuite," in *IBK* Vol. XIII no. 1 (January 1965) pp. 168–9.

30 *Seiten* p. 143.

31 *Ibid.*

32 *Seiten* p. 160.

33 cf. *Honzon Mondōshō* in *Seiten* p. 230–31.

34 See *Kyōkijikokushō* written during his exile in Izu, contained in *Seiten* p. 254.

35 *Senjishō* in *Seiten* p. 144; *Shōgumondōshō* in *Seiten* p. 285.

36 See the dialogue between Kino Kazuyoshi and Umebara Takeshi in *Eien no Inochi* p. 186.

37 *Ibid.*

38 cf. Furuta Shōkin, "Nichiren Kyōgaku no Shisō Seiritsu Keitai," in *IBK* Vol. VII no. 1 (December 1958) pp. 29–43.

39 contained in *Seiten* p. 335 ff.

40 later Nichidai was banished from this temple.

41 This is the opinion of the Nichiren scholar Motai Kyōkō, "Chūsei ni okeru Nichiren Kyōgaku no Tenkai" in *IBK* Vol. XX no. 2 (March 1972) pp. 573–81.

42 For a discussion of the origin of this group see Miyazaki Eishū, "Nichiren-shū ni okeru Shoki Fuju-fuse Shisō ni tsuite" in *IBK* Vol. IX no. 2 (March 1961) pp. 495–500 and by the same author, "Fuju-fuse-ha Seiritsu no Yōin" in *IBK* Vol. XIV no. 2 (March 1966) pp. 527–32.

43 For a critical Nichiren view of the claims of this school see Shigyō Kaishū, "Fuji Daisekiji-ha Kyōgaku no Tokushitsu" in *IBK* Vol. V no. 2 (March 1957) pp. 592–606.

CHAPTER IV— ZEN, THE WAY OF MEDITATION

1 Taga Munehaya, *Eisai* (Tokyo: Yoshikawa Kōbunkan, 1974) p. 47.

2 The Bodhisattva *śila* was a form of *vinaya* primarily based upon the precepts of the *Bommōkyō*.

3 See Tsunoda Haruo, "Eisai Zenji no Kairitsu" in *IBK* Vol. II no. 2 (March 1954) pp. 636–38.

4 Taga, *Eisai* p. 111.

5 Akamatsu ed. *Nippon Bukkyōshi* vol. 2 p. 58.

6 Taga, *Eisai* pp. 167–70.

7 quoted in Taga, *Eisai* p. 168.

8 quoted by Dōgen in the *Shōbōgenzō Zuimonki*, Reihō Masunaga tr. *A Primer of Sōtō Zen* (Honolulu: East-West Center Press, 1971) pp. 27–8, 110.

9 The *Azuma Kagami* incorrectly placed his death at the Jufukuji in Kamakura on the fifth day of the sixth month.

10 See Furuta Shōkin, *Kōza Bukkyō* vol. 5 p. 121.

11 four *dhyānas* compose the *Rūpa dhātu*, together with the four meditations of the *Arūpa dhātu*, these make eight *samādhi*.

12 For considerable research on this subject see Sekiguchi Shindai's articles in *IBK*: "Daruma wajō Zekkanron wa Gozuhōyū no Senjutsutaru o Ronzu" vol. V no. 1 (January 1957) pp. 208–11; "Shinshiryō Daruma Zenjiron ni tsuite," Vol. VI no. 2 (March 1958) pp. 417–8; and "Daruma to Daruma": Vol. XII no. 1 (January 1964) pp. 124–31. Also by the same author, *Daruma Daishi no Kenkyū* (Tokyo: Iwanami, 1957). For further discussions see Hu Shih, "P'u-t'i-ta mo k'ao in *Hu Shih wen-ts'un*" Vol. III pp. 293–304; Hu Shih, "The Development of Zen Buddhism in China," *The Chinese Social and Political Science Review* XV no. 4 (January 1932) pp. 476–87; H. Dumoulin, "Bodhidharma un die Anfänge des Ch'an Buddhismus," *MN* Vol. VII (1951) pp. 67–83.

13 For an explanation see *Foundation* Vol. I p. 157–8. Prof. Sekiguchi does find a Zen influence in this form of meditation in his article "Tendaishū ni okeru Daruma Zen," *IBK* Vol. VII no. 2 (March 1959) pp. 396–405.

14 Yanagida Seizan and Umebara Takeshi, *Mu no Tankyū, Bukkyō no Shisō* vol. 7 (Tokyo: Kadokawa, 1973) p. 131.

15 The late D. T. Suzuki spent a great deal of his life reconciling the two approaches and this was precisely what he meant when he found *Tariki* and *jiriki* to be identical in *Jōdokei Shisōnron* (Kyoto: Hōzōkan, 1967) pp. 307 ff.

16 *Jikishi ninshin* is derived from chap. V. of the *Laṅkāvatāra sūtra* and Chapter XX of the *Mahāprajñāpāramitā*, both of which stress the non-verbal nature of the Buddha's teachings.

17 *Śūnyatā* (Emptiness), *Śūnyatāyām prayojanam* (Function of Emptiness), and *Śūnyatā artha* (Practice of Emptiness).

18 We are primarily indebted to Prof. Yamada Mumon for the interpretation of this section from *Bukkyō no Shisō* Vol. 7 pp. 168–73; for differing English interpretations see Garma C. Chang, *The Practice of Zen* (New York: Harper-Row, 1970) pp. 175–84, and Chang Chung-yuan, *Original Teachings of Ch'an*

Buddhism (New York: Random House, 1969) pp. 97–101.

19 A dung scraper was an object of Zen life used in the place of modern toilet paper.

20 for a description see Matsunaga, *Foundation* Vol. I p. 264 f. 53.

21 from *Chinshū Rinzai Eshō Zenji Goroku*, in *Rinzaishū Seiten, Kokuyaku Daizōkyō* p. 6 ff. This analysis is closely related to Hua-yen philosophy and bears similarities to the T'ien T'ai concepts of 'emptiness, temporary and middle way.'

22 Akamatsu ed. *Nippon Bukkyōshi* Vol. 2 p. 161.

23 Prominent among Shōichi-ha movements were:
   1) Sanshōmon-ryū founded by Tōzan Kanshō (1231–91)
   2) Ryūgin-ha of Mukan Gengo (1212–91)
   3) Rikkyoku-ha of Hakuun Egyō (1228–97)
   4) Shōgakumon-ha of Sansōn Eun (1231–1301)
   5) Yōmeimon-ha of Zōzan Junkū (1233–1308)
   6) Shōtōmon-ha of Gessen Shinkai (d. 1308)
   7) Tōkōmon-ha of Mui Shōgen (d. 1311)
   8) Daijimon-ha of Chikotsu Daie (1229–1312)
   9) Mujū Dōgyō (1226–1318)
   10) Jōkōmon-ha of Jikiō Chikan (1245–1322)
   11) Honjōmon-ha of Senkei Shoken (d. 1330)
   12) Daiyūmon-ha of Tenkei Sōkō (d. 1332)
   13) Shōgonmon-ha of Nanzen Shiun (1254–1335)
   14) Keishōmon-ha of Sōhō Sōgen (1262–1335)
   15) Shōhōmon-ha of Mugai Jinen (dates unknown)
   Also Jinshi Eison (1195–1272), a fellow student of Bennen's under Gyōyū, and his followers became affiliated with the Shōichi-ha.

24 The Genjū-ha was based upon the teachings of the Chinese master Chungfeng Min-pen, who lived in the Huan-chu-an (Genjū-an) in China and taught a hermit life-style as well as the unification of Zen and Pure Land teachings. This school became extremely influential from the Warring States through the Tokugawa period.

25 cf. Akamatsu ed. *Nippon Bukkyōshi* vol. 2 p. 174.

26 *Ibid.* p. 494.

27 Tamamuro Taijō ed. *Nippon Bukkyōshi* Vol. 3 p. 89.

28 This is the opinion of Prof. Umebara, see Takasaki Jikidō and Umebara Takeshi, *Kobutsu no Manebi* in *Bukkyō no Shisō* vol. 11 pp. 215–30. Prof. Umebara interprets Dōgen's dislike of worldly power and sex in Freudian terms.

29 This has led some scholars to question whether Dōgen might have been a son of one of Michichika's brothers. See Takeuchi Michio, *Dōgen* (Tokyo:

Yoshikawa Kōbunkan, 1974) p. 7–10. Prof. Takeuchi maintains that Dōgen was Michichika's son and that the biographers are vague because he was not considered legitimate.

30 Tamamuro Taijō in *Kōza Bukkyō* Vol. 5 p. 184 maintains he did not since he places Dōgen's arrival at the Kenninji two years after Eisai's death.

31 *Shōbōgenzō Shisho* in *Sōtōshū Seiten, Kokuyaku Daizōkyō* (Tokyo: Tōhōshoin, 1929) p. 143.

32 Takasaki and Umebara, *Kobutsu no Manebi* p. 50.

33 *Ibid.* p. 190.

34 cf. Tamamuro, *Kōza Bukkyō* vol. 5 p. 199; Takeuchi, *Dōgen* p. 250–51.

35 Takasaki, *Kobutsu no Manebi* p. 247.

36 *Shōbōgenzō* in *Sōtōshū Seiten, Kokuyaku Daizōkyō* (Tokyo: Tōhōshoin, 1929) p. 235 ff.

37 *Sōtōshū Seiten* p. 131 ff; 453 ff.

38 *Seiten* p. 235 ff.

39 Takasaki, *Kobutsu no Manebi* p. 102.

40 *Ibid.* p. 109.

41 Masunaga, *A Primer of Sōtō Zen* p. 33.

42 Takasaki, *Kobutsu no Manebi* p. 110.

43 *Shōbōgenzō* in *Seiten* p. 29.

44 Takasaki, *Kobutsu no manebi* p. 126.

45 *Seiten* p. 383 ff.

46 *Ibid.* p. 25.

47 It is also quite possible Dōgen deliberately selected this chapter to contradict the famous *kōan* master Ta-hui, in whose school Dōgen briefly studied while in China and later severely criticized. Ta-hui is known to have composed a work of the same title as Dōgen's *Shōbōgenzō*, in which Ta-hui stressed the *kōan* as the means of attaining *kenshō*. cf. Takasaki, *Kobutsu no Manebi* p. 136–37.

48 "Genjō kōan," *Shōbōgenzō* in *Seiten* p. 23–24.

49 *Ibid.* p. 38.

50 quoted by Dōgen in *Shōbōgenzō, Seiten* p. 207.

51 *Seiten* p. 692.

52 *Seiten* p. 51–52.

53 *Ibid.* p. 52.

54 *Seiten* p. 199.

55 *Seiten* p. 49.

56 *Seiten* p. 731.

57 We are indebted for this excellent systematization to Prof. Masunaga Reihō, "Dōgen Zenji no Tachiba to Sono Jikanron" in *IBK* Vol. 1 no. 2 (March 1953) pp. 269–78.

58 *Ibid.* p. 273.
59 *Ibid.*
60 *Ibid.* p. 275.
61 *Shōbōgenzō* in *Seiten* p. 38.
62 Masunaga, *op. cit.* p. 275–76.
63 *Ibid.*
64 *Shōbōgenzō* in *Seiten* p. 674.
65 Akamatsu ed. *Nippon Bukkyōshi* p. 202.
66 Yamada Reirin, "Sōtōshū" in *Kōza Bukkyō* Vol. 7 p. 198.
67 Hashikawa, *Gaisetsu Nippon Bukkyōshi* pp. 244–45.
68 Tamamuro ed., *Nippon Bukkyōshi* Vol. 3 p. 97.

CHAPTER FIVE—ROLE OF THE OLDER SECTS DURING THE KAMA-
KURA AND MUROMACHI PERIODS

1 Akamatsu ed. *Nippon Bukkyōshi* Vol. 2 p. 295.
2 For his background, see *Foundation* Vol. 1 p. 248–49.
3 Narita Taikan, "Kamakuraki Nanto Shoshi no Shakanyorai Kan to Edo-
jōbutsu Setsu no Juyō ni tsuite" *IBK* Vol. XI no. 2 (March 1963) p. 684.
4 *Ibid.* p. 686.
5 For a description of the Zaō Gongen cult see *Foundation* Vol. I p. 245.
6 Narita Taikan, "Kamakuraki Nanto Shoshi no Taishikan" *IBK* Vol. XII
no. 2 (March 1964) pp. 718–21.
7 See Hiraoka Jōkai, "Tōdaiji Shūshō no Mirokujōdoron ni tsuite" *IBK*
Vol. IV no. 2 (March 1956) pp. 517–21.
8 For their biographies see *Honchō Kōsōden, Kokuyaku Issaikyō, Shidenbu* Vol.
28 (Tokyo: Daitōshuppansha 1961) p. 898 ff.
9 See Ishida Mizumaro, "Kakujō no Ritsushū no Fukkō ni tsuite," *IBK* Vol.
II no. 2 (March 1954) pp. 649–51.
10 See *Foundation* Vol. I p. 53.
11 The two major criticisms were that Hōnen advocated abandoning the *bodhi*
mind as a practice leading to *ōjō*, since it was motivated by self-power, and
secondly, that he compared those who followed the *Shōdōmon* (Holy path)
to robbers. In the first case, Myōe must have been aware of the varying interpretations of the *bodhi* mind among the schools, some of whom even considered it as a property of *Śrāvaka* and *Pratyeka-Buddhas*. The second criticism related to Hōnen's quotation of the famous 'White Path' story Shan-tao
used in his Commentary on the *Meditation Sutra* as an example of faith.
Myōe's charge in this instance, should have been directed against Shan-tao,
although even then it would be a misinterpretation. Other types of charges
Myōe made were that Hōnen placed the three evil existences within the Pure
Land, as well as stating that some individuals would drop from the Pure Land

to the evil existences.

12 The Eastern pagoda was located on the eastern side of Mt. Hiei, forming the centre of the mountain. Its principal buildings were the Konpon Chūdō (Main hall), Kaidan-in, Jōdo-in and Mudōji. The Western pagoda's main temple was the Hōdō-in (Shaka-dō, Jōgyō-dō and Hokke-dō). The Seiryūji was located in the Kurodani section of the mountain. Yokawa (also known as the Northern pagoda) was located several miles north of the Eastern pagoda. Its major temple was the Shuryōgon-in (Chūdō, Ruridō, Shikikōdō, and Eshindō).

13 Katsuno Ryūshin, "Eizan no Bukkyō" in Kōza Bukkyō Vol. 5 p. 86.

14 This was in contrast to the Nichiren tradition which stressed the honmon (original) section of the Lotus Sutra as superior.

15 This concept was a basis of the Pure Land development of faith.

16 See Wakamori Taro, Shugendōshi Kenkyū (Tokyo: Kawade Shobō, 1943) p. 204 ff.

17 Kiyohara Sadao, Shintōshi (Tokyo: Kōseikaku, 1942) p. 221.

18 Honchō Kōsōden, Shidenbu in Kokuyaku Issaikyō Vol. 30 p. 790.

19 An illusion is also made here to the Trikāya theory. See Matsunaga, Buddhist Philosophy of Assimilation p. 190-2, for a complete explanation.

20 The thirty-six schools of Tōmitsu are as follows:
   12 Major Schools (see Appendix chart III)
   4 Hirosawaryū minor schools—1) Yasuiryū 2) Jisoninryū 3) Jimyōinryū 4) Jōkiinryū
   20 Onoryū minor schools—1) Kojimaryū 2) Inzeiinryū 3) Shōchiinryū 4) Matsubashiryū 5) Miwaryū 6) Yamamotoryū 7) Jōshōryū 8) Kakuchiryū 9) Kamoryū 10) Iwakuraryū 11) Ryōshōryū 12) Hōoninryū 13) Jizōinryū 14) Igyōryū 15) Jimyōryū 16) Ginōryū 17) Shōdōryū 18) Gangyōryū 19) Kōhōryū 20) Shinkairyū

21 For the origin of this dispute see Foundation Vol. I p. 199-200.

22 It would seem there was considerable competition between the hereditary families controlling the Inner (Naigū) and Outer (Gegū) Shrines at Ise. Later the Watarai family in charge of the Outer Shrine established Ise Shintō to prove their superiority, and created a reverse of the honji-suijaku theory.

CONCLUSION

1 For an interesting article on this rare subject, see Matsuno Jyunkō, "Kamakura Bukkyō to Josei" IBK Vol. X no. 2 (March 1962) pp. 648-60.

2 Reihō Masunaga, "The Historical Meaning of Dōgen" IBK Vol. X no. 1 (January 1962) p. 32.

SELECTED BIBLIOGRAPHY

Akamatsu Toshihide. *Kamakura Bukkyō no Kenkyū*. Kyoto, 1957

Akamatsu Toshihide, Ed. *Nippon Bukkyōshi* Vol. II *Chūseihen*. Kyoto, 1968.

Akamatsu Toshihide. *Shinran*. Tokyo, 1961.

Anesaki Masaharu. *Nichiren, the Buddhist Prophet*. Gloucester, 1966.

Asai Endō. "Nichiren Shōnin no Gogihan no Seiritsu ni tsuite," *IBK*, Vol. XIII no. 1 (January 1965) pp. 168–9.

Bloom, Alfred. *Shinran's Gospel of Pure Grace*. Tucson, 1968.

Chang Chung-yuan. *Original Teachings of Ch'an Buddhism*. New York, 1969.

Chang, Garma, C. *The Practice of Zen*. New York, 1959.

Coates, Harper & R. Ishizuka. *Honen, the Buddhist Saint*. Kyoto, 1949.

Daitō Shuppansha pub. *Kokuyaku Issaikyō* Vol. 89, 90, 91. Tokyo, 1961.

Daizō Shuppan pub. *Kōza Bukkyō*, 6 Vol. Tokyo 1968–9.

Del Campana, Pier. "Sandaihihō-shō, An Essay on the Three Great Mysteries," *MN* Vol. XXVI (1971) pp. 205–24.

Dumoulin, H. "Bodhidharma und die Anfänge des Ch'an-Buddhismus," *MN* Vol. VII (1951) pp. 67–83.

Dumoulin, H. *A History of Zen Buddhism*. Boston, 1963.

Eliot, Sir Charles. *Japanese Buddhism*. New York, 1969.

Fujishima Tatsurō. *Eshin-ni kō*. Niigata, 1956.

Fujita Kōtatsu. *Genshi Jōdoshisō no Kenkyū*. Tokyo, 1970.

Fujiyoshi Jikai. "Bannen no Hōnen Shōnin," *IBK* Vol. XX no. 1 (December 1971) pp. 121–7.

Fung, Yu-lan. *A History of Chinese Philosophy*. 2 vol. Princeton, 1952–3.

Furuta Shōkin. "Dōgen to Ejō no aida," *IBK* Vol. XXIII no. 2 (March 1975) pp. 511–20.

Furuta Shōkin. "Kamakura Bukkyō ni okeru Jikaishugi to Hanjikaishugi," *IBK* Vol. VI no. 1 (January 1958) pp. 94–103.

Gorai Shigeru. "Ippen Shōnin to Hottō Kokushi," *IBK* Vol. IX no. 2 (March 1961) pp. 508–15.

Gorai Shigeru. *Kōyahijiri*. Tokyo, 1965.

Hakeda, Yoshito. *The Awakening of Faith*. New York, 1967.

Hanayama Shinshō. *A History of Japanese Buddhism*. Tokyo, 1960.

Hashikawa Tadashi. *Gaisetsu Nippon Bukkyōshi*. Kyoto, 1958.

Hori Ichirō. *Kūya*. Tokyo, 1974.

Hori Ichirō. *Wagakuni Minkanshinkō no Kenkyū*. 2 Vol. 1953.

Hirooka Jōkai. "Tōdaiji Shūshō no Miroku Jōdoron ni tsuite," *IBK* Vol. IV no. 2 (March 1956) pp. 517-21.

Hu Shih. *Hu Shih wen-ts'un*. Vol. III Taipei, 1953.

Ienaga Saburō. *Chūsei Bukkyōshisōshi Kenkyū*. Kyoto, 1966.

Ienaga Saburō, ed. *Nippon Bukkyōshi* Vol. 1 Kyoto, 1967.

Ienaga Saburō, ed. *Nippon Bukkyōshisōshi no Tenkai*, Kyoto, 1956.

Ienaga Saburō, ed. *Shinran Shōnin Gyōjitsu*. Kyoto, 1969.

Inaba Shūken. *Kyōgyōshinshō no Shomondai*. Kyoto, 1961.

Ishida Mizumaro. *Jōdokyō no Tenkai*. Tokyo, 1967.

Ishida Mizumaro. "Kakujō no Ritsushū Fukkō ni tsuite" *IBK* Vol. II no. 1 (March 1954) pp. 649-51.

Ishida Mizumaro. "Jitsuhan ni tsuite," *IBK* Vol. XI no. 1 (January 1963) pp. 76-85.

Ishida Mizumaro. *Shinran to Sono Tsuma no Tegami*. Tokyo, 1968.

Ishii Kyōdō. ed. *Hōnen Shōnin Zenshū*. Kyoto, 1974.

Itō Shintetsu. "Hōnen Shōnin no Tōdaiji Kōsetsu ni tsuite," *IBK* Vol. X no. 1 (January 1962) pp. 88-93.

Kabutogi Shōkō. "Nichiren ni okeru Hokekyō Honzon no Shisō," *IBK* Vol. V no. 2 (March 1957) pp. 588-91.

Kadokawa Shoten pub. *Bukkyō no Shisō*, Vol. 7, 8, 11, 12. Tokyo, 1968-71.

Kaneko Daiei. *Bangaku Monshiroku*. Tokyo, 1968.

Kaneko Daiei. *Fuhen no Hō, Tokushu no Ki*. Kyoto, 1968.

Kaneko Daiei. *Jōdosanbukyō to Jōdoron no Gaiyō*. Kyoto, 1963.

Kaneko Daiei. *Shinshū no Kyōgi to Sono Rekishi*. Kyoto, 1965.

Kaneko Daiei. *Shinshū Seiten*. Kyoto, 1960.

Kasahara Kazuo. *Shinshū no Hatten to Ikkō Ikki*. Kyoto, 1951.

Katsuki Jōkō. *Hōnen Jōdokyō no Shisō to Rekishi*. Tokyo, 1974.

Kikufuji Akimichi. "Kamakura Kyūbukkyō to Mappō Shisō," *IBK* Vol. XXIII no. 1 (December 1974) pp. 235-8.

Kino Kazuyoshi. *Hokekyō no Tankyū*. Kyoto, 1964.

Liebenthal, W. "The Sermon of Shên-hui," *Asia Minor* (1952) pp. 132-55.

Liebenthal, W. "Shih Hui-yüan's Buddhism as Set Forth in His Writings," *Journal of the American Oriental Society* LXX (1950) pp. 243-59.

Lu K'uan-yü. *Ch'an and Zen Teachings*. 3 vol. Berkeley, 1970-3.

Lu K'uan-yü. (Charles Luk) *The Secrets of Chinese Meditation*. New York, 1972.

Lu K'uan-yü. *The Sūraṅgama Sutra*. London, 1966.

Masunaga Reihō. "Dōgen Zenji no Tachiba to Sono Jikanron," *IBK* Vol. 1 no. 2 (March 1953) pp. 269-78.

Masunaga Reihō. *Eihei Shōbōgenzō*. Tokyo, 1956.

Masunaga Reihō. *The Sōtō Approach to Zen*. Tokyo, 1958.

Masutani Fumio. *Bussoshōden no Michi*. Tokyo, 1967.

Masutani Fumio. *Nichiren*. Tokyo, 1967.

Masutani Fumio. *Rinzai to Dōgen*. Tokyo, 1971.

Masutani Fumio. *Shinran, Dōgen, Nichiren*. Tokyo, 1956.

Matsunaga, Alicia. *The Buddhist Philosophy of Assimilation*. Tokyo, 1969.

Matsunaga, Daigan and Alicia. *The Buddhist Concept of Hell*. New York, 1972.

Matsunaga, Daigan and Alicia. *Foundation of Japanese Buddhism*. Vol. 1 Los Angeles, 1974.

Matsunaga, Daigan and Alicia. "The Concept of *Upāya* in Mahāyāna Buddhist Philosophy," *Japanese Journal of Religious Studies*, Vol. 1 no. 1 (March 1974) pp. 51–72.

Matsuno Junkō. "Kamakura Bukkyō to Josei," *IBK* Vol. X no. 2 (March 1962) pp. 648–60.

Matsuno Junkō. *Shinran*. Tokyo, 1959.

Merton, Thomas. *Zen and the Birds of Appetite*. New York, 1968.

Michibata Ryōshū. *Chūgoku Bukkyōshi*. Kyoto, 1965.

Miura, Isshu & Ruth Fuller Sasaki. *The Zen Koan*. New York, 1965.

Miyamoto Shōson ed. *Bukkyō no Konpon Shinri*. Tokyo, 1957.

Miyamoto Shōson. *Daijō Bukkyō no Seiritsushiteki Kenkyū*. Tokyo, 1958.

Miyazaki Eishū. "Fuju-fuse ha Seiritsu no Yōin," *IBK* Vol. XIV no. 2 (March 1966) pp. 527–32.

Miyazaki Eishū. "Nichirenshū ni okeru Shoki Fuju-fuse Shisō ni tsuite," *IBK* Vol. IX no. 2 (March 1961) pp. 495–500.

Miyazaki Eishū. *Nichirenshū no Shugoshin*. Kyoto, 1968.

Miyazaki Enjun. *Chūsei Bukkyō to Shominseikatsu*. Kyoto, 1951.

Miyazaki Enjun, *et al*. *Shinran Shōnin*. Tokyo, 1973.

Mochizuki Kankō. *Nichiren Kyōgaku no Kenkyū*. Kyoto, 1968.

Mochizuki Shinkō. *Bukkyō Daijiten*. 10 vol. Tokyo, 1960–63.

Mookerji, R. K. *Ancient Indian Education*. Delhi, 1974.

Motai Kyōkō. "Chūsei ni okeru Nichiren Kyōgaku no Tenkai," *IBK* Vol. XX no. 2 (March 1972) pp. 573–81.

Nakamura Hajime. "Gokuraku Jōdo no Kannen no Indogakuteki Kaimei to Chibettoteki Henyō" *IBK* Vol. XI no. 2 (March 1963) pp. 509–31.

Nakamura Hajime. *Indo Shisōshi*. Tokyo, 1956.

Nakamura Hajime. *Shūkyō to Shakairinri*. Tokyo, 1959.

Nakamura Hajime. *Ways of Thinking of Eastern Peoples*, Honolulu, 1964.

Narita Teikan. "Kamakura Jidai ni okeru Nanto Bukkyō no Tenkai," *IBK* Vol. VIII no. 2 (March 1960) pp. 663–665.

Narita Teikan. "Kamakuraki Nanto Shoshi no Shakanyoraikan to Edo Jōbutsu

Setsu no Juyō ni tsuite," *IBK* Vol. XI no. 2 (March 1963) pp. 684–88.

Narita Teikan. "Kamakuraki Nanto Shoshi no Taishikan." *IBK* Vol. XII no. 2 (March 1964) pp. 718–21.

Ōchō Enichi, *Hokekyōjosetsu.* Kyoto, 1962.

Ōno Tatsunosuke. *Nichiren.* Tokyo, 1972.

Ōno Tatsunosuke, *Nippon Bukkyōshi.* Tokyo, 1957.

Pandey, Lalta Prasad. *Sun Worship in Ancient India.* Delhi, 1971.

Renondeau, G. *Le Doctrine de Nichiren.* Paris, 1958.

Sekiguchi Shindai. *Daruma Daishi no Kenkyū.* Tokyo, 1957.

Sekiguchi Shindai. "Daruma to Daruma," *IBK* Vol. XII no. 1 (January 1964) pp. 124–31.

Sekiguchi Shindai. "Tendaishū ni okeru Daruma Zen," *IBK* Vol. VII no. 2 (March 1954) pp. 396–405.

Sekiguchi Shindai. *Zenshū Shisōshi* Tokyo, 1964.

Shibata Minoru. *Chūsei Shomin Shinkō no Kenkyū.* Tokyo, 1966.

Shigematsu Akihisa. *Nippon Jōdokyō Seiritsukatei no Kenkyū.* Kyoto, 1966.

Shigyō Kaishū. "Fuji Daiseki-ji Kyōgaku no Tokushitsu," *IBK* Vol. V no. 2 (March 1957) pp. 592–606.

Suzuki, D. T. (Daisetsu). *Essays in Zen.* 3 vol. London, 1949–53.

Suzuki, Daisetsu, *Jōdokei Shisōron.* Kyoto, 1967.

Suzuki, Daisetsu. *The Kyōgyōshinshō.* Kyoto, 1973.

Suzuki, Daisetsu. *Shin Buddhism.* New York, 1970.

Suzuki, Daisetsu. *Suzuki Daisetsu Senshū.* 25 vol. Tokyo, 1961–4.

Suzuki, Daisetsu. *Zen and Japanese Culture.* Princeton, 1970.

Suzuki, Daisetsu. *The Zen Doctrine of No Mind.* London, 1969.

Suzuki Jōgen. "Minobu ni okeru Nichiren no Seikatsu," *IBK* Vol. XIII no. 1 (January 1965) pp. 317–20.

Taga Munehaya. *Eisai.* Tokyo, 1974.

Takeuchi Michio. *Dōgen.* Tokyo, 1974.

Tamamuro Taijō. *Nippon Bukkyōshi,* Vol. III (*Kinsei Kindaihen*) Kyoto, 1968.

Tamamuro Taijō. *Nippon Bukkyōshi Gaisetsu.* Tokyo, 1951.

Tamura Enchō. *Hōnen.* Tokyo, 1964.

Tamura Enchō. *Hōnen Shōninden no Kenkyū.* Kyoto, 1956.

Tamura Enchō. *Nippon Bukkyōshisōshi Kenkyū (Jōdokyōhen)* Kyoto, 1959.

Tamura Yoshirō. *Kamakura Shinbukkyōshisō no Kenkyū.* Kyoto, 1965.

Tamura Yoshirō. "Nippon Chūsei Shisō to Tendai Hongakushisō," *IBK* Vol. XVI no. 2 (March 1968) pp. 554–60.

Tamura Yoshirō. "Shinran Nichiren Ryōshi ni okeru Kuonbutsushisō no Taihi," *IBK* Vol. V no. 2 (March 1957) pp. 584–7.

Taya Raishun, *et al. Bukkyōgakujiten.* Kyoto, 1961.

Tōhōshoin pub. *Nichirenshū Seiten, Kokuyaku Daizōkyō.* Tokyo, 1928.

Tōhō shoin pub. *Rinzaishū Seiten, Kokuyaku Daizōkyō*, Tokyo, 1929.

Tōhō shoin pub. *Sōtōshū Seiten, Kokuyaku Daizōkyō*, Tokyo, 1929.

Tsuji Zennosuke, *Nipponbunka to Bukkyō*. Tokyo, 1965.

Tsuji Zennosuke, *Nippon Bukkyōshi*. 11 vols. Tokyo, 1947-51.

Ui Hakuju. *Bukkyōjiten*. Tokyo, 1953.

Ui Hakuji. *Nippon Bukkyō Gaishi*. Tokyo, 1951.

Ui Hakuju. *Shina Bukkyōshi*. Tokyo, 1939.

Ui Hakuju. *Zenshūshi Kenkyū*. 3 vol. Tokyo, 1939-43.

Watanabe Shōkō. *Nippon no Bukkyō*. Tokyo, 1958.

Yamaguchi Kōen. *Tendai Gaisetsu*. Kyoto, 1967.

Yamaguchi Kōen. *Tendai Jōdokyōshi*. Kyoto, 1967.

Yamaguchi Susumu. *Seshin no Jōdoron*, Kyoto, 1953.

Yampolsky, Philip. *The Platform Sutra of the Sixth Patriarch*. New York, 1967.

Yomiurishinbunsha ed. *Nippon no Rekishi*. Vol. 4, 5, 6 Tokyo, 1972.

Yūki Reimon. "Indo ni okeru Shoki Jōdokyō no Itosurumono" *IBK* Vol. III no. 1 (September 1954) pp. 44-8.

APPENDIX CHARTS

DEVELOPMENT OF TENDAI SCHOOLS

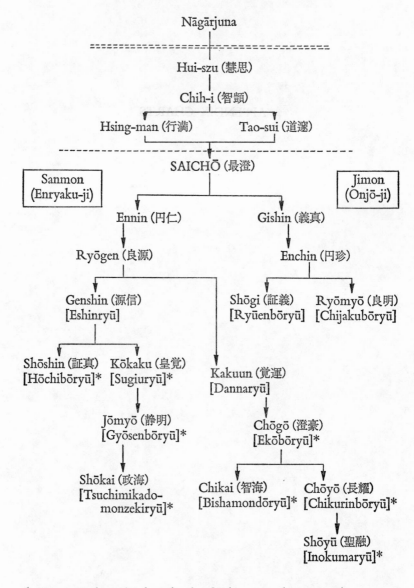

* *E-Dan Hachiryū* (Eight Schools of Eshinryū and Dannaryū)

DEVELOPMENT OF TAIMITSU SCHOOLS

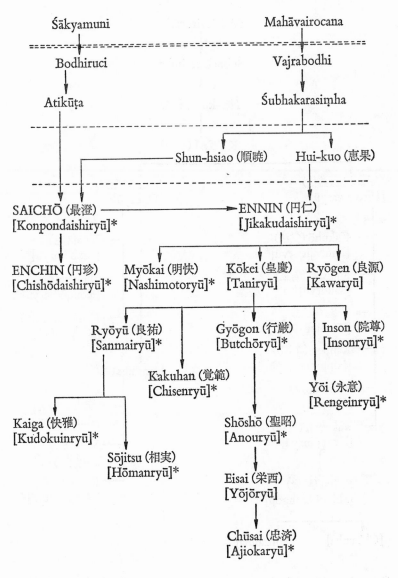

Śākyamuni

Mahāvairocana

Bodhiruci

Vajrabodhi

Atikūṭa

Śubhakarasiṃha

Shun-hsiao (順曉)   Hui-kuo (惠果)

SAICHŌ (最澄) ────────────► ENNIN (円仁)
[Konpondaishiryū]*   [Jikakudaishiryū]*

ENCHIN (円珍)   Myōkai (明快)   Kōkei (皇慶)   Ryōgen (良源)
[Chishōdaishiryū]* [Nashimotoryū]* [Taniryū]   [Kawaryū]

Ryōyū (良祐)   Gyōgon (行厳)   Inson (院尊)
[Sanmairyū]*   [Butchōryū]*   [Insonryū]*

Kakuhan (覚範)
[Chisenryū]*   Yōi (永意)
                                          [Rengeinryū]*

Kaiga (快雅)   Shōshō (聖昭)
[Kudokuinryū]*   [Anouryū]*

Sōjitsu (相実)   Eisai (栄西)
[Hōmanryū]*   [Yōjōryū]

                              Chūsai (忠済)
                              [Ajiokaryū]*

* *Thirteen Schools of Taimitsu*

DEVELOPMENT OF SHINGON SCHOOLS

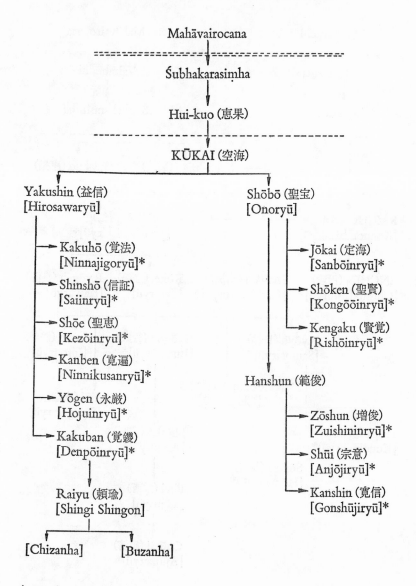

Mahāvairocana

Śubhakarasiṃha

Hui-kuo (恵果)

KŪKAI (空海)

Yakushin (益信)
[Hirosawaryū]

Shōbō (聖宝)
[Onoryū]

Kakuhō (覚法)
[Ninnajigoryū]*

Shinshō (信証)
[Saiinryū]*

Shōe (聖恵)
[Kezōinryū]*

Kanben (寛遍)
[Ninnikusanryū]*

Yōgen (永厳)
[Hojuinryū]*

Kakuban (覚鑁)
[Denpōinryū]*

Raiyu (頼瑜)
[Shingi Shingon]

[Chizanha]   [Buzanha]

Jōkai (定海)
[Sanbōinryū]*

Shōken (聖賢)
[Kongōōinryū]*

Kengaku (賢覚)
[Rishōinryū]*

Hanshun (範俊)

Zōshun (増俊)
[Zuishininryū]*

Shūi (宗意)
[Anjōjiryū]*

Kanshin (寛信)
[Gonshūjiryū]*

* *Twelve Major Schools*

DEVELOPMENT OF JŌDOSHŪ SCHOOLS

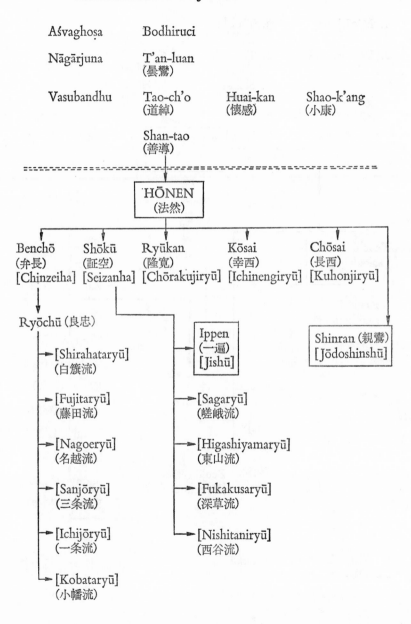

Aśvaghoṣa   Bodhiruci

Nāgārjuna   T'an-luan
                 (曇鸞)

Vasubandhu   Tao-ch'o   Huai-kan   Shao-k'ang
                 (道綽)   (懷感)   (小康)

                 Shan-tao
                 (善導)

                 HŌNEN
                 (法然)

Benchō   Shōkū   Ryūkan   Kōsai   Chōsai
(弁長)   (証空)   (隆寛)   (幸西)   (長西)
[Chinzeiha] [Seizanha] [Chōrakujiryū] [Ichinengiryū] [Kuhonjiryū]

Ryōchū (良忠)

                              Ippen   Shinran (親鸞)
                              (一遍)   [Jōdoshinshū]
                              [Jishū]

→[Shirahataryū]   →[Sagaryū]
 (白籏流)   (嵯峨流)

→[Fujitaryū]   →[Higashiyamaryū]
 (藤田流)   (東山流)

→[Nagoeryū]   →[Fukakusaryū]
 (名越流)   (深草流)

→[Sanjōryū]   →[Nishitaniryū]
 (三条流)   (西谷流)

→[Ichijōryū]
 (一条流)

→[Kobataryū]
 (小幡流)

DEVELOPMENT OF JŌDO SHINSHŪ SCHOOLS

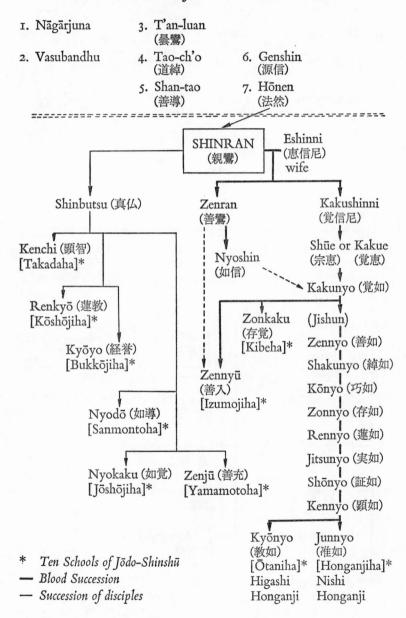

1. Nāgārjuna

2. Vasubandhu

3. T'an-luan (曇鸞)

4. Tao-ch'o (道綽)

5. Shan-tao (善導)

6. Genshin (源信)

7. Hōnen (法然)

SHINRAN (親鸞)

Eshinni (恵信尼) wife

Shinbutsu (真仏)

Zenran (善鸞)

Kakushinni (覚信尼)

Kenchi (顕智) [Takadaha]*

Nyoshin (如信)

Shūe or Kakue (宗恵) (覚恵)

Renkyō (蓮教) [Kōshōjiha]*

Kakunyo (覚如)

Kyōyo (経誉) [Bukkōjiha]*

Zonkaku (存覚) [Kibeha]*

(Jishun)

Zennyo (善如)

Shakunyo (綽如)

Kōnyo (巧如)

Zennyū (善入) [Izumojiha]*

Zonnyo (存如)

Rennyo (蓮如)

Nyodō (如導) [Sanmontoha]*

Jitsunyo (実如)

Shōnyo (証如)

Nyokaku (如覚) [Jōshōjiha]*

Zenjū (善充) [Yamamotoha]*

Kennyo (顕如)

Kyōnyo (教如) [Ōtaniha]* Higashi Honganji

Junnyo (准如) [Honganjiha]* Nishi Honganji

*   *Ten Schools of Jōdo-Shinshū*
—   *Blood Succession*
—   *Succession of disciples*

DEVELOPMENT OF NICHIREN SCHOOLS

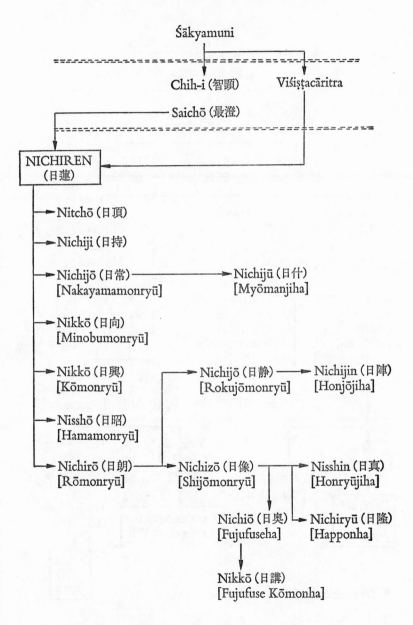

Śākyamuni

Chih-i (智顗)   Viśiṣṭacāritra

Saichō (最澄)

NICHIREN
(日蓮)

→ Nitchō (日頂)

→ Nichiji (日持)

→ Nichijō (日常)————————→ Nichijū (日什)
[Nakayamamonryū]   [Myōmanjiha]

→ Nikkō (日向)
[Minobumonryū]

→ Nikkō (日興)————→ Nichijō (日静)————→ Nichijin (日陣)
[Kōmonryū]   [Rokujōmonryū]   [Honjōjiha]

→ Nisshō (日昭)
[Hamamonryū]

→ Nichirō (日朗)————→ Nichizō (日像)————→ Nisshin (日真)
[Rōmonryū]   [Shijōmonryū]   [Honryūjiha]

Nichiō (日奥) → Nichiryū (日隆)
[Fujufuseha]   [Happonha]

Nikkō (日講)
[Fujufuse Kōmonha]

DEVELOPMENT OF CHINESE ZEN SCHOOLS

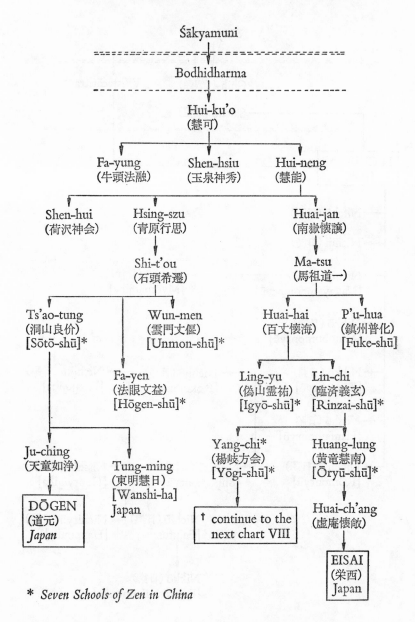

Śākyamuni

Bodhidharma

Hui-ku'o
(慧可)

Fa-yung   Shen-hsiu   Hui-neng
(牛頭法融)   (玉泉神秀)   (慧能)

Shen-hui   Hsing-szu   Huai-jan
(荷沢神会)   (青原行思)   (南嶽懐讓)

Shi-t'ou   Ma-tsu
(石頭希遷)   (馬祖道一)

Ts'ao-tung   Wun-men   Huai-hai   P'u-hua
(洞山良价)   (雲門丈偃)   (百丈懐海)   (鎮州普化)
[Sōtō-shū]*   [Unmon-shū]*   [Fuke-shū]

Fa-yen   Ling-yu   Lin-chi
(法眼文益)   (偽山霊祐)   (臨済義玄)
[Hōgen-shū]*   [Igyō-shū]*   [Rinzai-shū]*

Ju-ching   Yang-chi*   Huang-lung
(天童如浄)   (楊岐方会)   (黄竜慧南)
                  Tung-ming   [Yōgi-shū]*   [Ōryū-shū]*
                  (東明慧日)
                  [Wanshi-ha]
DŌGEN   Japan   Huai-ch'ang
(道元)   (虚庵懐敞)
Japan   † continue to the
                          next chart VIII
                                                        EISAI
                                                        (栄西)
                                                        Japan

Seven Schools of Zen in China

YANG-CHI SCHOOL OF RINZAI ZEN IN JAPAN

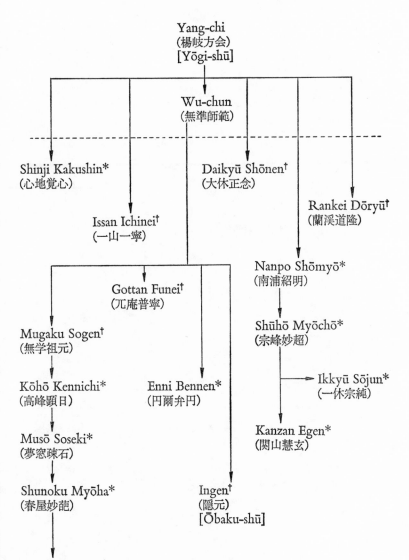

Yang-chi
(楊岐方会)
[Yōgi-shū]

Wu-chun
(無準師範)

Shinji Kakushin*
(心地覚心)

Daikyū Shōnen†
(大休正念)

Rankei Dōryū†
(蘭渓道隆)

Issan Ichinei†
(一山一寧)

Nanpo Shōmyō*
(南浦紹明)

Gottan Funei†
(兀庵普寧)

Shūhō Myōchō*
(宗峰妙超)

Mugaku Sogen†
(無学祖元)

Kōhō Kennichi*
(高峰顕日)

Enni Bennen*
(円爾弁円)

Ikkyū Sōjun*
(一休宗純)

Musō Soseki*
(夢窓疎石)

Kanzan Egen*
(関山慧玄)

Shunoku Myōha*
(春屋妙葩)

Ingen†
(隠元)
[Ōbaku-shū]

* *Japanese monk*
† *Chinese monk who came to Japan*

INDEX